The International Library of Sociology

PRIVATE CORPORATIONS AND THEIR CONTROL

I0891177

Founded by KARL MANNHEIM

The International Library of Sociology

THE SOCIOLOGY OF WORK AND ORGANIZATION
In 18 Volumes

I	Apprenticeship	*Liepmann*
II	Industrial Disputes	*Eldridge*
III	Industrial Injuries Insurance	*Young*
IV	The Journey to Work	*Liepmann*
V	The Lorry Driver	*Hollowell*
VI	Military Organization and Society	*Andrzejewski*
VII	Mobility in the Labour Market	*Jeffreys*
VIII	Organization and Bureaucracy	*Mouzelis*
IX	Planned Organizational Change	*Jones*
X	Private Corporations and their Control - Part One	*Levy*
XI	Private Corporations and their Control - Part Two	*Levy*
XII	The Qualifying Associations	*Millerson*
XIII	Recruitment to Skilled Trades	*Williams*
XIV	Retail Trade Associations	*Levy*
XV	The Shops of Britain	*Levy*
XVI	Technological Growth and Social Change	*Hetzler*
XVII	Work and Leisure	*Anderson*
XVIII	Workers, Unions and the State	*Wootton*

PRIVATE CORPORATIONS AND THEIR CONTROL

Part II

by

A. B. LEVY

Routledge
Taylor & Francis Group
LONDON AND NEW YORK

First published in 1950 by
Routledge

Reprinted in 1998 by
Routledge
2 Park Square, Milton Park, Abingdon, Oxon, OX14 4RN
Simultaneously published in the USA and Canada by Routledge

711 Third Avenue, New York, NY 10017

Transferred to Digital Printing 2007

Routledge is an imprint of the Taylor & Francis Group, an informa business

First issued in paperback 2013

British Library Cataloguing in Publication Data
A CIP catalogue record for this book
is available from the British Library

Private Corporations and their Control - Part Two

ISBN 978-0-415-17686-6 (hbk)
ISBN 978-0-415-86850-1 (pbk)

Publisher's Note

The publisher has gone to great lengths to ensure the quality of this reprint but points out that some imperfections in the original may be apparent

CONTENTS

PART II

LEGAL PROBLEMS OF PRIVATE CORPORATIONS (*Continued*)

PART II

Legal Problems of Private Corporations

(Continued)

CHAPTER III

SHAREHOLDERS' RIGHTS AND DUTIES

50. The Rights of Shareholders in General

From the fact that a corporation exists as a legal entity independent of the shareholders it follows that the legal position of the shareholders is to be clearly distinguished from that of the corporation. The shareholders are not the corporation; they have definite rights in its property and management, definite obligations towards it and to some extent definite liabilities with regard to it. But their rights and duties are not identical with those of the corporation itself.

This holds good even if one shareholder owns the majority of the shares. In principle it may be said that even if a single shareholder owns all the shares, his rights and duties are to be distinguished from those of the corporation, although in such a case the corporate status may be disregarded and the shareholder's acts may be treated as those of the corporation or the corporation is to be dissolved. This question is examined in § 94.

The rights of the shareholders are usually exercised in general meeting. This applies to the election of directors, to amendment of the articles and, where (as in the U.S.A.) by-laws as distinguished from articles exist, of by-laws, to assessment on the shares in excess of the unpaid part of their par value in so far as this is admitted, and to reorganisation, consolidation, merger and voluntary dissolution of the corporation.

There are some rights which may as a rule be exercised outside of meetings and belong to shareholders individually, such as examination of books and reports, pre-emptive rights, the right to dividend, the right to sue an officer of the corporation and to sue on behalf of the corporation or in proper cases to defend actions against it.

The management of the corporation is generally vested in the board of directors. This means that the board is empowered to perform all necessary acts in the course of management of the corporate affairs, and may disregard directions given by shareholders, unless a given act requires their assent.

A different view was adopted by Continental legislations until the later phase of German Company law. Under such legislations the shareholders in general meeting had the supreme right of direction of the management of the corporation, and directors and managers had to follow their instructions. This was generally held and in most legislations expressly provided by statute, although on the Continent the authority of directors as against third parties was and is much wider than in Britain, and even practically unlimited.

Under the Anglo-American system, if the directors disregard their wishes, the shareholders may refrain from re-electing them or may even remove them before the end of their term of office, but cannot otherwise undo their acts or fix on them responsibility for any disregard of instructions, *per se*. They may be responsible if their act was not reasonable.

In the latest phase of German Company law the so-called "leader principle" (*Führerprinzip*) was introduced, to the extent that managers (*Vorstand*) could not be removed without just cause, i.e. in case of gross mismanagement (see § 23).

It is obvious that under these circumstances the control of corporations by their shareholders is remote and ineffective. This applies especially to the question of damages; shareholders are not entitled to give instructions with the effect that disregard of them would involve the liability of the directors *per se*, and it may be impossible to decide whether an act or an omission of the directors was at the time reasonable or not.

It is true that the removal of directors is generally possible even before the end of their term of office, but usually it is a very hard task to organise the shareholders in order to obtain a resolution in general meeting for this purpose. If the practice as to general meetings (use of proxies and so on) is taken into account, the control of directors is in most cases ineffective, and an election may incidentally be fatal to the corporation and is without doubt a very risky undertaking.

It is generally agreed that in his dealings with the corporation the shareholder is in the same position as any third party. He may look after his own interests in making or implementing a contract; it is for the directors and officers to protect the corporation. This of course does not apply to frauds.

It has, however, sometimes been held that the shareholder is to some extent in a fiduciary position in regard to the corporation.

It has been said,[1] that a shareholder contracting with his corporation is properly held to a larger measure of candour and good faith than third parties. Similar tendencies in Continental legislations will be considered in § 75.

As a rule, however, a shareholder may purchase property from and sell it to the corporation by contract or authorised sale, make any other contract with it, engage in a competing business, acquire an adverse title or interest, purchase claims against the corporation, or, if he is its creditor, exercise a creditor's rights in the same way and to the same extent as if he were not a shareholder. If he is at the same time a director or officer of the corporation, his duties as such may operate as limitations or restrictions on the exercise of his rights as a shareholder (see § 82).

A special situation arises in cases of majority shareholdings. If one person holds the majority of the shares, or several shareholders assume control of the corporation in order to pass a resolution against the minority, it is held in the U.S.A. that they are under the duty to observe greater care for the interests of the corporation as a whole, i.e. for the equal interests of all shareholders. This greater measure of care has in some cases been described as a trusteeship or quasi-trusteeship. This is of course not true in the sense of its amounting to a technical trust, but it is true that such resolutions or a contract made by virtue of them will be more closely scrutinised than if made with third persons, and equity will interpose to prevent such a contract being used oppressively and in violation of the rights of the minority.[2]

Transactions between the corporation and the majority, whether it consist of one or several persons, are of course not void, but they "will be viewed by the Courts with jealousy and set aside on slight grounds".[3] This scrutiny is dependent on the discretion of the Court; the protection of the corporation and the minority shareholders is therefore neither certain nor very effective.

Even this rule is not everywhere accepted. Thus under the British Companies Act it is generally held that the shareholders, even if they constitute a majority, are in no way restricted in the exercise of their rights, especially their voting rights. If we bear in mind that under English law the directors are under no restriction in making contracts with the corporation, and that their

[1] E.g. in Twin-Lick Oil Co. *v.* Marbury (1875), 91 U.S. 587.
[2] Fletcher 5781, n. 45–6.
[3] Rothschild *v.* Memphis and C.R. Co., 113 Fed. 476, Fletcher 5781, n. 47.

only duty is to declare their interest, the protection is indeed very weak.

Continental laws have long ago observed the need for greater protection of minorities. Some legislations provide that a shareholder may not vote on contracts to be made with himself. In others the Courts have accepted the same view in the absence of statutory provision. Nevertheless, the Courts have been reluctant to apply the rules contained in the statutes or formerly accepted by the Courts and have done so mostly in the sense of restrictive constructions which were easy to evade by clever devices.

51. Contribution and Liability

(a) general

In considering the obligations of a company's shareholders to contribute to its capital, we shall here be concerned with the normal type of business corporation, namely, that which has a capital divided into shares with a par value. In many countries this is the only type that exists. The shareholders of such a corporation are as a rule bound only to pay up the par value of their shares, and their liability as against creditors of the corporation is limited to that amount. This, however, is not the only possibility, and the limitation of a shareholder's duty to contribute to the corporation in case of need (his internal obligation towards the corporation) and of his liability to its creditors is the result of a long evolution.

Originally, as we have seen earlier, the formation of a joint-stock company did not exclude the common law liability of the shareholders as partners, but was a privilege conferred by the Sovereign or the authority empowered to issue charters. Its basis was the charter.

In Great Britain it was not until 1855, and in the case of banks even later, that incorporators could choose whether to create a corporation with a liability limited to the par value of its shares, one with a limited liability in excess of that value, or one with unlimited liability.

Many American legislations have adopted the principle of limited liability in the sense of its limitation to the par value of the shares, and even under common law the rule there is that shareholders are not personally liable for a corporation's debts whether in law or in equity unless such liability is expressly imposed by constitutional or statutory provisions or by the charter (certificates or articles of incorporation) of the corporation concerned.[1] This applies equally to contractual obligations and to those originating from torts.

Certain of the State legislations by their constitutions or by their general corporation laws reject absolutely any modification of the principle of limited liability, though most of them give the same choice to the incorporators as British law does. Until the "New Deal", Federal legislation imposed on the shareholders of National Banks a liability up to the amount of the par value of their shares apart from and in addition to the obligation to pay that par value to the bank of which they were members. This liability could not be evaded or reduced either in the charter or by the by-laws. Many State legislations likewise adopted double liability in respect of certain classes of corporations, mainly banks, trust companies, and other financial corporations. This system did not work well in the case of banks, and experience led to its abolition by the amendment of the National Bank Act. In the case of State banks experience was even less favourable. Only about 40 per cent. of the assessments could be collected from shareholders of insolvent State banks. Consequently State legislations followed the lead of Congress; of the 38 States which had adopted the system of excess liability, 19 had already dropped it by 1937. Of these, six enacted that shareholders of State banks should not be subject to twofold liability if the banks insured their deposits with the Federal Deposit Insurance Corporation and became members thereof. Four others dropped it absolutely, while nine provided for the building up of a surplus equal to the nominal capital, and Florida prescribed the formation of a reserve fund out of profits to be invested in bonds until the fund should equal the full amount of the nominal capital. It may be presumed that the remaining 19 States will adopt a similar line, and that twofold liability will shortly be a thing of the past. In Canada a similar change in the law took place in 1934, when it was enacted that shareholders are liable only for notes and that this liability is proportionate.[2]

[1] Pollard *v.* Bailey (1877), 20 Wall. U.S. 520; Fourth National Bank of New York *v.* Francklyn (1887), 120 U.S. 747; U.S. *v.* Stanford (1895), 161 U.S. 412.

[2] cf. Ralph Marquis and Frank P. Smith, *American Economic Review*, vol. XXVII (1937), 490–502.

European legislations, following the example of the *Code de Commerce*, regarded the structure of the corporation as decisive. For joint-stock companies of the general type (*Sociétés anonymes* in French and *Aktiengesellschaft* in German law) the liability of the shareholder is restricted to his contribution, i.e. the par value of his shares and the premium, if any. Apart from cases in which personal liability arises in consequence of some irregularity, this is the limit of a shareholder's liability.

As we have seen earlier, French law recognises the partnership by shares (*commandite par actions*), i.e. a corporation which has one or more partners personally liable for all its debts and obligations, the corporation also having a capital consisting of shares whose holders are liable only up to the par value of their shares. As we saw earlier, this form was very popular under the *Code de Commerce* of Napoleon, because under this Code the *société anonyme* was dependent upon a charter, whereas share partnerships could be formed by the partners and shareholders without the necessity of applying for one. After the abolition of the individual charter system this form of corporation had less importance.

The same evolution took place in Germany up to 1870, when the system of governmental concessions was abolished. But partnerships by shares (*Kommanditgesellschaft auf Aktien*) were never so popular in Germany as in France. Their number declined, owing partly to their conversion into joint-stock companies, partly to dissolutions, so that by about 1939 only a very limited number were still in existence. Several big banks, however, continued to adhere to the old form of the K.A.G., although it is obvious that the personal liability of managers (*Geschäftsinhaber*) cannot have any material value or importance in cases where the amount of liabilities exceeds 100 or even 1000 million Marks.

Most of the legislations which in other respects are closely modelled on the German system have never accepted this form of corporation. The personal liability of the directors as partners of K.A.G.s is based not upon their shareholdings and their quality as shareholders, but upon their quality and functions as partners. Therefore strictly speaking it does not constitute an exception to the general rule that the shareholder's liability is limited to the par value of his shares.

The principle of limited liability is accepted under these

Continental laws with a rigidity which does not admit of any extension of it by the articles. German law, however, allows an obligation to be undertaken for periodical delivery of certain raw materials by shareholders to the factory of a corporation. It was fairly common in Germany to form joint-stock companies for the erection of beet sugar factories and in some cases of spirit distilleries the capital for which was subscribed by the landowners of the district, the articles providing that the holder of each share must either cultivate sugar beets on a certain fixed area in proportion to the number of his shares—say, five or ten acres per share—and deliver the beets to the company, or else deliver a certain fixed quantity yearly. Originally this obligation was based upon separate contracts with each shareholder. This system of ensuring deliveries was not very reliable, although the contracts provided against almost every eventuality, e.g. death, alienation of the shares, and so on. The cases gave much work to the Courts and many headaches to commentators on the German law. Eventually the German Commercial Code of 1897 allowed provisions to be inserted in the articles binding the shareholders to such supplementary performances as mentioned, namely, the compulsory production and delivery of the goods in question as a corporate liability. Court decisions show that the matter remained highly controversial, and on the whole the joint-stock company form is not suited to such enterprises. This economic necessity can be much better and more directly met by the co-operative form, as is done in the U.S.A., where in numerous cases members are obliged in virtue of their membership to sell and deliver their goods to the co-operative at a price to be fixed, or to conclude agreements with the co-operatives for the exclusive marketing of their products. Such agreements are made in the form either of an agency or of a sale and purchase contract. The agreements frequently provide for a penalty or for damages in case of a breach of agreement. It is sometimes provided by statute and is even generally held by the Courts in the absence of special provisions that the co-operative may apply for an injunction and may sue for specific performance in order to secure the delivery of the goods under the agreement.[1]

Although statutes and usually the Courts also favour co-operatives, the Supreme Court of the U.S.A. has held [2] that a

[1] Frost *v.* Corporation Comm. (1929), 278 U.S. 522.

[2] See Fletcher 8287, n. 95.

discrimination in favour of a co-operative against corporations or individuals engaged in the same public utility business is unconstitutional. On the other hand the Internal Revenue Code of 1939 has exempted the Farmers' Co-operative Marketing Association from Federal Income Tax.[1]

In all the countries of the European Continent there are special laws for co-operatives (*Sociétés à capital variable*, *Erwerbs- und Wirtschaftsgenossenschaften*, etc.). This was made necessary to a certain extent by the rigidity of the Company laws, which do not permit the extension of shareholders' liability to any amount exceeding the par value of their shares and the premium, if any. Furthermore the rules governing the capital structure of companies exclude the possibility of members leaving the corporation and the re-purchase of their shares. Consequently more or less elaborate statutes have been enacted covering co-operatives as a special class of corporations. In all these countries the law on co-operatives is a special branch of corporation law differing in many points from the law on companies proper, into the details of which we have not to go in view of the scope of this book (cf. § 36).

On the whole limited liability applies in practice to most corporations, and it may be said that the popularity and growth of corporations may to a large extent be attributed to it. Before the acceptance of that principle as a general rule of corporation law, only a relatively small fraction of business activities was carried on by corporations, the invasion of every aspect and field of economic activity by corporations arising subsequently to this alteration of corporation law.

The view voiced by Heckscher in his monumental work on Mercantilism that limited liability has not the importance generally attributed to it is therefore unconvincing. His main argument is that if corporations are correctly managed personal liability of shareholders does not arise, and in order to prove his argument he quotes the example of the Swedish banks which exist without any limitation of liability. Quite apart from the question whether this exceptional case proves the argument, Swedish legislation shortly afterwards, by the irony of events, dispensed with unlimited or extended liability in the same way as the U.S.A. had done.

[1] 26 U.S. C.A. 101 (12).

(B) LIABILITY FOR THE UNPAID PORTION OF SHARES

The shares, whether subscribed before or at the time of incorporation, or, as is possible under Anglo-American law, placed subsequently, may be fully paid in cash or may in certain cases remain unpaid, possibly for a considerable time. The position as to additional shares issued in connection with an increase of capital is considered in § 90.

The interests both of the corporation and of the creditors require that the obligation to pay the remainder to the company should be placed upon a solid basis.

In Britain, in view of the attitude of the law as to specific performance, it was necessary to enact that the company is entitled to sue at law for payment and is not restricted to suing for damages. This rule is now contained in sec. 20 (2) of the Act of 1948: "All money payable by any member of the company under the memorandum and articles shall be a debt due from him to the company and in England be of the nature of a specialty debt."

The shareholder must pay according to the terms fixed in the articles. In some cases these provide fixed terms for the instalments by which the remainder is to be paid and lay down the times of such payments. Generally, however, the directors are empowered by the articles to demand payment or to make "calls". Table A15 contains the following clause: "The directors may from time to time make calls upon the members in respect of any moneys unpaid on their shares". This clause is usually adopted; but there is no objection to the articles empowering any other person to make the calls.

Sometimes the maximum amount of a call is limited, and an interval fixed between consecutive calls. Table A15 suggests that no call shall exceed one-fourth of the par value, and that no instalment shall be payable less than one month from the previous one.

The company must observe the provisions of the articles, otherwise the call may be inoperative; but to make a call payable by instalments when that was not provided for by the articles, or to reduce a call, would not be regarded as a violation.[1]

[1] cf. Lawrence *v.* Wynn (1839), 5 M. and W. 355, and Ambergate, etc., Eastern Junction Rail *v.* Norcliffe (1851), 6 Exch. Reps. 629.

The power to make calls must be exercised for the general benefit of the company, and as a rule *pari passu.*

Shareholders may set up an effective defence by proving that the directors acted *mala fide*,[1] e.g. for their own benefit or for some purpose extraneous to the company's interest.[2] It has, however, been held that it may be proper to make a call in order to restrain a threatened transfer of shares,[3] or to increase the saleable assets of the company in view of an intended sale of the enterprise.[4] A call made not on all but on certain selected members needs special justification.[5] It is likewise inadmissible to favour a director in this respect.[6]

Shareholders sued may object that the call was irregular, e.g. that the directors making the call were not duly appointed [7] or not duly qualified.[8]

Where—as in most cases—the directors have power to make calls, they must be decided upon by a resolution of the board of directors in meeting, and it may be objected that there was no valid resolution because the meeting was not duly convened,[9] or there was no quorum,[10] or the resolution was not duly passed and recorded in the minutes.[11] Smaller irregularities, however, will not affect the validity of the resolution. Another line of defence is that the defendant is not liable because he is not a member or because his entry in the register of members is invalid. These questions are discussed in § 44.

In making the call directors must specify the times when and places at which payment is to be made, and the call may be ineffective for lack of definiteness.[12] Generally the articles require a notice; Table A15 suggests a notice of at least fourteen days, and this suggestion is often followed, but in some a period of twenty-one days is provided.

Shareholders are liable to pay interest according to the general

[1] Odessa Tramways Co. *v.* Mendel (1878), 8 Ch. D. 235.
[2] Alexander *v.* Automatic Telephone Co. (1900), 2 Ch. 56.
[3] Gilbert's case (1870), L.R. 5 Ch. App. 559.
[4] New Zealand Gold Extraction Co. *v.* Peacock (1894), 1 Q.B. 622.
[5] Galloway *v.* Hallé Concerts Society (1915), 2 Ch. 233.
[6] Alexander *v.* Automatic Telephone Co., *supra.*
[7] Howbeach Coal Co. *v.* Teague (1860), 5 H. and N. 151.
[8] Iron Ship Coating Co. *v.* Blunt (1868), L.R. 3 C.P. 484; Sharp *v.* Dawes (1879), 2 Q.B.D. 26.
[9] Garden Gulley, etc., Mining Co. *v.* McLister (1875), L.R. 1 App. Cas. 46; Faure Electric Accumulator Co. *v.* Phillipart (1888), 58 L.T. 525.
[10] Austin's case (1871), 24 L.T. 932.
[11] Cornwall, etc., Mining Co. *v.* Bennett, 5 H. & N. 423.
[12] *Re* Cawley and Co. (1889), 42 Ch. D. 209.

rules; the articles usually contain a provision to this effect. Table A18 provides that the rate of interest shall not exceed 5 per cent. from the day appointed, but the directors shall be empowered to waive the whole interest or any part of it.

It is usual to provide that shareholders may pay in advance even uncalled parts of the par value of their shares and that those who make such payments shall receive interest upon such advances. Table A21 is a clause empowering directors to receive from shareholders payments in advance of the uncalled parts of their shares if and to such extent as they think fit, and to stipulate for interest not exceeding 5 per cent. upon such payments, a higher interest being payable only with the assent of the general meeting. It has been held that such a clause does not as a rule apply to calls by the liquidators of the company.[1] In the absence of a provision to this effect interest on advance payments may be payable, or it may be the basis of a special agreement, and it has been held that the rate of interest should not be excessive.[2] Directors should receive advance payments only if they can be used by the company to its advantage.

If the company has to pay interest in virtue of these principles, it is to be paid whether or not there are profits or whether or not they are sufficient to meet the interest due[3]; the amount paid in advance ranks *prima facie* for repayment before capital not paid in advance in case of winding-up.[4] On the other hand if once such advance payment has been made it cannot be repaid without the assent of the shareholder concerned except in the case of a valid reduction of the capital.[5]

The payments are to be made in cash. Directors, however, may agree with a shareholder that a debt presently due to the shareholder from the company may be set off.[6] It has been held that so long as the company is a going concern the shareholder may be paid by a set-off.[7]

If the company is in voluntary liquidation the directors may

[1] *Re* Welsh Flannel and Tweed Co. (1875), L.R. 20 Eq. 360.

[2] Poole, Jackson and Whyte's case (1878), 9 Ch. D. 322; *re* Pyle Works (1890), 44 Ch. D. 534.

[3] Lock *v.* Queensland, etc., Mortgage Co. (1896), A.C. 461.

[4] *Ex parte* Maude (1870), L.R. 6 Ch. App. 51; Wakefield, etc., Co. (1892), 3 Ch. 165.

[5] London and Northern S.S. Co. *v.* Farmer (1914), W.N. 200.

[6] Spargo's case (1873), L.R. 8 Ch. App. 407; Laroque *v.* Beauchemin (1897), A.C. 358; North Sydney Investment, etc., Co. *v.* Higgins (1899), A.C. 263.

[7] *Re* Hiram Maxim Lamp Co. (1903), 1 Ch. 70.

make calls only with the sanction of the general meeting. Other aspects of the case of liquidation are discussed in § 95.

The estate of a deceased shareholder is liable for debts arising from calls.[1]

The company may sue and after judgment may enforce payment by way of execution; it may also proceed against the shareholder in bankruptcy.[2] In the bankruptcy of a shareholder the uncalled part of the share may be proved, but it has been held that if the company receives a dividend this is not equivalent to payment, and the bankrupt shareholder does not by virtue of the dividend become entitled to participate in the surplus assets of the company.[3]

If the estate of a deceased shareholder becomes insolvent, the amount of future calls in respect of the shares held by the deceased may be estimated and proved for, and it is immaterial whether the company is a going concern or in liquidation.[4]

The action to enforce a call may be futile if the shareholder's assets are not sufficient to meet the debt, and it may be of importance for the company to have the power to make forfeit the shares of a member in delay. The power to make the shares forfeit is not, however, inherent in a company.[5] A company has such power only if it is provided for in the articles, and it has been held that the articles may be amended by special resolution in order to give this power.[6] But this seems contrary to the principle that a shareholder's obligations cannot be increased without his consent. Actually, however, the articles of most, if not all, companies contain provisions to this effect. The power to make shares forfeit can be given only for failure to pay a call or instalment of a call, but not for any other debt; consequently if a company has a lien on the shares in respect of other debts it cannot make use of the lien to make the shares forfeit, and a clause to this effect would be inoperative.

The premiss of a forfeiture is a valid call, and the decided cases show that the Courts scrutinise the question of the validity of the call more closely where the company makes use of this

[1] New Zealand, etc., Co. *v.* Peacock, *supra.*
[2] *Re* Winterbottom (1886), 18 Q.B.D. 446.
[3] *Re* West Coast Goldfields (1906), 1 Ch. 1.
[4] *Re* McMahon, Fuller *v.* McMahon (1900), 1 Ch. 173.
[5] Clarke *v.* Hart (1858), 6 H.L.C. 633.
[6] Dawkins *v.* Antrobus (1881), 17 Ch. D. 615; Allen *v.* Gold Reefs of West Africa (1900), 1 Ch. 656.

power than in cases where it only sues the shareholder for payment. Thus it has been held that the forfeiture may be regarded as invalid if in the notice interest was demanded from the date of call instead of the date appointed for payment.[1]

The articles usually leave it to the directors' discretion to declare forfeit shares in respect of which a call or instalment remains unpaid after the expiration of the term appointed for such payment, with the proviso that they may declare the shares forfeit so long as the amount remains unpaid (Table A33–4).

The directors are to exercise this power for the benefit of the company. Thus a forfeiture made for the purpose of relieving a shareholder favoured by the directors of his liabilities to the detriment of the company may be attacked as an abuse of the power.[2]

The articles usually prescribe that before forfeiture a notice shall be served on the shareholder demanding the payment together with interest if any, naming a later day, usually at least a fortnight from the date of the notice, after which the shares will be liable to forfeiture. The shareholder in delay has a right to insist upon compliance with the terms of the notice.

A clause in the articles providing that the shares of a member who is bringing action against the company or the directors or threatens to begin such action, may be made forfeit on payment of the market value of the shares, has been held invalid.[3]

The member may sue the company for damages if his shares were irregularly forfeited.[4]

A shareholder may bring action to set aside an invalid forfeiture [5] and he may obtain an injunction to restrain the forfeiture pending the proceedings, though usually on payment into Court of the amount of the call.[6]

The forfeiture is usually to be made by resolution of the board of directors (Table A35); it may be challenged if the provisions of the articles are not complied with.

If forfeiture has duly been resolved on, the share concerned

[1] Johnson *v.* Lyttle's Iron Agency (1877), 5 Ch. D. 687; Faure Electric Accumulator Co. *v.* Philippart (1888), 58 L.T. 525.

[2] Spackman *v.* Evans (1868), L.R. 3 H.L. 171; *re* Esparto Trading Co. (1879), 12 Ch. D. 191; Lord Wallscourt's case (1899), W.N. 258.

[3] Hope *v.* International Financial Society (1876), 4 Ch. D. 327.

[4] *Re* New Chili Gold Mining Co. (1890), 45 Ch. D. 598.

[5] Sweny *v.* Smith (1869), 7 Eq. 324; Johnson *v.* Lyttle's, etc., Agency, *supra*, and *re* New Chili Gold Mining Co., *supra*.

[6] Lamb *v.* Sambas Rubber and Gutta Percha Co. (1908), 1 Ch. 845; Jones *v.* Pacaya Rubber and Produce Co. (1911), 1 K.B. 455.

passes into the property of the company. The usual provision of the articles is that "it may be sold or otherwise disposed of on such terms and in such manner as the directors think fit" (Table A36).

As a consequence of the forfeiture the shareholder loses his rights as to the share, but remains liable to pay the whole amount already due to the company. The articles, however, usually provide that the liability ceases if and when the company receives full payment of the money due (Table A37). But in the absence of express provision the membership ceases with the forfeiture, and the company has no action against the former member,[1] and the cancellation of the forfeiture cannot be exercised without the consent of the shareholder.[2]

If the company sells a forfeited share the sale may be effected at a discount; the rule against the issue of shares at less than par value does not apply to such a case.[3] The share in question may be sold as fully paid or as subject to calls.[4]

The company has by virtue of law no lien on the shares of its members. Such a lien may be created by agreement or by a clause in the articles; such provisions are usual (Table A11) and they generally include all debts due to the company. The question of liens and their effect is discussed in connection with the acquisition by the company of its own shares (§ 66).

In the U.S.A. the position is similar. Stockholders are bound to pay the par value of the shares subscribed or taken by them at the times and in the instalments fixed in the charter or articles; in the absence of such at the request of the corporation, i.e. at call. Certain States provide for a call in any case.

In the absence of a statute or charter (articles) or of provisions to the contrary the power to make calls is vested in the board of directors.[5] Many statutes make express provision to this effect, and there are only a few instances in which the power to make calls is conferred on other persons or is reserved to the general meeting.

Calls should be made for the legitimate purposes of the company, but the necessity or advisability of a call cannot be

[1] *Re* Stoeken's case (1868), L.R. 3 Ch. App. 412.

[2] *In re* Exchange Trust, Larkworthy's case (1903), 1 Ch. 711.

[3] Morrison *v.* Trustees, Executors and Securities Insurance Corporation (1898), 68 L.J. Ch. 11 C.A.

[4] Cf. New Balkis Eersteling *v.* Randt, etc., Co. (1904), A.C. 165.

[5] Oglesby *v.* Attrill (1883), 105 U.S. 605.

questioned by a shareholder; only a fraudulent call may be resisted by a stockholder.[1] It has been held that a call can be attacked on this ground collaterally.

A call when made must apply to all stockholders uniformly; if there is no equality it is inoperative.[2]

In so far as the power to make calls is vested in the directors there must be a resolution of a duly convened board with the necessary quorum, otherwise it is not operative. Similarly the call must be sufficiently clear and definite both as to amount and the date appointed for payment, and the provisions of the charter (articles) as to the call are to be observed.[3]

The corporation may enforce the debt created in respect of an unpaid subscription either at law or in equity; it may also be set off by a counterclaim. Even in States where in earlier times subscriptions were regarded as contracts of sale and purchase and as long as the contract was executory no action for payment was admitted (as in Pennsylvania), the statutes nowadays provide for such action. In Delaware, Maine, Massachusetts and New Hampshire it is held that without express promise to pay no action may be brought for payment.[4]

Corporations have a right to forfeit shares for default in payment only if this power is given them by statute or charter. In actual fact many legislations make express provision to this effect, as do numerous charters (articles).

As in Great Britain, the corporation has no lien on the shares for debts in the absence of express provision to this effect. Certain legislations give a lien for unpaid parts of the par value, and also power to sell the shares in order to satisfy the debt for unpaid calls.[5] Except in case of insolvency the stockholder has the right of set-off in respect of mature debts of the corporation due to him.[6]

French law contains no special provisions bearing on the obligations of shareholders towards the company in respect of the unpaid part of the par value of their shares. The matter is governed by Art. 1846 of the *Code Civil*, which provides that each partner must comply with what he has promised to contribute

[1] Oglesby *v.* Attrill, *supra*.

[2] Glenn *v.* Liggett (1890), 135 U.S. 533; cf. Fletcher 1808, Ballantine (1st ed.), 196.

[3] Nashua Saving Bank *v.* Anglo-American Land Mortgage and Agency Co. (1903), 189 U.S. 221.

[4] Fletcher 1838.

[5] See Fletcher, 1790–1933; Ballantine (1st ed.), 196 and 198.

[6] Ballantine (1st ed.), 204.

to the partnership, and that he is by virtue of law a debtor to the partnership in respect of that amount, and has to pay interest from the day appointed for payment without demand on the part of the *societas*. Further, damages may be claimed. This provision was extended and applied by the Courts to companies.[1]

German law provides a stricter regulation to ensure the payment of shares issued for cash. As we saw above, at least 25 per cent. of the amount and the premium, if any, must be paid before registration. The remainder is to be paid on the dates and in the instalments fixed by the articles. In the absence of such provisions the management has the power and the duty to make the calls. Notice is to be given, unless otherwise provided, in the same way as with other communications from the company to its shareholders, i.e. by advertisement in the *Gazette*, which is compulsory, and usually in one, or in the case of larger companies, in several, newspapers as provided in the articles (§ 57 (1), 18).

It is held that calls must be uniform; where several classes of shares exist there must be equality within each class. This applies both to the amount to be paid and the time of payment.[2] Earlier the R.G. held that the shareholder had no actionable right to enforce equality.[3]

The shareholder cannot plead a set-off (§ 60). This provision, however, does not prevent a set-off by mutual agreement.[4]

Shareholders who fail to comply with the call have to pay 5 per cent. interest. Claims for further damages are not excluded, and the articles may prescribe penalties (§ 57 (2), (3)), which may, however, be reduced by the Court in proper cases, except where the subscription is a mercantile contract (§ 343, Civil Code, cf. Gadow, pp. 193–4).

The company has a right to make forfeit the shares of shareholders who do not pay the call. This right is not dependent upon any provisions of the articles, but is given by the law. On the other hand the company is under no obligation; it may choose not to forfeit but to insist on payment and may enforce it by way of action and execution. If the company chooses forfeiture the shareholder concerned is to be given notice, which is to be published three times in those newspapers in which

[1] Supreme Court, 6 August 1862, D.P. 62,1, 427, and 14 November 1899, D.P. 1900, 1, 99.

[2] R.G.Z. 132, 396 (case of a G.m.b.H.).

[3] R.G.Z. 85, 367.

[4] Gadow, pp. 205–6.

by the articles communications to shareholders are to be published, and the company may declare forfeiture only after three months have elapsed from the first and one month from the third publication. Where the transfer of the share is dependent on the assent of the company a special written notice addressed to the shareholder is sufficient, and at least one month must be given for payment (§ 58 (1)). In the meantime the shareholder may avert forfeiture by paying the amount of the call with interest; on the other hand the company may change its mind and demand payment instead of forfeiture.[1] If after the time stipulated payment has not been received and the company has declared the shares forfeit, this fact is to be published by advertisement conformably to the articles. By the forfeiture the shareholder loses his shares and all payments made in favour of the company, which may sell the shares or cancel them by reduction of capital. The shareholder remains liable for the deficiency (58 (3), (4)).

The provisions of the Swiss law (O.R. 681–2) are similar in substance, as are those of most other European legislations.

52. Liability as against Creditors

The obligation of shareholders to pay the full par value of their shares holds with respect to and in favour of the company. It is an asset which must appear in the balance sheet. It is of eminent interest to creditors that this asset should be preserved and in case of need realised in order to satisfy the company's debts, and it is generally recognised that companies have no power to release shareholders from their liability. The question whether, how far and in what way creditors are entitled to assert their rights as against shareholders is dealt with on different lines by the various legislations.

In Great Britain it is for the company and in particular the directors to decide when and to what extent to make calls and collect the moneys due from shareholders. Generally directors will do their best to make calls if they are necessary to carry on the business and to satisfy creditors, but in a particular case it may be otherwise.

It has been asserted that a creditor may by *mandamus* compel

[1] R.G.Z. 51, 416; Gadow, p. 197.

directors to make calls. Receivers, however, have power to make calls only if the directors are authorised to delegate their power to do so; the Court may order a receiver to make calls or may order the directors to make calls and to hand over the proceeds to the receiver.[1]

The normal way open to creditors for obtaining satisfaction is to sue the company and in case of need to ask for a creditors' winding up. Further, as already stated, a company may mortgage uncalled capital if the directors have borrowing powers and there is nothing in the memorandum of association to the contrary.[2] Although no such case is to be found in the reports, it seems probable that creditors may attach unpaid capital after having obtained judgment against the corporation.

In the U.S.A. the liability of shareholders in regard to creditors when the corporation is unable to satisfy them and becomes insolvent is held to be a principle of common law.[3] It has sometimes been based upon the erroneous doctrine that the capital is a net fund for the benefit of creditors.[4]

Unless authorised by statute, the corporation has no power to exempt a shareholder from this liability, apart of course from the case of a reduction of capital. The statutes contain detailed provisions as to both the extent and the operation of this liability. These provisions are generally regarded in the U.S.A. as declaratory of the common law.[5]

Under most legislations the liability is a secondary one; it does not arise so long as the corporation is solvent and the creditors can obtain satisfaction from the company. In some States, however, the liability for unpaid subscriptions is primary.[6] Most States accept the rule that liability is restricted to whatever may be necessary to satisfy the debts of the corporation together with interest and costs. It is obvious that such restriction is difficult of operation although equitable. In many cases it would be pointless to demand payment in excess of the amount necessary. Nevertheless it would involve complicated questions if shareholders could object that the payment requested from them would not be

[1] *In re* Phœnix Bessemer Co. (1875), 44 L.J. Ch. 683.
[2] *In re* Phœnix Bessemer, *supra*.
[3] Ogilvie *v.* Knox Insurance Co. (1860), 22 How. (U.S.) 380; Sawyer *v.* Hoag (1873), 17 Wall 610; Upton *v.* Tribilcock (1876), 91 U.S. 45; Hatch *v.* Dana (1885), 101 U.S. 205.
[4] Cf. Fletcher 6052; Ballantine 340.
[5] Patterson *v.* Lynde (1883), 106 U.S. 519; Fletcher 6053, n. 42.
[6] Fletcher 6265.

necessary in future. Where such a defence is admitted the allegation and proof that the payment or a certain part of it is not necessary is imposed upon the shareholders.[1]

It is held in some States that liability extends to premiums which are to be paid in excess of the par value, whereas in others this is denied.[2] Under American law shareholders who have been compelled to pay more than others are entitled to contribution from them.[3] The existence of valid debts is a condition precedent of the liability. According to the better rule the liability extends to debts in tort.

Under legislations that regard the liability as merely a secondary one a judgment against the corporation and a failure of the execution are conditions precedent.[4] But a creditor may be excused from bearing the expense of an execution that would obviously be useless. Under legislations which reserve the exercise of the right of action on this liability to the receiver or trustee in bankruptcy, this question cannot arise.

A further question is whether the liability is actionable without a call or assessment. This is disputed in the U.S.A.[5] There are some decisions to the effect that although a call is necessary it could also be made by the Court. Where a call or assessment is required the call made by the Court or by the trustee, receiver, etc., is conclusive as to the necessity of the call or assessment. On the other hand, this question cannot be raised by collateral attack, and the shareholder is entitled only to file a bill in equity in order to obtain a judicial review.[6]

The call or assessment is not conclusive as to the liability of particular shareholders and its amount. They may set up their individual defences if sued: thus, e.g., that defendant is not a shareholder, that he has paid in full, etc.

Under common law the creditors were held to be entitled to sue on behalf of the corporation, and some States still maintain this rule. Many of the statutes, however, provide that it is

[1] See Scovill *v.* Thayer (1882), 105 U.S. 143; Fletcher 6062, n. 95–6.

[2] Fletcher 6064, n. 5–6.

[3] Fletcher 6070.

[4] Ogilvie *v.* Knox, *supra*; Terry *v.* Anderson (1877), 95 U.S. 628; National Tube Works Co. *v.* Ballou (1892), 146 U.S. 517; Swan *v.* Frank (1893), 148 U.S. 603; Hollins *v.* Brierfeld (1893), 150 U.S. 371, and Fletcher 6076, n. 73.

[5] See Harrigan *v.* Bergdoll (1926), 270 U.S. 560; Fletcher 6084, n. 20; for the opposite view Scoville *v.* Thayer, *supra*; Hawkins *v.* Glenn (1888), 131 U.S. 319; Glenn *v.* Liggett (1890), 135 U.S. 533, and Fletcher 6084, n. 20.

[6] See Glenn cases, *supra*; Great Western *v.* Purdy (1895), 162 U.S. 329; Fletcher 6092, n. 86.

only for the receiver, trustee or assignee of the corporation to bring action to enforce the liability.

Many complications arising from the granting of the action to individual creditors make it advisable to reserve it exclusively for the receiver or some other person acting for the community of the creditors. This is accepted by most, if not all, legislations outside the U.S.A. Even in those American States where individual creditors may otherwise bring actions they are held not to be entitled to do so after the appointment of a receiver or trustee in bankruptcy.[1] This rule does not apply if the receiver, trustee in bankruptcy, etc., fails or refuses to bring action against the shareholders or some of them; in such a case the creditor must be allowed to sue, and this exception is recognised.[2]

In case of bankruptcy or compulsory liquidation the claim based on the liability may be assigned. Correct analysis shows that it is not this claim but the obligation based on the subscription or purchase of the share which may be alienated and assigned by the corporation. Similarly the question whether the claim is an asset of the corporation is not put correctly under this heading. It is only the obligation of the shareholder as against the corporation which is an asset of the latter. The obligation and not the liability is the item which appears among the assets of the corporation. Whether this asset may be attached by individual creditors of the corporation in the course of execution, and whether it may be sold and assigned by the corporation, is settled by the various legislations in different ways.

In case of insolvency it is generally held that a shareholder sued cannot set off a claim which he has against the corporation. Some legislations hold that even apart from the case of insolvency a set-off is not admissible.[3]

The suit of creditors is held to be a suit in equity because there is no privity of contract between the shareholder and the creditor of the corporation. But there are decisions to the contrary.[4] Whether the action of the receiver or trustee in bankruptcy is taken in law or in equity is disputed. It is also disputed whether all the shareholders must be joined as defendants,[5] but the majority rule is that the shareholders may be joined at the discretion of the receiver or creditor but that such joining is not obligatory.[6]

[1] Fletcher 6121, n. 16–17. [2] Fletcher 6121, n. 16–17. [3] See Fletcher 6183, n. 20.
[4] Fletcher 6188. [5] See Fletcher 6202, n. 65–69. [6] cf. Ballantine 340.

The German law of 1937 provides that shareholders cannot be released from their obligation to pay the par value of their shares (§ 60). Any agreement in violation of this rule would be void. This is held to extend to any reduction of the obligation whether as to the amount or the time of payment. But if the company is in liquidation and there are no other creditors it is held that the company is not bound to observe the prohibition.[1] Since the prohibition is intended for the protection of the creditors, even shareholders in general meeting cannot resolve upon a release,[2] and a reduction of the obligation and liability could be brought about only in connection with a valid reduction of the capital.

The company is held to have power to assign claims arising from subscriptions. But it is held that such assignment is valid only against full consideration.[3] It is disputed whether in such case a call by the directors is necessary or whether the creditor may sue the shareholder independently.[4]

Mortgaging of uncalled capital is held to be admissible. Similarly, creditors may attach such capital, i.e. debts of shareholders to the company, although under German law this would involve the insolvency of the company.

53. Liability in respect of Shares for Property

The question of shares for property or services has already been discussed from the point of view of company formation (§ 45); here we have to examine it from that of liability. In Great Britain this is based upon the terms of the contract between the company and the shareholder concerned, and the Court will not review the contract as to the adequacy of the compensation. This applies also where the company was subsequently wound up. Fraud, however, is excepted.[5] The shareholder in such a case may be obliged to make good the deficiency.[6] On the other hand the company is entitled to exercise the rights arising from

[1] R.G.Z. 149, 298, 156, 25.
[2] R.G.Z., quoted by Gadow, p. 205, n. 4.
[3] R.G.Z. 124, 380, 133, 83, 135, 57.
[4] Gadow, p. 207, n. 11.
[5] *Re* Wragg, Ltd. (1897), 1 Ch. 796; Hong Kong and China Gas Co. *v.* Glen (1914), 1 Ch. 527.
[6] Re James Pitkin and Co. (1916), W.N. 112.

the contract, to sue for specific performance in a proper case, to bring action for damages or to repudiate the contract for non-performance. In a proper case the shares may be cancelled.

There is nothing in the Companies Act to prevent a company from taking property in satisfaction for calls. Lastly, although directors must deliver the contract under which the allotment of shares was made to the Registrar of Companies for registration within one month (sec. 52 (2)), and failure to do so makes them liable to a fine, it does not affect the validity of the contract.

In the U.S.A. this matter is dealt with under the heading of liability for watered stock.

In earlier days it was usually held that property transferred to a company in consideration for shares must at the time of the issue have had a value equal to the par value of the shares (the test of true value). Subsequently the Courts took a more lenient view, and not the actual value at the time of issue but good faith at that time became the test. Under this view errors of judgment were held to excuse from liability the shareholders receiving the shares.[1] Under the influence of this doctrine of good faith it was enacted in most States that in the absence of fraud the directors' judgment as to the value of assets given in consideration for shares is conclusive. It was also doubted whether constructive fraud was sufficient to establish the liability of directors. Eventually, however, the view prevailed that there must be actual fraud, in the absence of which shareholders cannot be sued for watered stock.

The evolution in Delaware is interesting. The constitution (Art. 11, sec. 3) required actual value. Corporation law in its turn made the directors' judgment conclusive. This limitation of liability was held to be unconstitutional, and in 1903 the constitution was amended by deleting the test of actual value. In this state of the law and in view of the changed attitude of the Courts very clear proof of fraud was required in order to establish the liability, all the more as an amendment of 1905 limited liability to cases of actual fraud. Error of judgment in cases where careful investigation had been made was held not to be fraud, although promoters paid a price much in excess of that which other purchasers would have paid.[2] On the other hand in a case where shares of a par value of $200,000 were

[1] Schenk *v.* Andrews (1874), 57 N.Y. 133.

[2] Henderson *v.* Plymouth Oil Co. (1928), 15 Del. Ch. 131.

issued with only $5000 covered by services actual fraud was held to have existed.

Some of the Statutes require valuation of the property, labour or services given as consideration. Such valuations are to be made either by the directors or by independent valuers. This is perfectly reasonable, but its effect depends on the consequences of an incorrect valuation. If it is only a deliberately false valuation that involves liability, this requirement is not very effective, since good faith is to be presumed, and both the fact of over-valuation and the *mala fides* have to be alleged and proved.

In the relation between the vendors of the property and the corporation the shares will be treated as fully paid in accordance with their agreement. This means that in so far as the agreement is valid the corporation is not entitled to demand the difference between the par value of the shares and the value of the consideration if it be subsequently proved that the consideration in property, labour or services is less than was agreed.[1]

As against subsequent *bona fide* creditors of the corporation the agreement does not give protection if the over-valuation was intentional, i.e. if the parties had knowledge of the fact that the value was less than the par value of the stock. The reason for this rule is that the *bona fide* creditors have a right to rely on the representation that the shares are fully paid, and have a right of action if this statement or representation was intentionally false or if both the corporation, i.e. its directors and the subscriber of the shares knew at the time of making the contract that the par value was not covered.[2] If, however, the consideration had no value at all, in other words if the shares were issued gratuitously, this violates the rights of the existing shareholders who did not consent and also of subsequent subscribers who make their subscriptions on the faith of the stated capital; they may sue for cancellation of the shares provided they have not in the meantime been acquired by a *bona fide* holder. Such shares violate not only the rights of subsequent creditors but also the rights of the above-mentioned two classes of shareholders.[3]

Under some legislations we also find decisions to the effect that the State may institute proceedings for the forfeiture of the company's charter in case of the issue of watered stock, and may accordingly, so long as the issue is not completed, bring a bill

[1] Fletcher 5202. [2] Fletcher 5201.
[3] Handley *v.* Stutz (1891), 139 U.S. 417.

for injunction.[1] This far-reaching remedy, however, is qualified by the limitation that such action lies only if the general public interest requires forfeiture; if only private rights are affected the State cannot maintain the action or a suit for injunction.[2] In view of this doctrine the remedy by way of forfeiture or injunction by the State is ineffective, and although the financial history of the U.S.A. presents examples of immense waterings of stocks, in none of them, such as the case of the Newhaven Railroad, have proceedings been started by the Attorneys-General of the State concerned.

If neither the rights of dissenting stockholders nor those of subsequent creditors are impaired the corporations involved are held to be bound by the transaction and estopped from demanding payment of the difference. Similarly the subscriber himself cannot attack the transaction. Remedy is thus restricted to dissenting shareholders and *bona fide* creditors. The shareholder has the right to rely on the representation contained on the face of the share certificate that the other shareholders have paid up the amount of their shares, and they have a similar right to expect that subsequent subscribers (purchasers) will enter the company on the same terms.

The prohibition of watering extends to increases of the original capital. It is accepted, however, that a company which becomes embarrassed may issue new shares at less than par value in payment of debts or to raise money for the continuance of its business.

The Supreme Court of the U.S. has held that a railroad company which was indebted to a construction company to the amount of $70,000 had a right to make a settlement whereby the construction company accepted shares of the par value of $350,000 as payment, since the shares had at that time no value at all on the market. It was held that under the circumstances the issue was not a fraud upon subsequent creditors nor *ultra vires*.[3] In Fogg *v.* Blair [4] it was held that a transaction by which a contractor received $185,000 in stock besides $12,000 in bonds per mile of the constructed road could not be attacked because it was not shown that the stock was of some value. The same was held in Handley *v.* Stutz,[5] where the corporation issued new shares as a bonus to purchasers of bonds.

[1] Fletcher 5225, n. 82–5.
[2] Fletcher 5225, n. 91–2.
[3] Clark *v.* Bever (1891), 139 U.S. 96.
[4] (1891), 139 U.S. 118.
[5] (1891), 139 U.S. 417.

This doctrine may be justified from the standpoint of efficiency, but it obviously impairs the future of the corporation. By issuing ordinary shares which at the time of issue have no actual value the corporation mortgages its future. In cases like that of United Steel, the common shares at the time of the issues contained water and acquired value only through the subsequent prosperity of the corporation. On the other hand corporations with a less fortunate development could never obtain real values for their common (ordinary) stock, and innocent purchasers of the shares suffered considerable losses. This was especially the case with many railway corporations.

The other accepted exception is for treasury stock and shares purchased or forfeited. It is qualified in this case to the effect that the exception does not apply where the transaction was not made in good faith.[1] But it is difficult to prove the absence of good faith, and therefore the qualification is not of much value. A better rule as to forfeiture would be to allow the issue only in cases in which the money paid by the shareholder in default and the sum to be paid by the purchaser of the forfeited share together represent not less than the full par value of the share.

Antecedent creditors and creditors with notice of or assenting to the transaction have no action for the discharge of their debts.[2]

In some States the certificates issued for watered stock are void; but in the majority of the jurisdictions they are voidable only. This of course applies to fictitious issues for which nothing at all has been paid. If the shares are unpaid only in part, i.e. are watered, the question of voidness cannot be raised since there is only partial voidness.[3]

The liability as against creditors arises only if the assets of the corporation are insufficient to pay its debts. The holders of watered stock are held to be liable *pro rata* for the debts to the extent of the balance due on their holdings.

Quite apart from the liability of the shareholders there is a liability on the part of the directors and other managing officers (see § 81). The liability of the shareholder may of course be enforced by the receiver or trustee in bankruptcy.

Although the remedies against the watering of stock are not

[1] See Fletcher 5238, n. 35–37.
[2] See Colt *v.* North Carolina (1886), 119 U.S. 343; Bank of Fort Madison *v.* Alden (1888), 129 U.S. 372; further the State Decisions quoted by Fletcher 5238, n. 43–5.
[3] Fletcher 5240, n.

very effective, their existence was influential in the introduction and spread of the device of stock without par value (see § 64).

By German law the conditions and terms for the issue of shares for property are, as shown in § 45 above, laid down in the articles. The law of 1937 (§ 60) provides that the shareholders cannot be released from their obligation and liability. Under this rule every agreement aimed at such release or reduction is invalid both as against the company and as against creditors. This applies also to resolutions in general meeting, which if they violate the rule are inoperative.

Compromises would on principle be inoperative, but in one case of a G.m.b.H. the R.G. found that a compromise was valid in view of the uncertainty of the legal position and the threatened damage to the company.[1]

It is further to be noted that the rule prohibiting alterations as to the terms of the issue during the first five years of the company's existence bars in the view of the commentators the conversion of the consideration fixed in property into cash.[2]

54. The Rights of Shareholders to Dividends

The essential right of a shareholder is that of participation in the financial results of the company. Some corporations, indeed, exist whose aims are of a non-profit-making character; in Great Britain even the form of a company limited by shares may be used for such altruistic purposes, and companies with such aims are likewise allowed under European legislations. The purpose of most companies, however, is to trade for profit, and in such companies the right of the shareholders to participate in that profit is essential. Although the corporation is a legal entity independent of its members, it is after all a means to ensure better results than could be attained by individual effort or by partnership, though this is sometimes forgotten. All other rights of shareholders are secondary to that of participation in the results, and are directed to ensuring it.

As we saw in the first part of this book, joint-stock companies were originally regarded as enterprises intended to last for one or a few ventures only, and after these were concluded their proceeds were distributed. The final distribution alone showed

[1] R.G.Z. 79, 274.

[2] Gadow 205, n. 5.

whether any profit had been made on the capital invested. The idea that during the company's lifetime the profits alone are distributable, and that at regular intervals, was one only of gradual evolution.

The earliest mention of dividends occurs in the charter of the Mines Royal, whereby the directors were empowered "to make divident of the commodities and profits". No mention is made of dividends proper, i.e. of distributed profits, in the charters of the other early companies. This is not surprising, since they mostly had no permanent joint stock, and distributions were made after the ventures had been wound up. The charter of the New River Company, however, provided in 1620 that dividends were to be paid out of profits. As we have mentioned, the East India Company paid its first dividend only in 1661.

In the case of the Bank of England the question of dividends was connected with the extension of indebtedness in excess of the loan made by the Bank to the State, which was equal to the capital stock. Dividends were to be paid only out of interest, profit or produce arising by or out of the said capital stock or fund or such dealing, buying or selling as was allowed by Act of Parliament. Furthermore, every shareholder was liable for debts in excess of the capital stock in proportion to his share (sec. 26 of the Act). It is to be borne in mind that the directors were prohibited from creating any excess liability without the assent of the General Court, i.e. the shareholders in general meeting. The Act of 1697 (sec. 49) extended the liability if any repayment were made to shareholders without reducing the debt. It appears therefore that the question of dividends was limited by two considerations, namely, that the Bank should not incur liabilities in excess of its capital and that repayments should not be made either in the form of dividends or otherwise so as to impair that capital.

Profit generally means the difference between revenue and expenditure. The possibility of the capital being reduced by factors other than an adverse balance of the revenue account was envisaged only in exceptional cases. One such was that of the New Mills Company, which from 1675 accounted for depreciation. The Bubble Act (1720) provided that for the two maritime insurance companies dividends should be a proper share of the profits and advantages attending the capital stock. This wording shows without doubt that dividends were thought of as distributions of profits without taking depreciation into account. Even as late as 1791 the Oxford Navigation Company still used the receipts and expenditure basis.

The companies that acted on this principle did not take capital losses into account and in many cases balance sheets were drawn up, not yearly, but only when the ledger was full or the business terminated. During the 18th century, however, it became usual to create reserves for bad debts and contingencies.[1]

Under the influence of English law and ideology the profit basis was adopted in the U.S.A. The Act incorporating the Bank of North America (1781) provided (sec. VIII) that the directors are to pay such dividends out of profits as they may think proper. Similarly in the case of the Bank of New York, created in 1784 and incorporated in 1791, the majority of the directors was to decide on the profits.

The Act incorporating the First Bank of the U.S.A.[2] provided (sec. 7) that "half-yearly dividends shall be made of so much of the profits of the Bank as shall appear to directors advisable". By the by-laws adopted in the same year (sec. 10), members who assented to distributions in excess of the profits and thus diminished the capital stock were made liable as individuals. Significantly, however, this limitation does not appear in the charter of the Second Bank of the U.S.A. So long as individual charters were used for the incorporation of companies the majority of them adopted the profit rule. Especially was this the case with banks. In the charters of turnpike, canal and bridge companies repairs and contingent charges, and in some cases even deductions for depreciation and improvement, are mentioned.

The actual practice is said to have varied. Charters of insurance companies contained prohibitions against impairing capital by dividends, and in the case of the Insurance Company of the North the charter (1794) contained a proviso that in the event of diminution of capital no dividends shall be paid before the loss is made good.

Gradually the U.S.A. drifted away from the unlimited profit rule, and in 1824 the Federal Court held [3] that capital must not be impaired although the charter contains only the profit clause.[4] The General Incorporation Act of New York [5] provided that

[1] Cf. Dubois, p. 414, nn. 142, 144, 146.
[2] 1 Statute, 194–5 *ex* 1791.
[3] Wood *v.* Dummer.
[4] (1824), 3 Mason 308 Fed. Cas. C.C. 17994.
[5] N.Y. Laws (1825), C. 325, § 2.

dividends should be paid only from "surplus profits", but at the same time it forbade companies to "divide, withdraw or to pay in any way any part of the capital stock". We may therefore conclude that the profit rule was not strictly adhered to, even if the language employed was similar to that used in England.[1]

The view of the modern law is that dividends may be paid only from profits, and that so long as the company is a going concern no distributions may be made out of capital. This rule does not prevent distributions in connection with and in consequence of a valid reduction of capital, which may be one resolved upon in general meeting in compliance with the special provisions applying to such resolutions or by redemption of shares as provided in the articles.

Every other distribution before the winding up of the company is therefore everywhere regarded as a violation of law, with consequential liability on the part of those responsible for it. In matters of detail, however, there is still much dispute. Thus there are dicta of prominent English judges to the effect that the company need not make good depreciations or losses suffered in earlier years provided there are current profits from which dividends may be paid. Lindley, L.J., said [2] that "a company may be formed upon the principle that no dividends shall be declared unless the capital is kept undiminished or a company may contract with its creditors to keep its capital or assets up to a given value". In the absence of such provision "even a sinking fund to replace lost capital by degrees is not required by law". He therefore concluded that "the law is more accurately expressed by saying that dividends cannot be paid out of capital than by saying that they can only be paid out of profits". This dictum found wide acceptance, and in view of similar dicta by American Courts it has been asked what is the true nature of company capital; is it a *quantum* or a *res*?

Actually every company law requires that the capital of a company shall be expressed in money, and that in the currency of the State in which the company is registered. The capital of a company is therefore necessarily a sum of money, whatever the assets in which the capital has been invested or of which it consists at a given time.

Even if a company does not carry on business and does

[1] Cf. Donald Kehl, *Early American Dividend Law*, H.L.R. 53, pp. 36–75.
[2] Verner *v*. General and Commercial Investment Trust (1894), 2 Ch. 239.

nothing but invest the cash paid by its shareholders, or does not use the property transferred to it as consideration for shares, the value of its assets may increase or decrease according to circumstances. Normally, however, a company will do business, and as a result thereof will either make profits or incur losses; and it is usual to review its business results and the consequent state of affairs at periodical fixed dates, usually once a year. On this basis the account of profits and losses is drawn up. Such profits and losses can be shown only in monetary units. We must therefore conclude that the capital of a company is always a quantum of money.

It was said in an early American case,[1] that capital is not a thing, but only the value in money of the thing owned by the corporation.

In this book the question of capital and profit is discussed only as regards Company law, and we are not concerned with questions connected with the taxation of companies, especially their income tax, or with the relations between the life tenant of stock and the remainderman. Cardozo as Chief Justice of New York rightly said [2] that "What is income in one relation may be principal in another". From our point of view the distinctions must be quite unambiguous.

The capital of a company is to be reviewed at the start of its activities and again at the end of any subsequent period for which accounts are to be made up. The realities of business life require the capital to be ascertained at the beginning of the company's life and at the end of every financial year as provided by the articles. Likewise a company's profit or loss is to be ascertained at the end of each financial year, always in money.

We have therefore to distinguish between a capital account and a revenue account. The capital account of a company would not be exact unless as its last item the result of the revenue account—whether it be a profit or a loss—were included. As we have said, the value of the assets is not static; it may be the same as at the time of the original acquisition, i.e. with the cost or purchase price; as a rule, however, it will either increase or diminish. It is a question of financial policy whether such alteration of values is to be taken into account and regarded as affecting business results or not.

[1] Earp's Appeal (1857), 28 P.A. 368.
[2] Equitable Trust Co. of N.Y. *v.* Prentice (1928), 250 N.Y. 1, at p. 11.

Sound financial policy requires that diminution of values should be inquired into and shown in the accounts, but that increases in value without any alteration in substance should be either neglected or, if shown, not added to profits, used to increase dividends or distributed among shareholders.

The English Companies Act contains no express provisions as to dividends; the question is therefore left to the articles. The only provision introduced by the Act of 1948 (sec. 59 (*c*)) deals with the method of apportionment of dividends where different amounts are paid up on the shares. Even on this matter the company may make its own arrangements in its articles. Table A, clause 116, provides, however, that dividends are to be paid out of profits, its wording being that "no dividend shall be paid otherwise than out of profits". Since the articles of most British companies either accept Table A or contain provisions identical with it, they are in fact governed by the rule that dividends may be paid only out of profits.

The meaning of this rule, however, is to some extent disputed. There is no doubt that articles could in no case provide that dividends may be paid out of capital, save of course for the payment of interest during the time of construction (sec. 65). Violation of this rule would be *ultra vires*,[1] nor could such payment be sanctioned or ratified by a resolution in general meeting.[2] Directors who are parties to any prohibited payment out of capital are of course jointly and severally liable for repayment of the amount. Furthermore it is clear that shareholders who in knowledge of the facts receive such dividends may be sued for repayment. The effect of this rule and of the limitation of the payment of dividends to sums taken out of profits depends, however, on the meaning of the term "profits"; and this is nowhere defined by law. English Courts consistently hold that it is for the company to determine what kind of profit should be available for dividends; in so far as the articles do not restrict them, shareholders in general meeting are free to determine the amount distributable. Consequently the Courts will not interfere with the company's decision unless the rule by which dividends may not be paid out of capital is violated. It has been held that profits means not only the current or business profits of the company, but that profits arising from realisation of fixed assets may also be

[1] Trevor *v.* Whitworth (1887), L.R. 12 App. Cas. 409.
[2] Flitcroft's case (1882), 21 Ch. D. 519.

distributed.[1] Such profits, however, may be excluded from distribution by special provisions in the articles.

This rule is sometimes commented upon in the sense that appreciations of capital not yet realised are equalised with realised profits provided they are immediately realisable.[2] Between the time of valuation and the payment of the dividend, or the actual sale, events may, however, occur which prove the valuation mistaken or cause a diminution in the value of the asset in question. On the other hand it has been held not to be necessary to account for losses or depreciations in respect of fixed assets in determining the amount of profits available for dividends,[3] and that a company was not bound to reduce the profits realised in the course of the year's business by a quota for depreciation of leased asphalt mines, since the articles did not contain compulsory provisions to this effect. In this case it was stated that the mining assets of the company did not depreciate, i.e. that in spite of the extraction of material their value was larger than when the company was formed, and the dicta were in the sense that depreciations of the capital sunk in the business by acquisition of fixed assets do not affect the profit realised, i.e. the difference between the income and the expenditure. The rule was in this case qualified by the distinction between fixed and circulating, i.e. current capital. In another case [4] it was held that mines, blast furnaces and cottages erected for workers could not be regarded as fixed capital, and the losses incurred by their realisation must be made good before the company could pay dividends. Everyone interested in sound financial policy will agree with this conclusion, but it is obvious that to try to maintain that this decision is in accordance with earlier decisions of the Court of Appeal is futile. The collieries and mines, furnaces and cottages of a steel company are fixed assets in the same way as those of an asphalt company, and the only reason for saying that the later decision is not contrary to the view taken in the Neuchâtel case is that in the Barrow Haematite case there was an actual loss in consequence of the realisation of the fixed assets in question.

A further question is whether losses incurred in earlier years

[1] Lubbock *v.* British Bank of South Africa (1892), 2 Ch. 198. This rule was followed in Foster *v.* New Trinidad Co. (1901), 1 Ch. 208, and Spanish Prospecting Co. (1911), 1 Ch. 92.

[2] See Palmer, p. 201.

[3] Lee *v.* Neuchâtel, etc., Co. (1889), 41 Ch. Div. 1.

[4] Bond *v.* Barrow Haematite Co. (1902), 1 Ch. 353.

are to be made good subsequently; in other words: Is the company prohibited from paying dividends until such losses have been made good out of the current profits of later years?

In Verner *v.* General Commercial, etc., Trust,[1] a company incurred substantial losses by depreciation of the market value of investments; on the other hand profit was received by the company from other investments. The question was whether the net amount of the profits received might be used for the payment of dividends or ought to be applied to reduce the depreciation and losses on other investments. Following the rule in Lee *v.* Neuchâtel the Court of Appeal held that the company had not to apply the current profit to the reduction of depreciation and loss incurred on investments and might use it for payment of dividends. It is to be noted that in consequence of depreciation a considerable portion of the capital seems to have been lost and that beside preference shares the company had debentures whose security was to some extent impaired. In connection with this decision the question was discussed of how the character of capital as fixed or circulating is to be decided. It was said that the term "fixed capital" is not restricted to physically fixed property, but that the ships of a shipping company or the rolling stock of a railway are similarly to be regarded as fixed capital, and that even securities with market values may be so regarded provided they were acquired not for re-sale but as a permanent investment. We shall see that in recent practice the same distinction is made not as a question of principle but as an exemption granted in order to alleviate the consequences which might be caused by fluctuations in prices of securities acquired for permanent investment.

With regard to losses incurred in previous years,[2] it has been held that although losses had been suffered on debts and the reserve for doubtful debts was not adequate, dividends could be paid up to the amount of current profits. It is true that this case related to the liability of a director, and the obvious absence of any bad faith may have influenced the decision; nevertheless the dicta of the Judges of the Court of Appeal are quite clear. In the House of Lords, Lord Chancellor Halsbury and Lord Macnaghten refrained from expressing any opinion on the

[1] (1894), 2 Ch. 239.

[2] National Bank of Wales (1899), 2 Ch. 629, approved by the House of Lords in Dovey *v.* Cory (1901), A.C. 477.

question of principle, and the case was eventually decided on the question of the directors' liability in respect of dividends paid out of capital. Nevertheless it seems that the decision of the Court of Appeal is not regarded by the Courts as overruled. Thus,[1] where a company had a loss which was made good by an increase of the valuation of the buildings, machinery and plant, it was said by Peterson, J., that: "If the losses are of earlier years and there is a profit, the dividend paid is not out of capital." He held that this question is distinct from that of whether the company may pay dividend when it had never made a profit, in which case of course dividends would be being paid out of capital. In the Court of Appeal Swinfen Eady, L.J., said (at p. 283): "The Companies Act does not impose any obligation upon a limited company nor does the law require that it should not distribute as dividend the clear profit of its trading unless its paid-up capital is intact or until it has made good all losses incurred in previous years." L.J. Scrutton expressed his view (p. 298) that the qualification made by Farwell, J.,[2] cannot be accepted and that Dovey *v.* Cory did not overrule the Lee *v.* Neuchâtel decision and those following the rule therein formulated. In this case also, however, the situation and legal position were obscured by the fact that it was an action against directors for the repayment of dividends paid by them in disregard of earlier losses and that the revaluation was made in good faith, which may have influenced the Court. The shareholders who sued the directors had acquired their shares after the dividends in question had been paid to preference shareholders, and L.J. Swinfen Eady stated (at p. 282) that this is immaterial.

Further, it has been held that profits carried to reserve remain profits unless capitalised,[3] which is unquestionable; the same decision, however, held that premiums paid by shareholders on the issue of shares may be treated as profits, which is obviously unsound.[4]

If in earlier years fixed assets have been written off in view of depreciation and subsequently their value has increased or the depreciation has in fact never taken place, the amounts applied for depreciation out of profits may be restored to the profit

[1] Ammonia Soda Co. *v.* Chamberlain (1918), 1 Ch. 266, at p. 273.
[2] Bond *v.* Barrow (1902), 1 Ch. 353.
[3] Hoare and Co., Ltd. (1904), 2 Ch. 208.
[4] This was followed in Drown *v.* British Gaumont (1937), Ch. 402.

account and applied for dividends.[1] This was extended to amounts written off against goodwill.[2] On the other hand it has been held that goodwill cannot be distributed as profit.[3]

It has also been held [4] that the profit resulting from the payment of debentures at discount cannot be distributed if there is depreciation in the value of the company's capital assets. This decision is undoubtedly contrary to the rule upheld in the Lee *v.* Neuchâtel decisions. There are obviously some contradictions between the various decisions, and it would be hard by collating them all to evolve a general rule.

The law in the U.S.A.[5] as to what funds may be applied to payment of dividends evolved slowly, and the common law position was obscure. In early decisions it was repeatedly held that a company may not pay dividends if it has debts. In other decisions this rule was stated in the terms that dividends cannot be paid out of borrowed money, and that the company may not pay dividends if it has not the necessary cash available. Eventually it was recognised that both formulas are erroneous: a company may be prosperous and may have earned profits in spite of its having debts. On the other hand it is possible for a corporation not to have sufficient cash at the time dividends are due, although its funds in stock-in-trade or debts warrant its liquidity.

The statutes of the various States in early times introduced provisions in this regard; but since these were neither clear nor exhaustive the Courts were amply concerned with the position at Common Law.

Two doctrines were alleged: first, that the capital of the company may not be impaired by dividends: second, that dividends may be paid only out of profits. There was, however, no definite agreement as to what capital or capital stock means, or how profits are to be determined.

It is hardly possible to reproduce the various provisions, and to do so would be futile, since there are many differences both in their material contents and wording. On the whole, four types of regulation may be observed. The first is that which is

[1] Bishop *v.* Smyrna, etc., Rail Co. (1895), 2 Ch. 596, and in Ammonia Soda Co. *v.* Chamberlain, *supra.*

[2] Stapley *v.* Read Bros. Ltd. (1924), 2 Ch. 1.

[3] Spanish Prospecting Co. (1911), 1 Ch. 92, at p. 105.

[4] Wall *v.* London and Provincial Trust (1920), 2 Ch. 582.

[5] Cf. Ballantine, 231–55; Berle and Means, pp. 283–377; Weiner, 29 Col. L.R. p. 761 seq.; Weiner and Bohnbright, 30 Col. L.R., pp. 341–358.

satisfied with the rule that no dividends may be paid when a corporation is insolvent, or when in consequence of their payment it would become so. While many statutes contain this rule, there are few in which it is the only one; many provide for other requirements as well.

In applying the rule it is important to be clear about the term "insolvency". Is a company insolvent only if it is unable to meet debts due, or also when its assets are not sufficient to cover all its obligations? It is obvious that if a company has a deficit, in other words has no surplus assets, its solvency can be only short-lived. On the other hand may a company pay dividends if its assets exceed its liabilities but its capital is not intact?

If the rule only prohibits dividends in case of actual insolvency, the company would be allowed to pay dividends even though its net assets were less than its capital; this all the more as the capital is not a debt. At this instance the common law rule frequently came into play, and it was held that dividends could not be paid in such a case because their payment would impair the capital.

The second type of regulation is that no dividends may be paid if the net value of the assets is less than a specified amount, generally the aggregate amount of the corporation's liabilities and its capital. In other words: in order to be able to pay dividends the corporation must have a surplus. This rule, however, was in some cases qualified, and dividends were held to be payable although it was doubtful whether the capital was intact. Thus in one case [1] it was alleged that the assets were over-valued and that their net value was less than the capital. The corporation, however, had no debts at all apart from transitory commercial ones, and earned substantial profits. It was held that dividends could be paid regardless of the alleged difference between the net value of the assets and the capital. This decision was affirmed.[2] In another case,[3] the company had a discount reserve in its assets, since shares had obviously been issued below par. The bill for injunction against payment of dividends was dismissed: it was held that although issue of shares below par was prohibited, in this relation the violation is immaterial and the rule means that the net value of the assets

[1] Goodnow *v.* American Writing Paper Co. (1907), 72 N. J. Eq. 645.
[2] (1909), 73 N.J. Eq. 692.
[3] Peters *v.* U.S. Mortgage Company (1921), 13 Del. Ch. 110.

in excess of liabilities must not be less than the amount which was paid on capital account.

On the other hand the New York Courts held that the so-called water is to be squeezed out before the company may begin paying dividends.[1] Earlier it was held by the New York Court of Appeal that under the New York statute capital means par value, i.e. nominal capital.[2] It was even held [3] that in an action for stock-watering the defendant shareholder could not offset notes of the company given for dividends because in view of the watering the dividends were illegally paid.

A special question arises in respect of premiums paid on shares at issue. It is usually held that such premiums could be used for dividends; but in California they could not be so used,[4] although the New York statute has nearly the same wording as that of California.

The Uniform Business Corporation Act and the Ohio Act require the corporation to state the source of any surplus, i.e. whether it comes from profits, premiums or some other source. Under the Delaware statute it is left to the company to declare what part of the premium—or, in the case of no par value shares, of the consideration—shall be capital or surplus.

The third type of regulation is that no dividend may be paid except from profits. This has been adopted by many statutes, but it is not always clear what is to be understood by the word "profits". The position is not made clearer by the use of the expressions "actual", "actually acquired" or "legitimate" profits. Some statutes use the expression "profits earned in business" or "arising from business", in which case extraordinary profits, e.g. such as those arising from the sale of fixed assets, might be regarded as excluded. This consequence, however, is not always drawn. On the other hand there are some statutes whose provisions are definitely ambiguous. Thus if it is provided that accumulated profits are distributable, we have still to ask what profits are meant. If a statute speaks of surplus profits the confusion is even greater: "surplus" may mean accumulated from regular profits or originating from share premiums or realised appreciation.

The fourth type is the introduction of the doctrine of wasting

[1] Shaw v. Ansaldi Co. Inc. (1917), 178 App. Div. 589.
[2] Williams v. Western Union Telephone Co. (1883), 93 N.Y. 162.
[3] Shields v. Hobart (1902), 172 Mo. 517.
[4] Merchants, etc., Company v. Schroeder (1918), 39 Cal. App. 226.

assets attributed to the well-known textbook of Morawetz. In his first edition published in 1885 this writer maintained that companies formed to exploit wasting assets such as mines, oil wells, patents, and so on, are formed and managed with a view to exploiting the object of the corporation regardless of replacement, and therefore the dividends represent both profits and part repayment of capital. This doctrine found adherents both in Courts and before taxation authorities. It has been said that if a company has only one class of shareholders nobody is injured by the distribution, and shareholders purchasing shares in such companies must be aware that the dividends they receive will consume the capital assets of the company. This doctrine was sometimes followed even in cases where the corporation had several classes of shares, in which case the preference shareholders may find themselves on the liquidation of the company in the position that nothing is left for distribution, and consequently their preferential rights will remain mere paper. Thus in Mellon *v.* Mississippi Wire Glass Co.[1] preferred shareholders complained that nothing was written off on patents and goodwill; nevertheless their action was dismissed.

The Delaware statute accepted the doctrine of wasting assets in full, and the Wittenberg *v.* Federal Mining and Smelting Co. case, begun under the old statute under which it was doubtful whether depreciation could be neglected, was eventually dealt with under the new statute, under which distribution could not be objected regardless of waste and depletion.[2]

The Uniform Business Corporation Act, sec. 25, and the new Ohio Act made it dependent upon the articles; a company may at the choice of the incorporators decide that depreciation, waste or depletion shall or shall not be taken into account. These two Acts are based on the view that there are corporations whose object is of a wasting character, and they name them wasting asset corporations. The fact that quite a number of corporations beside such assets have fixed assets of another kind which of course in many cases, if not in all, undergo depreciation is quite neglected.

A further question arises in connection with a reduction of capital. When corporations have full freedom to reduce their capital, they may frame the reduction in such a way that at the moment thereof they have a surplus, which may become

[1] (1910), 77 N.J. Eq. 498.

[2] (1929), 15 Del. Ch. 147.

distributable under the governing statute. This procedure may impair the interests of creditors immediately; in some cases it will considerably weaken the financial position of the corporation.

It has often been asserted that in spite of these defects of legal provisions both English and American companies follow on the whole the same sound financial policy with regard to distribution, and that in so far as they err, their error is rather in withholding dividends than in distributing them recklessly. Undoubtedly this is the case in respect of most of the large and even more of the giant corporations. Nevertheless following the recurrent financial crises cases have come before the Courts which have revealed the damaging consequences of the absence of legal restriction in a vivid light. On the other hand it is not at all unusual for mining companies to be left with minimal assets after the exhaustion of their mining property and for shareholders to receive very little as final distribution. The average shareholder is not aware that the dividend in wasting asset companies cannot be considered entirely as such but also represents some quota of the final distribution; he seldom if ever reinvests the dividends he receives from such companies, so as to retain his capital intact. The New Deal legislation left the law as it stood; Corporation law in general was not called upon to build up legal devices and restrictions; the difference between the various State legislations remained, and many of the Corporation Acts still give corporations more or less complete freedom to regulate this matter as they think fit. On the other hand in respect of all those corporations which fall under the two Securities Acts of 1933 and 1934, as well as the Public Utility Holding Companies Act and the Investment Companies Act, an administrative body, the S.E.C., has power to issue rules for the accounting of depreciation of every kind, including obsolescence and waste. It therefore depends upon the discretion of the Commission what part of the profits should be regarded as such and become distributable. It is as yet too soon to know whether this measure will lead to a satisfactory solution. We have to remember that since the passing of these Acts the U.S.A. has not faced any financial slump, and only the post-war years will give us the information and experience necessary to enable a well-founded judgment to be formed. In any case it seems doubtful whether the restriction of regulation to a defined class of corporations is justified, although it is true that their capital assets represent the larger part of corporate wealth.

Of Continental legislations it is the German law of 1937 which defines most clearly the rights of shareholders as to dividends. This follows the traditions of earlier legislation and the practice of the Courts. Its leading principle is that the contributions of shareholders are not to be repaid, and that so long as the company exists the shareholders are entitled only to the net profits which appear in the company's yearly balance sheet (§ 52).

This means not only that apart from a valid reduction of capital no distribution can be made save out of net profits, but also that profits are distributable only on the basis of the balance sheet drawn up at the end of the financial year. No interim dividend is therefore permitted.

If there is a loss from earlier years not met by legal reserves, or by free reserves if any (see § 34), no dividend is payable; this rule is accepted by all Continental legislations. When the loss is eliminated by reduction of capital and a corresponding reduction of the par value of the shares, no dividend can be paid unless there is a legal reserve equal to 10 per cent. of the capital. Furthermore as a rule for two financial years following the reduction no dividend exceeding 4 per cent. may be paid, and that only from current profits, not from a surplus resulting from the reduction of capital or from the dissolution of reserves (§ 182).

The doctrine of wasting assets was opposed from early times. This may have been connected with the system adopted in respect of the franchises of railways and public utilities; such franchises were usually granted for a certain number of years, e.g. ninety, after which the enterprise devolved without compensation upon the State or the municipality, as the case may be. This made it necessary to provide for the repayment of the capital by systematic redemption in yearly instalments or the formation of a sinking fund, and the charters of the companies concerned contained definite provisions to this effect. Under the influence of this system it became usual to provide for writing-off in the case of wasting assets of enterprises, even if the franchise was not limited to a certain number of years. Subsequently this became a compulsory rule.

As early as 1884 it was enacted that share premiums, whether paid by subscribers or by takers of additional shares in connection with an increase of capital, were to be put into legal reserve and must not be distributed as profits (§ 130 (2)). There is, however, no prohibition of payment of dividends from free reserves in so far as it is not otherwise provided in the articles.[1]

The regulation of the Swiss O.R. (74, 5) is identical.

Although the French law does not contain express provisions and regulates only the question of liability for the payment of fictive dividends, the French Courts have in practice evolved rules similar to those of the German and other Continental laws; on the other hand the financial policy of French companies has always been very sound and conservative.[2]

55. PROHIBITION OF PAYMENT OF INTEREST

The rule that dividends may be paid only out of profits necessarily operates against the payment of interest to shareholders and the validity of promises to pay such interest. But there is a need to provide for the possibility of such payments in the case of companies whose undertakings call for the construction of works, the erection of buildings, or the obtaining of plant or equipment which cannot be ready for use for a considerable period, as is the case with railways, canals, public utilities and even factories. Most legislations provide for such needs and allow for the payment of fixed interest during such transitional periods.

In Great Britain this was regulated by the Act of 1907 (sec. 9), inserted in sec. 91 of the Act of 1908, and is at present governed by sec. 65 of the Act of 1948. Under this section the payment of such interest must be authorised by the articles and be previously sanctioned by the Board of Trade. The Board, before giving its sanction, may investigate the circumstances of the case at the company's expense. When giving sanction it must determine the period for which such payment is to be made, which should terminate at the end of the half-year following that in which the works are completed or the plant provided. Lastly the interest may not exceed 4 per cent. or such other rate as may be prescribed by Order in Council.

The payment of interest shall not operate as a reduction of the amount paid up on the shares. The share capital on which such payment is made and the rate of interest are to be shown in the

[1] R.G.Z. 103, 370.

[2] Cf. for French judicial practice Pic 1178–9.

accounts of the respective financial year or years. The companies concerned may charge the amounts paid to their shareholders under this heading to the costs of construction or provision of the works, buildings or plant, and are thus not compelled to treat them as expenses.

In France in the absence of express provisions the question is disputed. Most of the textbooks argue that stipulations for interest are contrary to the idea of fixed capital, and therefore void, and consequently that its payment is prohibited in the absence of sufficient profits. Earlier the Courts shared this view; subsequently, however, the Cour de Cassation held the stipulation valid provided it is clearly stated in the articles that the interest is to be charged in the revenue (profit and loss) account as overhead expenses.[1] This view is strongly criticised and an opinion is held that it should be adopted only for the preparatory period.

In Germany the Commercial Code (1861) allowed interest to be paid during the period of construction or building, and this was maintained in the subsequent enactments. § 54 (2) of the law of 1937 provides that during the period necessary for the preparatory work until the enterprise can come into full operation the payment of interest may be stipulated in the articles. The rate of interest is to be stated as a definite percentage, and a time-limit fixed for its payment. After that date the payment is to cease, even though the building or setting-up is not finished. Should the enterprise come into operation earlier, the payment of interest is to cease forthwith.[2]

R.G.Z. 77, 255, held that such interest may be stipulated for in connection with an increase of capital if new buildings are erected or new plants equipped; but this view was strongly criticised, and under the Commercial Code of 1897 and the law of 1937 it is mostly held that the so-called building interest (*Bauzinsen*) could be paid only in respect of the original construction.[3] There is no limitation on the rate of interest, nor is the sanction of any authority, judicial or administrative, required.

The Swiss O.R. expressly permits the stipulation of interest in connection with an increase of capital. In such a case interest may be paid to the holders of the additional shares for the time needed for the erection of the new plant or building. Otherwise the provisions are identical with those of the German law (676).

[1] See Pic 1183–4. [2] Gadow, p. 183, n. 13. [3] Cf. Gadow, p. 183, n. 11.

The Italian Codice Commerciale (Art. 181) provides that the time during which such interest may be paid must not exceed three years, and it may not be higher than 5 per cent. Other legislations follow the German example.

It is obvious that there is nothing to prevent a guarantee of a certain fixed or minimum dividend if such guarantee is given by a third party and does not involve any burden upon the company itself. This was a much discussed question in Germany, where such guarantees were usually given, e.g. in the case of new railway lines, by the State or some municipal body and even by vendors in case of industrial enterprises.

56. Declaration of Dividends

(A) THE POWER TO DECLARE DIVIDENDS

Dividend is due only if and when it is declared.

By the British Companies Act, 1948, it is for the articles to decide who shall have power to declare dividends and how far the declaration is within the discretion of those so authorised. Table A (114) gives the power to the general meeting, but with the qualification that the dividend declared shall not exceed the amount recommended by the directors. The articles of many companies provide that the directors may declare dividends, though usually with the proviso that the declaration is to be sanctioned by the general meeting. Furthermore, under Table A (115), though the declaration is reserved for the general meeting, "the directors may from time to time pay to the members such interim dividends as appear to them to be justified by the profits of the company". Such interim dividends are as a rule paid half-yearly, but it may be resolved otherwise, and the period in respect of which they are paid depends on the terms of the resolution.[1]

The declaration of dividends is within wide limits a matter of discretion. It is held that in so far as the memorandum or articles do not otherwise provide the company, i.e. the general meeting or the directors, may set aside a part of the profits as reserve.[2]

[1] *In re* Jowitt (1922), 2 Ch. 442.

[2] R. Paterson & Sons, Ltd. *v.* Paterson (1916), W.N., 352; Evling *v.* Israel and Oppenheimer Ltd. (1918), 1 Ch. 101.

Table A (115) states that the declaration of dividends is merely optional; "the company in general meeting *may* declare dividends"; and clause 117 gives the directors wide discretionary powers recommending dividends; they may set aside such sums as they think proper as reserves, either to meet contingencies or to equalise dividends or for any other proper purpose.

If a dividend is declared and becomes due, any shareholder may sue the company therefor,[1] since it is a debt of the company; before and in the absence of a declaration shareholders have no action.[2] How far shareholders have remedies against the withholding of dividends is considered in § 78.

In the U.S.A. the power to declare dividends is held to be vested in the board of directors, even in the absence of statutory or charter provisions to this effect. Nowadays most statutes contain provisions authorising directors to declare dividends. This power is held to give them discretion to fix their amount as they think fit. Formerly some legislations limited this discretion and reserved it to the majority of stockholders in general meeting, or without even reserving this right to the majority provided that the net profits should be distributed. Nowadays, however, only a few legislations do this. Thus in North Carolina under § 1178 of the Code the directors are to pay the whole amount of the accumulated profits to the shareholders as dividend, unless the certificate of incorporation or the by-laws give them power to fix what amounts are to be reserved as working capital. Similarly the Statute of New Mexico (§§ 32–156) lays it down that unless otherwise provided in the original or amended certificate of incorporation or in the by-laws, or by the vote of the majority of stockholders, the directors are to distribute the whole of the accumulated profits except such amount as may be reserved according to the provisions of the certificate of incorporation or the by-laws or a resolution of the stockholders as aforesaid.

Most State legislations, however, either do not limit the discretion of the directors in any way, or directly confirm the power of directors to use their discretion. Thus the New Jersey law (14:8:20 of R.S.) says that in the absence of provisions in the certificate of incorporation or the by-laws, or a vote of the majority of stockholders, directors may at their discretion from time to time fix and vary the amount of the working capital of

[1] *Re* Severn, etc., Railway Co. (1896), 1 Ch. 559.

[2] Bond *v.* Barrow Haematite Steel Co. (1902), 1 Ch. 353.

the corporation and determine what dividends, if any, shall be declared and paid.

Under the influence of the prevailing trend of legal thought it is held even in the absence of such statutory provisions as aforesaid that the discretion of the directors should not be disturbed or varied by judicial review except where it is clearly shown that they have abused their powers or acted in bad faith in order to further their own interests. This rule is universally accepted. Actually, however, it is very difficult to produce satisfactory evidence of such abuse, and it is therefore not surprising that disappointed stockholders only exceptionally succeed in suits to compel directors to declare dividends or to increase those already declared.

Under European legislations it is the general meeting which has the power to declare dividends.

French law deals with this question indirectly, providing that at least once yearly a general meeting is to be held (Art. 27) and that the balance sheet and the profit and loss account are to be submitted by the board of directors at the end of each financial year to the general meeting for approval.[1] Although there is thus no express provision, it is undoubtedly the law that it is within the power of the general meeting to fix the dividend; the only function of the board of directors is to make a proposal, which may or may not be carried by vote in general meeting.[2]

German legislation similarly gave the power to declare dividends to the general meeting. The German Commercial Code reserved it to the general meeting to draw up the balance sheet and in connection therewith to resolve on the distribution of net profits. On the other hand Art. 217 of the Code was construed to mean that the shareholder is entitled to demand distribution of the net profits unless the articles otherwise provide. The general meeting was held to have no power to exclude any part of the net profits from distribution unless authorised by the articles, whether by putting it into free reserve or by transferring it to the next year's account, save for such amounts as owing to their relative insignificance would increase the dividend only by a minute fraction, e.g. ½ per cent.[3] It was even held that if in a given case the shareholders in general meeting approved the balance sheet but omitted to carry a resolution as to the dividend,

[1] Art. 34, as amended by the Order of 8 August 1935.
[2] Pic 1326. [3] Staub-Pinner, II, p. 605.

any shareholder had an action to demand his fractional share of the net profits appearing in the balance sheet.[1] This view was subsequently disputed.[2] Furthermore if by the resolution of the general meeting any part of the net profits distributable under the law (i.e. the whole of the net profits except the compulsory amount for reserve) and the articles was excluded from distribution, any shareholder had the right to sue for invalidation.

The trend, however, as shown in § 15, was to restrict the rights of the individual shareholder, and this was achieved by § 271 of the Revised Commercial Code (1897). By par. 3 of this section, action to invalidate a resolution on the ground that more has been placed to reserve than the law or the articles provided for is admissible only if brought by a shareholder or shareholders holding at least 5 per cent. of the share capital. This new provision made actions to invalidate resolutions of the shareholders in general meeting on the ground that the right to distribution was impaired extremely difficult, all the more so as the restriction also extended to excessive writings-off by undervaluation. This provision was maintained by the law of 1937 (§ 198 (2)). Another provision of this law, at least as construed by the commentators, practically excluded any such action in the following way: under § 125 (3) of the law, if the board of supervision agrees with the management as to the balance sheet, the general meeting is bound by it (§ 126 (3)). It is provided that the two boards may reserve the drawing up of the balance sheet to the competence of the general meeting if they choose to do so (§ 125 (3)), but it is hardly to be expected that such a case should ever occur. Apart from such exceptional cases, i.e. when the two boards do not agree or renounce their right to draw up the balance sheet, the general meeting may reduce the dividend proposed or dispense entirely with distribution provided they are empowered to restrict it under the articles.[3]

On the other hand it is held that if the balance sheet drawn up by the board of management has been approved by the board of supervision, an action based on excessive writings-off or excessive placings to reserve cannot be maintained, so that even shareholders holding 5 per cent. or more of the capital are unable to attack the balance sheet and enforce a fairer distribution.[4] In

[1] R.O.H. 19, 144. [2] Düringer-Hachenburg, III, 1, 64, *a*.
[3] Cf. Gadow, p. 537; Ritter to § 52, n. 4 (*a*) and (*cc*).
[4] Gadow, p. 174, n. 15, and p. 863, n. 14.

practice therefore the management and the board, if they agree on this matter, overrule the general meeting and deprive the shareholder of any remedy.

There are quite a number of legislations which still adhere to the two basic principles of the German Commercial Code of 1861, namely that the declaration of dividends is within the competence of the general meeting and that the shareholder has a right to dividends in so far as this right is not qualified by the articles. The Swiss O.R. maintains both principles, but its revised text (18 December 1936) enhanced the powers of the general meeting. According to § 674 it may be resolved by majority vote that any part of the profits may be put into reserve in excess of the quota of legal reserves provided by law and the articles if such a course is deemed advisable for the lasting prosperity of the enterprise or in the interest of a stable dividend policy. Furthermore, the general meeting may establish institutions for employees' and workers' welfare and may use part of the net profits for that purpose even if not provided for in the articles or in excess of such provision. The same may be done in respect of other welfare purposes (674). Under § 706 any shareholder may sue for invalidation of a resolution contrary to law or the articles; there is no provision similar to that of the German law, but it is obvious that in view of the wide powers granted to the majority in general meeting such an action could hardly be successful.

(B) PROPORTION OF DIVIDENDS

The general rule is that dividends are to be proportionate to the face value of the shares held. This principle is modified by the possibility, nowadays everywhere admitted, of the creation of preferential rights and the issue of preference shares (§ 61). Another question arises when the shares of a company are not all equally paid up.

None of the British Company Acts contained any provisions concerning the proportion in which fully and not fully paid up shares are entitled to take part in dividends; the matter is thus left to be regulated by the articles. In the absence of such regulation it is held that the shareholders are entitled to dividend in proportion to the nominal value of their shares, regardless of what proportion of the shares are paid up.[1] Table A of the Companies Act of 1862 actually contained a clause to the effect that dividend is payable "to the members in proportion to their shares", and this was construed as referring to the nominal value, regardless of the amounts paid up.[2] This clause became unpopular, and clause 118 of Table A regards the amount paid up as decisive, providing that "dividends shall be declared and paid according to the amounts paid or credited as paid on the shares". Only where nothing has been paid up on any of the shares may dividends be declared and paid according to their nominal value.

Obviously neither of these solutions is quite just and equitable. The former neglects the disproportion in payment, the second the risk incurred by the holders of partly-paid shares. In view of these considerations the articles of many companies provide that a certain percentage, say, 4 or 5 per cent., of the profits shall first be paid on the amounts paid up, and the rest distributed in accordance with the nominal value of the shares.

This is the solution adopted in Germany. The law of 1937 (52 (2)), in accordance with the Commercial Code of 1897 (214), provides that in case of unequal payments dividends are first to be paid in proportion to the payments up to 4 per cent. of the amounts, and the remainder distributed according to the par value of the shares. Payments made on the shares during the previous year are to be taken into account in proportion to the remaining part of the year. The articles, however, may provide otherwise.

Quite different is the question how dividends are to be apportioned as between a tenant for life of shares and the remainderman, or under Continental legislation, as between the owners of shares and the usufructuary. This question has everywhere raised many disputes, but since it is not a problem of company law proper we are not concerned with it.

56A. Payment of Dividends

As a rule dividends are paid in cash, and some legislations allow no other course. In Great Britain it is held possible to provide in the articles that they may be paid otherwise, by the

[1] Oakbank Oil Co. *v.* Crum (1882), L.R. 8 App. Cas. 65; Birch *v.* Cropper (*in re* Bridgwater Navigation Company) (1889), L.R. 14 App. Cas. 525.

[2] Oakbank Oil Co. *v.* Crum, *supra*.

distribution of specific assets. In the absence of such authorisation, however, the company is bound to pay dividends in cash and cannot pay them in shares or debentures, whether its own or those of other companies.[1] Cash means the currency of the country in which the dividends are paid.[2]

The legislations of the United States generally allow of the payment of dividends otherwise than in cash, i.e. in property or securities. One method is to make payment in the stock of the company itself; this is very popular, and will be considered presently.

In Germany it is held that declared dividends must be paid in cash, and that no shareholder can be compelled to accept dividends in other forms than money.[3] Such payment may, however, be effected with the unanimous consent of all shareholders. It is further held that a resolution which gives the choice of receiving the dividends either in cash or in property, e.g. in shares of another company, or in debentures, would be valid. Gadow (pp. 175–6) assumes that under the law of 1937 the articles may give the general meeting the power to resolve upon the payment of dividends in other forms than cash, and in such a case any shareholder would be bound to accept it. This view, however, is not warranted by any judicial authority.

STOCK DIVIDENDS

The practice of paying dividends in the company's own shares originated in the need felt by corporations to retain their profits in order to re-invest them in the business or to provide for contingencies. The payment of dividends by distributing shares is a simple matter if the company is in a position to issue and distribute shares; but if it has no outstanding shares, the capital must be increased.

Under European legislations, therefore, the device of stock dividends is seldom if ever practicable. Under the Anglo-American system of capital structure any company may have unissued shares or treasury stock and may issue them to shareholders in lieu of cash dividends. Nevertheless stock dividends

[1] Hoole *v.* Great Western Railway Co. (1867), L.R. 3 Ch. App. 262; Wood *v.* Odessa Waterworks Co. (1889), 42 Ch. D. 636.

[2] Adelaide Electric Co. *v.* Prudential Assurance Co. (1934), A.C. 122.

[3] R.G.Z. 107, 108; Fischer, p. 392; Staub-Pinner II, p. 176; Flechtheim (Düringer-Hachenburg), III, 1, 63 (*a*).

are not in use in Great Britain, though they have become popular in the U.S.A.

Until 1911 such dividends were rare; those which were distributed were substantial, and were rightly called extraordinary dividends. From 1912 onwards the practice of paying stock dividends gradually grew more usual, but it became really popular only after 1920. During the years 1920–6, in the case of 10,000 companies considered, the increase of cash dividends in comparison with the years 1913–19 amounted to 94·07 per cent., whereas the increase in stock dividends over the same period was 586·62 per cent. It is said that from 1926 onwards the popularity of stock dividends has been definitely at least as great, though exact statistical data are not available. This astounding popularity of stock dividends is attributed to the decision of the Supreme Court in Eisner *v.* Macomber [1] to the effect that stock dividends are not taxable as stockholders' income. Obviously the question of taxation may be important to shareholders, especially for the large shareholder. For the corporations themselves, however, this point is irrelevant. We may therefore certainly assume that beside the question of taxation the need for reinvestment plays a principal part in the choice between cash and stock dividends.

Owing to the regular practice of paying dividends in stock, the payments became relatively small. Consequently it may occur that the dividend accruing to an individual shareholder is not equal to the value of one share. Thus in the case of a 10 per cent. dividend, only a shareholder who holds ten shares will receive an amount sufficient to cover one new share. The same happens in the case of large holdings not equal to a multiple of the number required for new shares. Thus, in the case above mentioned a shareholder who holds 25 shares would receive two shares in lieu of dividends, but five shares bearing dividend will still remain uncovered. This difficulty may be overcome by the issue of fractional shares. Since the statutes of the United States generally contain no provision as to minimum par values, there is no legal objection to the issue of these. Nevertheless it is only in Ohio and South Carolina that the statutes expressly authorise them.

Though the law does not prohibit the issue of fractional shares, they lead in practice to many complications. The payment of dividends on them is hardly practicable; their registra-

[1] (1919), 252 U.S. 189.

tion in company books is impossible, and they cannot be given voting rights. In view of these inconveniences companies paying stock dividends resort to various means in order to avoid them. One such is to declare that if the stock dividends do not amount to full shares, the remainders are to be paid to the shareholder in cash. In cases in which the surplus is not fully capitalised this may mean a certain loss for the shareholder who cannot receive full shares and has to accept cash.

Another method is to provide that fractional shares must be exchanged within a certain period, after which the shareholder must accept cash. During this term the shareholders concerned may be able to sell their fractions or to acquire the additional fractional shares necessary for an exchange. They may, however, in both cases incur losses: a shareholder who sells fractions may be compelled to sell them cheap; those who buy additional fractions may have to pay too much for them. In view of this it is usual for the corporations concerned, or for their bankers, to provide for some marketing arrangement in order to minimise these losses. It is sometimes provided that after the expiration of the time limit the fractional shares that remain shall be sold by the company for the account of the shareholder. Another method is to grant a longer term for the exchange; cases with terms up to seven years are recorded. This method is usual in cases where it is foreseen that the company will regularly issue shares, i.e. pay stock dividends, so that in the course of time even small holdings will amount to full shares. A similar method is to credit the shareholders with the cash value of the stock dividends either by issuing scrip or without. These credits may accumulate until they equal the issue price of one or more full shares.

Either of these methods leads to some discrimination against small shareholders. This discrimination is increased if—as has occurred in several cases—the articles or a resolution of the board provide that shareholders who fail to exchange their fraction within a certain limited period lose their rights. Nevertheless if stock dividends are allowed at all, some discriminations are a matter of necessity. Legislation or the Courts may reduce such discriminations, but cannot provide full remedies. In the case of no par value shares (see § 64) some of these difficulties do not arise, but in any case in which the capitalisation is below book value there is a definite discrimination to the detriment of the shareholders who are unable to receive full shares.

On the whole the payment of stock dividends is not a sound financial practice. On the one hand directors may be more easily inclined to declare dividends in stock than in cash. In the statutes which expressly permit stock dividends it is generally stressed that they may be paid only out of profits; but it is doubtful whether such provisions are of much avail. On the other hand distribution of stock as dividend frequently involves difficulties, especially in the case of a wide dispersal of holdings. It is much simpler and more adequate to build up or strengthen the reserves, if such a course is indicated in view of impending capital requirements, or to resort to an increase of capital with full attention to the pre-emptive rights of shareholders.[1]

In the U.S.A. dividends are sometimes declared in scrip, i.e. certificates giving the right to a certain payment in cash or in property, usually stock, at some future date. This is done in cases in which the corporation is not in a position to pay a cash dividend, or a distribution in stock is inadvisable for the time being. The validity of such scrip depends on the real existence of profits.[2]

The limitations applying to stock dividends under German law apply also of course to distributions in scrip. A form of distribution is sometimes resorted to in Germany which is free from these restrictions: this happens when a company in general meeting resolves to distribute profit-sharing certificates (*Genuszscheine*) among its shareholders. These certificates give no rights whatsoever as to the capital of the company, but merely a certain participation in the profits with or without preferential rights as against the shareholders. In some cases such certificates have a nominal (face) value, which, however, means only that the company may redeem them out of profits by paying the amount stated.

57. Position after the Declaration of Dividends

All company laws agree that on a valid declaration the dividend becomes a debt of the company, and any shareholder may sue the company for the dividends accruing to his shares. This is the English law,[3] and the same is true of the United States,

[1] Cf. Berle and Means, pp. 197–9; Ballantine, 208.
[2] Cf. Ballantine, 239, at n. 46; Fletcher 5358.
[3] *Re* Severn and Wye and Severn Bridge Rail Co. (1896), 1 Ch. 559.

where it is held that if a dividend has once been declared the shareholders cannot be deprived thereof by subsequent withdrawal or alteration of the resolution in general meeting, or meeting of the board of directors, as the case may be. But it has been held that the board of directors may reserve its resolution until the shareholders have been informed.[1] The shareholders' remedy against the company in America is an action at law, usually on *assumpsit*; under some legislations the remedy is an action of debt.[2]

As a rule the shareholder is a general creditor of the corporation. Specific assets, however, may be appropriated for dividend; in that case the funds in question may become a trust fund for the dividends to the exclusion of other creditors, and this may be of importance in case of subsequent insolvency. Apart from such exceptional cases the shareholders may prove their claim for dividends accrued only in concurrence with other non-secured creditors. The corporation is entitled to set off a debt due to it from the shareholder against his claim for dividends.

The rule that the fixing of dividends by the general meeting makes them debts of the company has been upheld by German Courts in cases where the company subsequently suffered losses after the end of the relative financial year,[3] and the company was unable to invalidate the resolution as to the dividend, even by a special resolution for alteration of the articles.[4] Such a resolution would be void, and there is no need for a direct attack; the nullity may be asserted collaterally. It is otherwise if the resolution as to dividend was itself void as contrary to law [5] or was invalidated by judgment.

If the loss suffered by the company cannot be covered by reserves, the payment of dividends duly fixed may impair the capital, and it is held that the company cannot refuse the payment on this ground.[6] In the case of a private company, however, the provision of § 30 of the law on G.m.b.H.s on the prohibition of the repayment of capital is held to operate, and to entitle and bind the management to refuse the payment of duly fixed dividends.[7]

[1] Cf. decisions quoted by Fletcher, 5323, n. 75.
[2] Fletcher 5365, especially n. 95–7.
[3] R.O.H.G. 18, 153.
[4] R.G.Z. 22, 113, 37, 62, 87, 287.
[5] R.O.H. 18, 153.
[6] Flechtheim in Düringer-Hachenburg, n. 31 to § 213 of the Code (1897), III, 1, 65 (*a*).
[7] Hachenburg, n. 8 to § 30.

The shareholder may assign the dividend [1] even before declaration, so that future dividends are held to be assignable.[2]

BONUS

Frequently, especially in Great Britain and the U.S.A., companies distribute certain sums in addition to the dividend under the name of bonus. This may be a special dividend, the term "bonus" being then meant to indicate that it is paid out of extraordinary and non-recurrent profits. But the term is also used when specific assets are distributed or free reserves are applied for the distribution.

Many disputes have arisen as to whether a bonus is income or a distribution of capital. These disputes concern either its apportionment between a life tenant and the remaindermen or its position as regards income tax. With neither of these two matters is this work concerned, and it suffices to remark that bonuses are as a rule to be regarded under the same heading as dividends, i.e. as income, and that there must be weighty reasons for the assumption that they are distributions of capital.

The question of bonus shares is considered in § 90.

LIABILITY FOR UNLAWFUL DIVIDENDS

A dividend is unlawful if the formalities necessary for its declaration and payment have not been complied with, or if there are no profits or free reserves to meet it.

It is the aim of all company laws to prevent the payment of unlawful dividends, in the interest both of creditors, whose security may be impaired, and also of shareholders, who have a right to assume that the company's capital remains intact. The provisions as to the declaration of dividends and the drawing-up of balance sheets and profit and loss accounts are directed to such prevention. Nevertheless dividends may be declared and paid in cases where this should not be done. The question of redress and recovery thus becomes important.

In this regard the position of directors is quite different from that of shareholders. It is to be assumed that the directors have knowledge of the relevant facts, or at any rate means of ascertaining them, whereas shareholders generally have no or at least very limited notice, especially of the correctness of the accounts, and they are therefore generally not held liable in respect of

[1] R.G.Z. 98, 320.

[2] Wieland, 214, n. 6.

dividends received on faith of the balance sheet and on the basis of a lawful resolution. It is otherwise if a shareholder is in bad faith and receives the dividend in knowledge of the facts.

The British Companies Acts contain no special provisions as to the payment of unlawful dividends; the Courts, however, have evolved certain rules.

It is held that directors who are parties to the payment of an unlawful dividend are liable to repay its amount. Their liability is joint and several, and it is no defence that the payment was approved by the general meeting.[1] The person entitled to sue is the company or the liquidator, or any shareholder on his own behalf or on that of all the others, provided he or they accepted the dividend on the directors' representation that it was paid from profits.[2] Shareholders who received the dividend in full knowledge of the facts cannot sue the directors.[3]

Payment of unlawful dividends in order to influence the market price of the shares may involve criminal liability for conspiracy.[4]

Shareholders who have received a dividend *bona fide* on the representation of the directors are not liable for the amount received [5]; it is otherwise if they had full knowledge of the facts.[6]

In the United States the question is extensively dealt with by decisions of the Courts. In the first place, so long as the unlawful payment of dividends has not been effected, any stockholder may maintain a suit in equity to enjoin [7] such distribution [8]; the same remedy has been held to be available to any creditor.[9] It was held, however, that the Court of Equity will not interfere if the payment cannot injure the stockholders or the creditors, an eventuality which may probably occur in respect of creditors if the corporation remains solvent, but not in the case of stockholders, since every stockholder has a right to protest against the payment of dividends out of capital.[10]

[1] Flitcroft's case *in re* Exchange Banking Co. (1882), 21 Ch. D. 519.
[2] Flitcroft's case, *supra*.
[3] Towers *v*. African Tug Co. (1904), 1 Ch. 558.
[4] Dictum by L. C. Campbell in Burnes *v*. Pennell (1849), 2 H.L.C. 497, at p. 525, cf. R. *v*. Esdaile (1858), 1 Fos. and Fin. 213.
[5] Flitcroft's case, *supra*.
[6] Towers *v*. African Tug Co., *supra*.
[7] Here and elsewhere in this book the word "enjoin" is used in its American sense of "forbid" or "prevent".
[8] Fletcher 5419, n. 29.
[9] Mobile and O.R. Co. *v*. Tennessee (1894), 153 U.S. 486.
[10] See Chaffee *v*. Rutland R. Co., 55 Vt. 110; Fletcher 5419, *n*. 32.

If an unlawful dividend has been paid in bonds or notes, the corporation itself has an exception against the enforcement of the bonds or notes, and similarly the payment of stock dividends in the absence of profits may be contested by the corporation itself.

The remedies mentioned are in most cases ineffective, and in order to protect the corporation, its shareholders and creditors, it is important to have means for the recovery of unlawfully paid dividends. It has been held that the recovery of such dividends is in every case allowed if it be proved that there were no profits. The weight of authority, however, is for the qualification that dividends accepted in good faith cannot be recovered. This has been held by the Supreme Court of the U.S.A.[1] and the rule was followed by the Federal and some State Courts. There are, however, decisions to the contrary.[2] If the corporation at the time of the payment was insolvent, the remedy has been given regardless of the good faith of the stockholders.

It is disputed whether the corporation itself might recover the dividends unlawfully paid, but the Courts are in favour of such action.[3] This is contrary to the general principles relating to recovery in quasi contracts. It seems just, however, to give dissenting stockholders the right to maintain a suit in equity to compel repayment to the corporation.

For the creditor the remedy is undoubtedly available. The action can be maintained by a single creditor or by the receiver (assignee in bankruptcy). There have been cases in which the remedy was denied so long as the corporation was solvent and remained in control of its property and assets. This qualification is not without dangers.

A further question arises in respect of creditors who became such after the unlawful payment was made.[4] This qualification is in our view unsound in principle, and is surely not to be defended in cases in which the corporation became insolvent after the unlawful payment.

A director or officer of the corporation cannot be regarded as being in good faith, since he is bound to know the condition of the corporation; and therefore unlawful dividends received by a director or officer are deemed liable for repayment.[5]

[1] McDonald *v.* Williams (1899), 174 U.S. 397.
[2] Fletcher 5423, n. 64.
[3] Fletcher 5422, n. 38.
[4] Fletcher 5425, n. 53.
[5] Finn *v.* Brown (1891), 142 U.S. 56, and Fletcher 5426, n. 80.

Apart from this action for the recovery of unlawful dividends from shareholders, the directors are liable under common law. This liability is based upon negligence; therefore the remedy is available even against directors in good faith if they were in a position by the application of due care to know that there were no profits. The action is in tort in cases both of bad faith and of negligence.

Most statutes expressly grant remedy against directors. The general principles are identical with those accepted by common law; there are many differences of detail. Especially there are statutes holding the directors liable regardless of their good faith. As to the extent of liability the provisions are as a rule to the effect that the unlawful dividends are to be repaid. Some statutes, however, enforce liability only to the extent necessary to satisfy creditors. Others assert liability for all debts of the corporation regardless of whether they exceed the amount of unlawful dividends.

There are likewise differences on the question by whom this liability may be enforced. Action by the corporation and the shareholders is generally recognised. As to creditors, some statutes deny action to persons who became creditors only after the unlawful payment was made. Under some jurisdictions creditors may sue only after they have exhausted the possibility of recovery from the corporation; in others the previous suing of the corporation is not required. Similarly action on the part of the receiver or assignee in bankruptcy is not accepted everywhere.

Some possibility of exoneration of directors is generally admitted. The question of the steps to be taken to achieve it is differently treated. Under some statutes it is only assent to the payment which justifies the liability. This view does not take into consideration the obligation of directors to take part in the administration of the corporation. In pursuance of this duty they have to take part in the resolution of the board with respect to the payment of dividends, and therefore the absence of assent is not sufficient to exonerate them. Other statutes require express dissent and its recording. Thus the New York statute excepts only those directors who have dissented and have caused their dissent to be entered on the minutes of the board.

The difficulty with all these remedies is that the plaintiff has to show that the dividends were paid out of capital or were otherwise illegal. In order to prove the allegations, examination of the balance sheet and profit and loss accounts, and of the books of the company, will be necessary. This involves considerable expense, and so long as a corporation is solvent such proceedings will hardly ever be started.

The payment of unlawful dividends is also the concern of criminal law. Some statutes make the payment of dividends out of capital a criminal offence; as a rule criminal liability depends upon bad faith.[1]

By French law the liability of shareholders is restricted to cases where dividends are paid in the absence of an inventory or in excess of the amount appearing therein (Arts. 10 and 45 of law of 1867). If the declaration and payment do not violate these formal requirements no action can be maintained, even if the inventory was incorrect and the shareholder had notice thereof.[2] This view is attacked by nearly all leading textbooks, but nevertheless is still the law.[3] The action is for the repayment of the amount wrongfully distributed, and may be maintained by the liquidator or trustee in bankruptcy, and also by the company itself.[4] The term of limitation is five years.

The liability of directors is wider. Under Art. 44 of the law of 1867 they are jointly and severally liable if they pay fictitious dividends or do not oppose their payment. Those dividends are fictitious where either there was no inventory or where the inventory and consequently the balance sheet based thereon were materially incorrect, e.g. in consequence of undervaluation of liabilities or overvaluation of assets.[5] Good faith on the part of the directors is no defence; they are responsible for negligence, however slight.[6] The action is for damages, and it may be maintained by the company or by any shareholder individually,[7] or finally by any creditor. A resolution in general meeting granting release may be operative as against the company,[8] but not as against the individual shareholder suing for the damage caused to him[9] or as against a creditor.[10]

Where a director has been a party to the distribution of fic-

[1] Cf. Ballantine, §§ 253–5.
[2] Paris, 20 January 1888, D. 89, 2, 265.
[3] Cf. Pic 1214.
[4] Cass., 15 November 1869, D. 71, 1, 311.
[5] Cf. the decisions quoted by Pic 1213.
[6] Civ. C., 19 May 1903, D.P. 1906, 1, 63 and earlier decisions.
[7] Req., 26 January 1910, D.P. 1913, 1, 188.
[8] Req., 16 February 1909, D.P. 1913, 1, 188.
[9] Req., 26 January 1910, *supra*.
[10] Req., 16 March 1910, D.P. 1911, 1, 148.

titious dividend in the absence of an inventory or by way of a fraudulent inventory, he is liable criminally and also for damages (law 15.4). This liability, however, is dependent upon fraud [1]; the term of limitation is three years, but an action against a director not based on fraud is extinct by way of limitation only after 30 years.[2]

In German law one of the guarantees against declaration of dividends in the absence or in excess of profits is that any shareholder may bring action for invalidation of a resolution in general meeting which violates the law in respect of the approval of the balance sheet or the distribution of profits. The restriction provided for actions against undervaluations or inadequate distributions does not apply here. Similarly the board of management as a body may sue for invalidation on this ground, as may any member of the board of management or of supervision who would incur civil or criminal liability by carrying out the distribution resolved upon in general meeting (§ 198 (1), 1, 4 and 5).

On the other hand an action lies for repayment of amounts paid to shareholders. According to § 56 of the law of 1937 shareholders are generally liable for payments they have received from the company in violation of the law; but they are exempted from liability in respect of dividends received in good faith. It is held that the burden of proof is on the shareholder; he must produce evidence that at the time he received the unlawful dividend he was *bona fide* and had no knowledge of facts which would have shown that the declaration and payment were contrary to law. Gross negligence is held to be equivalent to actual notice. Under the Commercial Code of 1897 it was held that if a resolution as to dividends was not invalidated, their payment would not be unlawful unless a compulsory provision of the law were violated.[3] The liability is established in favour of creditors; but the company also may sue for repayment. If the shareholder makes a repayment to the company this extinguishes his liability, nor can the company claim repayment if and in so far as the shareholder makes a payment to the creditor. If the company is in bankruptcy, the trustee in bankruptcy (*Konkursverwalter*) is alone entitled to bring action during the bankruptcy.[4]

On the other hand the members of the board of management are liable both to the company and to the creditors if they have

[1] Cass., 24 April 1891, D. 93, 1, 49.
[2] Pic 1216.
[3] Staub-Pinner II, p. 190; accepted also by Gadow, p. 188.
[4] § 756 (2).

paid dividends in violation of the law (§ 84 (3), 1 and 2). But there is a fundamental difference between the two liabilities. That against the company is barred if the payment was made in pursuance of a valid resolution in general meeting, and after five years from the date of the unlawful payment the company in general meeting may renounce the claim or make a compromise, unless shareholders representing at least 20 per cent. of the capital oppose the resolution (§ 84 (4)). As against creditors neither the fact that the payment was authorised by a resolution in general meeting nor a renunciation or compromise is a defence. The liability as against creditors, however, is operative only if the creditor could not obtain satisfaction from the company. Liability is excluded if the managers have acted with the care of a conscientious agent (leader of business); the burden of proof is on them (§ 57 (2) and (5)).

The assent of the members of the board of supervision does not justify the unlawful payment (§ 84 (4)); furthermore they themselves become liable if they are parties to the payment or have made it possible by neglecting their duty to supervise the activities of the management. Their liability, in so far as it arises, is governed by the same rules as that of the management (§ 99). The liability of the two boards, in so far as it exists, is always joint and several (§§ 84 (2) and 99). The period of limitation for all these actions is five years (§ 84 (6)).

The payment of unlawful dividends involves criminal liability if it was made intentionally to the detriment of the company under the general clause of § 294.

Many European legislations embody the rule that dividends received *bona fide* cannot be claimed by the company, or like the Swiss O.R. (678) expressly provide that shareholders who have received unlawful dividends in bad faith are liable for their repayment.

58. Dividend Policy

It is always difficult to ascertain exactly the right measure to take in respect of distributions. The ascertainment of the real profits is a problem in itself, and legislations tend to grapple with it by drawing up detailed rules for accounting in general and especially for the balance sheet. Nevertheless a wide field remains for the exercise of the directors' judgment and discretion in showing the amount of profits and deciding what part of them should be appropriated to dividends when they declare the dividend or make their proposals thereon to the general meeting.

The use of sober judgment offers a difficult problem, since any deviation from a sound middle course may be harmful. Directors have often erred by being too optimistic in good times and overlooking possible contingencies, doing very little to provide the company with a comfortable cushion in the form of a reserve for the rainy days which would inevitably follow years of expansion and prosperity.

But there is danger in the opposite direction as well. Cautious managements are naturally inclined to withhold substantial parts of the profits in order to make provision for unforeseen contingencies, and also to make a stable dividend policy possible, so that the company may be able to pay dividends in lean years. Both aims are legitimate; the former will enable the company to weather even heavy storms, the second to evade violent fluctuations in dividends and thus make the distributions correspond to the constant earning power of the enterprise. This is of great importance, especially to small shareholders who would otherwise be shocked by sudden curtailments of dividends and be induced to part with their holdings at the most unsuitable moment. But sometimes the withholding of dividends goes farther, directors using or rather abusing their powers in order to starve and freeze out the minority; these will be discussed in § 78 in connection with the question of minority protection.

Apart from these rather exceptional cases there is a widespread inclination to curtail dividends in order to build up funds for new investments. It is an open question whether it is more advisable to resort to an increase of capital for such aims, or to prepare the way for self-financing by withholding a certain fraction of the profits from distribution and gradually building up reserves for possible enlargement or reconstruction of plant. So long as this is done openly and in accordance with the articles, there would be the less objection to such corporate finance, although on the whole it seems more appropriate to finance repairs alone from current earnings, and to set aside amounts sufficient to meet contingencies, whereas the decision to make new investments should be a matter for the shareholders, who should decide whether the company shall embark on the new line proposed and provide the means thereto by increase of capital and the issue of additional shares. This line of finance policy is to be preferred, the more so as self-financing easily leads—as experience shows—to a less responsible management. The withholding of profits becomes increasingly dangerous if it is done by building up secret or hidden reserves, thereby also withholding information as to the extent of profits.

The trend of legislation is more stringent in safeguarding the solidity of the balance sheet and preventing irresponsible distributions than in securing the rights and interests of shareholders as to distributions. In this connection the new developments of public policy as to undistributed profits should be mentioned.

In the U.S.A. the implications of a policy of amassing corporate profits by withholding dividends were clearly seen, and Federal legislation introduced a special tax on such profits. The German attitude was quite different. The law of December 1934 provided that companies (including A.G., K.A.G. and G.m.b.H.s) should not pay dividends in excess of 6 per cent., or, if in the previous year they had paid a higher dividend, in excess of 8 per cent. The surplus was to be placed with a public finance institution, the *Golddiskontobank*, which had to invest it in Reich bonds and hold these in trust for the companies concerned. This law was intended to give indirect financial help and to provide money for the vast rearmament plans of the Reich, and was meant to remain in force for three years only. Subsequently, however, the Nazi régime introduced measures by which payment of higher dividends was made subject to a special tax which was progressive to such an extent as to become prohibitive. This example was faithfully copied by all Continental legislations within the German orbit.

It is a rather remarkable coincidence that the slogan against excessive dividends was vigorously taken up by Mr. Hugh Dalton, Chancellor of the Exchequer of the British Labour Government. In his Budget speech for 1946–7,[1] he made an appeal to British companies to devote their funds to post-war developments rather than to increase of dividends, and said that if there was a wide departure from this course, the matter would have to be further considered. This was actually done, and the Finance Act for 1947–8 (10 & 11 Geo. VI, c. 35), provided for higher taxation on distributed profits in respect of the profits tax which took the place of the wartime excess profits tax from

[1] *The Times*, 1 March 1946.

1 January 1947. The Chancellor justified this discriminatory taxation with the observation that he was not satisfied with the "large increases in distributed profits and higher dividends. In his judgment too much has been distributed and too little ploughed back."

The Chancellor, however, seemed to feel a need to provide other reasons. These he gave by remarking that increased dividends would work in the direction of enhancing the inflationary trend, a view hardly in accordance with the fact that dividends are subject to income tax and in the case of larger shareholdings to surtax, so that very little would remain to increase purchasing power. Obviously more weight is laid on the consideration that higher dividends would impair the results of the cheap money policy embarked upon by the Government, and there is obviously a hope that the growing unpopularity of the 2½ per cent. issues will be counteracted by the obstacles placed in the way of increased distributions. Whether this hope is to be realised the future will show, and it is to be noted that the well-known slogans were not lacking. The Chancellor did not refrain from stressing that shareholders receive their dividends "for no work at all".

59. Transfer of Shares

Shares in a company are now everywhere recognised as personal property even if the company's sole purpose is the holding of real property; and shares are on principle transferable.

In the case of bearer certificates or warrants, since the transfer is made by delivery, the company is in no way concerned; it may even not be informed, and any restriction of transferability is inconceivable. This makes it desirable that bearer certificates should be issued only in respect of fully paid up shares, and most legislations in fact provide for this.

In the case of nominative shares, which are the prevailing type in Great Britain and the States of the British Commonwealth, and the only one in the U.S.A., no transfer is operative without the company's intervention, through the registration of the transfer, the entry of the new member's name in the register, and as a rule the issue of a new certificate.

In the case of shares not fully paid up the company's interest requires that it should have discretionary power to refuse registration if in doubt about the transferee's solvency. There may be other reasons to make transfer in general or in particular cases undesirable for the company or its existing members. The extent to which such claims for restriction of transfer are admitted varies under the different legislations.

In Great Britain, sec. 73 of the 1948 Act, in agreement with earlier enactments, provides that "the shares or other interest of any member in a company shall be personal estate, transferable in manner provided by the articles of the company". The rule therefore is that the shareholder has power to transfer his share or shares; this power is given by law and not by the articles. The articles, however, may curtail or even exclude it; they are therefore to be consulted to ascertain not only in what manner the transfer is to be made, but also whether they contain provisions affecting the power to transfer. In the absence of such restrictions the shareholder may transfer his shares to whomsoever he chooses.[1] On the other hand the articles may impose restrictions of any kind upon the power of transfer.[2]

A private company (sec. 28 (1) of the Act) must restrict the right of transfer, and if this restriction is removed by alteration of the articles ceases to be a private company (sec. 29 (1)). There is nothing to prevent a public company from imposing restrictions, though to do so would be contrary to the nature of a public company, and permission to deal in the shares of such a company on the Stock Exchange would be withheld. Table A (24) suggests a provision under which the directors may decline to register any transfer of shares not fully paid up to a person of whom they do not approve, and the transfer of shares on which the company has a lien. Such provisions cannot be regarded as restrictions in the strict sense of the term, and both serve to protect the company's legitimate financial interests. Real restrictions, while compulsory in the case of private, seldom if ever appear in that of public companies.

The usual restrictions in the case of private companies are that no transfer may be made without the assent of the directors, that shares may be sold only to members, or that the other shareholders shall have a pre-emptive right. This right may be coupled

[1] Weston's case (1868), L.R. 4 Ch. App. 20; Gilbert's case (1870), L.R. 5 Ch. App. 559.

[2] Stockton Malleable Iron Co. (1875), 2 Ch. D. 101; *in re* Cawley and Co. (1889), 42 Ch. D. 209; Delavenne *v.* Broadhurst (1930), W.N., 238.

with a fixing of the price, e.g. the par value of the shares. In some cases one or several shareholders have an option in respect of the shares of other shareholders. All these and similar restrictions are held to be valid—their validity cannot be challenged on the ground of the rule against perpetuities.[1] Furthermore, such restrictions operate against a mortgagee's power of sale in respect of the shares,[2] and similarly against a trustee in bankruptcy.

If the directors are empowered to accept or reject transfers for registration at their discretion the Court will as a rule not scrutinise the exercise of this power, but the refusal may be attacked if it is due to *mala fides*.[3]

If the articles are not quite definite as to the power to refuse registration of transfers the Court may inquire into the reasons of the refusal. The border-line is elastic. Interrogations have been allowed as to the reason of the refusal although the articles provided that the directors might decline to register a transfer "without assigning any reason"; [4] but in another case [5] this was not allowed, since under the articles the directors were not bound to specify the grounds of their refusal. If the directors give their reasons the Court may consider whether they are legitimate or not.[6]

In the course of the hearings of the Cohen Committee the awkward consequences of such restrictions were put forward by several witnesses, and various proposals to give relief to the parties aggrieved were advanced. The restrictions may operate with extreme severity against successors in case of death, especially where they are excluded from taking part in the company's management. The power of the directors to refuse transfers might make the shares unsaleable, and since the payment of dividends may be enforced only in exceptional cases the value of shareholdings might be impaired. Whether the right to demand winding-up on the basis of the "just and equitable" clause would bring real relief is doubtful (see § 95). Similarly the pre-emptive right of the other shareholders may also operate to the detriment

[1] Borland's Trustee *v.* Steel Brothers and Co. (1901), 1 Ch. 279.

[2] Hunter *v.* Hunter (1936), A.C. 222.

[3] Gresham Life Insurance Society *ex parte* Penney (1872), L.R. 8 Ch. App. 446; *re* Bell Brothers (1891), 65 L.T. 245; *re* Coalport China Co. (1895), 2 Ch. 404; Smith and Fawcett Ltd. (1942), Ch. 304.

[4] Duke of Sutherland *v.* British Dominions Land Settlement Corp. (1926), Ch. 746.

[5] Berry and Stewart *v.* Tottenham Hotspur Football, etc., Co. (1935), Ch. 718.

[6] *Re* Bell Brothers, *supra*.

of a shareholder if it is not coupled with the clause that if it is not exercised within a fixed time the shares may be sold freely. The same is true where some or all of the other shareholders have the right to purchase the shares at par.

Although such restrictions are practically non-existent in the articles of public companies, and for this reason are outside the scope of this work, it may be said that the unlimited acceptance of such restrictive clauses may be the source of exploitation and that a relief against such abuses is highly desirable. On the other hand if the articles give the directors no power to refuse transfers, a shareholder may transfer his shares to whomsoever he chooses, and the directors are not in a position to prevent transfers of partly paid up shares to transferees who have no means to satisfy calls.[1] In this way shareholders may evade liability, and the company would be unable to prevent such transfers up to the beginning of the winding-up. Only if the transfer was not a real one, the transferor having reserved beneficial rights in respect of the shares, can he be held liable in spite of the transfer. It is to be remembered that many articles actually authorise directors to decline the registration of the transfer of shares not fully paid up, and in such cases it is for them to accept or decline the transfer proposed; they may even cancel the registration and restore the name of the transferor to the register if they were induced to register the transfer by misinterpretation.[2] It may therefore be said that it is due to the company's and the promoter's negligence in framing the articles that such an awkward position can arise. Nevertheless it would be well to give the directors power to refuse the registration of transfers if the shares are not fully paid up and if they are not satisfied as to the solvency of the transferee.

It is unlawful to register a transfer of shares unless a proper instrument of transfer has been delivered to the company (sec. 75). In other respects the form and manner of transfer may be provided by the articles (sec. 73). Usually a simple instrument signed by both transferor and transferee is sufficient. Exceptionally a deed is required, and the directors may refuse registration if the transfer does not comply with the provisions of the articles.

In many cases blank transfers are executed, i.e. a blank place

[1] De Pass' case (1859), 4 De G. and J. 544; Lindlar's case (1910), 1 Ch. 312.

[2] Snow's case, Bank of Hindustan, China and Japan (1871), 19 W.R. 1057, reported as Roger's case, 25 L.T. 406.

is left in the declaration for the name of the transferee in order that the purchaser or mortgagee may complete the declaration by filling up the blank. In this way the same declaration may be used for several transfers and is completed only when presented for registration. This is particularly common when shares are being mortgaged. Where the articles prescribe deeds, blank declarations are inoperative, and the effect of a blank transfer can be attained only by means of a power of attorney, which in its turn must be under seal.

The registration is normally requested by the transferee, and in addition to the declaration he has to hand over the certificate to the company (cf. Table A25 (*b*)), and in due course a new certificate is issued in his favour. The company, however, is bound to register the transfer on the request of the transferor also (sec. 77). If only a part of the shares represented by the certificate is transferred, or the shares are transferred to more than one person, it is impracticable to hand over the certificate to the transferee; it is then lodged with the company, on whose behalf the secretary or some other officer certifies on the declaration of transfer by a written or stamped clause that the certificate has been so lodged. Such certified declarations of transfer are frequently used for the purpose of further sales, and according to the regulations of the London Stock Exchange certified transfers are accepted as good delivery of the shares to which they refer. It may happen, however, that the certifications give no actual title, because they are either erroneous or do not originate from the person authorised to act on behalf of the company. In Bishop *v.* Balkis Consolidated Co.,[1] it was held that although the person making the certification does not warrant the title of the transfer or the legal validity of the various documents which together purport to establish the title, the certification must amount to a representation that the transferor has produced to the person certifying either what purports to be a certificate of the title of the transferor to the shares mentioned in the transfer or the equivalent of such document; in other words what purports to be a certificate of someone else's title to the shares and one or more documents purporting to transfer those shares from such person to the transferor.

In two other cases,[2] however, it was held by the House of

[1] (1890), 25 Q.B.D. 512 C.A.

[2] George Whitechurch Ltd. *v.* Cavenagh (1902), A.C. 117, and Kleinwort Sons and Co. *v.* Associated Automatic Machine Corporation Ltd. (1934), 151 L.T. 1.

Lords that the company is not bound by a certification made by the secretary or other agent where the certificate was not in fact lodged with the company. Before the Cohen Committee several witnesses stressed that the interests of the security market require some safeguard to the effect that the company should be bound by certifications and that shareholders who buy shares on the faith of certifications may rely thereon. The Committee recommended (139) the insertion of a new section into the Act to the effect that if a transfer is endorsed with the words "certificate lodged" or other words to this effect and bears the signature or initials, whether written, printed or facsimiled, of any person authorised to make such certification, and is issued by the company, it should have the effect that the company has represented to any person acting on the faith of the document that the transferor has produced to the person making the certification documents which show a *prima facie* title of the transfer. The Committee, however, did not recommend that the certification should amount to a warranty of the genuineness of the documents.

Following these recommendations, sec. 70 of the Companies Act, 1947 (sec. 79 of the Act of 1948), provides that the company is liable to any person who acts on the faith of a false certification made negligently, to the same extent as if the certification had been made fraudulently, but the certification shall be taken merely as a representation that such documents have been produced to the company as on the face of them show a *prima facie* title to the shares in the transferor. The certification shall not, however, be taken as a representation that the transferor has any title to the shares or debentures.

An instrument of transfer is deemed to be certificated if it bears the words "certificate lodged" or words to the like effect, and the certification is deemed to be made by the company if the person issuing the instrument is authorised to issue such instruments on the company's behalf. The certification must be signed or initialled—whether handwritten or not—by a person authorised, whether an officer or servant of the company itself, or of a body corporate authorised to certify transfers on the company's behalf.

On the other hand the company may object that the certification was not signed or initialled by the person whose signature or initials it bears, and further that the signature or initials were not placed on the document for the purpose of certifying the transfer on the company's behalf.

Whether these provisions will prove sufficient to meet the exigencies of the market is doubtful.

As to transfers registered on the basis of a forged declaration, the company is entitled and even bound to scrutinise their genuineness, but such scrutiny is hardly practicable. Should it subsequently prove that the declaration of transfer was forged, the transferee does not acquire a valid title, and the owner has the right to require that his name be restored to the register. This is an old-established rule dating to before the first Companies Act, and is still maintained.[1] If the company discovers the forgery it may on its own initiative cancel the registration, remove the transferee from the register and restore the original holder.[2]

The company may, however, be liable for damages if a *bona fide* third party has acquired the shares acting on the faith of the registration.[3] The same is true for the transferee; he also is entitled to damages if he acted on the faith of the registered transfer, e.g. sold the shares. In such a case the company is estopped from setting up the forgery as defence, but to obtain damages the transferee must prove that he acted in good faith.[4] The position of the company is aggravated by the rule stated in Barton *v.* L. and N.W. Rail. Co., *supra*, where it was held that the transferor, if questioned by the company about the genuineness of the declaration, is not bound to reply, and if he omits to reply he is not estopped from asserting his ownership.

The company, however, may request indemnity from a person who under a forged transfer procured registration and the issue of a new certificate even if he acted *bona fide*.[5] The same was held in the case of a stockbroker who innocently acted under a power of attorney.[6] Furthermore, one who does not act within a reasonable time after having discovered the forgery and thus impairs redress on the part of the company may be estopped from asserting his title.[7] Even if a company is not liable for damages

[1] Davis *v.* Bank of England (1824), 2 Bing. 393; Sloman *v.* Bank of England (1845), 14 Sim. 475; Barton *v.* L. and N.W. Rail Co. (1888), 38 Ch. D. 144.

[2] Simm *v.* Anglo-American Telegraph Co. (1879), 5 Q.B.D. 188.

[3] *Re* Bahia and San Francisco Railway Co. (1868), L.R. 3 Q.B. 584; Otto's Kopje Diamond Mines (1893), 1 Ch. 618; Balkis Consolidated Co. *v.* Tomkinson (1893), A.C. 396; Bloomenthal *v.* Ford (1897), A.C. 156.

[4] Simm *v.* Anglo-American Telegraph Co., *supra*; Coates *v.* L. and S.W. Rail. Co. (1879), 41 L.T. 553; *re* Vulcan Ironworks Co. (1885), W.N., 120.

[5] Corporation of Sheffield *v.* Barclay (1905), A.C. 392.

[6] Oliver *v.* Bank of England (1902), 1 Ch. 610; Starkey *v.* Bank of England (1903), A.C. 114.

[7] Dixon *v.* Kennaway & Co. (1900), 1 Ch. 833.

it has power to pay compensation in certain cases under the Forged Transfer Acts of 1881 and 1892.

The company has time to make inquiries before registration, since under sec. 78 (1) the transferee is to be notified within two months after the transfer has been lodged that registration is refused.[1]

If the transferee has complied with the conditions prescribed by the articles the company is bound to register the transfer, and that without considerable delay. As we have seen, however, the company may take time for examination. But in the interest of administrative convenience companies are allowed to close their register once or several times every year, but not for more than 30 days in all; members are to be informed of such closing by public notice in a newspaper published at the place of the company's registered office (sec. 115).

The transferee has to insist on registration because until this is carried out the legal ownership of the share is not vested in him; he has only an equitable right which may be defeated, e.g. by a second transfer preceding as to the time of registration.[2] As between two claimants priority of title as a rule prevails. But the rule ceases to operate after the transfer has been registered in favour of a claimant with a later title.[3]

On the other hand the transferor also has a vital interest in registration, since so long as it is not carried out he remains liable for calls, and the one year's term during which he incurs liability as a past member for the unpaid part of the share begins to run from the date of registration (sec. 212 (1)). This interest is protected in that the transferor may apply to the Court in case of default or if unnecessary delay in registration takes place (sec. 116 (1) (*b*)).

Lastly it is not a matter of indifference to the company that transfers should be registered, and for this reason the company itself should have the right to apply for registration if the parties choose to omit it. Whether such right is given by sec. 116 (1) (*b*) of the Companies Act is in our view an open question.

Whether a transferor is by virtue of the registration freed from his liability for calls in arrear is not decided.[4] It is sub-

[1] Société Générale de Paris *v.* Walker (1883), L.R. 11 App. Cas. 20; Ireland *v.* Hart (1902), 1 Ch. 522; and Otto's Kopje Diamond Mines, *supra*.

[2] Ireland *v.* Hart (1902), *supra*.

[3] Moore *v.* N.W. Bank (1891), 2 Ch. 599.

[4] *In re* Hoylake Rail. Co. (1874), L.R. 9 Ch. App. 257.

mitted that the better solution would be in the negative. The transferee may be sued by the company in respect of such calls.[1] Quite apart from the case of a winding-up where the liability extends to the whole unpaid part of his share, the company has the power to make a fresh call for the arrears.[2]

The relation between transferor and transferee is governed by the law of contract, and therefore only some of the points arising need to be discussed. A contract to transfer shares for a money consideration is a contract of sale but not a sale of goods.[3]

The transferor has to deliver within a reasonable time to the transferee or his broker the certificate and the declaration of transfer duly executed. Reasonableness depends upon the circumstances normally occurring or those that were disclosed at the time of making the contract.[4] The obligation of the transferor is performed by delivery of the duly executed transfer and certificate; it does not include the obtaining of registration. Unless otherwise agreed it is for the transferee to procure registration.[5] In the period before registration the transferor is to be deemed a trustee for the transferee in respect of the shares.[6]

In case of death the transmission of shares is governed by the rules applying to personal property, and the personal representative of a deceased member has power to transfer his shares although he himself is not a member of the company (sec. 76). The executors or administrators are entitled to be registered as members unless the contrary is provided in the articles.[7] This is not a transfer (sec. 75, par. 2), and the grant of probate, the confirmation as executor, or the letters of administration, as the case may be, shall be accepted by the company as sufficient evidence of the grant notwithstanding anything in the articles (sec. 82). The validity of a provision in the articles excluding transmission of the shares in case of death has not been decided; the better view is that such a provision would be void. On the other hand restrictions imposed on transfers by the articles are

1 Herbert Gold Limited *v.* Haycraft, 27 March 1910, C.A., quoted by Palmer, p. 111.

2 Randt Gold Mining Co. *v.* New Balkis Eersteling (1904), A.C. 165.

3 Sec. 62, Sale of Goods Act, 1893; Colonial Bank *v.* Whinney (1886), L.R. 11 App. Cas. 426.

4 De Waal *v.* Adler (1886), L.R. 12 App. Cas. 141.

5 Skinner *v.* City of London Marine Insurance Corp. (1885), 14 Q.B.D. 882; London Founders' Association and Palmer *v.* Clarke (1888), 20 Q.B.D. 576.

6 Loring *v.* Davis (1886), 32 Ch. D. 625; Hardoon *v.* Belilios (1901), A.C. 118; Stevenson *v.* Wilson (1907), S.C. 445.

7 Scott *v.* F. F. Scott (London), Ltd. (1940), Ch. 794.

inoperative in respect of transfers made by executors or administrators.

In the U.S.A.[1] the transferability of stock is regarded as a right inherent in its ownership; it may, however, be restricted by statute or by the charter (articles). If so restricted, the restrictions prevail, and any transfer made in violation thereof is inoperative. An exclusion or restriction of transfer made in the by-laws depends for its validity upon the validity of the by-laws themselves. If these are authorised by a charter (articles) the restriction may be valid, otherwise it would be inoperative.[2]

The validity of a special agreement in restriction of the right of transfer depends in the first place on whether it is based upon a valid consideration; a further condition of validity is its reasonableness. It has been held that it would be valid only if it were concluded after all debts due from the shareholder to the corporation are paid.[3] Otherwise such an agreement is held to be in restraint of trade and contrary to public policy.[4] Similarly, an agreement by which the acceptance of a new shareholder is made dependent upon the assent of the board of directors has been held to be void.[5] But even the restrictions in the by-laws are regarded as binding only if they are reasonable. A restriction by which the shareholder is prohibited from transferring his shares for a specified time or until the par value is paid, or his indebtedness to the corporation is settled, is regarded as reasonable. The same is held of a provision which makes the transfer depend upon the assent of the directors, but this provision is subject to qualifications, as an absolute right on the part of the corporation, or of its directors on its behalf, to refuse assent would lead to awkward consequences. The shareholder may be compelled and may have to sacrifice a substantial part of the value of his share in order to obtain the assent; experience shows that apprehensions in this direction are well founded and that the shareholder may be subject to undue losses or extortions in consequence of such restrictions. It is therefore submitted that such provisions should be valid only to the extent that the directors should be entitled to refuse the acknowledgment for substantial reasons.

In practice corporations sometimes stipulate an option for the

[1] Cf. Ballantine, 320–38.

[2] Morgan *v.* Struthers (1889), 131 U.S. 246; Farmer's Loan and Trust Co. *v.* Chicago (1896), 163 U.S. 31; further, Fletcher 5452, n. 1.

[3] Fletcher 5455, n. 55.

[4] Fletcher 5455, n. 51.

[5] Fletcher 5455, n. 53.

repurchase of shares and pre-emptive rights. A stipulation for an option may be valid if based upon valuable consideration, but even so it is defensible only if restricted in time. An option without time limit would operate in the direction of excluding a transfer, since hardly any purchaser would be found to accept such an option. What time limit is to be considered reasonable depends upon the circumstances. Another consideration relates to the purchase price: an agreed purchase price may become unreasonable in particular circumstances, e.g. in cases where the market price or value of the shares had appreciated in the meantime in consequence of an accumulation of surplus or an increase of earning capacity. In such a case the option or its exercise at the agreed price may become inequitable. Generally the shareholder should have the right to refuse the exercise of the option, unless he purchased the shares with the express provision as to their repurchase. Even such stipulation should be valid only for a restricted period, say, five years. How inequitable such an option may become is clearly shown in certain cases, e.g. the famous lawsuit of C. H. Frick *v.* Andrew Carnegie, in which the fixed price of purchase in the agreement alleged by Carnegie amounted to only a small fraction of the actual value. The case ended in a compromise.

Another method of restriction is to grant a pre-emptive right to the corporation; in such a case the shareholder is under the duty to communicate any offer received for the share, and if the corporation is not willing to purchase it at the price offered to the shareholder by a third party he becomes free to sell. If the pre-emptive right is not coupled with an option it is less objectionable than an option.

Whether the restriction in order to be valid must be inserted in the share certificate is disputed. On strict legal grounds it would have to be regarded as valid even if it did not appear on the certificate, since the certificate is not the exclusive means of ascertaining the rights and duties of shareholders and a prospective shareholder is chargeable with the notice of the articles. On the other hand, if the restrictions are not made known in the text of the certificate, innocent persons purchasing the shares may be deceived and harmed. It is therefore advisable to make the validity of any restriction dependent upon its insertion in the text of the certificate, as is done by sec. 15 of the Uniform Stock Transfer Act.[1]

[1] Cf. Ballantine (1st ed.) 145.

The effect of a transfer is that the transferee steps into the place of the transferor as to both rights and liabilities. We have, however, to distinguish between the relation of transferee and transferor to each other and the position of them both with regard to the corporation.

As between transferor and transferee the position is governed by the terms of their agreement. As a rule it is held that the transferee is liable for calls made after the transfer, and thus that the liability for calls is fixed by the date when the call is made and not by the date on which it becomes payable. The same applies to dividends.[1] But the agreement may provide otherwise. If the transferor has to pay calls which under the terms of the agreement are to be borne by the transferee he may claim reimbursement. On the other hand he may claim dividends paid to the transferee which would belong to him under the agreement. The same applies if the transferee has to pay calls in place of the transferor or the transferor receives dividends which should belong to the transferee. The custom of stock markets and the regulations of the various Stock Exchanges as a rule settle the question from what time the dividends are to be deemed to belong to the purchaser of shares and the reimbursement of the transferor in respect of pending dividends. Generally the purchaser of a share acquires the right to dividends not yet paid at the time of purchase, whereas in the case of bonds the proportionate part of the current dividend up to the day of the purchase is to be paid over and above the purchase price.

The relation of transferor and transferee to the corporation depends upon the day on which all the conditions precedent are fulfilled. From that day on the corporation has to recognise the transferee as its shareholder; he is liable for all calls not yet made, i.e. made after the transfer, whereas the transferor remains liable for all calls already made but not yet paid.

Some statutes provide that the transferor remains liable regardless of the liability of the transferee until the par value, or in other cases until a certain proportion thereof, e.g. 50 per cent., is paid. In such a case the liability of the transferee is merely cumulative. On the other hand if the prescribed proportion is already paid in, the transferor's liability for the remainder is terminated.

[1] Webster *v.* Upton (1876), 91 U.S. 65; Pullman *v.* Upton (1877), 96 U.S. 328; and Fletcher 5464, n. 18.

There is controversy on the question whether the transferee is liable for the unpaid part of the par value if and when the certificate represents the share as being fully paid up. Some Courts hold that the transferee may rely upon such representation and would be liable only if he had notice that it was false. Other decisions hold that the representation cannot prevail against the facts and that the transferee is liable for the unpaid part of the share regardless of his good faith. A similar controversy exists as to the liability for watered or fictitious stock.

As already mentioned in connection with the issue of shares, the general view in the U.S.A. is that share certificates are not negotiable instruments. This has been held both by the Supreme Court and by most of the State Courts.[1] Consequently it has been held that a *bona fide* purchaser of such certificates acquires no better title to the shares than his transferor had; that he takes the share subject to equities against the transferor in favour of the corporation or of third persons. Similarly it has been held that a *bona fide* purchaser of a lost or stolen certificate endorsed in blank by the owner acquires no title against the owner, unless the latter were guilty of such negligence as would estop him from asserting his title. In recent times, however, the extensive dealings in shares by way of blank endorsements have prepared the way for the acceptance of a doctrine of quasi-negotiability by applying the doctrine of estoppel to a wider extent. It has been held that the title to shares will pass as between the parties by endorsement and delivery of the certificates, that the transfers are not subject to litispendence and delivery of the certificate, that the *bona fide* purchaser takes the share free from any secret liens in favour of the corporation created by contract or by-law and from any secret trusts or latent equities in favour of the corporation, of prior holders or of third persons. The Uniform Stock Transfer Act contains detailed provisions in this respect and protects the *bona fide* purchaser in respect of the title.

The rules of that Act are combined with provisions as to the manner of transfer. It is laid down that the "title to a certificate and the shares represented thereby shall be transferred only (*a*) by delivery of the certificate endorsed either in blank or to

[1] Hammond *v.* Hastings (1890), 134 U.S. 401; National Safe Deposit, etc., Co. *v.* Hibbs (1913), 229 U.S. 391; further, the Federal and State Decisions in Fletcher 5475, n. 1.

a specified person by the person appearing by the certificate to be owner of the shares; (*b*) by delivery of the certificate and a separate document containing a written assignment or a power of attorney to sell, assign or transfer the certificate or the shares. Such assignment or power of attorney may be in blank or to a specified person" (sec. 1). The transfer shall be effectual even though the transferor has received no consideration.

It has been held that the provisions of the Act are merely declaratory of the common law, although—as we have seen—as to the effect of the transfer the pre-existing rules were not quite the same. As to the formalities of transfer the Act did not introduce new law, since it had already been held earlier that in the absence of provisions to the contrary the shares may be transferred in the same manner as any other personal property. At common law it was held that the delivery of a stock certificate with a written transfer is sufficient to transfer the title to the share. Similarly it was held that the transfer endorsed on the certificate or contained in a separate document, and also the power of attorney to sell and transfer, may be executed in blank; [1] furthermore, that if the transfer or power of attorney is executed in blank, the certificate may be transferred by delivery from hand to hand without any further document, and any holder thereof has authority to fill in his own name or any other's as transferee or as attorney in fact.[2] Consequently the death of the transferor before the transfer is recorded does not affect the validity of the transfer of property.

In some jurisdictions it has been held that the methods provided by the respective Stock Transfer Acts are merely cumulative and a transfer of title may be made in any manner appropriate to the transfer of choses in action or other classes of intangible personal property.[3]

In order to execute a valid transfer the delivery of the certificate, whether actual or constructive, is of course necessary. An agreement to transfer without delivery, i.e. transfer of possession, is not sufficient, and has only the effect of a promise of transfer. On the other hand the delivery of the certificate without a declaration of transfer, i.e. endorsement, assignment by separate document, or power of attorney, does not suffice.

[1] Johnston *v.* Lalln (1887), 103 U.S. 800, and the State Decisions in Fletcher 5480, n. 15.

[2] Disconto *v.* U.S. Steel Corporation (1925), 267 U.S. 22; Fletcher 5480, n. 17.

[3] Fletcher 5483, n. 28.

There might be an action for the execution of the document in the case of a valid agreement for transfer, and it may be enforced by a suit for specific performance.

Besides the delivery of the certificate and the declaration of transfer many statutes, charters (articles) and by-laws require some record, as a rule the registration of the transfer by the company. Such registration became usual in order to protect the corporation, which has a legitimate interest in knowing who its shareholders are, who have the right to participate and vote at its meetings, who are entitled to receive dividends, and who are subject to the liabilities and obligations attached to the ownership of shares. Similar interests lie in the creditors of the corporation, the general public as prospective creditor and also the individual shareholders who have the right to know who their co-shareholders are. In consequence of the consideration of these legitimate interests most of the articles and many statutes adopted provisions requiring the registration of transfers with the corporation. Where such provisions exist they are to be complied with, and no transfer is valid until the registration has been effected.[1]

Though an unregistered transfer is inoperative as against the corporation, it is or may be valid and effective as between the parties.

Notice to the corporation can be given by any of the parties unless the contrary is expressly provided, and must be accompanied by the production of the certificate if the transfer is not endorsed on the certificate or accompanied by a written declaration of transfer or a power of attorney, as stated above. In the absence of provisions to the contrary the request for registration of transfer may even be oral.

The mode of registration is as a rule not specifically prescribed. In the absence of express provision the transfers may be entered in any book, even in a stock ledger or subscription list.[2] In many companies special transfer books are in use.

If the transferee has done all that is required and the failure of proper registration is due to the fault of the officers of the corporation the validity of the transfer is not affected.[3] This

[1] Johnston *v.* Lalln (1887), *supra*; Bridgewater Iron Co. *v.* Lissberger (1885), 116 U.S. 8; and Fletcher 5489, n. 75.

[2] Cecil National Bank *v.* Watsontown Bank (1882), 105 U.S. 217; Fletcher 5492, n. 17.

[3] Earle *v.* Carson (1903), 188 U.S. 42.

applies both to the rights of the transferee and to the termination of the transferor's liability.

It is not material to which of the corporate officers the communication of and request for the transfer is made. It is immaterial who is in charge of the office of the corporation during the usual business hours; some articles, however, require that the request should be made to a specific officer, as a rule the secretary.

It is generally provided that in case of transfer the certificate is to be surrendered and a new certificate issued by the corporation, but this is not held to be necessary unless expressly required by statute.[1]

Mere irregularities in registration or in requests therefor may be waived by the corporation; but if the corporation issues new certificates without requesting the production and surrender of the outstanding certificate it acts at its own risk.

A transfer, though not registered with the corporation, is not without some effect. It is true that in so far as registration is prescribed the transferee is not as against the corporation in a position to appear and to act as a shareholder. Nevertheless as between transferor and transferee the acts which are required to give a right to request the registration give the transferee at least an equitable title to the share.[2] There are even decisions to the effect that the transferee acquires the legal title, although not so that it would be exerciseable against the corporation and *bona fide* purchasers. This distinction has not much practical value and may even obscure the position. The relation between transferor and transferee having been already considered, it needs only to be added that the transferee may demand registration. In so far as the intervention of the transferee is required he has the right to compel the transferor to take all necessary steps. It has already been stated that the transferee may sue for specific performance if he does not choose to claim damages. But there are decisions to the effect that in order to do so he must show that an action for damages does not restore his position.

The corporation is not compelled to recognise the transferee as a shareholder before registration. This applies to dividends, to the right to vote, to liability for calls and also to qualification

[1] Cecil National Bank *v.* Watsontown Bank (1882), *supra*; Hawley *v.* Upton (1880), 102 U.S. 314.

[2] Black *v.* Zacharie (1845), 3 How. 483; Leyson *v.* Davis (1898), 170 U.S. 36; and Federal and State Decisions, Fletcher 5497, n. 15.

for office. Similarly the corporation is not bound to recognise the transferee in connection with the distribution of assets in the course of the winding-up of the corporation. This, however, is to be qualified in respect of cases in which the corporation has notice of a valid though unregistered transfer. In such a case the corporation will not be freed from its obligations by paying to a transferor who is known to have transferred the share.

If the corporation has wrongfully refused registration of a transfer, it has of course no right to regard the transferor as owner of the share.[1] Whether the creditors of the corporation may or must regard the transferor as shareholder in the case of an unregistered transfer is disputed.[2]

Following the principle that an unregistered transfer gives at least an equitable title as between transferor and transferee the accepted majority rule is that the transferee takes priority over subsequent execution and attachment by creditors of the transferor, although the minority rule is also followed in a number of jurisdictions.[3] Even the Courts which follow the minority rule make an exception if the failure of registration is due to the fault of the corporation.[4] Since transfer without registration gives only an equitable title, a purchaser or pledgee without notice of the prior transfer takes the share free of the title, though there are decisions to the contrary.[5]

We have already seen that the right to transfer the share *inter vivos* is an incident of ownership. Consequently the shareholder and his transferee have the right to demand registration and the issue of a new certificate provided they have observed the requirements laid down. In case of wrongful refusal the ordinary remedy would be an action for damages. According to recent practice, however, there is a suit in equity for specific performance even if a special interest for it is not stated or proved. This is the better view, since the amount of damages cannot be foreseen. "To say that the holder shall not be entitled to the stock before the corporation without any just reason refuses to transfer it and that he shall be left to pursue the remedy of an action for damages in which he can recover only a nominal amount would establish a rule which must work great injustice in many cases and confer a power on corporate bodies

[1] Whitney *v.* Butler (1886), 118 U.S. 655; Fletcher 5511, n. 6.
[2] Fletcher 5512. [3] Fletcher 5513. [4] Fletcher 5514.
[5] Bridgewater Iron Co. *v.* Lissberger (1885), 116 U.S. 8; Fletcher 5517, n. 5.

which has no sanction in the law." "The case bears a striking analogy to the one now presented and the same principle is manifestly applicable where the remedy at law is inadequate to furnish the proper relief." [1] Since this relief is one in equity, all qualifications recognised as to equitable remedies apply.

Many Courts hold that *mandamus* also will lie to compel a corporation to register the transfer and issue a new certificate. The parties injured by refusal have the choice of remedies. Especially is the right of the transferee to the choice recognised by the Courts.[2] As to the action for damages generally the premiss is the fault of the corporation; it has, however, been held that the corporation may be liable for damages caused by the refusal without any fault.[3]

In some jurisdictions the statutes provide that the corporation has the right to require proof of the transfer. It may refuse registration in case of forgery, but has no right to inquire into the transaction between transferor and transferee, nor can it raise the question of the validity of the transfer unless the transaction be void. On the other hand the corporation is liable for damages to the shareholders if it has failed to exercise ordinary care and diligence to prevent unauthorised transfers.[4] The issue of a new certificate and registration without requiring the production and surrender of the existing certificate makes the corporation liable to a subsequent holder in good faith.[5]

Under common law the transferee of a share certificate acquires no better title than that of his transferor. Consequently, unless the true owner is not estopped from the asserting of his right, the purchaser—even if *bona fide*—cannot prevail when the transferor had no better title.[6] This applies also to a case of theft and to cases where the transfer, endorsement or power of attorney was forged. The rule is a consequence of the doctrine that share certificates are not negotiable instruments. Since this doctrine is—as already shown—to some extent qualified by the Uniform

[1] Cushman *v.* Thayer Mfg. Jewellery Co., 76 N.Y. 365, quoted by Fletcher 5519 n. 28.

[2] Fletcher 5523, n. 5-6.

[3] Mackenzie *v.* A. Engelhard and Sons Co. (1924), 266 U.S. 131; Western Union Telegraph Co. *v.* Davenport (1878), 97 U.S. 369; Moores *v.* Citizens' National Bank of Piqua (1884), 111 U.S. 156; and Fletcher 5523, n. 7.

[4] Western Union Telegraph Co. *v.* Davenport, *supra*; St. Romes *v.* Levee Steam Cotton Press Co. (1888), 127 U.S. 614; Fletcher 5538, n. 2.

[5] First National Bank of South Bend *v.* Lanier (1871), 11 Wal. 369; Fletcher 5540, n. 27.

[6] Western Union Telegraph Co. *v.* Davenport, *supra*; National Safe Deposit, etc., Co. *v.* Hibbs (1913), *supra*; State Decisions: Fletcher 5542, n. 55.

Stock Transfer Act and some other statutes, in many of the jurisdictions the Common Law rules are no longer in force and the *bona fide* transferee may acquire a better title than the transferor had, or a good title, even though the transferor had no title at all.

In this connection we have to consider cases in which shares are held in trust. Under the American Common Law it is allowable to create valid trusts in respect of shareholdings and to insert note of trusts in the share register or books (records) of the corporation accordingly. If the person who appears in the share register is described as a trustee, or some clause to the same effect is inserted in the books or records, both the corporation and any third party is put on notice and is under the duty to make enquiries. If a transferee in such a case accepts the transfer without further enquiries, or the corporation accepts the transferee without such enquiries, the true owner may assert his rights against the transferee and the corporation may be liable to him. The owner's remedy against the corporation is an action at law for conversion or for damages. He may also at his choice maintain a suit in equity to compel the corporation to replace the shares on the register in his name and to issue to him a proper certificate. Instead of asking for replacement he may recover the value. Where new certificates would result in an over-issue a suit for value would be the only remedy.[1]

The true owner may sue at his choice either the transferee or the corporation. If the corporation has been sued and a judgment has been obtained against it the corporation may recover from the transferee, at least if he represented that he had a title to the shares. Whether it can do so where no representation was made is disputed.

As already mentioned, the true owner of the shares may be estopped from asserting his title as against a *bona fide* purchaser if the purchaser has acquired the shares from a person whom the owner has intentionally or through negligence clothed with the appearance of ownership.[2] The doctrine of estoppel is recognised to a very wide extent, and it may be doubted whether from a practical point of view it would not be better to recognise the character of shares as negotiable instruments. Such a reform

[1] Western Union Telegraph Co. *v.* Davenport, *supra*; St. Romes *v.* Levee Steam Cotton Press Co. (1888), 127 U.S. 614; Mackenzie *v.* A. Engelhard and Sons Co. (1924), 266 U.S. 131; Fletcher 5551, n. 2.

[2] Cowdrey *v.* Vandenburgh (1881), 101 U.S. 572; National Safe Deposit, etc., Co. *v.* Hibbs, *supra*; and Fletcher 5562.

would at least have the effect of providing clear and simple solutions.

A contract for sale and purchase of shares is governed on the whole by the same rules as the sale and purchase of personal property. From the point of view of the control of corporations it has no importance whatever, since it does not in any way affect the position of the corporation; the contract creates relations only between the vendor and the purchaser. Similarly, we have not to concern ourselves with the question of gifts of shares or with the devolution of property in shares under wills or intestacy.

As personal property shares may be pledged or mortgaged. The remarks made as to the importance of the contracts of purchase of course apply to pledges also. There are, however, some aspects relevant to our subject. In order to constitute a valid pledge the certificate must be delivered, and furthermore it is advisable though not necessary to register the pledgee with the corporation. Such registration is to be made in the form of ownership. Under the Common Law of the United States there is no provision for a special registration of the pledge; the pledgee therefore appears as the owner of the share. In this connection the question arises whether the pledgee has the right to vote in general meeting, and further whether he has the right to receive dividends and, in case of an increase of capital, to exercise pre-emptive rights. If we look at the question from the standpoint of the relation between pledgor and pledgee the answer is very simple: although the pledgee is in possession of the share and is entitled to make use of the rights inherent therein in order to secure payment of the debt, he is not otherwise an owner. This position is expressed in the maxim that the pledgee has the special property, whereas the general property is vested in the owner. It would follow that: (1) the pledgee has not the right to vote, at least without the assent or authorisation of the shareholder; (2) he has the right to receive dividends, but must account for them to the pledgor; (3) in case of an issue of new shares the pledgee is not entitled to take them, nor under duty to pay for them. He has to give all facilities to the pledgor to take the new shares, e.g. produce the certificates if required; he has to give the pledgor notice of the issue should he and not the pledgor receive such notice, and so on. If the pledgor refuses to take the new shares the pledgee has the right to sell the pre-emptive rights;

their purchase price is to be used for the reduction of the debt, whereas if the pledgee has taken the new shares they become subject to the pledge.

From the standpoint of public interest the only question of importance is to what extent the relationship between the two parties should affect the position as against the corporation. On this it is to be noted that the pledgee should not have the right to vote except as proxy of the shareholder. It is, however, very difficult to prevent his doing so unless some sort of special registration of the pledge is made possible. This is done by some of the U.S.A. statutes, and their example should be generally followed. The regulation should consist in a provision making possible the registration of a pledge in the form of a note in the share register; such regulation could be connected with a provision prohibiting the registration of a pledgee as shareholder. The question is on the whole of the same character and implications as that of nomineeship, which is considered in § 76.

As we saw earlier, the bearer certificate type of share was prevalent until recently on the Continent, and most companies chose this type by their articles. This facility is qualified by the rule that bearer certificates may be issued only after full payment of the par value and the premium, if any; but it was not until 1893 that the French legislation enacted this restriction, and still under some legislations the issue of bearer certificates is admitted after payment of a certain percentage—say, 30 or 50 per cent.

In case of bearer certificates the transfer of shares is made by mere delivery of the certificate. The company is not bound to examine the bearer's ownership, and it is generally held that it is not even entitled to do so. Consequently it became usual for delivery of the shares to be used as a means for obtaining exercise of the vote or of pre-emptive rights in case of the issue of additional shares, although the ownership of the share was not transferred. Banks in particular exercised the vote on shares deposited by their customers as collateral for loans or otherwise. The doctrine grew up that transfer of legitimation is possible without transfer of ownership. This means that the transferee is deemed to be entitled to exercise the rights arising from the shares as against the company and third parties, though in their relation *inter se* the transferor retains the ownership and is entitled to the benefits, e.g. dividends, or in case of sale to the purchase price of the share.

As a matter of fact German banks assumed and exercised all that could be included in the transfer of legitimation even if there was no agreement at all, and later they required from their customers the signature of forms with a long series of various clauses, *inter alia* one authorising their exercise of the vote. This practice was looked upon with disfavour, and the law of 1937 introduced special restrictions in respect of the vote (see § 72). Apart from these restrictions, however, the admission of transfers of legitimation remained.

In the case of bearer certificates the company has no means of restricting the transfer of shares. The case is different in respect of nominative certificates. Formerly it was held that the articles may restrict the transferability of shares in any way the company may choose, e.g. to the effect that only shareholders with special personal qualifications might acquire shares and become shareholders.[1] The law of 1937, however (§ 61), admits one kind of restriction alone, namely that transfer may be made dependent upon the assent of the company. Most commentators on the law agree that under it any further restriction would be inoperative.[2] The assent may be given by the management unless otherwise provided in the articles. It may be provided that assent can be withheld only for material reasons (§ 61 (3)).

The transfer may be made either by a declaration of transfer or by endorsement of the certificate, which may be either a blank endorsement or one on the name of the transferee, and we have seen that although as against the company only that person may exercise shareholders' rights who is entered on the register, the ownership of the shares is transferred by delivery of the endorsed certificate. Provided that the declarations of transfers or endorsements form an uninterrupted chain, the company is not bound, though it is entitled, to examine the genuineness of the signatures. In case of transfers by endorsement a *bona fide* holder, i.e. possessor of the certificate, acquires full ownership even though one or more of the endorsements be forged.[3] In such a case not only has the former owner no action but the company also is unable to refuse registration of the transfer.

The rule that as against the company only the person entered in the register is deemed to be the shareholder means that once he is registered he is empowered to exercise all rights incidental to

[1] R.G.Z. in Bankarchiv 14, 104. [2] Cf. Gadow 210.
[3] § 61 (2) of the law and § 16 of the Bills of Exchange law.

the share.[1] It is held, however, that the company may assert that the transfer was void, and there are even opinions that the company may prove that the transfer was of legitimation only and not of ownership, a view which seems contrary to the whole essence of a transfer.[2]

On the other hand the person entered on the register is liable for all obligations incidental to the share. His only defence is that the registration was made without his consent or is otherwise void,[3] but he is not entitled to contest the validity for duress, fraud or mistake if once he has given his assent.

The company has no action in respect of the obligations incidental to a share against a person who is not entered on the register, and cannot demand registration without the assent of the parties concerned. On the other hand some opinions hold that it may correct the register with the proviso that the person whose rights are impaired by such correction may bring action.[4]

The transferor remains liable for such part of the unpaid remainder of the par value as is not recoverable from the registered owner. If the company is unable to recover the amount of a call from the shareholder, it may request payment from his immediate predecessor, and at the same time must inform the next predecessor in the chain. On failure of payment within 30 days the predecessor may be sued, and so may the next in turn. This liability is operative within two years from the date on which the transfer was presented for registration. The payer of the call has the right to receive a new certificate. Should the call not be recoverable the company has power to sell the share if it is admitted to dealing on the Stock Exchange at the current price, or otherwise by public auction, and to sue for the deficiency (§ 59). Shareholders and former shareholders cannot be released from their obligations and a set-off is excluded (§ 62).

The Swiss O.R. restricts the liability of a transfer to the case of a subscriber, and even the subscriber is liable only if the company becomes bankrupt within two years. His liability is operative only if the share was forfeited (687). On the other hand the company may refuse to register transfers if the transferee does not give security for the unpaid remainder (686, par. 3).

If all the complications connected with the transfer of partly paid shares are taken into consideration, the right conclusion

[1] R.G.Z. 86, 158.
[2] Gadow 217.
[3] R.G.Z. 86, 159, 92, 318, 123, 285.
[4] R.G.Z. 86, 159, 123, 285.

seems to be either that the transfer of such shares should be forbidden, or that the company should be empowered to request security before the registration of transfers, since the liability of the transferor, even if carried as far as it is under German law, may not be satisfactory for the creditors of the company, while actually being an obstacle to the free marketing of the shares.

60. Bonds and Debentures

Any corporation engaged in business will necessarily incur obligations in the course of its operations. Industrial or commercial corporations order goods as raw materials or for resale, and make use of the customary credit facilities offered by the trade concerned, e.g. the payment of cash in 30 or 60 days or six months against a bill of exchange or note, and so on. It may procure an overdraft from its bankers or, if goods are purchased from overseas, arrange with a bank or an accepting house for financing the purchase.

Such transactions are dealt with under the head of borrowing powers (see §§ 43 and 65). In many cases, however, ordinary borrowing facilities are not sufficient: a corporation needs long or middle term credits with some degree of stability. The custom of securing part of the working capital by loans is therefore widespread. The corporation makes an agreement for a loan with one or more individuals or other corporations, which is evidenced in writing. Such written evidence of a loan is usually called a debenture. In many cases, however, a loan for more than one year cannot be had from an individual or corporation, even from a bank or financial house. The prospective creditor needs to be able to assign the whole or part of the loan to others, and either to deal with it through the Stock Exchange by way of an issue, or to place it among his clients or business friends.

To facilitate such assignments and placings it is usual to divide the loan into equal parts and to provide a written document as evidence for each such part, distinguishing it by a serial number. In commercial language the name debentures or bonds is applied to such documents, although from a legal point of view even a single document issued in favour of one person may be so called. Debentures or bonds are executed for a definite amount of money in the currency of the country of the corporation's registration or of the prospective creditors' domicile, and the bonds are made payable as to principal and interest. A British corporation as a rule issues debentures in sterling, an American in dollars. It was always exceptional for a British company to issue debentures in a non-British currency, and the same is, or at any rate was before World War I, true of any other corporation in the more developed countries of Western and Northern Europe. Companies in the countries of Central and Eastern Europe, however, not to speak of the Far East, fairly often obtained loans in foreign currencies from the richer countries of Western Europe and the U.S.A. Before 1914 France, the Netherlands and Switzerland were the main sources for financing the long-term needs of Eastern European corporations. Great Britain at that time did not take much interest in such credit transactions, and therefore, besides the public loans of the countries in question, many issues of Austrian, Hungarian and Russian corporations and of those of the Balkan countries were contracted in France, Holland or Switzerland in the currency of the creditor country and payable at some place within that country. After the First World War the U.S.A. became a creditor country of the first degree, and Britain showed a greatly increased interest in the financing of the European Continent. American and British banks did not grant credits or promote issues except in their own currencies. Consequently the debentures of Continental mortgage banks, industrial and commercial corporations were mostly expressed in sterling or in dollars. In many cases even it was usual to issue debentures with a clause securing the payment of principal and interest in gold.

The corporation by the debenture makes a promise to pay interest, usually half-yearly, and to repay the principal within a fixed time. As to the time of repayment practice varies. The debentures may mature after a fixed period, say, five or ten years or more, has elapsed. In other cases they are to be repaid by instalments; it is then usual to select which particular debentures are to be repaid at any one date by drawing lots. The corporation undertakes to devote a certain sum each year to repayment through such drawings and to the establishment of a sinking fund. It may, however, reserve the right to purchase in the market the amount of debentures to be redeemed. Sometimes the corporation reserves the right to repay the outstanding loan before maturity on calling in the debentures for redemption by public notice.

The relation between the debenture holder and the corporation is governed by the general law of debtor and creditor. This differs in many details as between the various legislations. Thus there are different views as to whether a debenture may be perpetual or not, and whether the corporation has the right to repay the debenture before maturity if this is not expressly stipulated. Such questions are outside the scope of this work.

The rule that a corporation is not forbidden to issue debentures at a discount is, however, universally accepted. A small discount is usual even in the case of quite solvent corporations whose bonds are very popular with the banks and the general public. An issue of 3 or 3½ per cent. debentures at 98 or 99 may be more attractive than one at par, even with an interest rate which would have exactly the same effect if the average life of the bond were taken into account. If the financial position of the debtor is not so good the discount may be substantial. The bond issues of United States railways, for example, were at the time of issue placed with the public at very substantial discounts. Their repayment and the payment of interest were a great burden on the railways, and were to a great extent responsible for their none too bright financial history.

As to the factors leading to the decision to issue bonds and to secure the money needed in this way, it seems contradictory but is nevertheless the case that the prospect of great prosperity and its opposite may be equally decisive for the issue.

If the business of a corporation looks very promising, it might be very lucrative for the shareholders to issue bonds at the usual rate of interest and thus increase the earning capacity of the shares and enhance the so-called equity. If a corporation has a share capital of, say, £1,000,000, wholly or mainly invested in fixed assets (land, buildings, machinery, tools, etc.) and needs further funds amounting, say, to £500,000, and if there is a prospect of earning 10 per cent. through the investment of £500,000 in current assets such as raw material, semi-finished products, etc., it makes a good deal of difference whether the corporation issues ordinary or preference shares for £500,000, or bonds for the same amount at 4, or, as is nowadays possible, 3 per cent.

It is therefore found that very prosperous corporations issue debentures (bonds) at rates of interest not much exceeding those of public loans, which nevertheless are quoted at par. On the other hand if the outlook for ordinary shares is not very bright the corporation will not have much chance of increasing its capital by the issue of ordinary shares, or even by creating preference shares, and the only way to secure the necessary funds will be to issue debentures. This is especially true if the law does not permit the issue of shares below par. In such an event, however, the issue of bonds will be possible only at a higher rate of interest, and even then at a discount and probably with substantial banker's commissions.

The laws of the various countries differ as to whether an issue must be authorised by the general meeting or can be decided upon by the board of directors. Some legislations provide that the issue of debentures invariably requires a resolution in general meeting, and that the necessary authority cannot be transferred or delegated to the directors. Others are satisfied with a resolution authorising the directors in general terms to issue debentures as the need arises.

In the former case the general meeting, after having resolved on the issue and settled its amount and conditions, may authorise the directors to fix the exact time of the issue and its details, e.g. the price at which the bonds are to be issued and the bankers' commission; but neither the amount nor the rate of interest and the conditions of repayment are to be left to the directors' discretion. All these questions must be resolved upon by the shareholders, and under most legislations are to be inserted in the by-laws. Under other legislations the board of directors may be authorised to decide on the issue of debentures and to settle all the relevant details.

Debentures may be nominative or to bearer. In the former case they are to be registered with the corporation and entered in a special book. It is a widespread practice to issue debentures to bearer even where bearer share certificates are not admitted, and since debentures give no right to vote in general meetings, there is less objection to the issue of bearer debentures than to that of bearer shares and warrants.

For the purpose of payment of interest special coupons are attached to the bonds, and these are frequently payable to bearer even though the bonds themselves are registered. It is, possible, however, in the case of registered bonds to dispense with coupons altogether, and to provide for the payment of interest to the registered owner by a dividend warrant.

The transfer of debentures is governed by rules similar on the whole to those for the transfer of shares (§ 59).

Debenture holders are creditors of the corporation both as to principal and interest; their rights do not depend upon the prosperity of their debtor, the corporation. They are entitled to the interest as due and to the principal on its becoming mature whether the corporation is operating at a profit or a loss. If the corporation is unable to pay the amounts as they fall due it becomes insolvent.

As a creditor, the debenture holder has generally no vote in general meeting; but in some cases voting rights have been conferred on debentures. Such rights are not only contrary to the nature of debentures, but also may lead to complications.

Debenture holders under certain legislations may be organised into a special body to deliberate and resolve concerning their rights in case of the corporation's insolvency or of attempts to alter those rights. In the absence of such legislation each holder is entitled to act independently.

As creditors of the corporation debenture holders take precedence, not only of ordinary or deferred shareholders but also of holders of preference shares. In the absence of special provision, however, they are not preferred to other creditors of the corporation. This position does not appeal to the investing public, and therefore debentures are in most cases secured by special assets. In the Anglo-American countries this is so usual that the name is usually restricted to those bonds which are secured by specific securities, generally mortgages.

In England, besides specific mortgages, debentures secured by a floating charge are also common. This means that the debenture holders have priority over all creditors of the corporation except those who may be secured by specific mortgages. In Scotland floating charges are unknown, as is also the case in several States of the U.S.A.

The Anglo-American law has no machinery for mortgages in the interest of unknown mortgagees other than the appointment of a trustee for the debenture holders. The trustee or trustees are appointed at the time the issue is made, and his (their) name is to be communicated to the subscribers to the issue in the prospectus. The mortgages are to be vested in the trustee, who holds them for the benefit of the debenture holders. The rights and duties of the trustee are to be defined in a special document: the trust deed. The main points of this deed are to be included in the prospectus, and a short summary thereof given in the text of the debenture certificates.

Up to 1947 the English Companies Act did not contain obligatory provisions as to the rights and duties of trustees; everything therefore depended upon the provisions of the trust deed. This generally contains very wide indemnity clauses, relieving trustees from their responsibility should they fail to fulfil their duties. By virtue of the indemnity clauses the trustee is responsible only in case of wilful breach of trust. If such an indemnity clause is contained in the trust deed any definition of the trustee's duties would be immaterial. How detailed the enumeration of those duties may be will not matter at all if the trustee is liable only for wilful default or neglect. The situation therefore is not at all satisfactory. Corporations and the issuing houses acting for them seek the co-operation of a well-known corporate or individual trustee in order to impress the prospective subscribers and purchasers of the bonds.

The public subscribes to or purchases the bonds on the assumption that the trustee will ensure the fulfilment of the conditions and stipulations of the trust deed. So long as the interest and the bonds which mature from time to time are paid all is well; in case of default, however, a most disappointing surprise may await the debenture holders, namely that the security has to a substantial extent disappeared or depreciated, owing to the fact that the trustees, on the faith of the indemnifying clause, are unwilling to act previous to a serious default, and when such a default occurs it is often too late.

The position, it is true, is not without difficulties. It is very simple to take the mortgage document into custody and to observe the terms of the trust deed as to its release. The trustee could easily ascertain whether the money has been paid to the company, and so on. The position is more difficult if the company seeks to change the mortgage, i.e. to obtain the release of a mortgaged asset from the trustee against another property to be mortgaged. In such a case the trustee should obviously release the mortgage property only if the new property offered as security in its place is equivalent in value to the asset to be released; this involves a great deal of technical knowledge, judgment and responsibility.

The position as to the use of the property by the company is even more difficult. As a rule the company has to and will reserve the use of the mortgaged property for itself. Thus, e.g. where a factory or other plant, or even an apartment house is mortgaged the public will rightly suppose that the trustee is keeping an eye on it and ascertaining whether it is in good repair, is properly insured, and that all other necessary steps are taken to safeguard its existence and value. The trustees are very often of another opinion, and take no trouble to be active in these respects. The man in the street would suppose that this question—at least so far as insurance is concerned—is very simple. In the discussions before the Cohen Committee, however, several witnesses gave evidence to the effect that the average trustee is not able to look after the proper insurance of the property in view of the difficulties of deciding against what risks, to what amounts and with what company the insurance contract is to be made. Yet the question of insurance is comparatively much simpler than that of repairs or of the exchange of one mortgaged property for another.

The difficulties encountered in the case of specific mortgages are infinitely smaller than those in the case of a floating charge. In such a case the security consists not in a specific property but in all the assets of the company excluding those exempted at the issue of the debentures. The company must have full liberty in the administration of the assets, e.g. in using the raw materials, selling the finished product, collecting the debts and so on. The trustee, therefore, in order to carry out his duties, would have constantly to examine the carrying on of the business and to take the necessary steps if serious deterioration should occur. It is this which is not done, and in the case of floating charges the trustee generally takes action only if and when the company is in default on the service of the debt. It is obvious that the last thing which the debtor company will do is to make default without urgent necessity, and consequently when the default occurs the mischief is presumably done and beyond repair. It has often been said that trustees are and should be faithful watchdogs; many who take an easier view say that they are watchdogs which do not bite but only bark. In the case of floating charges, however, the bark is only to be heard after the horse is out of the stable.

Some think that this situation cannot be improved, that a trustee cannot undertake such responsibilities, and that the indemnifying clause should be allowed to remain as it is at present. Otherwise, it is said, responsible persons would not be willing to act as trustees, at any rate for the fees now usual. Trustees of a less respectable class would give even less security than the trust corporations and other persons who are nowadays prepared to accept trusteeship.

Some witnesses before the Cohen Committee went so far as to suggest that not the function and responsibilities of trustees, but their name, should be altered: they should be called custodians, i.e. custodians of the mortgage documents. This view cannot be accepted. The issue of debentures or bonds secured either by specific mortgages or by a floating charge is not and should not be allowed without a trustee being appointed. Whether the trustee should be a corporation or an individual should be left for the parties to decide. In many cases it will be advantageous to have a corporation as trustee, particularly one specially organised for undertaking trusteeships, a trust corporation or insurance company. It has the advantage of continuity regardless of death, illness, and other events which affect real persons, and it may have further benefits. Sometimes, on the other hand, an individual is to be preferred. This will be the case with floating charges, especially if the debtor corporation has special types of production whose supervision calls for special knowledge. In practice it will be advisable in many cases to have one or several individuals as co-trustees beside the corporate trustee.

The trustee's duties should be clearly defined in the trust deed. It is not for the legislator to make rigid rules as to these duties, for circumstances vary in each case. On the other hand for legislations which provide models for articles of incorporation, such as the English Act of 1948, it would be advisable to provide such a model for trust deeds and especially for the duties of the trustee. Should the company not wish to make any alteration of the model rules, they would apply as they stand, and special provisions would be necessary only where the parties so desired. In this way it could be clearly declared what the bondholders are entitled to expect from the trustee, e.g. whether he is to look after insurance, repairs, the necessary valuations in case of the exchange of mortgaged properties, supervision of the business, and so on. As to indemnity, the trustee should not be allowed to contract out of his responsibility for the fulfilment of the duties which he undertook in virtue of the trust deed. Consequently he should be responsible for the exercise of reasonable care and diligence, and no contract should be valid against this provision of the law. In other words the position of a trustee should in this regard be identical with that of a director. A beginning was made in this direction by sec. 152 of the English Companies Act of 1929 for directors; the extension of this provision to trustees would be fully justified. It might be that such an alteration of the law and the abolition of the wide indemnity clauses would be followed by an increase in the fees required by trustees; this, however, should not operate to induce the legislature to refrain from such a reform. It is essential that bondholders should know what they can expect, and that the trusteeship should be a serious support for the issue and not a mere formality. If the expenses of a serious trusteeship should stand in the way of the issue of debentures, it would be better for the issue to be made without any security and openly declared to be such than to offer securities and establish trusteeships which in fact offer no support for the enforcement of the trust deed. Should the public not be willing to accept bonds without special securities and trusteeships, and corporations be unwilling to accept trustees who take their duties seriously, it would be better to refrain from the use of bonds altogether than to persist in the issue of debentures which give only apparent security.

In this regard it is to be borne in mind that the issue of bonds to secure funds is not always advantageous for a corporation. The interest and the payments into the sinking fund or for the instalments as they become due are fixed burdens on the company's budget which have to be met regardless of profits. In the case of corporations with variable prospects the issue of shares, even of preference shares, is much to be preferred in the interest of their stability. Dividends are never a burden if profits decline or losses are experienced. It is not in the interest of the common weal to make the issue of bonds too easy.

As already stated debenture holders have no voting rights, and on principle none should be given to them. Whether it is advisable to organise bondholders so that majority votes could be taken is quite a different question. Without some machinery of this kind every debenture holder has an individual right and claim against the corporation for the principal and the interest of his debentures. Consequently, if the corporation should wish to come to an arrangement with the bondholders, say, with regard to a change in the rate of interest, time of repayment and so on, the assent of each several bondholder would be required. It is obvious that such assent is not in the ordinary course of events to be obtained, or at least is faced with difficulties which are increased by the dispersal of ownership of the debentures. It is therefore advisable that some machinery should be established by which in such a case the debenture holders can be called together for a meeting to discuss the proposed alteration of terms, and that at such a meeting a fixed majority of votes should be required. The votes should be taken according to holdings, and the majority should be a substantial one both in respect of the number of bondholders taking part and of the amount of bonds outstanding. A provision requiring only a quorum of holdings represented regardless of the percentage of the whole outstanding issue which they represent would not be equitable; in many cases this would mean the representation of only a small part of the total issue. A resolution agreed to by only an insignificant part of the issue could not be accepted as a ruling as to a change in terms. It is to be remembered that under sec. 206 of the Companies Act the Court may sanction a compromise or arrangement if the holders of three-quarters of the outstanding debentures give their assent.

Special questions arise with regard to the winding-up of the company and the realisation of securities; these are considered in § 95.

In view of the frequent and manifold complaints it is surprising that the Cohen Committee was very moderate in its recommendations and that its line was adopted by the Companies Act, 1947. Two amendments only were adopted. The first deals with the register of debentures; according to sec. 74 (sec. 87 of the Act of 1948) the publicity of the register of debentures is to be extended so that any persons although not interested as share or debenture holders shall have the right to inspect the register and to receive a copy of it or of any part of it for a fee not exceeding one shilling. The second and more essential amendment related to the indemnity clause (sec. 75, incorporated in sec. 88 of the Act of 1948). Any provision of a trust deed for securing an issue of debentures, or of a contract with the holders of debentures secured by a trust deed, shall be void in so far as it would have the effect of exempting a trustee from his liability or indemnifying him against such breach of trust where he fails to show the degree of care and diligence required from him as trustee having regard to the provisions of the trust deed or absolving him from showing the degree of care and diligence ordinarily required of a trustee having regard to the provisions of the trust deed conferring on him any powers, authorities or discretions.

The draft of the Bill declared it admissible to entitle the trustee to rely on opinions formed or on information supplied by others. It was not laid down that if a trustee makes use of such information or opinions he has a duty to show due care in selecting the expert on whose opinion he chooses to rely and in scrutinising the information received. It is fortunate that this provision was abandoned in the committee stage in the House of Lords and thereby a dangerous loophole was stopped.

On the other hand the rule is qualified by two far-reaching exceptions. A release otherwise validly given in respect of anything done or omitted to be done by a trustee before the giving of the release shall remain operative. Further, it shall be valid to provide that a release may be given by a majority of not less than three-quarters in value of debenture holders present in person, or, where proxies are permitted—which as a rule is the case—by proxy, at a meeting summoned for that purpose. The release must be either with respect to specific acts or omissions or on the trustee dying or ceasing to act. Lastly, the new enactment is to operate only for the future; it is not to invalidate any provisions in force so long as any person entitled to the benefit of that provision remains a trustee under the deed. Nor will any person be deprived of his exemption or right of indemnification in respect of anything done or omitted while the provision remains in force. Thus the indemnity clauses will die a very slow death.

The position in the United States is similar to that in England, but debentures are there generally called bonds. Bonds with a floating charge are very seldom issued in America; on the other hand by virtue of law bonds have no specific fund or property as security in the absence of special stipulations. If bonds are issued with a specific fund or property as security they are usually called mortgage debentures.[1]

Short-term obligations, i.e. obligations with a run not exceeding five years, usually appear in the form of notes, which may be sealed or unsealed, whereas obligations running for a term exceeding five years are usually in the form of bonds or debentures and are generally sealed.[2] Bonds or debentures may also

[1] Fletcher 2636.

[2] Fletcher 2638.

be issued to bearer or nominatively. If issued to bearer they are provided with interest-warrants called coupons, and usually with a talon, i.e. a warrant for the issue of new coupons after those annexed are exhausted. The coupon bond may be convertible, i.e. the bearer may have the option of converting it into a registered bond. Such convertible coupon bonds are to be distinguished from convertible bonds in general, i.e. from bonds which may be converted into stock (shares) of the corporation.[1] They are also to be distinguished from stock purchase warrants, i.e. warrants delivered together with the issue of bonds entitling the holder to purchase shares in the company as part consideration for the money paid by the bondholder. Whether such warrants give this right independently of the production of bonds or only in connection with such production depends on the conditions of the issue. Another category is the income bond, i.e. a bond or debenture which gives a right to interest only if the corporation has a net income of a defined amount. The conditions are to be laid down in the instrument, and are to be construed according to the general rules of construction, especially with regard to the existence and the amount of net profits.[2]

The power to issue bonds is dependent on the power to borrow money: if a corporation has such power it has the implied power to issue bonds, and the same follows from the power conferred upon the corporation to mortgage its property. Generally this power may be exercised by the general meeting; under some jurisdictions, however, it may be vested in the board of directors. There may of course be restrictions or prohibitions in the statutes or the charter; in such a case bonds issued in violation of them would be void. Perpetual or irredeemable bonds are not usual in the U.S.A., but their issue is not illegal.[3]

In the case of public service corporations many States require the assent of a public authority, usually the Public Service Commission. Similarly the Federal Transportation Act gives the Interstate Commerce Commission exclusive control over the issue of securities by interstate railroad companies. These and similar provisions are to be construed in the sense that the issue of bonds in violation of the respective provisions is void.[4]

Provisions of a State constitution or of statutes prohibiting

[1] Fletcher 2640.
[2] Fletcher 2644–5.
[3] Fletcher 2653.
[4] Fletcher 2656.

the issue of bonds except for money, property or services (labour) are generally held to cover the funding of previously existing debts by the issue.[1] As a rule the consideration for which the bonds are issued is not material; therefore an issue below par cannot be objected to. This rule cannot, however, be construed in the sense that an issue at an insignificant fraction of the par value may be regarded as valid.[2] The issue of bonds for property or services is, so far as concerns consideration, subject to the same rules as those for cash.

Certain corporations are prohibited from issuing bonds at less than a certain percentage of their nominal value.[3] The validity of bonds issued as bonus depends on the existence of a consideration.

Generally the conversion of bonds into stock is held admissible. This question is considered in connection with the increase of capital.

If the bonds comply with the requirements for negotiable instruments they are to be regarded as such. There is, however, a conflict of opinion whether registered bonds are to be regarded as negotiable instruments. In States where the Negotiable Instruments Law is adopted the provisions of that law govern both the requirements as to bonds and the form and effect of transfers, including the position of a *bona fide* holder in due course.

In the absence of specific provisions the bondholder is held to be entitled to sue on the coupons and the bonds themselves at maturity, to obtain judgment and to enforce it. This right, however, does not as a rule extend to the security pledged for the whole issue in question, i.e. for all bondholders of the same class. Such security is held to be enforceable only at the request of the trustee. If, however, the trustee refuses to take action, the bondholders may apply to the Court for an order to compel him to act, or, where the law gives such a right, to bring action on behalf of all bondholders of the same class.

As already shown, the bondholders are on principle wholly independent of each other as to their rights, and therefore a majority of bondholders cannot deprive any bondholder of his right or of part of it without his consent. There are, however, special statutes providing for such majority resolutions to be binding on dissenting bondholders.

As a rule the corporation has a right to acquire a bond or

[1] Fletcher 2673. [2] Fletcher 2674. [3] Fletcher 2679.

coupon by purchase. In the case of such purchase the corporation may sell the bond or coupon without the necessity of reissue, whereas in case of redemption the bond or the coupon is extinct. Whether in a given case a purchase has been made or the bond or coupon has been redeemed is a question of fact.

A company which has power to issue bonds is generally held to be authorised to pledge such bonds and deposit them as collateral for loans. This may be done in respect either of bonds which have never been sold to investors or of bonds which have been repurchased by the company and not cancelled. The position of the latter class is that the company has the right either to withdraw the bonds definitely from circulation and formally cancel them, thereby reducing the amount of the issue, or to retain them in its treasury while awaiting an appropriate occasion to sell them. In the meantime it is entitled to cash the dividends and to treat the bonds in the same way as would be done with bonds issued by the State or by another company. In accounting, such bonds are to be reckoned as assets at a valuation in accordance with the principles of sound financial policy. Under some legislations there are express statutory provisions which prescribe accounting at the market price of the date of the balance sheet. It is to be borne in mind that the prohibition of issues below par does not extend to bonds, and therefore companies are almost without exception held to be authorised to issue their bonds below par.

Further it is held that there is no compulsory relation between the nominal value of bonds pledged as collateral and the amount of the loan for which the bonds are deposited.

Wide use has been made of this method of financing in the U.S.A. It appears that the La Crosse and Milwaukee Railway Co. pledged its whole bond issue for a loan, and similar cases were also reported earlier. This practice again became widespread during the depression period in the 1930s; it is recorded that in 1932 railroads issued $1000 million dollar bonds to secure loans amounting to $650 millions. On the average the ratio of par value to loan seems not unreasonable, but there were cases in which loans were granted against a collateral of 300 per cent. The Interstate Commerce Commission sanctioned such loans, and even the Reconstruction Finance Corporation granted loans on a similar basis. Companies were induced to resort to this device in cases in which the current market price of bonds was unfavourable, and the company believed that in course of time the bonds might be placed at more favourable rates. This may or may not be a successful policy, but there were cases in which the company could not satisfy its most urgent financial needs without pledging a block of bonds far in excess of the amount of the loan actually granted. Under the rules already mentioned the American Courts held such pledges valid. It is true that several statutes enacted provisions prohibiting fictitious increases of stock, and this rule was also applied to the issue of bonds. Such a provision is contained, e.g. in the Pennsylvania Constitution (Art. XVI, par. 7), and many other States have adopted similar provisions. It has been held, however, by the Supreme Court of the U.S.A.[1] that the rule does not mean that the face value of the bonds must correspond dollar for dollar with the face value of the loan. Following this decision any pledging being a real transaction was and is held to be valid. The only limit is that corporations are not empowered to issue and pledge bonds as additional security for a debt already existing, even where the creditor simultaneously grants an extension of the term of repayment.

It is obvious that the facility to pledge bonds and to make issues for such a purpose is not without great dangers. If a company remains prosperous, and even more if its financial position is improving, it may redeem the pledged bonds and after redemption obtain more favourable prices and conditions. If, however, the company's position does not improve, the expectation will fail, a notice by the bank and the ensuing maturity of the loan may place the company in an awkward position, and in certain cases may lead to bankruptcy. Strict adherents of *laisser-faire* in company matters will say that it is a matter for the company in question whether it adopts one or another way of financing itself, and it is not for legislation to interfere. But if we take into account that soundness of financial policy in the corporate field is a matter of public concern, we cannot agree to such passivity. However unfavourable the conditions of a bond issue might be, the loss is precisely known at the issue. The consequences of a pledge on the other hand are not accountable; they may involve the total loss of the bonds pledged without any substantial reduction of the indebtedness. In view of this possibility the only method is to prohibit corporations from pledging their own bonds.

[1] Memphis and Little Rock R.R. *v.* Dow (1887), 120 U.S. 287.

We have lastly to refer once more to the qualifications of trustees. On a report of the S.E.C., Congress in 1939 enacted a regulation in respect of trust deeds.[1] This Trust Indenture Act applies to all corporations subject to the Securities Act in so far as they issue debentures or bonds. The S.E.C., however, has power to grant exemptions. The Corporations concerned must include in their registration statement particulars of the issue and the indenture. It is provided that at least one of the trustees must be a corporation with a paid-in capital and surplus amounting to at least $150,000. Conflicting interests exclude appointment, and are defined in the Act. Conflict of interest is deemed to exist if the trustee is at the same time trustee for another issue of the debtor, or where the trustee controls or is controlled by the debtor. Such control is deemed to exist in the case of the ownership of five per cent. of the voting power or ten per cent. of the issue, or where the trustee is a creditor of the corporation, with certain exceptions. The trustee, in case of a subsequently arising conflict, has to communicate it and to withdraw from the trusteeship. Should he collect money from the debtor, he has as a rule to share the amounts collected with the debenture holders.

The debtor under the trust indenture is under obligation to submit a report at least half-yearly, and the trustee must give access to these reports on request by three or more debenture holders. The trustee on his part is under obligation to prepare at least yearly a report in respect of the trust property and to procure certificates of fair value from independent experts, and counsel's opinion whether conditions precedent have been complied with.

The Act provides that before the debtor comes into default the trustee must perform the specific duties set out in the indenture, and generally he has to examine the evidence submitted to him by the debtor, but in this respect he may rely upon the statements and opinions contained in the certificate. In case of default he has to act with the diligence and skill a prudent man acting in regard to his own affairs would exercise under the circumstances. The trustee is liable for negligence in acting, or for negligent failure to act, and cannot be relieved of his liability; he is, however, exempted from liability for *bona fide* errors in judgment.

A release may be granted by a simple majority of the votes

[1] Public Act 283 of 3 August 1939, Ch. 411.

of the outstanding issue; securites owned by the debtor, however, are excluded. For a postponement not exceeding three years in respect of any payment due a three-fourths majority of the shareholders' vote is required.

The S.E.C. exercises a wide power of supervision, and the Act undoubtedly marks a substantial progress.

In Europe the financing of companies by the issue of debentures first came into use in the case of railways. Their issue was regulated by the statute chartering the railway company, and they were granted a special charge over the railroad, its buildings and rolling stock. As a rule special registers were made in which the debentures were to be entered with effect that entry in the register gave a priority against not only shareholders but also the unsecured creditors of the company. Both in business circles and in enactments and in the articles debentures were called priority debentures, being distinguished in this way from ordinary and preference shares. On the nationalisation of the railways these debentures became State debts; in many cases, however, they were not exchanged for Consols or other bonds, but remained until redeemed, just as if the railway company concerned had continued to exist as an independent enterprise.

The enforcement of the debenture holders' rights in case of insolvency was regulated in detail by special enactments.

Another wide field for debentures is the satisfaction of the financial needs of agriculture and housing. Mortgage banks, joint-stock companies or co-operatives created for these purposes provided the means needed for the loans which they gave to owners of agricultural or house property by issuing debentures, usually called mortgage bonds (*Pfandbrief*). The loans themselves were secured by mortgages in favour of the mortgage bank. As most European legislations adopted the system of land registration, the mortgages were to be entered in the land register. The security of holders of mortgage bonds was built up by making the whole amount of the loans granted by the bank security for the bonds outstanding at any time. The fact that the loan is a special security for bonds issued by the mortgage bank was to be recorded in the mortgage deed and on the land register. Thus if a mortgage bank issued mortgage bonds to the amount of 10,000,000 francs, marks or kronen, as the case may be, it had to earmark mortgages of at least the same amount as security for the issue and to record this fact in the register.

On the other hand the bank was to have some freedom in dealing with the mortgages. Thus some legislations were content with imposing on mortgage banks the duty of always keeping the balance between the sum of the outstanding bonds and the amount of the loans and of withdrawing bonds from circulation by redemption or purchase if the stock of loans was reduced by repayment or otherwise. To ensure compliance fines were imposed in case of violation. On the other hand there were provisions for publicity in the form of compulsory publication (quarterly or half-yearly) of particulars as to the loans and the bonds, and mortgage banks had to keep a special security fund up to a certain percentage of the bonds, apart from the loans. Some legislations were not satisfied with these provisions, and a trustee for the custody of mortgage deeds was appointed whose signature was required for the release of mortgages. Apart from these special fields the issue of debentures, especially by industrial enterprises, was relatively moderate.

Debentures on the Continent are usually to bearer. Nominative, i.e. registered bonds are the exception. Coupons for the interest are always attached to the bonds, usually payable half-yearly, as well as a warrant (*talon*) for a new sheet of coupons for a future period. Debentures are always regarded as negotiable instruments.

In connection with the issue of debentures we have first to take into account that under European law the borrowing powers of the board are unrestricted, and this principle is absolute, so that any curtailment of it would be void. Certain legislations, however, while maintaining that the board is empowered to contract a loan irrespective of its amount, nevertheless regard the issue of debentures, divided into certain units, as a matter of major importance which requires a resolution in general meeting.

The position under German law is somewhat peculiar; the issue of debentures is held to be within the competence of the management (§§ 70–1); a restriction in the articles or by a resolution in general meeting would be inoperative as against third parties, and would only have the effect of an instruction whose violation might possibly involve a liability for damages but would not affect the validity of the issue.[1] On the other hand if the debentures are to bearer—as in most cases they

[1] Cf. §§ 74 and 103, Gadow, p. 36.

are—their issue is dependent upon the consent of the Government.[1]

It is possible under German law to give the debenture holders, besides or in place of fixed interest, a share in the profits,[2] but they cannot have a vote, since even in such a case they are not regarded as shareholders. Debentures with participation in profits may be issued only by a resolution in general meeting, carried by a three-fourths majority of those present (§ 174 (1)). The articles, however, may provide otherwise. The same requirement applies to convertible bonds, which are considered in § 90. The issue of debentures below par is allowed; similarly companies are free to repurchase their own debentures.[3] The questions connected with accounting are considered in §§ 84 and 85.

61. Preference Shares

In principle the rights of shareholders are equal. In early corporation practice they were so also in fact; but where the enterprise needed a lengthy period for construction or building and the expenditure thereon could not be exactly foreseen or owing to unforeseen eventualities had to be increased, companies were compelled, in order to raise the necessary additional capital, to grant special preferential rights to the capitalists who provided it. In this way the issue of preference shares came into use. This was particularly the case with railway companies. Although earlier there had been exceptional cases of the issue of such shares, they became common only in railway financing; and their use for other varieties of enterprise, especially for industrial companies, came later. Nowadays, however, they are widespread, and the financial structure of many large companies has become extremely complicated.

Preference shares are to be considered as a separate class of share, their rights being defined by the articles (charter). They may be issued on the formation of the corporation or later in connection with an increase of capital. If issued at the formation as a part of the original capital their position is to be defined in the original act which creates the corporation.

Whether preference shares may be issued in connection with an increase of capital was formerly disputed. The question was

[1] § 795 Civ. Code and § 6 of the Order of 8 December 1931.

[2] R.G.Z. 118, 152.

[3] R.G.Z. at Holdheim 11, 259.

finally resolved everywhere in the affirmative, and it is nowadays a recognised practice, provided that the necessary formalities, which are generally identical with those required for an alteration in the articles, are complied with. Furthermore, under some legislations ordinary shares may be converted into preference shares by additional payments, provided that such payments are voluntary, and that shareholders who do not opt for such conversion are not disproportionately discriminated against. There have thus come to be many companies with more than one class of shares. The shares which enjoy preferential rights are called preference or preferred shares, the others ordinary or common, or sometimes deferred, shares.

Nowhere is there a rigid rule as to how or to what extent preferred shareholders may be favoured. This depends upon the provisions of the articles, original or altered, and these in turn are governed by circumstances. Normally no corporation would grant more privileges than were necessary for the success of the issue or the procuring of the additional capital. It may be otherwise if the majority is bent on a policy of exploitation.

The usual preference concerns dividends; the holders of preference shares enjoy the right to receive out of the net profits a dividend up to a certain limit, say, four per cent. or more, before the holders of ordinary shares take anything. If the company prospers the dividend will be met, and in such a case the position of the preference shareholder is somewhat similar to that of the holder of a bond or debenture. Nevertheless there is a fundamental difference; the company has no power to guarantee the preferential dividend if profits are not sufficient to cover it, for such a stipulation would violate the prohibition against paying interest to shareholders, and would therefore be void.

It may therefore happen that preferred shareholders will not receive dividend at the rate which is shown on the face of their certificate. They may receive less or even nothing, according to the amount of profits earned. In other words they have a priority, but not a vested right to the percentage. The articles may provide either that the unpaid dividend shall lapse, or that arrears are to be met from the profits of later years; the shares are accordingly called either cumulative or non-cumulative.

It is likewise for the articles to decide whether the preference shares entitle their holder to participate in the remainder of the profits after the holders of ordinary shares have received a dividend

—usually the same as that stipulated for preference shares—or are excluded from further participation: the shares may be called participating or non-participating preference shares accordingly.

Priority may be given also in respect of the distribution over in case of winding-up, the liquidation quota, and in such a case the question of further participation arises and may be settled by the articles in either sense.

The financial structure of corporations may be still more complex where there are several varieties of preference shares with different priorities; these are usually called senior and junior issues.

It is often provided that preference shares may or must be redeemed, of course only out of profits, in accordance with a fixed plan or at the choice of the corporation (redeemable or non-redeemable preference shares). Redemption is most usual in the case of non-participating preference shares. It may be effected by way of yearly drawings or by the creation and periodical reinforcement of a sinking fund, or by purchase in the open market.

In all these respects many variations in the rights given to preferred shareholders are possible, and thus the simple name of preference share, even when qualified as "cumulative" or "participating", does not fully explain the position. The articles have to be carefully examined by the prospective investor, and failure to do so may result in bitter disappointment.

The existence of different classes of shares does not necessarily involve differentiation as to voting rights; but this is often found, its motive being the implications of differential participation in dividends. It may lead to awkward consequences if the holders of preference shares have a vote in deciding what the ordinary shareholders shall or shall not receive. For this reason it has become usual, especially in Great Britain and the U.S.A., to provide that preference shares shall carry no voting rights: they may be deprived of a vote once and for all, or for so long as they receive dividends. Further, there were cases, especially in Germany, where companies, mostly very prosperous ones, issued shares with a very low dividend preference, e.g. four per cent., without further participation and correspondingly with a limitation of their quota to the par value of the share in the event of winding-up, but with a voting preference in the form of a multiple vote. In this way it became possible to secure the control of large corporations by means of small investments.

In Great Britain preference shares are fairly widespread. They were invariably found in the case of railway companies, and frequently in industrial enterprises.

The issue of preference shares may be authorised by the memorandum of association; but it is more usual to create them on the basis of an authorisation in the articles. If it is the memorandum of association which gives power for the issue and defines the preferential rights, those rights cannot be altered (sec. 4) except with the sanction of the Court (sec. 206).[1] If, as is usual, the memorandum of association contains a clause giving the power of alteration, such clause is operative.[2]

It is nowadays usual to authorise by the articles the creation of preference shares, and even though the original articles do not give such power it is held that the issue can be authorised by a special resolution for the alteration of the articles.[3] Most articles provide that the preferential rights may be altered by the creation of a new class of preference shares or otherwise. Such a clause is of course effective, but even in its absence the issue of preference shares with identical or even greater preferences has been held permissible.[4]

It was formerly disputed whether a direct abrogation or variation of preferential rights is possible by special resolution if the creation of the shares was authorised by the articles and not by the memorandum, and there was no clause therein authorising the variation. The dispute seems to be settled in the affirmative.[5] On the other hand an oppressive or unfair variation may be restrained regardless of whether there was specific authorisation or not.[6] If under the articles the variation or abrogation of the preferential rights is dependent on the consent of any specific proportion of the holders of the preference shares concerned or upon a resolution of a special meeting of the holders, the variation may be contested by holders of at least 15 per cent. of the shares of that class. Application is to be made to the Court in writing within seven days after the consent or the passing of the resolution. The Court, after hearing the parties, may

[1] Ashbury *v.* Watson (1885), 30 Ch. D. 376.
[2] Welsbach Incandescent Gas Light Co. (1904), 1 Ch. 87.
[3] Andrews *v.* Gas Meter Co. (1897), 1 Ch. 361.
[4] Andrews *v.* Gas Meter Co., *supra*; Underwood *v.* London Music Hall Ltd. (1901), 2 Ch. 309.
[5] Underwood *v.* London Music Hall, Ltd., *supra*.
[6] Menier *v.* Hooper's Telegraph Works (1874), L.R. 9 Ch. App. 350, and dictum of Romer L.J. in Allen *v.* Gold Reefs of West Africa (1900), 1 Ch. 656.

disallow the variation if it finds that it unfairly prejudices the class concerned, or may confirm it if it is found to be proper (sec. 61, Act of 1929). It is obvious that this remedy was hardly practical in view of the short time limit; moreover it is held by the Court of Appeal that the ownership of 15 per cent. must be operative at the time the application is made, and the joining of shareholders after the expiration of the seven days until the hearing is to be disregarded. The Companies Act, 1947, extends this time limit to 21 days (sec. 10; sec. 72 (2) of the Act of 1948).

The substance and extent of preferential rights is to be defined at the creation of the class of shares concerned. The drafting must be clear, and usually is so in fact. Nevertheless doubts and disputes arise, and we may note the view of the Courts on specific disputed questions.

It has been held that a preference as to dividends is *prima facie* cumulative.[1] If it is intended that the preference shares should be restricted to participation in the profits of each separate year, this must be expressed.[2] The meaning of the clause of the articles in question is of course a matter of judicial construction.

If there are unpaid arrears on cumulative preference shares when a company goes into liquidation, the question arises whether such arrears are to be paid prior to any payments to ordinary shareholders. There can be no doubt if the articles expressly give the right to arrears.[3] The question is answered in the negative if the preference shares give only the right to arrears "due", i.e. declared at the commencement of the liquidation.[4] In the absence of any express or implied provision the question is disputed. In two cases [5] it was held that in such an event cumulative preference shareholders have no rights as to arrears, whereas in another [6] it was held that they have a right to arrears at the fixed rate of dividend before any payment is made on the ordinary shares. It is to be noted, however, that in this case the holders had under the articles also a preference as to the capital.

In the absence of any special provision the preference is

[1] Henry *v.* Great Northern Railway Co. (1857), 1 De G. and J. 606; Webb *v.* Earle (1875), L.R. 20 Eq. 556; Foster *v.* Coles (1906), 22 T.L.R. 555.

[2] Staples *v.* Eastman Photographic Materials Co. (1896), 2 Ch. 303; Thornycroft and Co. *v.* Thornycroft (1927), 44 T.L.R. 9.

[3] New Chinese Antimony Co. Ltd. (1916), 2 Ch. 115; Springbok Agricultural Estates Ltd. (1920), 1 Ch. 563.

[4] *Re* Roberts and Cooper Ltd. (1929), 2 Ch. 383.

[5] Crichton's Oil Co. (1902), 2 Ch. 86, and in W. J. Hall and Co. (1909), 1 Ch. 521.

[6] *Re* Walter Symons Ltd. (1934), 1 Ch. 308.

restricted to dividends, and the holders of preference shares have no priority as to the capital in the event of winding-up [1]; they rank with the ordinary shareholders in proportion to the par value of their shares.[2] In practice articles often confer such priority, and then the ordinary shares get nothing until the par value of the preference shares is paid in full.[3] As to the further question whether preference shares give a right to further participation, it is held that as to profits they do not confer such rights in the absence of express provisions.[4] On the participation in the distribution over after the ordinary shares have been repaid in full the question is disputed. It was held in the negative in certain cases,[5] in others [6] in the affirmative. The Courts were obviously influenced by the wording of the articles in each case, otherwise it is hard to see why judicial opinion should differ on the question of participation according to whether it refers to dividends or to capital.

The matter of redeemable preference shares is regulated by sec. 46 of the 1929 Act. Preference shares may be issued with a clause in the articles authorising their redemption either compulsorily or at the option of the company. Such redemption cannot be undertaken except out of profits available for dividend or out of the proceeds of a fresh issue of shares made for the specific purpose of such redemption; shares not fully paid up may not be redeemed.

If the redemption is met out of profits, a sum equal to the amount applied for redemption is to be transferred into a "capital redemption reserve fund". If the shares are to be redeemed at a premium, such premium must have been provided for prior to the redemption out of the profits of the company, even though the redemption is effected from the proceeds of a new issue. The company must include in every balance sheet a statement specifying what part of the issued capital consists of redeemable preference shares together with the date on or before which their redemption must or may be effected. Any company may issue

[1] *In re* London India Rubber Co. (1868), L.R. 5 Eq. 519; *re* Madame Tussaud and Sons Ltd. (1927), 1 Ch. 657.

[2] *Re* Bridgwater Navigation Co.; Birch *v.* Cropper (1889), L.R. 14 App. Cas. 525.

[3] *Re* Bangor and Port Madoc Slate and Slab Co. (1875), L.R. 20 Eq. 59.

[4] Will *v.* United Lankat Plantations Co. (1914), A.C. 11.

[5] *In re* National Telephone Co. (1914), 1 Ch. 755; Collaroy Co. Ltd. *v.* Giffard (1928), 1 Ch. 144.

[6] The latest are *re* John Dry Steam Tugs (1932), 1 Ch. 594; Wm. Metcalfe Ltd. (1933), 1 Ch. 142 C.

new shares in place of those redeemed, and is empowered to use the "capital redemption reserve fund" to pay the par value of such shares as are to be issued to existing shareholders as bonus shares.

The provisions of this section are amended by the Companies Act, 1947, in some details. The amount to be put into the capital redemption reserve fund shall be equal, not to the amount which was paid for the redemption, but to the par value of the redeemed shares (sec. 71 (1)). This amendment will prevent the use of the discount for distribution or free reserves. The power to use the fund for paying up bonus shares is to be exercisable whether or not new shares have been issued up to the nominal amount of the redeemed shares, and shall not be limited by reference to the amount of such shares. In other respects the amendments proposed are of a technical character. They are now incorporated in sec. 58 of the Act of 1948.

In the United States the financing of corporate enterprises is largely carried out by the issue of preferred stock. The position was stated by the Supreme Court [1] as follows: "In organising corporations it is not unusual to issue different classes of securities with various priorities as between themselves to represent different kinds of contribution to capital. In exchange for cash bonds may be issued; for fixed properties like plant and equipment, preferred stock may be given, while more speculative values like goodwill or patent rights may be represented by common stock." This apt definition is a moderate hint at the evolution, since, as we have shown, in many corporations a part even of the preference stock did not represent tangible assets, and common stocks were to a large extent watered. Owing to this system of financing the question of preferred stock frequently occupied the Courts.

It is recognised that the holders of preferred stock are stockholders and not creditors. Their right to demand the payment of dividends is subject to the same limitations as is that of the holders of common stock, and they are subject to the same liabilities as other stockholders.[2] It is often said that the dividends of preference stock are guaranteed, but this means as a rule nothing more than that they have a limited preference in respect of the distribution of profits. It is possible, of course, in a given

[1] Labelle Iron Works *v.* United States (1921), 256 U.S. 377.

[2] See Warren *v.* King (1882), 108 U.S. 389, and the Federal and State Decisions quoted by Fletcher 5290, n. 57.

case for the holder of a certain class of corporate securities to have an absolutely guaranteed right to a fixed or minimum distribution: in that case the securities are not stock but bonds, and the guaranteed payments are strictly speaking not dividends but interest. Such rights may be guaranteed by the statutes or by the charter (articles), provided they do not violate the statute governing the legal relations of the corporation in question; such securities, however, are actually bonds. Under the earlier Massachusetts statutes a corporation has the power to issue "special stock". For such special stock dividends could be paid which did not depend on the existence of profits, so that the corporation was obliged to pay the so-called dividends and was in fact a debtor to the holders of such stock.[1] Apart from such cases a security must be either a share or a bond, and the holder is either a stockholder or a creditor of the corporation; he cannot on the basis of the same security be both. His legal position is to be determined by the construction of the contract as embodied in the articles or by-laws and the context of the security. In this respect, as in all other cases, it is not the name but the essence of the contract which determines its effect. If the holders of a security are in fact creditors of the corporation there is nothing to prevent the allotting of a special security, such as a mortgage, for the benefit of such stock.[2]

It was held formerly that without express authorisation by its charter a corporation cannot issue preferred shares, but only one class of stock, and consequently that preferential rights cannot be created by adopting by-laws, unless by unanimous consent.[3] It has been held further that the consent of all registered stockholders authorising the issue of preferred shares does not bind those who were not registered. Nowadays, however, most legislations expressly permit the issue of different classes of stock. Consequently the power to create and to issue preferred shares is regarded as inherent, and the majority of stockholders in general meeting has the power to resolve on the issue of preferred shares and to determine their rights and privileges, even if the original charter (articles) did not authorise such issue. Generally, however, a specific majority is required for the resolution.

The issue of preferred shares may of course be excluded by the articles, in which case it is possible only if an alteration of the

[1] Fletcher 5292. [2] See Warren *v.* King (1882), 108 U.S. 389.
[3] Fletcher 5284 at n. 14, 5286.

articles is allowed and the special formalities for such an alteration have been observed.

It is stated that preferred shares cannot be issued if the issue would violate or impair the contracts made with existing stockholders. On this basis it has been held that if the articles provide for only one category of shares, i.e. common shares, an issue of preferred shares could be made only by unanimous resolution or the consent of all stockholders, and not by a majority decision.[1] On the other hand it has been held that the authorisation of the issue of preferred shares cannot be regarded as a substantial change of the purposes of the original organisation.[2] Under the majority rule the power to borrow money is not as a rule regarded as authorising the issue of preferred shares, though it has been held that if the preferred shares are redeemable by the corporation by repayment of the money and therefore serve merely as security for the repayment, their issue would be valid under the power to borrow.[3] If the charter (articles) contains a provision leaving the regulation of the manner of an increase of capital to the general meeting, this would give the power to issue preferred stock.

The rights of dissenting stockholders against unauthorised issues are the same as in general: they may maintain a suit in equity to enjoin the issue to or cancel the issued stock, provided the rights of innocent third parties have not intervened. The relief may be lost by ratification, waiver or laches.[4]

The rights of holders of preferred shares cannot be altered without their consent, but some legislations authorise such changes by a majority resolution of preferred stockholders in a special meeting. Where a variation of preferential rights is allowed, a specified majority (e.g. two-thirds or three-fourths) is as a rule required.

The issue of a new category of preferred shares giving equal or superior preferences is obviously an impairment of the rights of the existing preferred shareholders. Therefore an increase of capital by issue of such shares is valid only if it is not in violation of the rules as to the variation of the rights and privileges of outstanding preferred stock.

State legislations in the U.S.A. in general admit the converti-

[1] See Banigan *v.* Bard (1890), 134 U.S. 291.
[2] State *ex* Rel. Chapman *v.* Urschel, 104 Ohio St. 172, quoted Fletcher 5284, n. 12.
[3] Fletcher 5285.
[4] Fletcher 5288–9.

bility of stock into bonds and *vice versa*. Even where such conversion is not admitted, preferred stock can be converted into common and common into preferred. If the conversion is provided for at the issue it is of course valid and enforceable without the consent of individual holders. Otherwise it is subject to the same rules as any change or impairment of the position of stock or bondholders.

It is frequently stressed that in the U.S.A. preferential rights are based on a contract. We have, however, to bear in mind that the real basis of the preference is the power conferred by the statute or charter, and that under some legislations a majority resolution of the holders of preferred stock is sufficient for the abolition or alteration of the preference.

The dividends on preferred shares are payable only out of profits, either of the last year or those accumulated during previous years, and cannot be paid out of capital in the event of absence or insufficiency of profits.[1] Cases in which securities called preferred shares are in fact bonds and therefore lawfully authorise the payment of dividends in the absence of profits have already been considered.[2]

Whether an issue is actually one of bonds or of preferred shares depends on its terms and on the powers of the corporation; if it is an issue of preferred shares neither a valid promise nor a valid guarantee may be given to its holders. Similarly the rules as to the distribution of dividends and especially as to the discretion of the board in respect of their declaration are the same as in the case of common shares.[3] The remedies of stockholders against abuse of discretion are also the same as in the case of common shares. Even in the case of preference "the profits or net earnings may be allowed to accumulate and remain invested in the business" if no abuse is proved,[4] and it was said in the New York *v.* Nickals case, *supra*, that the mere fact that profits exist for the particular year does not necessarily entitle the holder of preferred shares to a dividend. The terms of the issue, however, may impose stricter limits on the exercise of discretionary power.

[1] Warren *v.* King (1882), 108 U.S. 389; New York, etc., Co. *v.* Nickals (1886), 119 U.S. 296; further, the decisions quoted by Fletcher 5444, n. 25.

[2] See St. John *v.* Erie (1874), 22 Wal. U.S. 136.

[3] See Wabash Railway Company *v.* Barclay (1930), 280 U.S. 197.

[4] Spear *v.* Rockland Rockford Lime Co., 115 Me. 285, quoted by Fletcher 5446, n. 58.

As we have seen, preferred shares may or may not be cumulative. It is held that unless a contrary intention appears dividends on preferred shares are cumulative.[1] Some of the U.S.A. statutes even prescribe that the articles must provide to this effect. If there is a cumulative right, the holders of common shares cannot receive dividends until the arrears have been paid. The rule accepted in the U.S.A. is that the dividend for the current year is to be paid first, and the arrears for earlier years afterwards. In principle it would be more natural to pay the arrears in the order of their dates, and the dividend for the current year only after they have been satisfied.

We have already seen that preferred shares may or may not participate in the profits remaining after the common shares have received equal dividends. It depends on the terms of the issue whether in the absence of an express stipulation such participation is attached to preferred shares, and it is a matter of controversy.[2] A similar controversy exists as to priority in case of dissolution, and many Courts hold that in the absence of express provision the preference does not extend to the liquidation quota and that common and preferred stock share alike rateably.[3]

A further matter of dispute is whether in the event of a surplus appearing at the liquidation unpaid arrears are to be met; this is disputed even in the case of cumulative preferred stock.

The position of preferred stockholders is therefore somewhat precarious, especially in view of the discretionary power of directors to declare dividends or to withhold profits for reinvestment. Whereas it may be argued that in respect of cumulative preference stock this means only postponement, in the case of non-cumulative preferred stock the shareholders lose their right if no dividend is declared.

In some cases the amounts withheld from non-cumulative preferred stock in order to make provision for additional working capital have been earmarked as a special reserve, and the holders of such stock have claimed that if and when that reserve should become distributable it should be used to satisfy them in respect of their unpaid dividends. On the other hand holders of common stock asserted that dividends should be paid only out of the profits of the current year, and that the holders of non-cumulative pre-

[1] Fletcher 5447, n. 70; Ballantine 215 at n. 36.

[2] Fletcher 5448, n. 90, and on the other hand n. 93, Ballantine 216, Berle 26 Col. L.R., p. 303.

[3] Cf. Fletcher 5449, n. 98, and Ballantine 217.

ferred stock have no priority as against them in respect of unpaid dividends earned but not declared.

In some cases the withholding of dividends from non-cumulative preferred stock was abusive, and in some jurisdictions, especially New Jersey, the Courts gave relief, ruling that dividends withheld from non-cumulative preferred stock must be paid before the holders of common stock could have any dividend,[1] but the time of payment should remain discretionary. Professor Berle evolved the doctrine [2] that amounts earned but not distributed should be segregated in the books for the benefit of the non-cumulative preferred stock, that such funds can never be distributed as dividend on common stock, and that the corporation is bound to pay the dividends withheld as soon as there is opportunity so to do. The Supreme Court in Wabash Ry. Co. *v.* Barclay [3] took a view unfavourable to the holders of non-cumulative preferred stock. In this case the articles provided that each fiscal year the dividends of preferred stock should be paid before any dividends upon any stock of the company but without cumulation, and that in case of liquidation the holders should be entitled to priority as to the par value and dividends declared but unpaid. From 1916 to 1928 the corporation paid either no dividend at all or a smaller one than was stipulated in the articles, and reserved an aggregate amount of $16 million during these years, applying this amount for justifiable improvements, although dividends could have been paid without impairing the safety of the railway. In 1929 the preferential dividends of the preferred shares were duly paid, and in 1930 dividends were declared upon common shares also. Holders of non-cumulative preferred shares contended that they had priority covering the aggregate amount of dividends not declared for the past years. The Supreme Court decided against this claim.

It has been held that it is the common understanding of lawyers and business men that holders of non-cumulative preferred shares cannot claim a dividend if profits are justifiably applied to capital improvements, and that if no dividends have been declared the claim has completely expired. The question whether there is a right to dividends if profits have been merely set aside has not been discussed. The Supreme Court obviously did not find that in this case dividends were withheld in order

[1] Cases quoted by Ballantine 232, n. 8. [2] 23 Col. L.R. 360.
[3] (1930), 280 U.S. 197–204.

to deprive preference shareholders of their rights, nor was the question argued whether existing remedies against abuses are adequate or not. The Supreme Court referred to the earlier cases.[1]

The judgment in the Wabash case was followed in another.[2] In this case the corporation during the years 1925–8 paid no dividends, and the profits were applied to capital improvements. In 1929 dividends were paid to the holders of preference shares, and in 1930 dividends were declared on both categories. The Massachusetts Court felt itself bound by the rule in the Wabash case; in this respect the decision was contrary to earlier decisions of the same State. It is to be noted that in Morse *v.* Boston etc. Co.,[3] the Court declared that holders of preference shares will not necessarily be deprived of their share in profits; it may be only a postponement.

Although it may be asserted that the construction of charters (articles) is a matter of State law, it is to be assumed that the judgment in the Wabash case will settle this question for a long time to come. In view of this state of the law the only remedy for non-cumulative preferred shareholders against the withholding of dividends would be a suit in equity based upon clear evidence of the abusive reservation of profits. This remedy, however, is not available apart from exceptional cases, and not at all where profits were used for investment. Even in cases where profits were not reinvested it might be argued that the withholding of dividends was justified in view of contingencies not yet known at the time at which dividends were to be declared.

For the holders of cumulative preferred shares the position is of course more favourable. So long as the corporation is a going concern they retain their priority, although they cannot claim dividends unless they have been declared. The question becomes crucial in the event of liquidation. In this regard we have to bear in mind that priorities cannot be attributed to preferred shares unless provided for in the articles. This seems hard on preference holders; in practice, however, it means only that lawyers have to be careful in drafting the articles and buyers of this class of securities cautious before they decide on purchasing them. With regard to dividends of cumulative preferred shares

[1] Bailey *v.* Railroad Co. (1873), 17 Wal. 96 N.Y., etc., Co. *v.* Nickals (1886), 119 U.S. 296; Continental Insurance Co. *v.* U.S. (1922), 259 U.S. 156.

[2] Joslin *v.* Boston and Mo.R.R. (1931), 274 Mass. 551.

[3] 263 Mass 318.

accrued but not paid American Courts generally adopt a rather favourable view. In Fawkes *v.* Farm Land Inv. Co.[1] it was held that on the basis of the articles provision was made that in case of dissolution the assets should be applied first to the payment in full of the principal of the preferred stock at par with all cumulative dividends thereon, and the holders of such stock should enjoy priority with regard to unpaid dividends, regardless of whether such dividends had been declared in the respective years or even whether any profits had been earned during those years. Similar views have been accepted in Delaware in other cases.[2] It is held generally that in order to enjoy participation in any surplus after common shares have received full payment up to their par value, there must be an express provision in the articles to that effect. This view is based on the consideration that it was for the holders of preferred stock to stipulate for themselves the priorities which they require, and the privileges secured should be regarded as full compensation, so that they are not entitled to claim participation if it was not expressly stipulated.

Generally in America preferred stock is made redeemable on the terms of the issue, but frequently at the choice of the corporation. Some statutes provide that such redemption may be effected not only out of profits or surplus originating in earlier years, but also out of capital, provided that the redemption does not reduce the assets to less than the amount of all debts and liabilities plus the par value of the capital remaining after redemption.[3] Certain statutes allow redemption at the choice of the stockholder, e.g. Ohio.[4] Even then, however, the stockholder cannot enforce the redemption and payment if it would impair the capital or disable the corporation from meeting its obligations.

Nowadays the holders of preferred stock are generally deprived of a vote. Such exclusion is held to be admissible, in accordance with the American view that even common stock may be issued without voting rights. The articles generally provide that a vote may be exercised if the corporation fails to pay the dividend as fixed over a certain period, usually two or three consecutive years. In some cases the vote is restricted to the election

[1] (1931), 112 Cal. Ap. 297.

[2] Pennington *v.* Commonwealth Hotel Co. (1931), 17 Del. Ch. 394; Wilson *v.* Laconia Car Co. (1931), 176 N.I.

[3] See e.g. New York S.C.L. s. 18 as amended by L. (1941), c. 838, and Del. Rev. Code (1935), §§ 19 and 27.

[4] G.C., s. 8623–4, as amended by L. (1939), S.B. 47.

of directors. On the other hand there are cases in which holders of common stock are debarred from voting if the corporation does not pay dividends on preferred stock, and remain so as long as the payment of dividends is not resumed.

The rule of Art. 34 of the French *Code de Commerce*, that shares must be equal in value, was for a long time interpreted to prohibit the creation of preference shares. Only in 1882 did the Cour de Cassation by its decision of 20 December [1] declare their issue valid. Even under that decision preferred shares could be issued only if provided for in the original articles. A subsequent issue on the basis of an alteration of the articles was admitted only if the original articles by express provision authorised the issue of such shares by way of a special resolution, or, in the absence of such authorisation, if there was unanimous assent of all the shareholders. Such assent was seldom, if ever, attainable, especially in the case of larger companies.

The law of 9 July 1902 admitted the issue of preference shares by special resolution only for newly formed companies, and did not extend it to *commandites par actions*. In the following year, however, an amendment was effected by the law of 16 November 1903, and issue by special resolution was generally admitted. Nevertheless preference shares did not attain the same popularity in France as in the U.S.A. or Britain.

In Germany and in the Austro-Hungarian Monarchy in the days preceding the codification of company law preference shares were connected with the financing of railway companies. These companies, created by acts of the legislature or by special charters, secured much of the capital needed for construction and equipment by the issue of such shares, giving priority in respect of dividends, as a rule fixed at five or six per cent., and also of the par value of the shares. The usual type was that of cumulation of the arrears. Since the franchise was invariably given for a definite term, usually of 90 years, the nominal value was to be repaid by systematic redemption over the whole period, to be made by drawings. On the other hand the shares were invariably participating, and therefore if a share was drawn and actually redeemed, the holder received a certificate (*Genuszschein*), which gave the right of participation in the profits remaining after the ordinary shares had received a dividend at a rate equal to that promised to the holders of preference shares. In years of pros-

[1] D. 83, 1, 301.

perity the *Genusschein* gave a more or less substantial yield. Similarly, the *Genusschein* gave title to participation in the surplus remaining at the winding-up of the company after the par value of both the preference and ordinary shares had been repaid. The nature of preference shares and of the *Genusschein* as shares was clearly recognised, and voting rights were conferred on both equal to those of ordinary shares.

The German Commercial Code was silent on the question of preference shares. But in the practice of German companies outside the field of railways, under the regulation provided by the special charter, and after 1870 by the articles, there were in a number of cases issues of preference shares whose validity was recognised, though in the absence of legal regulation there were frequent disputes as to details.

The amending law of 1884 provided that the articles might provide for several classes of shares, conferring upon them different rights as to the distribution of profits and in case of dissolution of the net assets. This provision was taken over by the Commercial Code of 1897 (§ 185), and was in force until the adoption of the Companies Law of 1937.

Preference shares could be issued if provided for in the original articles, or also by special resolution. Companies could give a preference in respect of dividends or of the final distribution, or both, in their original or amended articles. It was usual to give both ; in many cases preference shares were cumulative in respect of dividends and also participating both in respect of dividends and of the final distribution. There was, however, no presumption in favour of any of these alternatives.[1]

The issue of preferred shares was not resorted to frequently by industrial companies. When the crises occurring in the eighteen-nineties compelled many companies to procure additional capital, this was frequently done by the issue of additional shares with preferential rights, but in certain cases also by shareholders converting their ordinary into preference shares by additional payments. In this way the necessity for an increase of capital could be avoided, and the amounts paid could be used as working capital and employed to write off losses or strengthen reserves. The validity of a resolution to this effect carried by a majority, i.e. without the unanimous consent of the shareholders, was disputed. It was argued that such a resolution would amount

[1] Cf. Staub, 6–7 ed. to § 185.

to indirectly compelling the shareholders to make the payment or to suffer a loss in respect of their rights to dividends and/or other distributions.[1] The Courts, however, decided in favour of the validity.[2] In certain cases the transaction was coupled with a reduction of capital by reducing the nominal value of the shares and by providing for a compulsory conversion of a block of shares into one should the reduced value be below the legal minimum. Shareholders who paid a certain amount per share would be exempt from the reduction and enjoy preferential rights, whereas those who refused to pay the additional amount would have to suffer the reduction; their shares would become ordinary shares. In this direction also the validity of the resolution was accepted, provided the reduction was proportionate to the additional payment required.[3] Thus, if the shares had a nominal value of 1200 M. each and the reduction was one of 50 per cent., the resolution would be valid if the additional payment was likewise 50 per cent., i.e. 600 M. per share, but voidable if it were less, say 500 M. In so far as such additional payments were not to be applied to the writing-off of assets or to meeting extraordinary losses, they were to be put into legal reserve (§ 262 (3)).

Voting rights under German law were regarded as inherent in the share, and therefore preference shares could not be deprived of a vote, but discriminations as to voting rights in favour of one class of shares or against another were held valid.[4] Earlier, under Art. 190 of the Code of 1861, such discriminations were not admitted. Furthermore in 1900 it was asserted that a class of shares might be created with priority merely as to voting, so that, e.g. the preference shares had a multiple vote but no preferential rights in respect of dividends and final distribution.[5]

After the 1914–18 war, as we have seen, a new type of preference shares evolved, owing to the fear that foreign groups might make use of the currency depreciation to acquire large blocks of shares and gain control of the most important German corporate enterprises. In order to defeat such infiltrations many German companies issued preference shares with priority as to dividends restricted to from about four to five per cent., and as to distribution

[1] See Staub, 6–7 ed., I, p. 568–9; Lehmann, I, 219.
[2] R.G.Z. 52, 287, and other decisions.
[3] R.G.Z. 80–85.
[4] § 252 of the Commercial Code, 1897.
[5] Staub, 6–7 ed., I, 760; *contra*, Makower 377.

to the nominal value of the share, excluding further participation in both directions. On the other hand these preference shares gave plural voting rights. Pre-emptive rights were generally excluded, and the shares were placed with persons in close relation to the management and board of supervision, frequently with an undertaking not to alienate the shares without the assent of the two boards. If it is remembered that the preference shares were mostly issued at par, and thus in view of the currency depreciation at merely nominal prices, it is obvious that control could thus be secured by a minute contribution without any risk or sacrifice. This device, hailed as a patriotic weapon against illegitimate intrusion, was subsequently used in cases where not the slightest trace of foreign aspirations appeared, and it became a means of perpetuating the control of the ruling clique, who were able to sell their ordinary shares if market opportunities arose and nevertheless to dominate the company by the multiple vote of the preference shares.

Basing themselves on the doctrine that preference may be given as to votes, and even in the sole form of a multiple vote, the Courts intervened only in cases where the issue of preference shares with the exclusion of pre-emptive rights resulted in serious financial detriment to the holders of ordinary shares, and thus—as shown elsewhere—the bulk of German companies were controlled by holders of preference shares of this type (see § 21 and § 23).

The law of 1937, after stating (§ 11) that classes of shares may have different rights, particularly in respect of profits and assets, declares (§ 12 (2)) that the multiple vote is illegal; the Government, however, may grant exemption if it is required in the interest of the company or of the national economy. On the other hand the cancellation of the existing multiple votes was left to the Government (§ 9 of the introducing law), and this step was never taken.

The law further allowed exclusion from voting in respect of cumulative preference shares with the limitation that their amount must not exceed half the nominal amount of the other shares; in other words preference shares without vote might be issued up to one-third of the share capital (§ 115). If the dividend as fixed by the articles was not fully paid in any one year and the arrears plus current dividend were not met in the following year, the holders of preference shares were free to exercise the vote until the arrears were fully paid. Otherwise the law as to preference shares remained unaltered.

Under the Swiss O.R. the issue of preference shares by special resolution is dependent on the presence of at least two-thirds of the existing capital at the general meeting.

In case of any variation of preferential rights the assent of the majority of the shareholders concerned given at a special meeting is likewise required, and to this the same rules apply as to minimal participation (654, 655). Preferences may be created in respect of voting rights, but only within certain limits.

62. Share Certificates as Means of Transfer

From the beginnings of corporate enterprise one of its attractions was the transferability of shares. This made it necessary for shareholders to possess documentary evidence of their holdings, which was provided by the issue of share certificates. This became so usual that in many languages the word "share" or its equivalent is used as a synonym for "share certificate".

The whole subject of share certificates is much influenced by the view taken as to method of transfer. Some legislations require shareholders' names to be recorded by the company, while others allow of the issue of shares to bearer, i.e. without record of any particular holder, so that production of the share certificate is the only evidence of ownership. Anglo-American law is based on the principle that the names of the members should be known to the company, to each other and to the public. Every company therefore has to keep a register in which those names are entered, and the certificates must accordingly contain their owner's name. This principle was qualified in Great Britain by the Companies Act of 1867, which permitted the issue of warrants to bearer in respect of fully paid up shares. Since on the Continent of Europe, as we shall presently see, the bearer type of share was prevalent, many companies which sought an international market for their shares availed themselves of this possibility; but even to-day the great majority of British companies still issue only nominative share certificates. In the U.S.A. bearer warrants for stock are not allowed.

The British Companies Act (sec. 80) provides that the company shall complete the certificates and have them ready for delivery within two months after allotment. In the event of the company failing to comply with his request a subscriber may serve a notice, and ten days thereafter may apply to the Court for an order directing the company to make good the default. The company, or the officer responsible for the default, is liable for costs and a fine. The delivery of a share certificate may also be enforced by an action.[1]

This rule, however (sec. 80 (1)), applies only "unless the conditions of the issue of the shares provide otherwise". In other words the articles may stipulate that share certificates are to be delivered on other terms or even not at all, a course which may be convenient in the case of private companies or of public companies of small size. Usually, however, the articles provide that every shareholder, i.e. every person entered on the register of members, is entitled to a certificate, and that without any payment (see Table A, 8).

The contents of the certificate are not expressly defined by the Act; sec. 81 mentions only that it must specify what shares the member holds. It must of course state their nominal value, their serial numbers, the amount paid and the holder's name, otherwise it would not serve its purpose. It is to be under the company's common seal (sec. 81) and is to be signed by persons who have power to represent the company, usually at least one director and the secretary.

The share certificate, if under the common seal of the company, is *prima facie* evidence of the member's title to the shares (sec. 81); consequently it may be rebutted by other evidence. When a *bona fide* person has acted on the faith of an incorrect certificate the company may be estopped from asserting its incorrectness, and may in the circumstances be liable for damages, a question which mostly arises in connection with transfers (see § 59). It is to be noted that only one certificate is to be issued for each member. This makes it voluminous if it is for a large number of shares, since all their serial numbers have to be given.

In order to relieve companies the Companies Act, 1948 (sec. 74), provides that if all the issued shares of a company or all the issued shares of a particular class are fully paid up and rank *pari passu* for all purposes none of those shares need have a distinguishing number.

The Companies Act allows of the conversion of fully paid up shares into stock, in which case it is the nominal value as

[1] Burdett *v.* Standard Exploration Co. (1899), 16 T.L.R. 112.

recorded in the books of the company which alone matters, and the stockholder is entitled to sell and transfer any part of the stock registered in his name; no numbers are to be recorded. It is usual in such a case to speak of units and not of shares. Such conversion is to be made by resolution in general meeting; it can be made in respect of the whole share capital or of any part of it, and stock may be reconverted into shares in the same way, i.e. by a resolution in general meeting (sec. 61). It is usual to provide by the articles what minimum amount of stock may be transferred, or to leave the fixing of the minimum to the directors; such minimum is generally the par value of a share as fixed previous to the conversion into stock (cf. Table A, 41).

By sec. 83 of the Companies Act a company has power to provide in its articles—original or as altered by special resolution—for the issue of bearer warrants. Such warrants may be issued only in respect of fully paid up shares, and the conversion need not include the whole share capital. These warrants are called by the Act "share warrants", and must be issued under the company's common seal; they must state that the bearer is entitled to the shares specified in the warrant.

The company may provide for the payment of future dividends in any way it thinks fit, e.g. by requiring that the holders shall present the warrant for marking, but the most usual method is to attach to the warrants coupons likewise drawn to bearer, the dividend being paid against their surrender.

The share warrant entitles the bearer to the shares specified therein, and these may be transferred by its delivery (sec. 83 (3)). This means that the warrant represents the share, and is to be regarded as a negotiable instrument, although the Act is silent in this respect. At any rate warrants are so treated in practice.[1]

If a share warrant is issued, the fact of its issue, the particulars of the shares concerned, including their numbers, and the date of issue of the warrant are to be entered in the register and the shareholder's name is to be struck out. Unless the articles otherwise provide, the holder of a share warrant may surrender it at any time for cancellation and may demand that his name be entered on the register. The company has to exercise due care, for it is responsible under the Act for any loss if the entry in the register of the members was made without cancelling the warrant (sec. 112 (1), (2) and (3)).

[1] Webb, Hale and Co. *v.* Alexandria Water Co. (1905), 21 T.L.R. 572.

Since the number of warrants may from time to time change, all relevant particulars must be stated in the annual return, i.e. the number of share warrants outstanding at the date of the return, the amount of shares represented by each and all of them, and the number issued and surrendered since the last return (sec. 124 (1) (*b*) and Sixth Schedule, Part I, para. 5).

It has been held that share warrants may also be issued for stock.[1] In principle share warrants give their holders the same rights as the shares they represent. Share warrants, however, are not to be taken into account if the articles require a minimum shareholding as a director's qualification (sec. 182 (2)). It is left for the articles on the other hand to provide what rights the holder of a share warrant may exercise (sec. 112 (5)). Thus they may deny him a vote, but hitherto this has been done only in exceptional cases.

Share warrants are secured by penal provisions against forgery and impersonation.

American law is similar, except that bearer shares or bearer warrants are not admitted. The purpose of facilitating transfers is attained by another means: the blank transfer (see § 59).

A subscriber whose subscription has been accepted becomes a stockholder and has the right to request the issue and delivery of a certificate. Payment is generally not a condition precedent; but many statutes require the payment of a certain part of the nominal value, and some prescribe full payment prior to the issue as a condition precedent.[2] The articles or by-laws may fix the conditions of the issue and of the delivery of the certificate, in which case the stockholder on complying with such conditions has the right to demand the issue and delivery of the certificate.[3] The majority rule is that *mandamus* is the appropriate remedy; certain Courts hold that the stockholder may sue in equity for specific performance.[4]

If the corporation is prevented from delivering the certificate because its authorised capital is already exhausted the only remedy would be an action for damages, since the corporation has no power to make an over-issue and any issue without authority would be void.[5] There may or may not be an actionable breach

[1] Pilkington *v.* United Railways (1930), 2 Ch. 108.
[2] Fletcher 5161.
[3] Cecil National Bank *v.* Watsontown Bank (1882), 105 U.S. 217.
[4] Fletcher 5165, n. 62, 63 and 69.
[5] Scovill *v.* Thayer (1881), 105 U.S. 143.

of contract; in the latter case damages could not be claimed, but the amount paid in by the stockholder would be recoverable.[1]

As in Great Britain the certificate is merely an evidence of the share. It may for various reasons be invalid, but its invalidity does not affect the validity of the share itself if that is otherwise valid. In such a case the stockholder may demand delivery of a valid certificate on returning the invalid one for cancellation. If the issue of the share of stock is itself void or voidable, the corporation is not only entitled to refuse delivery of a new certificate but must request the return of the invalid certificate for cancellation.

It is held that wrongful refusal to deliver the certificate entitles the stockholder to rescind his contract with the corporation. On the other hand the certificate is held to be a continuing affirmation and representation on the part of the company that it is valid and genuine, and also that the person named therein is the owner of the stock therein specified.[2] Therefore the corporation is liable for damages to purchasers or pledgees of the certificate who are deceived and injured by relying upon its genuineness. The only condition for reliance on a certificate representing an authorised issue is that it be executed by an officer or agent of the corporation (as a rule two directors) acting within the apparent scope of their authority. In such a case the corporation is estopped from denying its validity, or the ownership of the person named in it. On the other hand the shareholder is equally estopped from denying its validity as against the corporation or its creditors for irregularities in the issue or for lack of formalities.[3] The corporation is likewise liable if the certificate is forged by an officer in charge of the stock-books of the corporation having authority to issue certificates.[4]

Whether the officer has or has not authority to issue certificates is a question of fact, and it depends upon this fact whether this authority extends to the issue of certificates in general, although the issue of the false certificate in question may have been unauthorised and was in fact not for the purposes of the corporation. Apparent authority, equally with actual authority, is

[1] Congress and Empire Spring Co. *v.* Knowlton (1881), 103 U.S. 49; Fletcher 5167, n. 6.

[2] Fletcher 5168, n. 23.

[3] Scovill *v.* Thayer (1881), 105 U.S. 143; further, C. H. Chubb *v.* Upton, Pullman *v.* Upton (1877), 95 U.S. 665 and 96 U.S. 328.

[4] Fletcher 5171, n. 57.

sufficient to establish the corporation's liability. In the case of an unauthorised or spurious issue wrongfully made by an officer or agent for whose acts it is responsible, the corporation is liable for damages to a *bona fide* purchaser or pledgee. The liability of the corporation is parallel with that of the officer responsible for the issue.[1] The agent may be sued either alone or jointly with the corporation. On the other hand the corporation may bring a suit in equity to cancel such invalid certificates and to enjoin their transfer, the payment of dividends in respect of them and the exercise of a vote by the holder. The agent guilty is liable to the corporation for the damage caused by his act.[2]

The right to relief depends upon the equity of the person claiming it.[3] Therefore the relief may be claimed only by *bona fide* purchasers or pledgees without actual or constructive notice. The false affirmation in the certificate must have been the proximate cause of the loss or injury to the person relying on the certificate.[4]

The view taken by the legislations of the European Continent formerly was that the ownership of shares depends upon entry in the register of members and that the certificates are merely documents of evidence. Share certificates to bearer, however, were already in use in France under the *Ancien Régime*, and the *Code de Commerce* provided that the certificates may be either to bearer (Art. 35) or nominative. If a company chooses the former alternative, transfer is effected by delivery. This rule was followed in the other Continental countries, and it was thus generally left to the choice of the companies whether their certificates should be to bearer or nominative.

Certain legislations deprived some classes of companies of this free choice; thus the law of Norway (sec. 30) and of Denmark (sec. 14) provided that banking companies may issue nominative certificates only. But even where the certificates are nominative and transfer is made by entry in the register of members there are two characteristic differences from Anglo-American law and practice. One is that not only in the case of bearer, but also of nominative, certificates coupons are attached, which in both cases are usually to bearer. The second is that all certificates are

[1] Moores *v.* Citizens' National Bank of Piqua (1883), 111 U.S. 156; Fletcher 5174, n. 75.

[2] Fletcher 5175, n. 89, 90.

[3] Supreme Court of Pennsylvania *in re* Kisterbock, 127 P.A. St. 601.

[4] Fletcher 5178, n. 27.

regarded as negotiable instruments which may be transferred by endorsement. The register of members has consequently lost much of its importance, since although the shareholder if he is entered in the register is secured as against the company, one who comes into possession of the certificate with an endorsement, either blank or in his name, acquires ownership and may enforce the entry of his name on the register. There are many differences in details. The French, Italian and Spanish legislations still regard entry in the register as decisive, whereas under German law and the systems that follow it the endorsement has an effect similar to that of a bill of exchange.

In earlier times it was not necessary that bearer shares should be fully paid up. It was permissible to issue bearer certificates with only a part, usually 50 per cent., paid up, in which case the remaining 50 per cent. was covered only by the subscribers' liability which was of little value, especially where this position of part payment remained for a longer period. Gradually, however, the drawbacks of this system became obvious, and it was enacted by nearly all the legislations concerned that certificates to bearer may be issued only for fully paid up shares.

In view of the numerous though mostly immaterial differences in details, only the provisions of two of the latest laws, the German and the Swiss, will be reviewed here, since it is these that most clearly express the characteristic traits of Continental legislation. Both of these admit the two alternatives on an equal footing.[1] The German law provides that if the articles are silent, the certificates are to be nominative (§ 17 (1)). Both laws leave it to the articles to permit bearer to be converted into nominative certificates and *vice versa*. In addition Swiss law allows the articles to fix the proportion of bearer to nominative certificates (622, 2). This is allowed also under German law, though there is no express provision to this effect.[2] Furthermore it is held in Germany that a special resolution may convert all the certificates into one kind or the other and compel the shareholders to exchange their certificates.[3]

Every shareholder is entitled to demand the issue of a certificate in respect of his shares,[4] and Wieland [5] maintains that the articles may not provide to the contrary; in his view such a provision would involve the nullity of the company. He admits,

[1] German law of 1937, § 10 (1); Swiss O.R. 622. [2] Gadow 54, n. 3.
[3] Gadow 54 (55). [4] R.G.Z. 94, 64. [5] II, p. 40.

however, that the shareholders by unanimous consent could dispense with the issue. The validity of such an agreement, however, is recognised,[1] and there seems to be no objection to the incorporation of such agreements into the articles. If no certificates are issued, transfer is governed by the general rules applying to the transfer of debts; no formalities are required, and the same applies to mortgaging.[2] In practice it is only in the case of small family businesses that share certificates are not issued; in the case of G.m.b.H.s the issue of certificates is prohibited.

As we saw above, share certificates are regarded as negotiable instruments. If they are to bearer they are governed by the rules regulating bearer instruments (*Inhaberpapiere*), with the exception that the company is not prevented from objecting against the holder that they are void, e.g. for over-issue, or that they were not actually issued by the company, or were stolen from it. Otherwise the ownership of the certificate and consequently of the share itself is effected by the delivery of the certificate.

If the shares are not fully paid up, only nominative certificates may be issued.[3]

Consequently the Swiss O.R. provides that bearer certificates issued in respect of shares not fully paid up are void (683, 2). The German law does not so enact; in accordance with the Commercial Code of 1897 it is held that the certificate is not void, and moreover a *bona fide* holder is not liable for the unpaid part.[4] The company is protected only by the liability of the management and the board. On the other hand interim certificates, i.e. certificates issued prior to the issue of the definitive certificates and entitling their holder to receive the latter, are under German law always to be nominative; if to bearer they would be void (§ 10 (4)). In this respect too the Swiss O.R. is more consistent, since it requires that they should be nominative only if the shares are not fully paid up (688). If a nominative certificate is issued before full payment, the amount paid is to be stated thereon.[5] It is held that violation of this rule does not affect the validity of the certificate, and its holder is liable for the amount outstanding on the share, though in the case of *bona fide* transfers liability is excluded.[6]

Under both German and Swiss law the transfer may be made

[1] R.G.Z. 52, 423, and a number of earlier decisions.
[2] R.G.Z. 86, 157; as to mortgages R.G.S.T. 64, 82.
[3] German § 10 (2); Swiss 683, 1.
[4] R.G.Z. 144, 145.
[5] German § 10 (2).
[6] Gadow 32.

by endorsement, and the endorsement is governed by the law on bills of exchange.[1] This means that by delivery of the endorsed certificate the transferee acquires ownership thereof and thereby ownership of the share, unless of course transfer is restricted by the articles (see § 60). It is to be remembered that under both systems the endorsement may be in blank, i.e. without naming the transferee (endorsee), and he or any subsequent holder of the certificate may insert his name.

As against the company the transferee is recognised as a shareholder only if the transfer has been recorded in the share book (register of members). This, however, is relevant only for the right to take part in general meetings and if occasion arises to exercise pre-emptive rights. Otherwise the holder is in no way prevented from selling his share in the same way by delivery and endorsement, or where there is a blank endorsement, by delivery alone, whereas he is able to cash the dividends declared by detaching and presenting to the company the dividend coupons which are, as already stated, nearly always to bearer.

Thus the regular practice is for nominative shares to circulate for years without being presented to the company for their transfer to be recorded. Moreover, if and when the certificate is presented to the company, it is only the formal regularisation of the chain of endorsements—but not the genuineness of the signatures—which the company is under duty to examine.[2] The company is entitled to examine whether the endorsements are genuine or forged, but it is to be remembered that a holder of the certificate acquires ownership provided the chain of endorsements is formally in order even though one or more of them be forged, except in case of negligence or *mala fides*.[3] This rule applies equally as against the former holder and the company.

The rule makes the transfer of nominative shares to a large extent similar to that of bearer certificates. It does not apply if the transfer of a nominative share is made not by endorsement on the certificate but by a declaration of transfer. In such a case the company has to examine the signature, and a forged declaration gives no title.

The remedies in case of the loss of share certificates are to a large extent determined by the attitude of the country concerned as to the legal character of the certificate. Where the certificate

[1] German § 61 (2); Swiss 684.

[2] German § 62 (2).

[3] German law on Bills of Exchange § 16; Swiss O.R. 1006.

is merely evidential its loss or destruction does not affect the ownership of the share, and the shareholder has a right to demand the issue of a new certificate. The corporation, however, can be compelled to issue the new certificate only if there is no danger that two certificates will be in existence at the same time for one and the same share or group of shares should the allegation of destruction or loss prove to be incorrect. Both the owner's and the corporation's interests need protection in such a case.

The English Companies Act contains no provisions; regulation is left to individual companies, which nearly always deal with the matter in their articles. Clause 9 of Table A suggests that in case of a share certificate being defaced, destroyed or lost it may be renewed on payment of a fee—if any—not exceeding one shilling, and on such terms—if any—as to evidence and indemnity as the directors think fit.

In the U.S.A. many statutes provide for the issue of a new certificate against indemnity, but it is held that in the absence of statutory provisions the corporation may be compelled to issue one.[1] The Uniform Stock Transfer Act contains provisions to this effect (sec. 17), and in all States where it is in force its provisions apply. In States where the statutes do not contain such provisions it is usual to insert provisions for the issue in the by-laws.

If a corporation refuses to issue new certificates, the shareholder, in some States, has in proper cases an action at law, in others a suit in equity. Furthermore in some States remedy by summary proceedings is also granted, as a rule as a cumulative remedy.[2]

Under the Uniform Stock Transfer Act the Court may order the issue of a new certificate on service of process on the corporation and on reasonable notice by publication to all persons interested, and in any other way which the Court may direct, upon satisfactory proof of such loss. The Court may at its discretion order the shareholder to pay the corporation reasonable costs. The issue of a new certificate cannot be ordered where an over-issue would result. The indemnity is as a rule to be furnished by a bond. The Court may at its discretion compel the corporation to the issue if the proof of the loss or destruction is quite clear, or if the corporation has caused the destruction or loss by its own carelessness.[3] The Uniform Stock Transfer Act (sec. 17) requires the

[1] Fletcher 5179, n. 2. [2] Fletcher 5179, n. 15. [3] Fletcher 5180, n. 36.

giving of a bond with sufficient surety to be approved by the Court.

Under the Continental legislations in the case of loss or total destruction the special procedure is to be followed which is established in the country concerned for cancellation of negotiable instruments. The general lines of these regulations are an application to the Court, which in the case of *prima facie* evidence of loss or destruction issues a public notice to be inserted in the official *Gazette* by which the unknown holder is called upon to appear and show cause within the time limit fixed by the law, usually one year from the publication. In the meantime the company is forbidden to recognise the holder. If after the notice the holder presents himself the question of ownership is to be settled by trial; if the holder does not appear the Court, after expiry of the time limit, issues an order declaring the certificate cancelled, and after such order the company is under duty to issue a new certificate. The procedure takes a considerable time and involves expense. A simplification is everywhere desirable.

The question of coupons causes further complications. Some legislations provide that lost coupons cannot be cancelled and renewed, and that if they are presented the dividends due are to be paid even though proceedings for the cancellation of the certificate have already been begun or the certificate has already been cancelled. At the same time it is usually provided that if during the term of limitation the coupons have not been presented the company is to pay the amount to the holder in whose favour an order for cancellation has been made and enforced.

The German law provides (§ 66 (2)) that the cancellation of the certificate extends also to coupons not yet due at the time of the cancellation.

For defacement or partial destruction of certificates no judicial procedure is required, and if the certificate is sufficiently identifiable the holder may demand the issue of a new certificate on payment of the expenses (see e.g. German law, § 68).

It is usual to attach to the certificates coupons for a number of years—e.g. 20—on a separate sheet, together with a document entitling the bearer to demand a new sheet of coupons after the last coupon has become due; this is called a *talon*, and the production of the certificate itself is not usually required. If, however, the holder of the talon does not hold the certificate, the holder of the certificate may oppose the delivery of a new sheet of coupons against the talon. By German law (§ 69), the holder of the certificate is in such a case entitled to the coupons.

It is to be noted that German law [1] allows the signatures on the certificate to be made by mechanical reproduction. The articles may require special formalities, but these must appear on the certificate. The same is provided in 14 of the Swiss O.R. for all negotiable instruments issued in large numbers, which equally covers share certificates.

63. Register of Members

The keeping of books and records, a record of membership among them, has always been a part of corporate routine. Even apart from any change of membership by transfer or transmission, the corporation needs to know and to possess an exact record of the names and addresses of its members and the amount of their holdings; similarly the shareholders have a legitimate interest in knowing who their co-shareholders are, and what changes may occur in the holdings in consequence of transfers or transmissions in case of death or otherwise. If the shares are not fully paid up, the exactness of the record is fundamental to the corporation's financial security.

But when bearer certificates or bearer warrants are issued in respect of shares, the membership cannot be recorded; even if any particulars of holdings are known, such information is unofficial and may at any moment be out of date, since the shares can be sold and their ownership transferred at any time without the company's knowledge.

As we saw earlier, if bearer warrants are issued the names of persons entered in the register must be struck out. In their place is to be entered the fact and date of the issue of the warrant, together with a statement of the shares it covers, with the number of each share (sec. 112 (1) Companies Act 1948).

Where, as under European laws, a company's whole share capital may be represented by bearer certificates, the keeping of a share record is not necessary. A company may, however, need such a record to show the numbers of the shares issued, to enter particulars of certificates lost or destroyed by cancellation, and so on. Such a book is a mere record for the internal use of the company. A register of members, on the other hand, is a

[1] § 13 of the law of 1937, in accordance with the Commercial Code of 1937.

document which concerns not only the company and its shareholders, but also its creditors and even the general public.

By the Company legislation of Great Britain full publicity is provided for. This is the result of a gradual evolution. Thus in England the Act of 1844 (sec. 50) gave the right to inspect the register of members to shareholders alone, but the Companies Act of 1862 (sec. 32) extended this right without limit, so that anyone might inspect the register without giving a special reason. It is a consequence of this publicity that persons who contract with the company have a right to rely on the register, and those who are entered therein as shareholders have an interest in taking the necessary steps for their removal on ceasing to be members without any unreasonable delay; otherwise they have to bear the consequences and to make good their liability for the unpaid part of their shares, even though they may have had good grounds for avoiding being entered on the register.

Under the Companies Act of 1929 (sec. 95) every company must keep in one or more books a register of its members; in case of default the company and every officer in default is liable to a fine. This register is to contain the name, address and occupation of each member, the numbers of the shares he holds, the amounts paid on them, the date on which he was entered in the register as a member, and if any person has ceased to be a member the date of termination of his membership. If the company has converted any of its shares into stock, the register must show the amount of stock held by each member with all the particulars aforementioned. If a company has more than 50 members an index of their names is to be kept with sufficient indication to enable the particulars relating to any member to be readily found in the register, every change in which must be recorded within 14 days in the index: this may be in the form of a card-index. If the register itself is in index form, e.g. is kept in alphabetical order, the index may be dispensed with (sec. 96).

The register and index must be kept at the registered office of the company and be open to inspection during business hours; the company in general meeting may impose reasonable time limits, but not less than two hours are to be allowed daily (sec. 98 (1)). The company may close the register once or more each year, though only for periods not exceeding 30 days in all, on giving public notice in a newspaper circulating at the place where the registered office of the company is situate (sec. 99). Members may inspect the register and its index without charge, and other persons may do so on payment of a sum to be fixed by the company not exceeding one shilling (sec. 98 (1)). A creditor or member may inspect through his solicitor or agent.[1] The company on request must deliver copies at a charge not exceeding sixpence for every 100 words or part thereof within ten days from the receipt of the request (sec. 98 (2)). But persons who inspect the register are not entitled to take copies therefrom themselves.[2]

The company must allow access to the register and index to everyone and must deliver the copies requested whatever the motives of the request.[3] In case of refusal of inspection or default in delivering copies the Court may issue an order for compliance (sec. 98 (4)); a fine may also be imposed (sec. 98 (3)).

Publicity, however, is not restricted to the keeping of a register by the company. Every company must make at least once yearly a return of its members and also of those who have ceased to be members. This list is to contain the same particulars as to shares and stock as the register (sec. 100); it is to be made up on the 14th day after the first or only ordinary general meeting and must be completed within 28 days; a copy thereof, signed by a director, manager or secretary, is to be presented forthwith to the Registrar of Companies (sec. 110). If the return is not in alphabetical order it must be accompanied by an index. This list of members is equally open to inspection at the Registrar's office.

It is to be noted that the register of members and the list contained in the annual return show only the membership, the amount of shares and stock held by each member, and the changes that have occurred during the year, with the dates of any important alterations (see § 54). In respect of companies registered in England (but not in Scotland) no notice of any trust expressed, implied, or constructive shall be entered in the register or be receivable by the Registrar (sec. 101). Accordingly it is held that a company cannot enter a memorandum of lien in the register.[4]

The register of members is *prima facie* evidence of any matters directed or authorised to be inserted therein (sec. 102). It is

[1] Bevan *v.* Webb (1901), 2 Ch. 59.
[2] Balaghat Gold, etc., Co. (1901), 2 K.B. 665.
[3] Davies *v.* Gas Light and Coke Co. (1909), 1 Ch. 708.
[4] *In re* Key (W.) and Son Ltd. (1902), 1 Ch. 467.

not conclusive evidence.[1] It may be rectified on the application of any person aggrieved or of any member of the company on the ground that the name of any person has been entered therein without sufficient cause, or has been omitted, or that default has been made, or unnecessary delay has taken place, in entering the termination of the membership of any person. The Court has power to decide any question relating to the title of any person being a party to the application to be entered upon or struck off the register of members (sec. 100).

A person who asserts that he has been improperly entered in the register has every reason to make application as soon as possible, since he may be held liable as against third parties in respect of the unpaid par value of the shares registered in his name. On the other hand if a person is wrongfully omitted from the register, the company will not regard him as a member until his name is entered; consequently he has to apply for rectification or bring an action against the company.[2]

In the U.S.A. most legislations provide that corporations must keep a stock-book, frequently called the stock-ledger, and regulate what particulars are to be recorded in such book.

Thus under the New York Stock Corporation laws the stock-book must contain the names of all stockholders in alphabetical order, their places of residence, the number of shares of stock held by each member, the time when they became members and the amounts paid by them on the stock. The stock-book is to be kept at the office of the corporation, or if the corporation has a stock agent, at the office of such agent. It must be open to inspection during at least three business hours daily. The right of inspection, however, is restricted. No persons are entitled to inspect the stock-book other than those who: (1) are judgment creditors of the corporation; (2) have been stockholders for at least six months immediately preceding the demand; (3) produce a written authorisation signed by holders of at least five per cent. of all outstanding shares, provided that the inspection is not aimed at communication with stockholders in the interest of any business or object other than the business of the corporation. Inspection may further be refused if the person making the request has within five years sold or offered for sale any list of stockholders in this or any other corporation or has collaborated in

[1] Reese River Silver Mining Co. *v.* Smith (1869), L.R. 4 H.L. 64.
[2] Reese River Silver Mining Co. *v.* Smith, *supra.*

such sale or offer for sale. The corporation is entitled to ask for a written statement clarifying this matter, and in case of refusal may deny inspection. Persons who have a right to inspect the stock-book are entitled to make extracts therefrom. The stock-book is presumptive evidence of the facts stated therein.[1]

Some statutes have more liberal provisions as to the right of inspection. Thus in California any shareholder or holder of a voting trust certificate may inspect the share register at any reasonable time and for a purpose reasonably related to his interests as a shareholder or holder of such certificate.[2] Under the law of Delaware the stock-ledger shall at all times during business hours be open to inspection by any shareholder.[3] The same right is granted by the statute of Massachusetts.[4] Several statutes require that before any election, usually for ten days, a list of stockholders entitled to vote shall be open for inspection by stockholders. Other statutes provide that a specified minority holding, e.g. five or ten per cent. of the stock, have the right of inspection. The unrestricted right of inspection given by the Companies Act of Great Britain is quite unknown in the U.S.A.

Although the *Code de Commerce* (art. 36) provides that the ownership of shares other than to bearer is established by entry in the register of the company, French law leaves the keeping of the register of members to the company; nor is its publicity in any way guaranteed.

The German law of 1937 provides that every company having nominative shares must keep a stock-book (*Aktienbuch*). The holders are to be registered in the book; the entry is to contain the names, addresses and occupations of the shareholders (§ 61 (1)).

The duty of keeping a stock-book arises only if the company issues nominative share certificates. In such a case every shareholder has an actionable right to demand the keeping of a stock-book and his entry therein.[5] If an entry is erroneous or incorrect the person aggrieved may sue for correction,[6] and a shareholder may bring action if he has been wrongfully struck off the register.[7]

[1] S.C.L. § 10, as amended by L. 1933, ch. 641.
[2] C.C. § 355, as amended by L. 1933, ch. 533, § 54.
[3] R.C. § 29.
[4] G.L. ch. 155, § 22.
[5] R.G.Z. 86, 155.
[6] R.G.Z. in J.W. (1918), 503, 3.
[7] R.G.Z., Bank A, 31, 411.

It is held that the recording of a mortgage or life interest (usufruct) by entry is permissible though not necessary.[1]

As against the company only those persons are to be regarded as shareholders who are entered in the register as such. The same applies to holders of interim certificates if such are issued (§ 62 (3) and (4)). We must remember that interim certificates are invariably nominative.

It was formerly held that it is by the actual act of the entry that the position of a shareholder is established, and the entry was construed as a contract between the company and the shareholder.[2] This doctrine was later abandoned, and it was accepted that the registration is merely evidence; it is the means of "legitimation" as the German decisions and literature put it. One who is entered as a shareholder on the register may or may not be the lawful owner of the share or shares concerned, but he is in any case bound to perform the obligations arising under the articles in respect of the holdings. Thus it is no defence that he has sold his holding, even though he has delivered the certificate to the purchaser and the company has had notice of the sale.[3] His only defence is that he never gave his assent or that his assent was void.[4] In one case simulation of assent was accepted as a good defence;[5] the correctness of this decision under German law is doubtful, since it is generally held that the validity of the acquisition cannot be attacked on the ground of duress, mistake or fraud.[6] Conversely the company cannot sue a person for obligations arising from the ownership of a share unless he is on the register, and the action cannot be based on the fact that the defendant acquired the ownership of the share by a valid endorsement or otherwise,[7] though it was held in one case that a company may sue the successors of a shareholder in case of his death.[8] Whether the company could rectify the register without the consent of the person concerned is disputed.[9] On the other hand a person who is on the register is entitled to exercise the rights of a shareholder; the company, however, is held to be entitled to object that the entry was void.

The regulation of the Swiss O.R. (684–5) is on the whole identical.

[1] Gadow 218; Flechtheim-Duringer-Hachenburg III, 1, 168 (*a*).
[2] R.G.Z. 3, 163, 4, 17.
[3] R.G.Z. in J.W. (1931), 2997.
[4] R.G.Z. 86, 159, 92, 318, 123, 285.
[5] R.G.Z. in J.W. (1934), 363, 19.
[6] R.G.Z. 72, 294.
[7] Flechtheim 194 A, n. 11; Gadow 216.
[8] R.G.Z. 79, 164.
[9] See Flechtheim 195 A, n. 12; Gadow 217.

This survey shows that full publicity for the register of members is guaranteed only by the British Companies Act, but even under this Act the register may reveal little or nothing as to the real ownership of shares. It is possible for the persons whose names are entered on the register to have actually no beneficial interest in respect of the shares, but to hold them for the beneficial owners merely as nominees. Where the shares are not fully paid up the financial security of the company may be endangered if the registered shareholders are not solvent; by the use of this machinery the beneficial owners enjoy the advantages if the venture prospers and abandon the company in case of failure. Moreover in so far as prospective shareholders or creditors have an interest in knowing by whom the shares are held at any time, they will learn nothing from the register.

The terms of reference of the Cohen Committee included the question of nominee holdings of both shares and debentures. The Committee did not recommend a general register of beneficial ownership, but only a declaration thereof in specific cases. In the course of the debate in the House of Lords, however, even this modest proposal was dropped, and in its place power is given to the Board of Trade to order investigation as to the beneficial ownership if and where public interest requires it. This question is discussed in its other aspects in § 76.

Apart from this point only technical improvements, mainly simplifications, are introduced by the Companies Act, 1947. Thus the occupations of shareholders need not be registered (sec. 57). The register may be kept at any office of the company or where the work of making it up is done with the register agent appointed to make up the same (sec. 50). The annual return must not be contained in a separate part of the register of members (sec. 53 (3)). The company has to include a full list of members in its return only every third year; at other times it is only bound to include the changes which have occurred during the year (sec. 53 (3)).

The Companies Act, 1947 (sec. 74), extends the provisions relating to the register of members to the register of debenture holders. This applies to the keeping of the register, its contents, its inclusion in the annual return and its publicity. Under the 1929 Act it was not clear whether a company was bound to keep a register of debenture holders, or whether, if such a register was kept at all, it was open to inspection only by members and debenture holders (sec. 73). The extension of publicity secured by the Bill is undoubtedly a susbstantial advance.

These amendments are now incorporated in sections 110–118 of the Companies Act, 1948.

64. Shares of No Par Value

In the earliest days of incorporation some companies had no fixed capital expressed as a definite sum of money, and their shares had accordingly no par value. Such companies soon almost entirely disappeared, and it became axiomatic that every company must have a capital expressed as a definite sum of money, and that the shares into which it is divided must have a nominal or par value likewise expressed in money. The par value of a share is the amount of money which the shareholder has to contribute to the company; if the par value is not contributed the share is not paid up (or in American terminology "paid in"), and the shareholder is subject to call. Further, it is generally accepted that when shares are issued for money, they cannot, save for certain exceptions, be issued below par. The value of a company's assets may be more or less than its capital, and therefore the par value of shares may not be identical with their actual value: it may be either more or less.

In the case of shares issued for property or services it is desirable that the contribution should be equal to the par value; and as we have seen, every legislation seeks to provide guarantees against the watering of stock, a danger difficult to avoid.

The problems connected with this question have led to the introduction of shares with no par value. This occurred under the New York legislation in 1912, and the example was followed by other American States, with the result that at present 44 States of the U.S.A. have legalised no par value shares, only four still requiring that shares must have a nominal value. No par value shares have also been adopted in Canada. Even earlier they were known, though not in frequent use, in Italy and Belgium. Their introduction in other countries has been advocated, but so far without result.

The simplest form of no par value share is that found when the corporation in question has no other kind of share; in other words when it has no shares of par value, and all the no par value shares have equal rights. Each share then represents a quota of the net value of the corporation's assets; they are therefore sometimes called quota shares (*Quotenaktien*). But under existing statutes corporations may either issue no par value shares in addition to shares having a par value, or may have shares of one or other class alone.

The no par value shares may have priorities either against all or any class of par value shares, or against other classes of no par value shares. If shares without par value are issued on a company's formation, the particulars relating to them are to be laid down in the document of incorporation. In the case of subsequent issues the consideration for which they may be issued or, as it is generally expressed, be sold may be fixed in the articles or by-laws, but under most statutes the directors may be empowered to settle the consideration. The law of Delaware (R.C. § 14) even provides that they have such power unless the articles reserve it to the general meeting. But if the power belongs to the general meeting, a majority of two-thirds of the total outstanding stock, and—if there is more than one class—of each class, is usually required. The directors generally have full power to decide what part of the consideration received for no par value shares is to be appropriated to capital and what to surplus.

Such shares are advocated on the ground that the par value of a share has no meaning in relation to its real value; it serves only to raise unwarranted assumptions in the minds of the ignorant, who will be induced to accept the share's par value as an indication of its actual value. It is even on record that in the days of large-scale railway building in the U.S.A. the not over-honest promoters of railroad companies preferred to issue stock with a higher par value than the assets warranted, in order to induce the gullible public to purchase it. This is said to have been a very successful device. No par value shares dispense with such pretences. We may, however, presume that it was not this academic interest in better information which gave rise to their use, but their greater ease of issue.

If a share to be issued for cash has no par value, the prohibition of issues below par does not apply, and the corporation can issue the share at any price it thinks suitable. There is no obligation for further calls, and liability for watered stock cannot arise. In issues for property the corporation may give the vendor any number of no par value shares as consideration for the property transferred. Again, if an increase of a company's working capital becomes necessary, the new shares can be issued at any price the corporation thinks fit.

On the other hand it cannot be denied that no par value shares are not free from dangers. At the original issue there is the possibility of over-capitalisation if an excessive number of shares is given in consideration for property or services. If the company is a going concern and issues additional no par value shares the existing shareholders may be injured: if the new shares are issued for cash and their price is less than the value of the shares already issued would warrant, the value of the latter will necessarily be reduced. This injury may be avoided if all the new shares are taken by the existing members. In practice, however, the protection of the pre-emptive rights of shareholders is not complete, and also the original shareholders may not be in a financial position to take up the new shares.

If the new shares are issued as consideration for property to be acquired, the shareholders can hardly be protected against an over-valuation of that property if compared with the value of the existing shares.

Furthermore there are dangers as to the management of companies with no par value capital and shares. At first there was no effective protection against the use as dividends of the amounts paid into the treasury of the corporation. Since in such a case the corporation has no fixed capital, there was no theoretical limit to the use for dividends of the consideration received. The unsoundness of such a state of affairs was obvious, and prohibitions were soon introduced; yet even now some legislations allow the distribution as dividends of a certain part of the amounts paid by the shareholders in the same way as in the case of a surplus, i.e. a free reserve accumulated from profits. Even where such distributions are prohibited, there is still the possibility of a corporation paying a dividend out of the profits of the current year although a part of the amounts paid in for the additional shares may have been lost. In order to avoid this it has become usual in the case of no par value shares to require a *stated* capital, e.g. the stating of the aggregate amount of the contributions paid by the shareholders. If, however, this principle with all its implications is accepted, there is not much difference between par value and no par value shares.

Again, the possibility of the issue of no par value shares at any price the board thinks fit gives the board much greater possibilities of making injurious increases of capital.

So far we have considered only the simple case in which a corporation has only one class of shares, namely no par value shares with equal rights. The position is much more difficult if there are no par value shares of several classes, e.g. ordinary (common) and preferred, and more so still if, beside no par value shares, there are ordinary or preferred shares with a par value. It is obvious that against these dangers and complications some protection is needed.[1]

One of the main reasons which led to the introduction, or more correctly the revival, of no par value shares was to evade any responsibility for the watering of stock. If the shares have no par value and the corporation is in no way restricted in fixing the price which is to be paid by subscribers of original shares or of shares issued in connection with an increase of capital, the question of any further liability beyond the payment of the price agreed on cannot arise. It has been said [2]: "The manifest danger of an over-valuation of assets given in exchange for par value stock and the risk of liability consequent thereon in the cases of both new and going concerns and the rigid strait jacket into which corporate financing by sale of stock of a going concern was placed if the actual value of its stock has fallen below par were the prime considerations which prompted corporate organisers and managers to evolve some plan for stock issues which would liberate shares of stock from the thraldom of the par value feature."

Similarly, H. W. Ballantine has said that the great beauty of no par value stock is that the holder of the shares is not liable to creditors beyond the price fixed by the corporation.[3] But this opinion as to the desirability of this position is not shared by all. It has been said that it would not be a serious exaggeration to say that in such a case "the shareholder's liability has disappeared and the outstanding feature of corporations has now become not limited liability but no liability".[4] On their introduction William W. Cook said that: "Shares without par value conceal what money or property a share really represents." [5] His attack

[1] Fletcher 5124–8.
[2] Bodell *v.* General Gas and Electric Corp. (1926), 15 Del. Ch. 119.
[3] 57 Am. L. Rev. 233.
[4] 24 Colum. L. Rev. 449.
[5] 19 Mich. L. Rev. 594, quoted by Fletcher 5259, n. 13.

against the propriety and wisdom of the authorisation of no par value shares was mainly based on this point.

In the type of case discussed the liability of shareholders is restricted to the payment of the consideration for which the shares were issued. In cases of the other type, however, where the no par value shares have a stated value, i.e. where the amount for which they may be issued is fixed at the formation of the corporation and this amount governs subsequent issues, their effect is very similar to that of par value shares. Therefore it has been said [1] that the former type alone, and not that of stated value, is really no par value stock.

W. W. Cook said in the essay quoted above that "on the whole stock without par value looks like a skilfully devised scheme for issuing a maximum of watered stock at a minimum of risk. In the hands of reliable men it may be all right, in the hands of unreliable men it is all wrong; it conceals the mystery of the water."

This, however, is only a consideration as to the advisability of no par value shares as long and in so far as they are allowed; the rule is that the subscriber has to pay the consideration and nothing more, regardless of whether it is adequate to the proportionate part of the net assets which it represents.

The dangers of the position, especially if the pre-emptive rights of existing shareholders are not guaranteed, have already been exposed. In the case of Bodell *v.* General Gas and Electric Corp., *supra*, the Court said that in a case of manifest abuse of power on the side of the directors the Court may give relief in equity. "Notwithstanding the obsolete character of the language in which the power of the directors is expressed (i.e. in the Delaware Statute) it cannot be that a court of equity is powerless to circumscribe it. The section requires the directors to fix the consideration. It certainly would be out of all reason to say that no Court could review their action in fixing it."

Nevertheless this right of judicial review is fairly strictly circumscribed in the judgment quoted. The Judge of the Delaware Court of Chancery said that in the case of newly founded corporations he did "not see that it can make any difference how much or how little in the way of consideration is received for its original no par value stock so long as the consideration is lawful in its quality. If the assets received are one thousand dollars in money, it is of no consequence whether five shares or

[1] 25 Colum. L. Rev. 53.

ten shares or ten thousand shares are given for it". It is true that in such a case every share is simply a proportionate part of the total assets unexpressed in terms of money, but it is obvious that the issue of a large number of shares where a small amount of money is paid or property of little value is contributed is not without dangers, and may be apt to incite assumptions on the part of the lay public at least as erroneous as those which arise in consequence of par values not warranted by the actual value of the assets.

As to subsequent issues the judgment quoted recognised the vital interest of the existing shareholders that the value of the fraction representing the present aliquot interest in the assets held by each shall not be diminished by the issue of the additional shares at a lower price than is warranted under the circumstances. On the other hand it was stated that the market price cannot be accepted as a safe guide for the fixing of the sales value for unissued stock, and that book value in itself likewise cannot be accepted. The leading principle would be that the issue price be "fair to the corporation and the existing shareholders and best calculated to yield the largest possible capital." This is admirably stated in general terms. The Court, however, accepts that there is a presumption in favour of the propriety and fairness of the directors, and on the other hand states that "it would be hazardous to venture an examination of all the possible considerations which directors might take into account in fixing the price." It is a poor consolation that such crass violations of equity as the issue of no par value stock of "a demonstrable value of three hundred dollars if made to outsiders at ten will not be allowed to proceed" since the cases coming up for judicial review will not show such "glaring" abuses, but may nevertheless harm stockholders to a large extent without remedy.

Thus an effective protection for holders of no par value stock, in spite of the improvements introduced by the latest amendments and decisions, is still an unsolved problem.

In the opinion of the author substantial progress could be achieved by providing that a corporation may at the choice of the incorporators have either shares with par value or without, but not both; further that the consideration received for shares of no par value may be appropriated either to capital or to surplus (reserve), but that even in the latter case surplus arising from such consideration should not be distributable.

As to subsequent issues it is obvious that the judicial remedy against abuse of power, however beautiful it sounds, will operate only in extreme cases, and that transactions will ordinarily be unassailable. The only real remedy in our opinion lies in an absolute right of pre-emption.

The introduction of no par value shares was strongly advocated before the Cohen Committee. The Committee, however, did not recommend it, and the 1947 Act made no change in the law in this respect.[1]

[1] Cf. Ballantine, 203–7; Dodd and Baker, pp. 1001–30; Berle and Magill, pp. 174–210; Bonbright, 24 Col. L. R., pp. 449—68; Berle, 25 Col. L.R., pp. 49—63; Wickersham, 37 Harv. L.R., pp. 464—78.

CHAPTER IV

MANAGEMENT AND CONTROL

65. THE POWERS OF CORPORATIONS. THE DOCTRINE OF ULTRA VIRES

We have already considered the doctrine of *ultra vires* in its historical evolution, as well as in connection with the objects clause. Here we shall examine its practical implications.

The formation of a company is always undertaken with some definite and particular aim, be it wide or narrow. In the days of the South Sea Bubble one enterprise was announced whose purpose was to be communicated only subsequently to the shareholders; actually, however, it is a prerequisite for the creation of any corporation that it should have some definite purpose. How far this object should be defined at the time of formation, and how far the corporation should be bound by such definition, is, however, a matter of legislative politics.

The early English chartered companies without exception were given corporate powers for a clearly defined purpose, such as trade with the East Indies, the Levant or Russia, the colonisation of various areas in North America, and so on (see § 5). At the same time it was consistently held after the Sutton's Hospital case,[1] that a corporation created by royal charter has the same capacity as a natural person to do anything not forbidden by law, and to conclude any contract not specially prohibited or against public policy, whether within the corporation's original scope as foreseen and defined at the time of its creation or not. This doctrine was even extended to maintain that if a charter contained some express prohibition, the violation of that provision would not affect the validity of the act in question. It might lead to forfeiture of the charter, but never to an avoidance of the contract. Some of the corporations created by royal charter were in fact prohibited from entering into certain contracts, but the breach of these rules was not held to invalidate the contracts entered into or other acts done in violation of the charter.

Such restrictive measures were applied mainly to corporations

[1] (1612), 10 Co. Rep. 24, 30, 16.

created with Parliamentary assent, such as the Bank of England, since Parliament always liked to define clearly the objects of companies, and special Acts authorising companies were always accompanied by plain definitions of their purpose. The Courts accepted the view that corporations so created were bound by the provisions of the Act that brought them into being, and every contract not within the scope of the Act or ancillary to the defined purpose was beyond the power of the company and therefore void. In short, the rule is that a company created by Act of Parliament can do nothing which is not authorised by its constitutive act, and that a contract made in violation of such act is void.

When the formation of companies was made possible under a general statute without any special intervention on the part of the legislature or government, it became the duty and the right of the persons forming a corporation under the enabling law to define and settle its purposes. The Act of 1856 already provided for such definition, and the Companies Act of 1862 prescribed that the memorandum of association should contain a declaration of the objects or purposes. It was for the incorporators to decide for what purpose they intended to call the company into being, the Registrar having only to ascertain whether that purpose was lawful and did not require any special authorisation or franchise. The memorandum of association was to govern the whole life of the corporation, and its provisions could not be altered by the articles.

This state of affairs was marked by two main features. On the one hand the founders were free to draw up the memorandum of association as they wished, and to make it as narrow or as wide as they chose. They were restricted by law only in as much as no company can be created for any purpose that is unlawful or contrary to public policy. The second restriction was that if the purpose or one of the purposes of the company required a special franchise, the company could not be registered until it had secured whatever Act of Parliament or Governmental Order might be necessary for that purpose. If, however, the incorporators had already made their decision and the company had been registered under its memorandum of association, they were bound by that decision. The consequences of this rule were twofold; not only was the company unable to change its declared objects by resolution of the shareholders in general meeting or by any alteration of its articles of association, but the memorandum of association was itself not alterable by special resolution, whether by a bare or a special majority, or even by the unanimous desire of the shareholders. This line of legislative thought was maintained until 1890, and up to that year an alteration of objects was possible only by a special Act of Parliament. The Memorandum of Association Amendment Act of 1890 (53 and 54 Vic., c. 62), however, allowed the object clause to be altered by special resolution, subject to confirmation by the Court. The provisions of this Act were embodied in sec. 5 of the Companies Act of 1929, which allows alteration of the memorandum in so far as may be necessary to carry out one of the following purposes: (*a*) to carry on the business more economically or efficiently; (*b*) to attain the main purpose by new or improved means; (*c*) to enlarge or alter the locality of operations; (*d*) to carry on some other business which may conveniently be combined with the existing business of the company; (*e*) to restrict or abandon any of the objects specified in the memorandum (sec. 5 (1)).

The Court has wide powers; it may confirm or refuse to confirm the resolution, or may prescribe such terms or conditions as it thinks fit. Judicial scrutiny extends to the question whether sufficient notice has been given to the debenture holders and any other persons whose interests, in the Court's opinion, are affected. The Court must also be satisfied that other creditors, in so far as they are entitled to object and have in fact objected in the manner directed by the Court, have either consented to the alteration or have been paid off or secured. The Court may for special reasons dispense with the notice (sec. 5 (4)). The leading rule for the exercise of the power conferred on the Court is that due regard must be had to the rights and interests of all or any class of shareholders, and also to those of creditors. The Court may facilitate the purchase of the shares of dissentient minority shareholders by adjourning the proceedings and giving directions or orders to that effect, provided that no part of the capital is expended for such purpose.

In view of the requirement of confirmation by the Court alterations of the memorandum were relatively rare. On the other hand the Courts were fairly cautious in construing the object clause, and, as shown in § 43, avoidance of *ultra vires* contracts frequently occurred.

To counter the consequences of this doctrine, solicitors in preparing draft memoranda of association gradually adopted the practice of drawing up exhaustive definitions of the company's purposes and of the ancillary and incidental powers required to further them, so that in current practice the objects and powers clauses of memoranda are very long, enumerating many branches of industry and trade regardless of their actual connection with the company's real purposes.[1] They thus seek to ensure that the various contracts which a company may make in furtherance of its actual purposes shall not be open to objection as *ultra vires*, and also that the company shall be able to extend its activities without difficulty, unfettered by its memorandum. This state of affairs is unsatisfactory; the objects clauses of memoranda are as a rule too voluminous and unwieldy, while on the other hand it often happens that some eventuality which arises in the course of the company's operations is not provided for.

During the hearings before the Cohen Committee the drawbacks and difficulties of the existing situation were fully discussed. One suggestion was that the whole doctrine of *ultra vires* should be abandoned, and that the position should revert to what it was under the system of charters and still is even to-day in respect of the few remaining chartered companies, i.e. that a company should have power to do everything which its memorandum of association does not expressly prohibit. Another proposal was that only the real objects and purposes of the company should be stated in the memorandum of association, but that the company should have the inherent power to do everything necessary or reasonable in furtherance of the objects stated.

It is, however, obviously against public policy as well as opposed to shareholders' rights that a company formed for a particular purpose stated at the time of its formation should be entitled to extend its activities to other and unconnected fields. This would frustrate the rights of those who subscribed for shares in the expectation that the company would operate on the lines of its objects clause. It is not a matter of indifference to them that they should some day find that the company is operating in other branches of economic life as well as or instead of its original field. Nor is it indifferent to a creditor who has given credit to the company with knowledge of its purpose as defined in its memorandum. One case quoted during the hearings is highly

[1] See p. 373.

characteristic: a company originally formed to manufacture rayon after a time abandoned this activity and established a plant for making jam. If the objects clause in the memorandum was wide enough, this could have been done without difficulty, and still could be if the suggestions mentioned were adopted.

On the other hand it is not easy to see what the supporters of the idea that the real objects alone should be included in the memorandum have in mind. How could this be controlled? How could the Registrar know in advance that the object stated was in fact the real one? All that he could ascertain is that the objects as enumerated were consistent. It is obvious that if a company were formed to acquire an iron and steel plant, dealing in, say, agricultural products would be inconsistent therewith, but if the memorandum mentioned among the company's objects ore or coal mining, or even the acquisition of ships for the transport of its products, no such objection could be raised.

Whether from the point of view of industrial policy the creation of so-called vertical combines or undertakings should be facilitated is quite another question. This, however, is beyond the scope of our investigations, and we should be content with the postulate that inconsistent objects clauses should not be registered.

The only other practicable measure would be to give the Registrar power to check the activities of companies after a certain period—say, two or three years—from registration, objects which are not being pursued at that time being deleted from the memorandum.

As stated above, during the Cohen Committee hearings objections were also raised against the whole doctrine of *ultra vires*. It was asserted that it would be unjust for the Courts to be able to declare a contract void as *ultra vires*, thereby throwing the onus of the violation on the third party contracting with the company. That it should be for the shareholders to see that the directors do not violate the objects clause, to supervise and restrain them, to hold them responsible, and eventually to remove them from office, sounds very convincing. In most cases, however, the mischief would be done before the shareholders had the smallest knowledge of the *ultra vires* acts, and to secure compensation for the damage done to the company would be possible only in very few cases. On the other hand it is clearly hardly right to speak in such a case of innocent third parties. One who makes a contract with a company knows or should know what limitations are imposed upon its management by the memorandum of association. Frequently the company's name or style will in itself give sufficient information as to what activities are justified. If, for example, a rayon factory proposes a contract for the sale and delivery of 50 tons of jam, it would clearly be for the prospective purchaser to institute some enquiries, and we are hardly asking too much of third parties in demanding that they should know the contents of the memorandum, and if the law so requires, should have a constructive knowledge of the objects of the company.

In the United States the doctrine of chartered companies as it evolved in England was never accepted, though there were some *obiter dicta* to the effect that a corporation may act precisely as may an individual.[1] It was always in fact held that corporations have only such powers as are conferred by their charter, and that therefore any act not covered by the definition of the corporation's purposes in the charter and not incidental or auxiliary thereto is *ultra vires*. It is of course only just and equitable that the Court should take a liberal view as to the ancillary powers of companies.

The introduction of general corporation laws affected this position only in as much as the powers are now contained in and defined by the articles or certificate of incorporation. There can be no doubt that the powers so conferred belong to the corporation; but since the articles (certificate) are to be construed in the same way as a statute, it is to be and in practice is held that the express powers do not cover all the powers conferred upon the corporation, but that any stated express power carries with it all powers which may be implied from or are incidental or auxiliary to it. The corporation is therefore empowered to do everything convenient, suitable or necessary to enable it to exercise fully the powers designated in its charter and to do the business for which it was created.[2] An act need not be absolutely necessary provided it is directly appropriate and immediately within the powers.

There is much casuistry about the matter of implied powers, and some conflicting decisions. It is, however, accepted that acts done in the normal course of business to secure debts owing to a corporation, and to protect or aid employees, are within its

[1] Cf. Fletcher 2676, n. 25.

[2] Fletcher 2487.

powers. To embark on a different business, on the other hand, is in excess of the powers, and occasional acts belonging to a different kind of business are within the powers only if they serve the purposes covered by the charter.

There is much conflict over the question whether acts directed to increase business are within the powers or not. The articles may restrict the powers of the corporation, and the by-laws are not competent to enlarge powers in contrast with the charter (articles, certificate). On the other hand the consent or acquiescence of the shareholders does not suffice to confer powers which are neither expressly given nor implied by the charter.[1] The corporation may surrender a portion of its chartered powers; as to their alteration, the statutes provide differently. Some allow it, others give no such right.

The position of National Banks is exhaustively defined by the Act of Congress, 12 U.S.C.A. 24, and special rules apply to quasi-public corporations, such as railway, street railway, electric light and power, gas and water companies, and so on.

It is held that in the absence of express restrictions a corporation has implied power to enter into any contract necessary for the conduct of its business and the accomplishment of its corporate purposes.[2] Whether the contract is beneficial or not is of course immaterial. Contracts prohibited by the charter or by the general law, or contrary to public policy, are invalid. On the other hand the corporation is bound by an implied contract in the same way as a natural person.[3]

A corporation's borrowing powers are generally unlimited; in particular there is no limitation on the amount of the capital or any multiple of it. In some States, however, there are statutory or even constitutional limitations, and the borrowing powers may be limited by the charter.

It is generally held that a corporation has no implied power to enter into a contract of guarantee or suretyship. Such contracts may, however, be within the corporation's purpose, as in the case of surety and guarantee corporations, or they may be incidental and in furtherance of the business. In what cases the contract is incidental or in furtherance of the corporation's purposes depends on the circumstances of the case.[4] There is some authority for the rule that a contract is valid if there is a

[1] Fletcher 2493–4.
[2] Fletcher 2564.
[3] Fletcher 2580.
[4] Fletcher 2591–5.

reasonable expectation that the business of the corporation will be directly furthered or increased by it.[1] If the contract of guarantee or suretyship is in excess of the powers of the corporation, it is void, or under some legislations voidable, and the guarantor must return any benefit received thereunder.

It is held that a corporation is entitled to act as agent if this is not forbidden by the statute or charter governing the corporation, and if the matter is incidental to its main business.[2] The rule as to trusteeship, at least nowadays, is almost identical. It was formerly held that a corporation could not hold any property, real or personal, in trust for another person because the whole institution of trust is based on conscience, and coercive measures, particularly imprisonment for contempt of Court, could not be applied to a corporation. This view, however, has long been abandoned, and as Story said: "The doctrine has been long since exploded as unsound and too artificial, and it is now held that where a corporation has a legal capacity to take real and personal estate, there it may take and hold it upon trust in the same manner and to the same extent as a private person may do."[3] Many corporations are expressly authorised to act as trustees; there are even some whose main business consists in undertaking trusts, but even without such express authorisation a corporation may act as trustee in matters which will promote its general purposes.[4] The majority rule is that a corporation has power to act as executor or administrator. It is provided that National banks may act in a fiduciary capacity if no State or local law is thereby violated.[5]

Borrowing powers in general have already been considered. It must be added that power to borrow is not a principal but an incidental power, i.e. the corporation has such power not only where the statute or charter expressly so provides, but also where it empowers the corporation to purchase and hold property.[6] The power may be affected by the nature or character of the corporation, and in a given case the purpose or object of the loan may be of importance. As a rule, however, contracts for loans are valid as against third parties in ignorance of the violation of the limitations imposed upon the corporation, and in any case the corporation has to return any benefit which it has received

[1] Fletcher 2696. [2] Fletcher 2600.
[3] Vidal *v.* Philadelphia (1844), 2 How U.S. 127.
[4] Fletcher 2601. [5] Fletcher 2609. [6] Fletcher 2610.

from the invalid loan on the principle of an implied contract.[1] Similar rules apply to negotiable instruments. In this connection the question of accommodation papers arises. It is very exceptional for a corporation to have power to become an accommodation party to a negotiable paper, and as a rule no corporation can do so, but as against *bona fide* holders for value of such papers the corporation is not entitled to use the character of the paper as a defence.[2]

If an act is not within the powers, i.e. is neither in pursuance of the objects nor incidental to them, it is *ultra vires*. As to the consequences of an *ultra vires* act there is considerable conflict of opinion. The Supreme Court of the U.S.A., the Federal Courts, and some State Courts accept the rule that such an act is void and consequently can have no effect in law, and neither the corporation nor the other party is entitled to ask for specific performance of the contract, or to sue for damages.

By the National Bank Act as amended in 1928, National Banks were not expressly granted power to act as agents in purchases of stock. It has accordingly been held that a National Bank instructing its brokers to purchase stock acts *ultra vires*, and the contract is void whether the principal was disclosed or not.[3] In this case the action was brought by the broker for damages, and it was held that he could not sue the Bank.

If the contract is performed in full by both parties, neither is entitled to bring an action for rescission and repayment of what was paid or delivered. If the contract is performed by one party only either in full or in part, this in the light of the rule gives no right to action either for performance or for damages, but only for restitution of what has been paid.

It is held, however, by a number of State Courts that an *ultra vires* contract is not void but only voidable by the corporation, and if it has accepted the performance and by it the benefits of the contract it must perform it for its own part. Furthermore under this rule a ratification of the contract *ultra vires* is possible, and the corporation may be estopped from the assertion of *ultra vires*. In a case where the contract is prohibited by Common or Statute Law or is against public policy there is of course no difference between the two opinions. In such a case the contract is void according to either view, and the parties being *in pari*

[1] Fletcher 2612–8.
[2] Fletcher 2632–4.
[3] Casatt *v.* First National Bank of N.Y. (1933), 111 N.J.L. 536.

delicto have no action whatever against each other based on an implied contract (quasi contract). Similarly, both opinions are in accord that a merely executory contract without performance on either side is not actionable against the corporation. Whereas under the Federal rule it is not actionable even by the corporation, under the other rule an action can be maintained, since the bringing of an action is equal to ratification.

Shareholders are entitled to prevent a corporation from entering into an *ultra vires* contract by injunction if it intends to do so. This, however, will probably be helpful only in very rare cases, since generally shareholders will have no notice of the directors' intention. Whether and to what extent directors are responsible for *ultra vires* acts will be discussed separately.

Furthermore the State has the right to declare the charter forfeit if the corporation engages in *ultra vires* acts, although there is not much evidence of this power having been exercised.

The Common Law rule was that by incorporation the purposes and powers of a corporation are determined for the whole term of its existence, and cannot be extended or altered. Under many legislations, however, it is now possible to alter the purposes clause of the articles (certificate) of incorporation by a resolution in general meeting. Such resolutions as a rule require a specific majority, e.g. two-thirds of the total capital. These largely disputed rules of the Common Law are superseded in a number of States by express statutory provisions.

Under the influence of the Model Business Corporation Act published by the Commissioners of Uniform State Laws certain States adopted a definition of the powers of corporations but without going into the question what would be the fate of acts in excess of these powers.

Thus the Code of Idaho (1932) provides that a corporation "shall have the capacity to act possessed by natural persons, but shall have the capacity to perform only such acts as are necessary or proper to accomplish its purposes which are not repugnant to law" (§ 29–114 (1)) and further that a corporation shall have authority "to do all acts permitted by the Act and all such other acts as are necessary and expedient to accomplish its stated purposes" (subsec. 2 (*k*)).

The provisions of the General Corporations Act of Indiana of 1929 (§ 3) are on similar lines and differ only in drafting, but there is an express provision that any act in excess of the corporation's powers shall be avoidable by direct proceedings instituted by the prosecuting attorney of the county in which the principal offices of the corporation are located.[1]

The Statute of California takes a fundamentally different view. After enumerating the acts to which a corporation is authorised [2] it is provided that no limitation on the business purposes or powers of the corporation or upon the powers of the shareholders, officers or directors, or the manner of the exercise of such powers contained in or implied by the articles shall be asserted between the corporation or any shareholder and any third person. Consequently such limitations give only the right (*a*) to the shareholder or to the corporation to bring action in order to enjoin the directors or officers from performing or continuing acts in excess of their powers; (*b*) to the State to start proceedings for injunctions or for dissolution of the corporation; and (*c*) to the corporation to bring action against officers or directors for damages. Similar action may be brought by shareholders in a representative suit.

No action for injunctions can be brought in so far as third parties have acquired rights under unauthorised contracts. Similarly, contracts or conveyances made or ratified by the directors or done within the scope of their even merely apparent authority shall bind the corporation unless the act concerned falls under a special limitation of the law. On the other hand the corporation shall acquire the rights arising from each contract whether the contract is executed or partly or wholly executory (§ 345). Thus the position as it was under Common Law is in nearly every respect reversed.

The law of Illinois follows the same principle, but empowers the Court in proceedings for enjoining to perform a contract *ultra vires* to set aside the contract if it thinks equitable and to allow compensation to the other party or parties, or to the corporation for the loss or damage arising in consequence of the injunction, with the exclusion however of damages for loss of anticipated profits.[3]

The corporation laws of Michigan,[4] Minnesota,[5] and Ohio,[6]

[1] Gen. Corp. Act, § 54.
[2] Civ. Code, § 341, as amended by law (1933), c. 533, § 44.
[3] Business Corp. Act of 1933, § 8.
[4] § 10-11 of Gen. Corp. Act of 1931, as amended by Act of 1935.
[5] § 11 of Business Corp. Act of 1933.
[6] § 8 of Gen. Corp. Act of 1927.

whilst generally adopting the same rule, allow the defence of *ultra vires* if the other party had actual knowledge of the *ultra vires* character of the contract.

The Model for State Business Corporation Acts prepared by the Corporation Law Committee of the American Bar Association (October 1946) contains in its § 6 provisions very similar to those of the law of Illinois.

On the European continent alteration of the purposes of companies is nowadays generally allowed.

In France a resolution for this purpose requires a quorum of three-fourths of the total capital and a majority of two-thirds of the shares represented at the meeting.[1]

German law is satisfied with a majority of three-fourths of the shares represented, but there is no quorum. The articles may provide for stricter requirements, e.g. for a larger majority or for a quorum (§ 146 (1)).

Under Swiss law a resolution to alter the purposes of a company requires a two-thirds majority of the total capital (648, par. 1); this requirement cannot be reduced. But if the resolution is aimed merely at the adoption of new kinds of business within the ambit of the company's stated purposes, and similar to those laid down in the articles, a simple majority is sufficient, provided that two-thirds of the total capital is represented at the meeting. Where this quorum is not obtained, a second meeting may carry the resolution with a quorum of one-third, and the articles may provide for another and smaller quorum, or even dispense with a quorum altogether (649).

On the other hand the doctrine of the unlimited authority of the board of management to act on the company's behalf, as held under German law, means that the validity of contracts is not affected by the fact that they are not covered by the purposes of the company. This was so even before the law of 1937,[2] and under §§ 70 and 74 it is clear that the management has authority to enter into any contract which can be concluded by a company. The limits following from the definition of the purposes and objects contained in the articles are operative only in internal relations. Violation of the articles by the conclusion of contracts beyond the purposes of the company may involve liability for damages, but in no case affects the validity of the contract.

[1] 31 as amended by the law of 1 May 1930.

[2] R.G.Z. 115, 246.

The Swiss law adopts the German doctrine with a substantial modification. The directors (718) are empowered to make contracts which may follow from the purposes of the company. It seems that contracts obviously outside the scope of those purposes would be inoperative. In most cases, however, it would be difficult to say that a contract, though outside the purposes of the company, could not be regarded as within what the articles might be taken to imply.

The doctrine that the rights of third parties ought not to be affected by any omission in the memorandum or articles undoubtedly has its attractions, and this favourable view is promoted by the above-mentioned practice, evolved in Great Britain, of drafting the articles widely and at great length.

The Cohen Committee recommended an amendment of the law to the effect that every company, whether incorporated before or after the anticipated new Act, should have the same powers as regards third parties as an individual, notwithstanding anything omitted from its memorandum; likewise that the provisions of memoranda, whether as now existing or as adopted in future, as to the powers of the company, should operate merely as a contract between the company and its shareholders as to the powers exercisable by the directors.[1] This recommendation was welcomed by many lawyers, especially by those imbued with German legal traditions. For the reasons already explained we think it fortunate that this recommendation was not followed by the Companies Act, 1947, which refrains from altering the existing law in this respect.

A second recommendation of the Cohen Committee, however, was adopted in sec. 76 and is now incorporated in sec. 5 of the Companies Act of 1948. In future the confirmation of the Court will not be required for resolutions altering the objects clause of the memorandum. Holders of not less than 15 per cent. of the issued share capital, or of not less than 15 per cent. of debentures secured by a floating charge issued or first issued before the coming into force of the Act, or forming part of the same series, may make an application to the Court directed against the resolution within 21 days after its adoption. In view of this right of application to the Court, holders of debentures entitled so to apply are to be notified of the meeting in the same way as shareholders. The Court has power to confirm

[1] Report 12 (p. 9).

the alteration wholly or in part, and to impose such terms and conditions as it thinks fit, and to exercise in general the same powers as under sec. 5 of the Act of 1929. The decision of the Court is final.

In this way alteration of the objects is substantially facilitated, and it may be anticipated that in most cases the resolutions will not be the subject of applications to the Court. Whether it was proper to withhold the right of objection from holders of debentures with special security future experience will show.

66. Acquisition by a Company of its own Shares

Although it may be maintained on principle that a company cannot be a member of itself, many companies have in fact indulged in the practice of purchasing, directly or indirectly, their own shares. Well-known cases are those of the South Sea Company in England and the Mississippi Company in France. In both these instances the directors used the company's funds to enhance a speculative movement in shares by purchasing large blocks of them; in both cases disaster followed. In the case of the South Sea Company Parliament and the Government averted total ruin (see § 6); in that of the Mississippi Company the Regent of France was not so circumspect, and in consequence both the investing public and the credit of the State suffered.

It is obvious that for a company to advance loans on its own stock may lead to similar results; yet for a long time this fact was not appreciated, and during the 18th century even the Bank of England made occasional advances on such security. The unreasonableness of such loans was, of course, soon realised, and they were stopped for ever. But this was not the case in general, and after almost every financial boom and subsequent slump instances of this practice came to light. Hardly ever did a company, especially a financial company, collapse without having made a more or less substantial purchase of its own shares.

After the great crisis of 1873 on the European Continent the bankruptcy of a large number of companies, especially of banks, was attributed to their having speculated in their own stock and diverted their corporate funds for this purpose. After the notorious collapse of the French bank, the Union Générale, in 1882, investigation revealed that a large part of the stock had been repurchased by the bank in order to keep the market price of the shares at a high level. The bank succeeded in the autumn of 1882 in increasing its capital by 50 per cent., but could not keep up the market price of the shares, and collapsed only three months later. No exact particulars as to the proportion of shares repurchased by the company are available, though it is alleged that it amounted to 25 per cent. of the capital. It was partly the conservatism of the French business world, and partly no doubt the attitude of the Courts in regarding such transactions as illegal and void, that prevented the spread of the abuse.

In Great Britain this practice was never widespread, although occasionally cases were found in which a company repurchased even more than 25 per cent. of its own stock, as in that of J. Schofield and Sons, Ltd.[1]

In Germany operations by companies to control the market in their own stock were popular, especially in the case of banks. During the slump which followed the collapse of the American Stock Exchanges in 1929 the leading German banks, with only one exception, acquired their own shares to an extent hitherto quite unknown. The Barmer Bankverein acquired 63·9 per cent. of its own stock; other leading German banks a percentage varying from about 50 to 60 per cent., and even the Deutsche Bank Diskonto Gesellschaft purchased 36·8 per cent. of its capital of 285 million marks. All these banks were near to bankruptcy, which was averted only by Government intervention.

The movement spread to industrial companies also; several large concerns actually went bankrupt, and even the largest single industrial unit, I. G.-Farben (dye trust) repurchased 114 million nominal of its shares, i.e. 10 per cent. of its whole capital of 1100 million marks, of which, however, nearly a quarter in par value, 260 million marks, were *Vorrats-Aktien* at the company's disposal and not in the hands of the public. Similar occurrences took place in the U.S.A. after the slump of 1929, though not to such a grotesque extent.

Business circles, especially in earlier times, saw nothing wrong in such operations. It was argued, and is even to-day, that every corporation should see to the marketing of its own stock, at least to the extent of stabilising its current market price. It was stressed that it is not in any company's interest for its shares to be the subject of wild speculation and the consequent excessive fluctuations of market prices.

[1] See Trevor *v.* Whitworth (1887), 12 App. Cas. 409.

In industrial enterprises such speculative movements may lead to extensive changes in the ownership of shares. The small investor is as a rule frightened by depressions in the price of his securities, and will sell in time of slump regardless of the intrinsic value and future prospects of his shares. The speculator who has bought shares on margin, i.e. to a large extent with borrowed money, is even compelled to sell if the price fall affects the margin and he is unable to meet it. In the U.S.A. the grandiose campaigns of famous bear speculators, such as Jay Gould, in railway shares and in the shares of Western Union will be remembered. The typical course of such campaigns is as follows: large blocks of shares are sold short, and subsequently rumours are spread as to the future prospects of the corporation. The irritated public begins to sell, and the fall in prices is increased by successive short sellings, until at last the price is reduced to a level at which it is worth while for the campaigner to buy not only enough to cover the margin of his sales, but in some cases a substantial block of shares also, and thereby acquire control of the corporation. The possibility of such operations is undoubtedly a great evil, but experience shows that to allow a corporation to purchase and resell its own shares is not the right way to counter such speculations and may lead to consequences which can bring ruin on the corporation. The causes of this are obvious when a corporation begins to operate in its own shares; it is very difficult to come to a halt if prices get out of control. The directors convert more and more of the company's funds to purchase shares or to give advances secured by the shares as collateral. The real business is neglected and starved of funds, profits diminish, and in some cases the corporation even incurs debts in order to support the market. The financial basis of the enterprise is shaken and eventual collapse cannot be averted.

The dangers of such manipulations were appreciated only gradually, and legislative steps to counter them taken, as will presently be shown. In the meantime new varieties of technique came into use aimed at concealing these transactions which were frowned upon by the public and under some legislations by the law also. One of these was for the company not to purchase its own stock but to give financial assistance to those who did so. It has often been urged that there can be no objection to such loans if the borrowers are solvent. The trouble is, however, that the management are actually too anxious to further such transactions and are inclined to neglect careful scrutiny both with regard to personal solvency and to collateral other than the purchased shares themselves. It therefore often happened that at the ensuing collapse there was no security, or only a negligible security, for such advances.

With the evolution of the group systems another device was found, namely that not the corporation itself, but one or more of its subsidiaries, purchased the shares or gave financial assistance for the purchase by way of loans. This practice was fairly widespread in Europe, and during the hearings before the Commission of the U.S.A. Senate it was revealed that one of the leading banks, the National City Bank of New York, had indulged in such transactions through the National City Company, whose stockholders were identical with those of the National City Bank itself, and that moreover by special arrangement the whole capital of the National City Company was held by the Bank in trust for the stockholders. The aim of the scheme was to keep the price of National City Bank stock in line with other bank stocks, and it is on record that a large block of stock was sold short and the necessary shares borrowed from the president of the bank. The tragic consequences of such manipulation of the bank's own stock did not fail to appear.

The attitude of the law towards repurchase by a company of its own stock varies. In England the question was for a long time disputed, and was discussed mainly from the point of view of *ultra vires*.

There were decisions holding that such purchases are admissible if authorised by the memorandum of association, while others held that such purchases may be incidental to the purpose of the company and therefore *intra vires*, although not expressly authorised by the memorandum. The House of Lords, however,[1] held that a company's purchase of its own stock is void and *ultra vires* whether the memorandum of association gives such power to the board of directors or not, and since then this has been the law. The *ratio decidendi* was mainly that the Companies Act prohibited repayment of capital to shareholders save in the case of a reduction of capital in legal form. It was, however, said by Lord Watson that a company cannot be a member of itself, and therefore such an acquisition of shares would be void on this ground. Lord Herschell said that such a purchase

[1] Trevor *v.* Whitworth (1887), *supra*.

would be either a trafficking in a company's own shares, which is absolutely forbidden, or a reduction of capital, which could be effected only by special resolution and with the sanction of the Court.

This judgment was followed in British and American Trustee and Finance Corporation *v.* Couper.[1] In Kirby *v.* Wilkins [2] it was held that shares surrendered without repayment could be held in trust for the company. This decision is remarkable in two directions: it was held that a trustee could hold surrendered shares in trust for the company without the necessity of cancellation and reduction of the capital, in order to use them *per accidens* as treasury stock for sale. Secondly, it was held that a provision of the agreement by which the trustee had to exercise the vote according to the instructions of the company was valid.[3] The question whether such shares held in trust for a company carry dividends was not under discussion.

It was held in Investment Trust Corporation Ltd. *v.* Singapore Traction Company Ltd.,[4] that it is not *ultra vires* for a company to make payment to a shareholder for the cancellation of the special privileges attached to his shares if such payment is for the benefit of the company.

Until the Act of 1929 there were no express provisions with regard to loans on the security of a company's own shares: the question was disputed. The right view was against the validity of such loans.[5]

Eventually sec. 45 of the 1929 Act declared it unlawful for a company to give financial assistance for the purpose of a purchase of any shares of the company made or to be made by any person. This extends to any indirect assistance, and includes the granting of a loan, the giving of a guarantee, the provision of a security, or any other means leading to the same result. This rule, however, is qualified by three exceptions:

(1) A company whose ordinary business is *inter alia* lending of money is allowed to lend money for the purchase of its own shares in the ordinary course of business.

(2) A company may provide for a scheme to acquire by trustees fully paid shares in the company to be held by or for the benefit of employees of the company, and may make loans for this purpose.

[1] (1894), A.C. 399. [2] (1929), 2 Ch. 444. [3] *Per* Romer, J., p. 453.
[4] (1935), Ch. 615. [5] Rex *v.* Lorang (1930), 22 Cr. App. Rep. 167.

(3) A company may grant loans to persons *bona fide* in its own employment to enable them to purchase fully paid shares in the company to be held by themselves by way of beneficial ownership.

A scheme of the kind mentioned under (2) may include directors holding salaried employment or office in the company, whereas in the absence of such a scheme loans to directors or even to salaried executives for such purposes are prohibited.

The aggregate amount of the loans granted to employees is to be shown as a separate item in the company's balance sheet, whereas the loans granted by a bank or financial company on the security of the company's own shares are not to be so shown.

The Act does not provide any civil consequences for violations of sec. 45; the right view seems to be that loans granted in violation of this section shall be payable to the company at any time, and furthermore that directors or other officers taking part in such transactions shall be liable to the company for any loss. In case of violation the company and any directors or officers taking part in prohibited transactions are liable to a fine not exceeding £100 (sec. 45 (3)). The prohibition has been extended by the Act of 1947 (sec. 73) to subsidiary companies, otherwise the provisions are the same (sec. 54 of Act of 1948).

In the U.S.A. conflicting views are held. Some of the Courts adhere to the view formerly held in England that a corporation has power to purchase its own stock only if such power is expressly conferred on it by statute or by its charter. This rule is sometimes applied even in cases where the purchase was made with the intention of withdrawing the stock after purchase. The reasons given for the rule are that purchase by a corporation of its own shares is foreign to the ends for which the corporation was created and such purchase is a diversion of its funds for an unauthorised purpose. The so-called trust fund doctrine is also quoted sometimes, and it is stressed that such a purchase might affect the position of creditors. On the other hand the purchase of stock with the intention of withdrawing and cancelling it would be a contravention of the rules provided for the reduction of the capital.[1] In most jurisdictions, however, this rule is not recognised, and it is held that unless prohibited by statute or charter a corporation has power to purchase its own stock; but national

[1] Cf. Fletcher 2647; Ballantine 256*a*–9; Nussbaum 35 Col. L.R., pp. 971–1006.

banks are expressly prohibited from purchasing or holding their own stock, except when the transaction is necessary to prevent the loss of a debt previously contracted in good faith.[1] The same rule has been enacted by many States in respect of State banks, trust companies and similar corporations.

Only a few State legislations prohibit a company from purchasing its own shares in general, e.g. Wyoming [2] and Kentucky,[3] in the latter case with certain exceptions, and nowadays most statutes allow the purchase by companies of their own shares with more or less qualification provided there is no express limitation or prohibition in the charter.

The essence of the regulation contained in many statutes is that a company's purchases of its own stock are valid if they are made for legitimate purposes and in good faith, not in overvaluation, there being a surplus, if the company's capital is not impaired or at least if it is not insolvent, and the position of the creditors is not affected. But there are many differences in detail. Certain statutes are fairly liberal. Thus Delaware [4] makes only the condition that the use of corporate funds shall not cause any impairment of the capital stock. Minnesota on the other hand [5] permits purchase only out of earned and paid-in surplus, and if there are preference shares, the paid-in surplus may be used only for the repurchase or redemption of these. It is further provided that in order to ascertain whether a surplus exists, unrealised appreciation of assets shall not be counted, except for a readily ascertainable market value of securities other than those issued by the corporation itself.

The law of Connecticut allows such purchases only if made to prevent losses, or if the purchase is approved by the holders of 75 per cent. of the shares at a meeting called for this purpose.[6]

The statute of New Jersey provides no special regulation; the majority rule is followed.

In New York, sec. 664 of the Penal law [7] forbids the purchase by a company of its own stock, except out of surplus.

The law of California contains a detailed regulation which reflects in many respects the present impact of the majority rule. It admits purchase out of earned surplus, and further, subject to

[1] Rev. Stat. sec. 5201, 12; U.S.C.A. sec. 83.
[2] Rev. Stat. (1931), c. 28, §§ 28–122. [3] (1942), § 271-120.
[4] Rev. Code (1935), c. 65, § 19. [5] B.C.A. 21, g. ss. 7492, § 21, VI.
[6] Conn. Gen. Stat. (1930), § 3423.
[7] Consol. Laws (1909), c. 60, as amended by L. 1941 ch. 838.

certain limitations, out of paid-in surplus. Where redemption is provided for by the articles, redemption or repurchase is allowed at a price not exceeding the redemption price, except where there is reasonable ground to believe that the corporation is unable, or by the purchase or redemption will be rendered unable, to satisfy its liabilities or to meet the lowest liquidation preferences of outstanding shares of at least equal priority. Apart from such transactions the purchase is allowed if made in the collection or compromise in good faith of a debt, claim or controversy with any shareholder, or to satisfy the claim of a dissenting shareholder entitled under the law to a repurchase, from an employee other than an officer or director under a repurchase agreement, or for the elimination of fractional shares.[1]

Under the statutes and the majority rule respectively the board generally has power to authorise or ratify the corporation's purchases of its own stock, and a resolution in general meeting is required only exceptionally. Within the limits mentioned repurchase agreements are held enforceable unless the corporation is insolvent at the time of the action.[2]

The taking of stock as collateral for or in discharge of a debt due to the corporation is generally allowed, and the same holds where the acquisition is made pursuant to a compromise.[3] It must, however, be remembered that National banks are expressly prohibited from making loans on the security of their own shares unless the taking of the stock as security is necessary to prevent a loss on a loan previously made in good faith.

It is usual for agreements with employees to provide that they must resell and the corporation must purchase the stock held by them when they leave the corporation: such agreements are generally upheld.

Whether a purchase contrary to law is void or merely voidable is disputed. In jurisdictions where it is held to be voidable, the corporation may or may not sue for its invalidation, though it may use the voidability as a defence against the enforcement of an executory contract. The other party has no defence against an action for the purchase price. Thus when a National bank sold its repurchased stock the vendee was held to be liable for the purchase price.[4]

Shareholders and creditors have an action when their rights

[1] Civil Code (1937), §§ 341–2. [2] Fletcher 2849.
[3] Fletcher 2855–7. [4] Cf. Ballantine, 1st ed., p. 229.

are impaired by the purchase; whether persons who became creditors after the purchase have such an action is disputed.

In the case of National banks the Government of the U.S.A. has the right to attack the transaction.

As to the effects of a valid purchase, it is to be noted that in no case has the corporation a vote in respect of repurchased stock. Whether in case of a purchase made for retirement and cancellation of shares the purchase itself is a reduction of capital is disputed.[1]

It is held that the absence of good faith, i.e. the presence of fraud, is to be proved by him who attacks the transaction. As to the presence of surplus, the company as defendant or the directors—as the case may be—will be able to refer to the book values, and the books will certainly show a surplus if such transactions have occurred. The plaintiff attacking the transaction will hardly—if ever—be able to show that there was no surplus and that the valuations were exaggerated. The case is similar with insolvency: it will hardly be possible to show that the company did not meet its mature obligations. Furthermore in States where insolvency means material insolvency, i.e. excess of debts over assets, the question will be decided on book values.

Some of the cases are highly illustrative. In Copper Belle Mining Corporation *v.* Costello,[2] the corporation purchased a block of shares from one of the directors. Part of the price was paid out of borrowed money; for the remainder the corporation gave notes. The following year the corporation became bankrupt, and it was held that the transaction was valid, and the director could assert his claim for the remainder as a creditor because it was not proved that he had knowledge of the financial position of the corporation. In another case,[3] the corporation purchased shares from its general manager, who was leaving. The company was not able to pay the purchase price, but there was a surplus in the books, and an action by a preference shareholder was dismissed. In Wolff *v.* Heidritter Company[4] the company purchased 150 of its own shares for $40,000 by instalments, and after having paid $13,500 became bankrupt. The seller was allowed as creditor for the remaining $26,500 and interest. In Thompson *v.* Shepherd,[5] the company purchased

[1] Fletcher 2860, n. 38–9.
[2] (1908), 12 Ariz. 334.
[3] Barrett *v.* Webster Lumber Company (1931), 275 Mass. 302.
[4] (1932), 112 N.J. Eq. 34.
[5] (1932), 203 N.C. 310.

the majority of its own shares in 1925 and became bankrupt in 1929. An action by the receiver attacking the transaction was dismissed.

It is to be noted that not only the absence of good faith but also the presence of surplus and solvency are to be determined according to the state of affairs at the time when the contract was made. Later developments do not affect the validity of the contract, and, as appears from the cases quoted, the Courts do not go deeply into the question whether a subsequent insolvency was due to later events or must have been present or impending, though not yet apparent from the company's books.

Even where the minority rule is adopted, it is subject to several qualifications. Firstly, stock may be taken in payment of debts; this qualification is very dangerous, for, in order to comply with it, a corporation may grant loans on collateral other than its own stock but insufficient to cover the debt, and subsequently accept its own shares in payment. Secondly, it is held that shares could be accepted under the terms of a compromise. There is a third qualification which may do and has in fact done much damage. It is held that in connection with a sale of stock a clause for repurchase or the granting of an option to the purchaser may be inserted in the agreement. A conspicuous example of such an agreement is found in Grace Security Company *v.* Roberts.[1] Shares were sold by the corporation in September 1927 at the price of $44·25 with an option to the purchaser to resell the shares at his choice. After the crash of 1929, when the price fell to $8 bid, $15 asked, the purchaser exercised the option, which was upheld.

The events of the boom which ended in the collapse of 1929 drew public attention to the abuses relating to dealings of corporations in their own stock especially through their affiliated or associated companies. The New Deal legislation, however, refrained from a fundamental regulation; artificial booms and slumps only were made unlawful by the Act of 1934 (sec. 9 (*a*) (2)).[2] Only transactions of considerable volume, therefore, were affected by this provision. Purchases and sales which by their amount were not able to influence the current market prices in either direction were not *per se* unlawful. It is true that under sec. 9 (*a*) (6) the Security and Exchange Commission may issue prescriptions against pegging, and such prescriptions may affect

[1] (1932), 158 Va. 792. [2] 48 Stat. 887.

even purchases of smaller amount; in fact, however, no such rulings were issued. On the other hand the Federal Trade Commission, at that time entrusted with the administration of the Securities Act of 1933, required in 1934 the registration of treasury stock with the Commission.

Much more effective steps were taken by the New York Stock Exchange in December 1933. Companies whose securities were subsequently listed were put under obligation to report any transaction in treasury stock to the Stock Exchange and also to agree that further trading in treasury stock should be dependent on a permit from the Stock Exchange Authorities, and many companies voluntarily complied with this ruling. Since under the 1934 Act the companies had to register their securities, the ruling could be extended, and up to the end of 1935 about 75 per cent. of companies had complied with it. It seems that the other stock exchanges did not follow the example given by the New York Stock Exchange, and therefore a not unimportant part of corporations retained the former position.

In France neither the *Code de Commerce* nor the law of 1867 and its amendments contain any express prohibition of purchases by companies of their own shares. Nevertheless the Courts hold them void on general principles if they are made out of capital.[1] Not only the creditors but even the company itself has an action for nullity.[2] On the other hand it is held that a company may act as agent (on commission) in contracts for the purchase of its own shares and even make loans with these shares as security.

The German Commercial Code of 1861 provided no special rules against transactions by companies in their own shares. Abuses observed in the sixties led to a provision being inserted (art. 215 (3)) in the Code by the law of 1870 which declared that a company must not acquire its own shares. This was construed to mean that such purchases were void, but it was held that repurchase agreements made in connection with subscriptions are valid, and that the making of advances on the security of such shares is not prohibited. On the other hand it was generally held that a company may not purchase its own shares on the charge or account of a third party. This latter extension of the rule was regarded as oppressive and unjustified, and the law in this respect was amended in 1884. The amendment, however, went further: by the new subsection (*d*) of art. 215 it was enacted that a

[1] Cf. the decisions quoted by Pic 1157.

[2] Pic 1158.

company ought not to (*soll nicht*) purchase its own shares in the course of its business. This was held to have the effect that the violation of this rule involves the liability of the members of the boards of supervision and management, as expressly provided in arts. 226 and 241, but the validity of the transaction is not affected. It was only the purchase of so-called interim shares which was prohibited absolutely with the consequence that it was void.

It has further been enacted that a company may purchase its own shares for the account of a third party as an agent on commission. In the case of interim shares, however, even such transactions as these were declared invalid, even though made on the instructions of a third party, e.g. a customer of a bank. On the other hand the prohibition was extended to the taking of shares as collateral for loans; but this did not exclude the possibility of purchasing shares of the company itself on behalf of a customer on margin. Such transactions were well known to German banks. It was held under the new law that shares could be acquired by way of gift, attached by way of executive proceedings, and purchased on ensuing public sales. It is remarkable that the most prominent commentator on the law, Ring, assumes that none of these restrictions apply to dealings in shares through connected companies: an interesting prediction of the events of a later period.

The revised Commercial Code of 1897 accepted the provisions of the law of 1884, extending the prohibition of the acquisition of interim shares to shares not fully paid up (§ 226). The position therefore was that the absolute prohibition with its consequence of voidness was maintained in respect of interim and any other not fully paid up shares, whereas for fully paid shares the only consequence was that the members of the boards of management and supervision were liable for any damage caused by the violation of the said provision (§§ 241 (3) and 249).

It is alleged that up to 1929 German companies did not purchase their own shares, nor advance money on their security to any considerable extent. Banks, however, followed the practice of controlling the market in their own shares and concentrating dealings in them at their own counters or those of their affiliates. Especially did they transact business for the account of their customers on "commission", contracting in their own name but at the charge of their principals. From 1884 this was expressly allowed, and it was usual to advance a more or less substantial part of the purchase price on the security of the shares.

As already mentioned, the crisis of 1929 induced the German banks to purchase their own shares to an extent hitherto unknown. They aimed at stabilising market prices, but without result; the situation went from bad to worse, quotations constantly declined, and the whole position of most of the leading German banks became untenable. In one case a Court of first instance declared void the resolution of a general meeting authorising a company's board of management to purchase its own shares. This decision met with unfavourable criticism, but it became obvious that the situation had to be regulated. This was done by an emergency decree issued in October 1931, providing that any company might purchase its own shares, even interim shares and those not fully paid up, if and when such purchase was necessary to avert substantial disadvantage. The amount purchased was not to exceed ten per cent. of the share capital, or such smaller fraction as the Government should prescribe. What circumstances would justify purchase was not defined in detail. Commentators on this decree were of opinion that events endangering the existence of the corporation were sufficient reason for such transactions. Such circumstances must really exist, and error in judgment does not excuse the management. In normal circumstances the prohibition stands, and companies therefore remained prohibited from controlling dealings in their own shares.

Violation of this rule, however, was not to impair the validity of purchases in excess of the ten per cent. or in absence of an emergency; the only consequence was that managers and members of the board of supervision were to be liable. Apart from cases of emergency the provisions of the Code have been maintained and to some extent widened. It has further been enacted that fully paid shares may be acquired up to ten per cent. of the share capital even in the absence of any emergency, provided the purchase is made for the purpose of cancellation and that the shares purchased are actually cancelled within six months after their acquisition.

In view of the frequent use of subsidiaries for such transactions the prohibition was extended to purchases and to loans on the security of shares to controlled ("dominated") companies, and vice versa. It was enacted that the acquisition of shares and financial assistance for such acquisition is to be deemed to have been made by the company itself if made by a third party on the company's account, the prohibition extending also to price guarantees.

The dispute relating to dividends and voting rights on repurchased shares was settled in the negative. Apart from the acquisition of interim and not fully paid up shares the act of acquisition and the advancing of money on the security of shares was declared not to be void.

The provisions of the decree did not prevent the continuance of the practice. The Reich Government was compelled to give assistance to banks by acquiring large blocks of stock which they had already purchased. This was subsequently legalised in 1936, and the absorption of these stocks was gradually effected in the subsequent years.

The law of 1937 on the whole maintained the provisions of the decree. Significantly, however, the Government was empowered to allow an increase of the ratio of ten per cent. at its discretion. Furthermore, the six months' term for the cancellation of shares acquired apart from emergency cases was dropped. On the other hand it was provided that the acquisition of shares for the purpose of cancellation may be made at any time pursuant to a previous resolution in general meeting and in compliance with the rules governing reduction of capital. Otherwise the law introduced minor corrections, among which it may be noted that although the violation of the prohibitive rule does not invalidate the transfer of the property in the shares, nevertheless an action based on the contract, e.g. for payment of the purchase price, cannot be maintained (§ 65).

Of the legislations following the French model, both the Belgian (art. 134) and the Italian (art. 144) Codes contain express prohibitions, the Belgian legislation also providing penalties for violation. The Hungarian Code of Commerce (§ 161) follows the Belgian rule.

The Swiss Law of Obligations as early as 1911 prohibited the acquisition by a company of its own shares. The provisions of sec. 628 were amended in 1936 and re-enacted by sec. 659 of the new law. These provisions are fairly complete: acquisition by a company of its own shares and lending on them as security is in principle prohibited. Such acquisitions, however, are allowed: (1) if the shares are acquired for cancellation on the basis of a resolution in general meeting for the reduction of capital, in which case they are to be cancelled immediately; (2) where the company acquires them for the satisfaction of debts due to it, other than debts arising from subscriptions to shares; (3) in connection with mergers or the acquisition of business units as a whole with their assets and liabilities; (4) when the acquisition or lending is connected with a kind of business authorised by the articles—in other words banks were authorised to acquire shares and lend money on their security; (5) members of the management, directors or employees of the company may deposit shares with it as security for the performance of their duties. In all these cases the company has to disclose such purchases and investments in its annual reports. The shares are to be resold as soon as possible, and they carry no vote.

During the last 15 years no instances of considerable dealings of corporations in their own stocks have been recorded in the U.S.A.

In Great Britain they never attained similar dimensions, and the only direction in which a strengthening of the law was found necessary was to extend the prohibition to transactions through subsidiaries and thus to fill a gap. Sec. 73 of the Companies Act, 1947 (now sec. 54 of the Act of 1948) provides that the provisions of sec. 45 of the Act of 1929 prohibiting financial assistance for the purchase of a company's own shares shall apply to shares in a company's holding company, and further that they shall apply to subscriptions for shares in a company or its holding company, as they apply to a purchase of such shares.

After this survey of the most important legal enactments we may consider the question from the point of future legislation. It is obvious that business circles, especially the managements of corporations, insist on the necessity of controlling the market in the corporation's own shares. On the other hand it is equally obvious that legislation allowing a company to purchase its own stock is dangerous in spite of manifold guarantees and restrictions. A quantitative limitation such as was adopted in Germany and earlier in Denmark may mean that any company can purchase yearly up to ten per cent. of its ever-outstanding capital.

One method of regulation would be to restrict a corporation's power to make such purchases to cases of emergency. This was done in Germany and maintained by the law of 1937. But it is difficult to say what would constitute such an emergency. It has been said that sudden falls in market prices of the shares may have such an effect upon the credit of the company as to lead to financial collapse, even though the corporation were quite sound. Especially is this said of banks, with their large volume of deposits mostly on call, payment of which may be requested at any time. This may be true to a certain extent, but it is equally true that if the fall in price is due to the general trend of the market, purchases made by the corporation will not reverse this trend, unless they amount to such a portion of the share capital as would impair the liquidity of the bank. This is not a question of pure imagination or hypothesis, but a fact that has been observed in times of slump in many countries. Furthermore, purchases by the corporation are apt to create an artificial price level and will induce shareholders to sell, since their other investments show more substantial losses. It may also provoke bear speculations, i.e. speculative short selling, and so increase the inducement to further purchases by the company concerned.

Beside these general considerations the possibility of abuse cannot be overlooked. It has been observed that purchases of their own stock by corporations are frequently made at levels quite disproportionate to the current prices. On the other hand it is very easy to allege an emergency if there are other reasons for purchase, such as to favour shareholders in close relations with the directors, or to buy out shareholders who importune or annoy the board, e.g. by questions or by demands for the inspection of books and records. All these objections are based upon facts frequently observed in many countries.

It has been suggested, and sometimes even enacted, that a corporation should be able to use its surplus, in other words its free reserves, for such purchases. We are not concerned here with purchases for the systematic redemption of shares, a problem which will be examined in § 91. Apart from such redemptions the admission of purchases up to the amount of the surplus is open to serious objection. A surplus or reserve is either a cushion for possible losses, or an amount set aside for improvements and extensions of the company's business or for later distribution. None of these purposes is served if it is used for investment by the company in its own shares. Especially is this true in respect of a paid-in surplus from share premiums or other reserves not arising from undistributed profits. We must therefore conclude that the best and simplest course is to prohibit companies from purchasing their own shares on principle without any qualification or exception.

This is not meant to exclude purchases for reduction of capital. Such purchases, however, should be subject to the special regulations and requirements provided for capital reductions (see § 91). Nor need we concern ourselves with such extraordinary cases as gifts and bequests by shareholders, i.e. the surrender of shares without payment or the acquisition of shares in consequence of amalgamations or purchase of other businesses. In all these cases, however, the only way to exclude the possibility of abuse and danger to the corporation is to require the immediate cancellation of such shares. The need for control of the market should be met by majority shareholders who enjoy the direct and indirect advantages of the welfare of the corporation and should therefore bear risks and endure sacrifices for the sake of its preservation.

It is further obvious that such a prohibition would be futile if it did not extend to financial assistance by way of loans on the security of shares. The exception, allowed by a number of legislations and frequently advocated, that banks should be exempt and should therefore be authorised to grant such loans in the usual course of business, is not acceptable. At first sight there seems no reason why a bank or financial company should not have power to assist its customers by making loans for the purchase of its own shares. It is often said that it would be both awkward and pointless to compel customers to go to other banks if they should wish to purchase shares on margin or to borrow on the security of such shares. But if the position is scrutinised more closely, it appears that the position of the company itself is quite different from that of another bank. A creditor who is not directly interested in the company will be governed by merely objective financial considerations in requesting repayment and eventually in selling the shares. A corporation, however, which has lent money for purchases on margin or on the security of its own shares will necessarily be influenced by considerations of the price level, and therefore—as experience has shown—will neglect to take the necessary steps to liquidate the investment even though that would be advisable on the basis of an objective judgment. Similarly, it is not advisable to allow a corporation to accept its own stock as collateral in case of advances. Even if the shares are not the sole securities, such acceptance is dangerous. The only exception should be for the corporation to be entitled to attach its own shares in the course of executive proceedings against a debtor in default. In such a case it should be obliged to dispose of them by public sale and only if they cannot be sold should it be allowed to purchase them on account of the debt. The corporation should then be compelled to resell the shares within a short period, say, six months, as is provided by U.S.A. legislations for National banks, or if such sale is not feasible or advisable, to take adequate steps to reduce the capital by cancelling the shares within a reasonable time.

Financial assistance to employees of the company other than directors is motivated by considerations which lie outside corporation law or finance. Such measures are due to the desire to operate schemes enabling employees to become shareholders on easy terms and to tie them as interested parties to the welfare of the enterprise. The grant of exemptions for such schemes may be justifiable provided that directors and such officers as are virtually equal to directors by their occupation of managerial positions are excluded. Secondly it would be advisable to limit the extent of such investments to a definite fraction of the capital, say, five per cent. It can hardly be assumed that such a limitation would be detrimental to the scheme; in the cases actually observed employees' shareholdings did not reach such limits; especially in the case of large corporations, they fell far below such a percentage. On the other hand the limitation would prevent any danger to the corporation.

So long as purchases by companies of their own stock are not prohibited the question arises how the company should deal with the shares purchased. Should they be retained as treasury stock, and should the directors be empowered to retain or sell them at their discretion and according to market conditions? This was generally the practice, and in most cases the board had a free hand for resale. The accumulation of treasury stock in the company's portfolio is a constant danger to the shareholders; the market price will always be influenced by the existence of unabsorbed treasury stock, and it may also be detrimental to the company, since the directors cannot devote the funds to current business. If therefore purchases of a company's own stock are allowed at all and its cancellation is not required, the only reasonable provision would be to require its sale immediately or within a reasonable time, say, six months at most.

As to accounting, a widespread practice is to include such shares as an item among the securities owned by the company. This is misleading, and the least requirement should be that they be shown in the balance sheet as a separate item. The general rule as to valuation should be applied, namely, that the shares in question should be shown at cost price or at the market price at the end of the financial year, whichever is the lower. It has frequently happened that companies have shown at par shares they have purchased at a discount, thus seeking to improve their financial status. This is inadmissible. Similarly it would be misleading to deduct the shares retained in the portfolio from the capital.

A closely connected question is, how the corporation is to deal with profits arising from the repurchase and resale of such shares. Generally such profits are looked upon and dealt with as current profits, but such a policy is surely not sound. Such price differences should be placed to a special reserve and not be distributable as dividends.

It is unnecessary to go into detail in order to show that transactions by subsidiary companies in shares of the parent company should be treated on a like basis (see § 92). Similarly, it goes without saying that dividends should not be paid and accounted for on shares in portfolio, and that the vote attached to them should be suspended for so long as the shares are owned by the corporation or a subsidiary, or even by a trustee.

We have lastly to consider the consequences of violation. So long and in so far as the contract of sale is executory, the interest of the company surely demands that it should be regarded as void, and therefore that the seller should not have an action for the purchase price or its remainder against the company. If the contract were regarded as merely voidable, the company's position might be impaired, since it is hardly to be supposed, even if it could be maintained from the standpoint of law, that the directors who made the contract in violation of the rules would subsequently attack the transaction. In respect of completed transactions it should depend upon whether the transaction was made directly; if not, a *bona fide* vendor should not be open to attack from the side of the corporation, its shareholders or creditors. Knowledge, actual or constructive, should involve making the contract equal to a direct contract with the company.

The right to attack the transaction should be subject only to the normal term of limitation, since in most cases the consequences of abuse come to light only after a considerable time.

In accordance with the general plan of this work, the penal side of legal guarantees against abuses is not considered.

67. The General Meeting. Preliminary Remarks

The carrying on of a business requires constant day-by-day attention, the settlement of a general policy. and from time to time the making of decisions on major matters. In the case of a small business all this can be seen to by the owners themselves without difficulty or formality. This is not so in the case of larger units, even when they are not organised on corporate lines. Since from its beginnings the corporate form was intended specially for such larger units, methods suited to the needs of individual cases were laid down in their charters, and at a later stage the various Companies Acts provided rules for the administration of company affairs. Their provisions gradually became, and are still becoming, more and more detailed.

The simplest form of such a legislative framework requires that in every company one or more persons shall be appointed or delegated by the members as a whole to manage day-to-day business, to enter into contracts and see to their performance, such persons being usually called directors, while decisions of major importance shall be made by the members in meetings which are similarly regulated by the law.

Some legislations make a distinction between the settlement of policy and its execution and require a board of directors in addition to the managers. In some countries this division of function is carried so far that the managers are prohibited from being directors, whereas under other legal systems the same persons may perform both functions. The supervision of the management and the checking of the accounts is sometimes entrusted to a special board or committee to be elected in general meeting generally from among the ranks of the members, whereas under other legislations this task is entrusted to experts in accountancy, acting as auditors.

Such a framework is on the whole more suitable to units of some size. But legislations do not generally take the size of the individual unit into consideration, and it is only when the incorporators have a choice between several types of corporate existence that some, though not all, legislations lay down simpler and less exacting requirements.

We will first deal with the general meeting, bearing it in mind that, owing to the interdependence of functions, some repetition will be inevitable when we examine the powers and duties of the board.

It has always been a ruling principle of every *societas* and partnership that, unless otherwise stipulated in the formative contract, decisions can be made only by unanimous consent. In the case of corporations, however, it has been recognised from early times that majority rule must prevail, in order to secure a smooth and uninterrupted corporate life. Questions which could not be decided by majority vote were always exceptional, and the tendency is to extend the rule of the majority, and to narrow the field reserved for the volition of individual members.

In order to limit and counterbalance the power of the majority, specific quorums or majorities are required for certain major decisions, and to-day legal remedies exist for the protection of minorities. On the other hand every company law attempts to provide adequate guarantees to ensure that shareholders shall have sufficient information about matters that come up for decision and opportunity to discuss them before voting on a resolution.

It is a generally accepted rule that shareholders may pass resolutions only in meetings duly convened and in compliance with the rules governing the procedure at such meetings. It is the directors' duty, on the other hand, to convene meetings from time to time, and if they fail to do so, there are rules enabling a minority of specified size to enforce such convocation.

It is important that general meetings should be attended, and desirable that they should be attended largely. Dispersal of share ownership, however, has resulted in a gradual decrease in attendance. Sometimes, of course, shareholders obtain sufficient information on corporate matters without attending meetings, from invitations and from circulated accounts and reports, so that they are in a position to decide whether it is worth their while to attend a meeting in person or not. Nevertheless their non-attendance is usually a sign of lack of interest, the deplorable result of which is that they increasingly lose control.

It is rightly said that in normal times shareholders, satisfied with receiving their dividends, take no further interest in the company's affairs, the meetings are over without any ado in a couple of minutes, and it is only when a company gets into difficulties that meetings are well attended and stormy. Both legal and other remedies have been used to combat this indifference.

Of legal remedies we need mention only the quorum, i.e. the minimum of attendance required sometimes by law, or more generally by the articles, and also the possibility of attending and voting at meetings by proxy. In certain countries again, e.g. in France, some companies have offered a fee or premium for attendance which, small as it was per share, nevertheless operated as an inducement. On the other hand many managements by no means dislike the present disinclination of shareholders to take an interest in the activities of their companies, since in consequence they are able to dominate them even through small or negligible holdings.

68. The Annual General Meeting

The Companies Act of 1929 provided that, apart from the statutory meeting to be held before the commencement of business, every company must hold a general meeting at least once in every calendar year, and not later than 15 months after the last preceding meeting (sec. 112 (1)). In case of default the Court may, on the application of any shareholder, call or direct the calling of such a meeting; besides this the company and every director or manager who is knowingly a party to the default is liable to a fine not exceeding £50 (sec. 112 (2)).

The purpose of this annual meeting is to consider the accounts and reports presented by the board of directors, and to resolve upon their proposals as to the distribution of profits and the declaration of dividends. This meeting is usually called the annual or ordinary general meeting. The Companies Act, 1947, introduced several amendments which have now been inserted into the Companies Act of 1948. The meeting in question shall be held as the "annual general meeting" of the company, and it is to be specified to be such in the notice convening it; it is made clear that this meeting is additional to any other held during the year. The rule that not more than 15 months shall elapse between two consecutive annual general meetings is maintained, but so long as a company holds its first annual general meeting within 18 months of its incorporation, it need not hold one in the year of its incorporation or the year following (sec. 1 (1); now sec. 131 (1) of the Act of 1948).

The power to call or to direct the calling of an annual general meeting in case of default is to be exercised in future by the Board of Trade. This Board is also given power to give such ancillary or consequential directions as it thinks expedient, including directions modifying or supplementing the operation of the company's articles in relation to the calling, holding and conduct of the meeting (sec. 131 (2) of the Act of 1948).

A meeting held pursuant to the direction of the Board of Trade is to be deemed to be an annual general meeting of the company, but the Board of Trade may direct otherwise. If the meeting is not held in the year in which the default occurred, it shall not be treated as the annual general meeting of the year in which it is held, though the company in general meeting may resolve otherwise. If this be done the company must forward a copy of the resolution to the Registrar of Companies within 15 days. Lastly, a fine up to £50 is to be imposed in case of non-compliance with any direction of the Board of Trade (sec. 131 (3)–(5)).

Every other meeting of a company is called an extraordinary meeting. Such meetings may be held whenever the directors choose to call them, in order to resolve upon matters which are reserved for the company in general meeting, and clause 49 of Table A provides that "the directors may whenever they think fit convene an Extraordinary General Meeting".

The holder or holders of not less than one-tenth of the paid-up capital having voting rights may also call for an extraordinary general meeting by depositing their written and signed requisition in one or more documents at the registered office of the company (sec. 132 of the Act of 1948). The articles may reduce the fraction provided for by the Act, but any provision for a higher one would be inoperative.

The requisition must state the object for which the meeting is to be called, and the directors must convene it within 21 days from the date of deposit of the requisition, whatever its objects. Should the directors not comply with the requisition, the requisitioners or any of them representing more than one-half of their voting rights may themselves convene a meeting, but not for an earlier date than three months after the expiration of the 21 days (sec. 132). Any reasonable expense occurred in consequence of the default is to be repaid to the requisitioners by the company, which must deduct any sum so paid from the fees and other remuneration due from the company to the directors in default (sec. 132 (5)).

If for any reason the calling of the meeting would be impossible the Court may convene the meeting on its own motion or on the application of any director or of any shareholder who would be entitled to vote at the meeting (sec. 135 (1)). We may, however, agree with Buckley (p. 272) that such cases must be rare.

In the U.S.A. the importance of general meetings is reduced owing to the power of the directors to declare dividends. Therefore there is no common law rule that corporations must hold general meetings annually, and it is left to the board of directors to call them whenever they see fit. Certain States, however, prescribe the annual holding of general meetings, and some even lay down in detail the time of such meetings. Thus the law of California [1] provides that an annual general meeting is to be held at 11 o'clock on the first Tuesday of April of each year, unless the by-laws provide another time. Under the statute of Massachusetts an annual meeting is obligatory, and it is to be held at the time fixed in the by-laws, or in any case within 90 days after the end of the financial year of the corporation.[2]

The necessity of electing directors, even in States whose statutes do not prescribe the holding of annual meetings, operates to make them essential from time to time; in practice meetings are called regularly.

The right of a specific fraction of stockholders to demand the calling of a general meeting is not held to be vested in them at common law, but many statutes contain such a provision. In some States stockholders holding ten per cent. or some other fraction of the total voting power are given such a right. Thus in Massachusetts [3] this right is made to depend on the holding of one-fifth of the voting power. Moreover, it is to be borne in mind that in view of the widespread practice of issuing non-voting shares, the right to convene a meeting without or against the wishes of the directors will rarely be exercisable.

Under the Continental legislations the power to resolve upon the accounts and the distribution of profits is reserved exclusively

[1] C.C. § 312, as amended by L. (1933), c. 533, § 20. [2] G.L. c. 156, § 28.
[3] G.L. c. 156, § 30, as amended by L. (1937), c. 533, § 21.

to the general meeting, and in view of this the holding of annual general meetings is prescribed everywhere. Even the German law of 1937, while excluding the matter of accounts from the competence of the general meeting where there is agreement between the boards of management and supervision, reserves to the meeting the power to decide on the distribution of profits within the limits proposed by the two boards and that of the release of the members of the two boards from their liability in respect of the last financial year; the law consequently maintains the compulsory holding of the annual meeting (§ 104).

The time of the annual meeting may be laid down in the articles; but the more modern laws limit this freedom. Thus the German law requires it to be held within five months following the end of the financial year (§ 104); the Swiss O.R. allows six months (699, 2).

Generally a minority of ten per cent. is entitled to demand the calling of a general meeting; the German Commercial Code of 1897 gave this right to a minority holding five per cent. of the share capital, and this is maintained in the law of 1937 (§ 106 (2)); the articles may provide for any smaller fraction. The remedy in case of default is an application to the Court.

Under certain legislations the Court may order the convocation of the meeting, as e.g. under the Swiss O.R. (699, 4), whereas by German law the Court's interference will consist in authorising the requisitioners to convene the meeting if neither of the boards has complied with their request. At the same time the Court may appoint a chairman for the meeting.

It is left to the meeting itself to decide whether its expenses shall be met by the company (§ 106 (4), (5)). It is hardly to be supposed that a majority opposed to the calling of the meeting would be disposed to bear this expense, and thus the provision amounts in practice to a denial of its payment out of the company's funds.

The French Company laws contain no express provisions for the convocation of general meetings at the request of members where the directors fail to comply with their duty. The position would be quite unsatisfactory did not the Courts take the view that in case of default they have the power to compel the board of directors to convene a meeting, or else to authorise the complainants to convene it themselves.[1]

[1] Pic 1283.

69. Notice, Time and Place of Meeting

An important matter regarding the general meeting is the notice by which it is convened. Such notice is always given, but there are differences in details of procedure.

It is held in Great Britain that in principle every shareholder is entitled to notice, the omission whereof invalidates the meeting and the resolutions carried at it.[1] But it has been held that holders of a class of shares precluded by the articles from voting are not entitled to notice.[2]

The notice is to be served on the members entitled to it, i.e. it must be in writing, and is to be communicated in the manner provided in Table A, except where the articles otherwise provide. Clause 131 of Table A requires the notice to be given personally or to be sent by post to the member's registered address, or if he has no registered address within the United Kingdom, to the address supplied by him for this purpose. When a notice is sent by post by a properly addressed and prepaid letter, it is deemed to have been effected at the expiration of 24 hours after posting (131). Accidental omission to give notice to a member or non-receipt of notice shall not invalidate the proceedings (clause 51).

Under the Act of 1929, in the case of an ordinary meeting, i.e. one where no special resolution is to be moved, seven days' notice was sufficient (sec. 115 (1) (*a*)) unless the articles provided otherwise; they seldom if ever required longer notice than this. In the case of a special resolution 21 days' notice was required, whether for an ordinary or an extraordinary meeting, and Table A (clause 44) provided that all business other than the sanctioning of dividends, the examination of the accounts and balance sheets, the receiving of the ordinary reports of the directors and auditors, the election of directors and other officers to replace those retiring by rotation, and the fixing of the auditors' remuneration should be treated as special business.

It became obvious that seven days' notice is too short to enable shareholders to attend a meeting in person or to make arrangements to appoint proxies of their own choice. Moreover, if shareholders are dissatisfied with the board, or have objections to raise to the accounts or to the dividends proposed, there is no time for them to communicate with each other and to organise

[1] Smyth *v.* Darley (1849), 2 H.L. cases 789.
[2] *Re* Mackenzie and Co. (1916), 2 Ch. 450.

joint action. This is one of the factors which strengthen the power of the board and tend to divest the shareholders of control. The Companies Act, 1947, and now sec. 133 of the Act of 1948, requires for the normal general meeting a notice of 21 days and for extraordinary meetings, unless called for a special resolution, 14 days. The notice must state the date and place of the meeting, and Table A (clause 50) requires the specification of place, day and hour.

The Act contains no provisions as to the place of meeting, nor is it usual for the articles to restrict the directors' discretion; it is for them to fix both time and place. Some companies are accustomed to hold their meetings at their registered office, but many larger ones, especially if their registered office is situated at a small place or at their works, hold them in some public hall in a large commercial centre, especially when a large attendance is expected. Cases have been known in which "directors anxious to pass resolutions without thorough scrutiny by the shareholders have convened meetings of the company to be held at times and places calculated to be inconvenient to the shareholders".[1] The committee, however, found that such abuses were exceptional, and that it would be difficult to deal with them by legislation; it made no recommendation on the matter.

An essential part of the notice is a statement of the business to be transacted at the meeting; in respect of special business this is expressly prescribed (clause 50, Table A). In such a case the general nature of the business is also to be communicated. It is not sufficient to notify, e.g. that an alteration of the articles is to be proposed; what the alteration is must also be specified. In the case of a proposed increase or reduction of the capital it is essential to show to what extent and how this is to be effected.[2]

The Act, moreover, requires that where a resolution is intended to be passed as an extraordinary or special resolution, this is to be specified in the notice, and without such specification the meeting is not deemed to have been duly convened (sec. 141 (1), (2)). In respect of the annual general meeting there is only the provision (sec. 158 (1)) by which a copy of the balance sheet, including every document required by law to be annexed thereto, and a copy of the auditor's report, is to be sent at least 21 days before the meeting to all members entitled to receive notice.

[1] Comm. Rep. 127, p. 78.
[2] Cf. e.g. MacConnell *v.* E. Prill and Co. (1916), 2 Ch. 57.

No business can be transacted at any meeting which is not put on the agenda in the way described after the shareholders have been informed thereof, and a resolution passed without such communication would be void. But it is a matter of judicial construction whether any particular notice is to be regarded as giving sufficient information and as covering the substance of the matter in hand, and the Courts do not construe notices with strictness. There is rather a tendency to uphold the resolution if its substance could be gathered and understood from the notice, if it were read as a business man would understand it in the ordinary sense.[1] Thus, if the articles are to be replaced by a new set, the inclusion of the suggested text is held not to be necessary if the terms of the proposed alterations have been communicated.

An annual general meeting called by shorter notice than 21 days or the longer term specified in the articles is deemed to have been duly called if it is so agreed by all the members entitled to attend and to vote at the meeting. The same applies to any other meeting called by shorter notice than prescribed, provided a simple majority in numbers of the members holding not less than 95 per cent. in nominal value of the shares giving a right to attend and to vote so agree (sec. 133 (3) of the Act of 1948).

The Companies Act, 1947, introduced a new kind of notice called special notice (sec. 3), and its provisions are now contained in the Act of 1948. In every case for which such special notice of a resolution is required, notice of the intention to move it is to be given to the company not less than 28 days before the meeting at which it is to be moved. The company on its part has to give notice thereof to the members at the same time and in the same manner as it gives notice of the meeting, or if this is not practicable, by an advertisement in a newspaper having an appropriate circulation, or in any other mode allowed by the articles, but not less than 21 days before the meeting. On the other hand, if after the said notice has been given to the company a meeting is called for a date less than 28 days after the giving of the notice, the same is deemed to have been properly given even though it was not given within the time required (sec. 142).

Such special notice is required in case of motions for the appointment of an auditor other than the retiring one (sec.

[1] Cf. the cases quoted by Palmer, pp. 146–8.

160 (1)), for the removal of a director (sec. 184 (2)) and for any resolution appointing or approving the appointment of a director over 70 years old (sec. 185 (5)).

The Cohen Committee came to the conclusion that although the annual general meeting should be the occasion on which the ordinary members can introduce resolutions on their own account or oppose the resolutions submitted by the directors, this opportunity has become largely illusory because, with the great increase in the number of shareholders, it is difficult for a single shareholder or even a group of shareholders to seek the support of their fellow-shareholders.[1] In order to enable minorities to overcome this difficulty the Committee recommended the granting to a certain minority of the right to request the circularisation of their views and statements. This recommendation has been followed by sec. 3 of the Companies Act, 1947, the provisions of which are incorporated in sec. 140 of the Act of 1948.

Any number of members representing not less than five per cent. of the total voting rights existing at the time of the meeting, and similarly not less than one hundred members holding shares in a company on which there has been paid up an average sum per member of not less than £100, are entitled to request the circularisation among the members of a notice of the resolutions which they intend to move at the next annual general meeting and of any statement of not more than one thousand words related to any matter on the agenda of the meeting.

The requisition is to be in writing, and one or more copies thereof containing the signatures of all the requisitioners are to be deposited at the registered office of the company. Together with the requisition a sum reasonably sufficient to meet the expenses of the circularisation is to be deposited or tendered.

A requisition for the notice of a resolution must be deposited not less than six weeks before the meeting; but if after the requisition has been deposited the annual general meeting is called for a date less than six weeks following the deposit of the request, the request shall be deemed to have been properly deposited for the purposes of the meeting.

If the requisition complies with these conditions, the resolution or statement is to be circulated in any manner permitted for service of notice of the meeting to the members of the company who are entitled to have notice of the meeting, and notice of the

[1] Report, par. 128, pp. 78-9.

general effect of the resolution is to be given to any other member of the company in any other manner permitted for giving him notice of meetings.

The circularisation is to be made in the same manner as the notice of the meeting itself and as far as practicable at the same time; should this not be practicable, it is to be done as soon as practicable thereafter.

The business which may be dealt with at an annual general meeting shall include notwithstanding anything in the company's articles any resolution of which due notice has been given, and accidental omission in giving it to one or more members shall be immaterial.

On the application of the company or of any person aggrieved the Court may declare that the company is not bound to circulate any statement if the Court is satisfied that the rights conferred by sec. 140 are being abused to secure needless publicity for defamatory matters, and in such case the Court may order that the costs of the company are to be paid in whole or in part by the requisitioners notwithstanding that they are not parties to the application.

In case of non-compliance every officer in default is liable to a fine not exceeding £500.

In the U.S.A. the autonomy of corporations in respect of the place and the notice of general meetings is usually recognised. The majority view was that meetings cannot be held outside the State of incorporation, but some Courts have held that the validity of resolutions is not affected by the fact that the meeting was held outside the State.[1] The question is now dealt with by most of the statutes. In certain States it is provided that the meetings must be held within the State, as e.g. in Massachusetts. Other States, such as California, Delaware, New Jersey and New York —and their number is increasing—allow meetings to be held either within or outside the State, as the articles or by-laws provide. Furthermore, if companies incorporated in different States are merged into one, it is held that meetings may be called and held in any of the States in which the former constituent companies were incorporated.[2] It is held that meetings may be called at any reasonable time and with any reasonable notice. Many statutes leave the regulation to the articles or the by-laws;

[1] Cf. Ballantine, 172.

[2] Graham *v.* Boston, etc., Co. (1886), 118 U.S. 161.

some of them provide for a minimum, e.g. Massachusetts for seven days.

The earlier European laws left full freedom for the articles to regulate place, time and notice of meetings; this freedom was later curtailed. Under the German law of 1937 general meetings are to be held at the seat of the company or at a place on the Stock Exchange whereof the shares are quoted, but the articles may provide otherwise (§ 105).

QUORUM

It is for the articles to settle the quorum, i.e. the number of members and the amount of shareholdings that must be present or represented in order to make the proceedings valid. Clause 53 of Table A prescribes a quorum of three members, but no quorum of holdings. If that quorum is not present the meeting is to be adjourned to a fixed date, when no quorum will be required, i.e. the members present, whatever their number, will be considered as forming a quorum. Table A (clause 54) makes a distinction between a meeting called on the demand of members and one convened by the directors; the former is to be dissolved, the latter adjourned to the same day of the following week.

For major matters some legislations require a quorum of a definite portion of the shareholdings, and this course seems to us desirable. It is to be noted that the Companies Act, 1948, provides that at a meeting convened by or at the direction of, or in pursuance of an order of the Court the attendance and vote of one member present in person or by proxy shall suffice if it is so directed (sec. 135).

70. PROCEDURE

The articles usually prescribe who is to preside at the meeting. This is usually the chairman of the board or his deputy, or if they are not available, such person as the articles shall designate, e.g. a director (see clause 55 of Table A). In case of need the meeting itself may appoint a chairman. Under sec. 134 (*d*) of the Act of 1948 anyone elected by those who are present may be chairman unless the articles provide otherwise; the procedure, if not prescribed by the articles, is generally held to be governed by the rules of parliamentary practice. The motions are to be put to the members; every member has a right to speak on all matters on the agenda. It is the duty of the chairman to arrange for taking votes and to declare resolutions carried. Gross defects in the proceedings may lead to invalidation, though the Courts are everywhere rather disinclined to void resolutions approved by a substantial quota of members.

One point of importance is how far members who are not satisfied with the information furnished in the accounts, in the directors' and auditors' reports, and in the chairman's speech, may raise questions on them in general meeting and demand explanations or interpretations to supplement them. The chairman and directors are generally not favourable to such requests, and are often disinclined to give the explanations asked for.

The restrictions with regard to proxies, especially the rule contained in most articles that shareholders alone may be appointed proxies, are mostly due to a desire to prevent the attendance of solicitors, accountants, and generally of all persons who have professional experience in dealing with company meetings. It is therefore not surprising that debates in general meetings very seldom lead to practical results in securing information which was not given in the documents submitted to the meeting.

Under the present law directors always have recourse to the majority at the general meeting to defeat a request for additional information. If and when a dissatisfied shareholder presses his request in spite of the hostile attitude of the chairman and the board of directors, only extraordinary circumstances and suspicion of grave irregularities are likely to secure a vote from the majority ordering explanations to be given, when the directors oppose the motion.

The only matter on which the Act of 1929 gave a right to demand information is the remuneration of directors. By sec. 148 members holding not less than one-fourth of the total voting power might request information as to the aggregate amount of remuneration paid them during the previous three years; but even this could be defeated by a majority. This provision has been repealed by sec. 38 (10) of the Companies Act, 1947. It is our view that a stated minority—say, five per cent. of the shares issued if represented at the meeting—should be entitled to request information and explanations at the general meeting, with the proviso that such a demand cannot be defeated by a majority vote. In this connection it is worth noting that by German law a minority of ten per cent. had the right to demand explanations: the only sanction, however, was that the general meeting must be postponed. If the board of management declined to furnish information and the majority affirmed this decision by a resolution, there was no way of pressing for the information and the action was futile.

71. Voting Rights

The British Companies Act (sec. 134 (*e*)) states that, if the articles do not otherwise provide, every member of a corporation has one vote for each share or each £10 of stock held; this of course applies only to voting by poll. The articles, however, frequently make other provision, thus clause 62 of Table A provides that each share held gives one vote and clause 65 denies a vote in respect of shares if the calls or all sums presently payable have not been paid. The articles may also deny voting rights to preference shares or limit them to certain contingencies, and there is nothing to prevent the issue of non-voting shares. Formerly the voting rights of large shareholders were sometimes curtailed; nowadays it is rather the little man against whom the articles are weighted, though actually voting rights have comparatively the widest recognition in Great Britain and the member States of the Commonwealth.

In the United States exclusion of shareholders from the vote is nowadays widespread. This was not always the case; W. S. Stevens [1] states that until about 1900 there were few restrictions on voting rights in America. Railroad corporations especially, which without exception had large issues of preferred and common shares, generally gave full voting rights to shareholders of both categories. For industrial corporations his data were not so complete; nevertheless he is able to assert that in most corporations shareholders had full and unrestricted rights. Even during the great wave of consolidation in the years 1898–1903 there was no move towards restrictions. Thus United States Steel Corporation, International Paper, and United Shoe Machinery Corporation gave their shareholders full voting rights. Stevens explains this by the financial structure of the great combines. Since the previous owners of the consolidated industrial units

[1] Qu. J. of Ecs. 40, 353–92 (1926).

received both preferred and common shares, the latter partly for goodwill, they had no interest in restricting their own voting rights. But there were some exceptions: thus the common shareholders of the International Silver Company had for a limited period no vote at all, and thereafter only one vote for each two shares. The holders of preferred shares in Federal Mining and Smelting Corporation had no vote.

From 1910 onwards restrictions of voting rights became more and more frequent. Stevens examined 350 companies whose stocks were listed on the New York Stock Exchange; of these 42 were railroads, 74 public utilities and 234 industrial corporations. He found that in only 16 cases out of 225 were preferred shareholders excluded from voting. One instance of non-voting preferred shares was the issue of Standard Oil of Ohio. More frequently the votes on preferred shares were restricted to special questions, such as the issue of new shares, the contracting of mortgages, or other exceptional matters. Apart from these cases they generally had contingent votes, a matter with which we shall deal presently.

Non-voting common (ordinary) shares were not frequent. Total exclusion was found in one case only, and partial exclusion, i.e. the parallel existence of voting and non-voting common shares, was likewise infrequent. Such cases occurred mainly in the tobacco industry and in some smaller corporations. There was one case, however, in which only one per cent. of the common shares, 2000 out of 200,000, had voting rights. Otherwise the ratio of voting to non-voting stock varied from 12·5 to 75 per cent.

The contingency vote of preferred shares was found under widely varying forms; mostly they had a vote if dividends were not paid on them for a certain period. The usual contingency is failure to pay dividend for one year. There were some cases in which failure for a single quarter made the contingent vote operative, and others in which the term exceeded one year, e.g. two consecutive years of default were required for the vote. The effect of contingency as a rule was that preferred shares acquired full voting rights to be exercised concurrently with the votes of other issues. In some cases, however, preferred shareholders on default became entitled to exercise exclusive voting rights, at least in the election of directors. This was the case with industrial corporations. Stevens found fewer restrictions for public utilities than for industrial companies. But he admits that this may be due to the lack of material, or possibly to the fact that the device of holding companies was sufficient to secure control to an active majority. In the case of the United Gas Light and Railway Company, however, there were 12·5 million dollars of voting stock and 37·5 millions of non-voting stock. In this case one-eighth of the share capital could secure absolute control. In the case of railroad companies the old method, unrestricted voting rights for all shares, was generally maintained.

After 1926 the device of non-voting stock and the restriction of voting rights went further, so that relatively small minorities became able to secure full legal control of large companies. If this device is coupled with the pyramiding of several holding companies, the results may be surprising, and effect a real distortion of control by legitimate interests. This question is fully discussed in connection with holding companies. In the case of public utilities, American legislation took effective steps against this abuse.

Outside this field American companies are still allowed to restrict voting rights quite freely, and it may be asked whether this freedom of restriction should remain undisturbed. The adherents of *laisser-faire* will certainly maintain that incorporators should be free to regulate the question of voting rights at their choice, that a later buyer of shares must know the situation, and if he purchases the shares in actual or constructive knowledge of the charter, has to take the consequences. Those experts who are very tolerant do not go so far, and even Stevens condemns the total and absolute exclusion of voting rights, though he is not opposed to restrictions, especially in the case of preferred shares, in regard whereto he finds the restriction to cases of contingency justified. But he is aware that the usual definition of contingency is not adequate; thus if failure to pay a dividend constitutes contingency, it might be that preferred shares had no vote, even though the position of the company was deteriorating and dividends were being paid not from profits but from surplus. It would be much more effective to make the vote dependent upon failure to earn profits. On the other hand, Stevens is not for legislative reform and would prefer action by the Stock Exchanges. Important issues are mostly dealt in on at least one Stock Exchange, and in his view the public interest would be sufficiently safeguarded if Stock Exchanges were to permit dealings only if they were satisfied with the provisions of the articles. In order to be effective, voting rights in case of contingency should be full, i.e. should extend beyond the election of directors to all other matters, and should be exclusive; otherwise preferred may be outvoted by common shareholders.

The impact of voting trusts is considered in § 74.

On the European Continent the earlier legislations gave companies full freedom to regulate voting rights by their articles as they should think fit. There were some cases in which only a multiple holding gave a vote, others where the votes were on a diminishing scale. The German Commercial Code of 1897 established as compulsive the rule that each share has a vote. There were nevertheless gaps: thus partly paid shares had also a full vote, and in this way control could be secured through small capital investments. Furthermore, § 252 allowed different voting powers to be given to different classes of shares, and as shown in § 23 the issue of shares with multiple votes thus became possible, and after 1918 even usual. The law of 1937 makes this abuse impossible on paper. It is provided (§ 113) that each share, even if not fully paid up, has a vote; fully paid up shares have proportionately more votes. Since the rule is compulsory, the votes are to be proportionate to the amounts paid up; the only possible exception is for a maximum of votes to be fixed or a diminishing scale adopted; non-voting preference shares may be issued. The issue of shares with a multiple vote is prohibited; the government may, however, grant exemption if it is required in the interest of the company or by considerations of public economic policy (§ 12). Furthermore § 9 of the introducing law provides that the date at which existing multiple voting rights are to be abolished is to be fixed by the government. But this was never done, and we know from reliable sources how wide was the extent of plural voting rights.

Under the Swiss O.R. (692–3) the vote depends upon the nominal amount of the shares, though the number of votes may be limited. In respect of fully paid up nominative shares the articles may provide that they have one vote in spite of the difference in nominal amounts. On the other hand this privilege does not extend to votes on the appointment of the *Kontrollstelle*, or of directors and experts, and on the institution of actions against directors.

It is our view that general considerations both of the interests of shareholders and of public policy require that voting rights should depend exclusively upon the amounts paid up by members, and that every restriction to the detriment of the small shareholder should be made inoperative.

72. Proxies

Members of companies are often unable to attend a meeting in person, and may wish to appoint a proxy to take their place and to exercise their votes. By common law the vote was to be exercised in person; attendance and vote by proxy was not recognised.[1] Later, however, it was accepted that the articles of association might permit proxies and thus confer the right to appoint them and to prescribe forms and conditions for doing so.

Gradually the articles generally came to allow proxies. Clause 58 of Table A to the Act of 1929 provided that on a poll votes might be given either personally or by proxy, and according to clause 62 the instrument appointing a proxy was to be deemed to confer authority to demand or to join in demanding a poll.

Although clause 59 of Table A provided that a proxy need not be a member of the company, many articles required that only members may be appointed. This made representation by proxy difficult, as the short notice, which was allowable and customary, often made it impossible to choose suitable persons for proxies. A further difficulty was that the articles generally required the instrument appointing a proxy to be deposited at the registered office of the company not less than 48 hours before the meeting or adjourned meeting, and that failing this the appointment should not be treated as valid (clause 60, Table A). In this way shareholders could seldom appoint independent proxies at their free choice.

On the other hand directors used to send out to shareholders forms in which they or persons closely connected with them were named as proxies. This inducement to the large mass of inactive members to accept the suggestion was only too often successful. The directors were then in a position to control the majority at the meeting even without having substantial holdings. Moreover it was held admissible for the directors to send out such forms at the company's expense, so that the postage was at the company's charge.[2] In some cases directors sent proxy forms only to

[1] Harben *v.* Phillips (1883), 23 Ch. D. 14.
[2] Peel *v.* N.W. Rail Co. (1907), 1 Ch. 5.

specially selected members, e.g. those with substantial holdings. Even this has been held to be allowable.[1] In this way the possibility of representation by proxy frequently operated not to the members' advantage but to strengthen the position of the board of directors.

It is to be noted that although proxies are *per se* revocable, and shareholders who have appointed proxies are not prevented from attending the meeting and voting in person, there is nothing to exclude the validity of an agreement by which a proxy is made irrevocable for valuable consideration, and a proxy may be given for several meetings without restrictions.[2]

In America[3] at Common Law the vote was to be given in person, unless otherwise provided in the charter, articles or by-laws.[4] Nowadays the statutes generally confer on members the right to vote by proxy.

If the right to vote by proxy is given by the statute or by the charter, any by-law depriving the shareholders of this right, or imposing unreasonable restrictions thereon, would be inoperative. A provision that only shareholders may act as proxies is held to be unreasonable.[5]

Some statutes provide that in absence of an express limitation a proxy's appointment shall be valid only for a limited period, and prescribe a maximum therefor. Thus in California,[6] the appointment of a proxy, in absence of express limitations, is valid for eleven months from its date and its validity cannot exceed seven years.

The proxies are as a rule revocable, and irrevocability cannot be stipulated unless the proxy is coupled with some interest in the shares. In such case it is generally held to be irrevocable. In New York an agreement by which a shareholder gave an irrevocable proxy to his creditor as security for a debt was held to be void.[7] Shareholders may limit the authority of their proxies, but even an unrestricted proxy does not extend to resolutions involving fundamental changes.

The use of proxy machinery, and particularly the solicitation of proxies at the corporation's expense, enables managements to

[1] Wilson *v.* L.M.S. Railway (1940), Ch. 393.
[2] Cousins *v.* International Brick Co. (1931), 2 Ch. 90.
[3] Cf. Ballantine 178–87; Dodd and Baker, pp. 190–3.
[4] Ballantine 178, and the decisions quoted in n. 87.
[5] Ballantine 178, n. 39.
[6] Civil Code § 321.
[7] Ballantine 179, n. 46.

retain control, and the observed abuses led to the regulation contained in the Securities Exchange Act of 1934, and the Public Utility Holding Company Act of 1935.[1]

The position in Britain is now substantially improved by sec. 5 of the Companies Act, 1947 (sec. 136 of the 1948 Act). Thereunder any member who is entitled to attend and to vote at a meeting shall be entitled to appoint any other person, whether a member or not, as his proxy, to attend and to vote on his behalf, and in the case of a private company the proxy shall also have the right to speak on the member's behalf.

Without a provision in the articles to the contrary a member of a private company is not entitled to appoint more than one proxy for the same meeting. Further, in the absence of provisions in the articles to the contrary, no proxy may vote except on a poll. In every notice a statement to that effect is to be inserted with reasonable prominence. No longer time than 48 hours previous to the meeting may be required for the production of the instrument appointing a proxy. The sending of invitations to a restricted circle of members to appoint a given person or persons as proxies at the company's expense is prohibited on pain of a fine not exceeding £100.

Table A contains some noteworthy provisions. In case of a poll it is sufficient to deposit the instrument appointing a proxy not less than 24 hours before the time appointed for the taking of the poll (clause 69).

Clause 70 contains a form for the appointment, and clause 71 a form for the instrument authorising the proxy to vote for or against the resolution.

According to clause 72 the instrument shall be deemed to confer authority to demand or join in demanding a poll, and clause 73 provides that facts or events invalidating the authority of the proxy, namely death, insanity of the principal, revocation of the proxy or of the authority under which the proxy was executed, or the transfer of the share do not affect the validity of the vote unless written notice thereof has been received at the office of the company before the commencement of the meeting at which the proxy was used.

[1] See § 22.

73. Mode of Voting

In Great Britain it is left to the articles to settle the mode of voting. The usual method is by show of hands, a poll being taken only if demanded, according to the provisions of the articles.

Under the Act of 1929 clause 50 of Table A provided that three members present in person or by proxy entitled to vote may demand a poll, as may one or two members if they hold not less than 15 per cent. of the paid-up capital. If such demand is put to the chairman before the resolution is carried the poll is to be taken as the chairman may direct.

If the vote is taken by show of hands, each member has one vote, and the chairman declares the result, whether the motion be carried unanimously or by a given majority or lost. The entry of the chairman's decision in the minutes shall be conclusive evidence of the fact without proof of the number or proportion of the votes recorded in favour of or against the resolution (Table A, clause 50).

If a poll is duly demanded, the votes are to be taken and counted in such manner as the chairman directs, and the result of the poll is deemed to be the resolution of the meeting (clause 51). The articles of some companies contained even more oppressive conditions.

Hitherto the right to refuse or restrict the demand for a poll was limited only in respect of special and extraordinary resolutions (sec. 117 (4)). The Companies Act, 1948, now provides that a demand for a poll may be refused only in respect of a resolution to elect the chairman of the meeting or to adjourn the meeting. Five members regardless of the amount of their holdings are entitled to demand a poll, as may any one or more members whose holdings represent not less than one-tenth of the voting rights or one-tenth of the paid-up capital having the right to vote at the meeting (sec. 137). Lastly, the instrument appointing a proxy to vote at a meeting shall be deemed also to confer authority to demand or to join in demanding a poll, and such demand by a proxy shall be counted as a demand by the member (sec. 137 (2)). Clauses 58–61 of Table A are amended accordingly.

Resolutions as to appointments or elections are generally carried in the same way as those on other matters; but the

Companies Act, 1948, prescribes that motions to appoint directors are to be voted on individually, and resolutions appointing two or more directors shall not be passed unless before the vote a resolution that the vote should be so taken has been agreed upon by the meeting, without any vote given against it. Any appointment made in violation of this rule shall be void, even if not objected to at the time (sec. 183). This restriction does not apply to private companies.

In certain States of the U.S.A. cumulative voting is possible in the matter of elections, i.e. the votes of members may be multiplied by the number of posts to be filled; e.g. if a member has ten voting shares each normally carrying one vote, and ten directors are to be appointed, he may exercise 100 votes in favour of a single candidate. In this way a minority may more easily obtain representation on the board. Whether this is an adequate protection of minority rights may be doubted.

74. Voting Trusts

The voting trust [1] is an institution peculiar to the United States, and hardly found elsewhere. Its main feature in practice is that several shareholders agree with one or several trustees to transfer to these latter the legal ownership of their shares in order to enable them to exercise at their discretion the voting rights attached to those shares. The transferors of the shares reserve for themselves the beneficial ownership, especially the right to dividends and other distributions.

Technically the procedure generally consists in a surrender of the share certificates. These are cancelled by the corporation, which then issues new certificates to the trustees, who on their part execute and deliver voting trust certificates to the shareholders, transferable in the same way as the shares themselves. The trustees undertake to pay the dividends received from the corporation to the owners of the voting trust certificates, with or without deduction of expenses. After the term of the voting trust has lapsed, the shares are reconveyed to the holders of the certificates.

Voting trusts are of relatively recent origin. The laws of several of the States contain no provisions with regard to them; other States provide more or less complete and elaborate rules.

[1] Cf. Ballantine 184.

With regard to the legislations in which there is no statutory authority for voting trusts opinion is widely controverted. One view, which seems now to prevail, is that they are highly beneficial to the shareholders, who as a rule have neither the time nor the knowledge necessary to exercise their votes judiciously and to control the management effectively. By entering into a voting trust agreement they select trustees in whom they have full confidence, who have the necessary qualities, and enough time to devote to the exercise of voting rights. Those who accept this view hold that the period and other terms of the trust should be fixed by free agreement between the shareholders and the trustees.

In this view a voting trust, unless prohibited by statute or the charter of the corporation, is to be regarded as valid, unless of course it is aimed at some unlawful purpose or at injuring the corporation or other shareholders.

A contrary view is that the voting trust is against public policy because it severs the vote from the beneficial ownership. This was held especially in earlier cases.[1]

Another view is that shareholders who transfer their shares under such an agreement are entitled to terminate it at any time, without regard to the period set out in it, and that the trustees are not entitled to resist such a demand by virtue of the agreement. This view was accepted in, e.g. Venner *v.* Chicago City Railways Co.[2]

Another matter affecting the validity of voting trusts is the position of the other shareholders. It is not only the right of the cestuis qui trustent under the agreement which is affected by the voting trust, but the interest of the other shareholders also, since as a consequence of the trust resolutions may be carried at general meetings which do not correspond with the intentions of the holders of the voting trust certificates, who might have adopted another attitude if they had been present at the meeting in person and taken part in its deliberations. On this ground some decisions recognise a suit on the part of other shareholders to restrain the trustees from voting.

Certain decisions seek to mediate between these opposed views, recognising voting trusts if they protect some lawful interest, such as indebtedness on the part of the corporation which makes

[1] E.g. in Harvey *v.* Linville Impr. Company (1896), 118 N.C. 693; Shepaug Voting Trust cases (1890), 60 Conn. 553; Warren *v.* Pim (1904), 66 N.J. Eq. 353.

[2] (1913), 258 Ill. 523.

control of the management by the creditor necessary and advisable, or if the shares are under option, and so on.

The statutes which deal with voting trusts recognise their validity in principle. Generally they cannot be entered into for a longer period than the statute provides; this does not generally exceed ten years; in California, however, it is 21 years.[1] A restriction as to time does not absolutely exclude the existence of voting trusts for a longer period, since according to the majority of the statutes an extension may be arranged for in the last year of the term. Some statutes even admit such extension by a majority resolution of the shareholders, whereas under others an extension by majority vote is possible only if the voting trust is to protect some legitimate interest, of the kind already mentioned.

Voting trust agreements must be in writing; a duplicate or copy is to be filed with the corporation, and is to be held open for inspection by the shareholders at the principal office. The share certificates are to be surrendered; the corporation issues new certificates in favour of the trustees. On these certificates a note is to be made to the effect that they are issued to a trustee, and some statutes provide that a similar note is to be recorded in the proper books of the corporation. The issue and delivery of voting trust certificates is under most of the statutes left to the discretion of trustees or to the trust agreement; but one statute makes such issue compulsory. Many statutes provide that vacancies may be filled by the remaining trustees.

There is a diversity of opinion with regard to the trustees' liability. Under most of the statutes they are not liable except in their own person. Some provide that a trustee is liable only for his individual malfeasance; others extend liability to individual neglect.

Some statutes regard voting trusts as beneficial to such a degree that they reserve to all other shareholders the right to join the voting trust on the same conditions. Schmey,[2] a German lawyer, who examines American voting trusts from the German point of view, thinks that their evolution is due to the absence in the U.S.A. of a board of supervision or any other organisation to supervise and check the activities of the directors. Under the American corporation laws the board of directors has a

[1] Civ. Code (1937), § 321*a*.
[2] Z.H.R. (1932), vol. 97, p. 249.

wider competence than the German board of management, and no organ similar to the German board of supervision exists. Thus the board of directors is not restricted to management, but exercises powers which exceed even the combined powers of the board of management and the board of supervision as defined by the German Code.

Voting trusts are formed to exercise the main and almost the only power which American law leaves to the shareholders, namely, the election of directors, and it is by this election that they are able to influence the board's business policy. Besides this, in Schmey's view, the trustees appointed in the trust deed may meet in order to give instructions to the directors. He forgets, however, that the directors are not bound to follow the instructions, and the only way to make them obey is the power of dismissal or removal, which is greatly restricted in the by-laws.

Although it cannot be denied that in some circumstances voting trusts might have improved the position of shareholders, it is obvious that on the whole they are dangerous. It may be that, exceptionally, persons may be found who are both ready and able to occupy themselves with the careful protection of shareholders' interests and to extend their activities to a constant supervision and judicious exercise of voting rights. In most cases, however, trustees under voting trusts do not fall into this category. It is usually a shareholder who holds a substantial block of shares or persons acting under his instructions who undertake the formation of a voting trust. The voting trust agreement, once signed, will be irrevocable for a fairly long period, during which many circumstances may, and as a rule will, change. There is little opportunity to cancel a voting trust on the ground of malfeasance, and to do so expensive litigation would be necessary. Moreover, the trustees are able under the respective laws to restrict their liability so far as to make it largely inoperative. These considerations lead to the conclusion that a law which would recognise voting trusts even for a short period is undesirable. A voting trust should be regarded as a proxy; proxies in their turn should be made revocable, and any agreement stipulating irrevocability even for a short period should be regarded as void.

Whereas nowadays voting trusts are either expressly admitted by statute or are regarded by the Courts to a fairly liberal extent as valid, so-called voting agreements by which shareholders undertake to vote in a certain manner for a consideration are generally held to be void,[1] and this sometimes even if the vote is only for the election of a manager, director or officer.[2] But there have been cases in which voting agreements were held valid if made in connection with the sale of a member's holdings or any part of them.[3] The agreements in question were as a rule confidential and not known to the other shareholders; whether the *ratio decidendi* was their secrecy may be doubted.

Outside the U.S.A. voting trusts are practically unknown, but voting agreements are in fairly common use.

In Great Britain agreements to vote or not to vote in a particular manner have been upheld.[4] In the latter case a mandatory injunction was granted to enforce the agreement. The remark of Buckley (p. 713), that this rule should not apply to cases of fraud is undoubtedly correct.

On the Continent, particularly within the German orbit, agreements by which shareholders, especially majority shareholders, bind themselves for a certain period to exercise their voting rights in a certain manner, e.g. to vote for the election of their candidates to the board, or to vote against motions by outsiders, were frequently made, and were known as syndicate or consortial agreements. Such agreements were usually made for the period of about five years, with renewal clauses in absence of notice. In one case the R.G. upheld an agreement made for ten years.[5] Such agreements are held to be governed by the provisions of the law on *societas* and may be terminated before maturity for substantial reasons and by notice if the term stipulated is oppressive by reason of its length. They are generally held to be valid, unless the agreement aims at private gain [6]; and a stipulation to vote for the election of certain persons is not held to be so aimed.[7] Since 1884 the sale and purchase of votes has been penalised, and the provisions of Art. 279 were re-enacted in § 317 of the Rev. Com. Code (1897), and with minor amendments in § 299 of the law of 1937. Both a person who accepts or stipulates for special con-

[1] See Palmbaum *v.* Magulsky (1914), 217 Mass. 306; Stott *v.* Stott (1932), 258 Mich. 547.

[2] Cf. Hellier *v.* Achorn (1926), 255 Mass. 273.

[3] See, e.g. Roosevelt *v.* Hamblin (1908), 199 Mass. 127; San Remo Copper Mining Co. *v.* Mineuse (1912), 149 App. Div. 133, N.Y. Supp. 509.

[4] Greenwell *v.* Porter (1902), 1 Ch. 530; Puddephatt *v.* Leith (1916), 1 Ch. 200.

[5] R.G.Z. 111, 405.

[6] R.G.Z. 107, 67; 119, 368; 133, 94.

[7] Cf. Staub-Pinner, II, pp. 887–9.

sideration or advantage for refraining from voting at a general meeting or for voting thereat in a particular manner, and one who gives a promise so to do, are liable to imprisonment not exceeding one year or a fine not exceeding M10,000. Contracts in violation are void and not enforceable; moneys paid are not recoverable.

The R.G. held in one case that a contract by which the purchaser of a block of shares bound himself to vote for the appointment of the vendor would be invalid if this stipulation were of importance in the fixing of the purchase price, and that no part of the consideration was expressly stipulated as being for the vote would be immaterial.[1]

75. Conflict of Interests

The British and American laws do not debar members from voting on matters in which they have an interest.

In England it is held that the vote is a right of property; the shareholder is entitled to vote as he thinks fit even from a motive of personal interest.[2] Thus where the vote was on the question whether a steamer should be purchased by the company, the owner was held to be entitled to vote even though his vote turned the scale.[3] Similarly, a member could vote where the question was whether the company should adopt a bill impeaching his title to his shares.[4] In this respect a shareholder's position is held to be different from that of a director or of a creditor in a creditors' meeting.

This right, however, is qualified. If a member seeks to perpetrate fraud, e.g. to make a present to himself through the purchase at a nominal price, the vote will be nullified; [5] similarly, his vote would be inoperative if the passing of the resolution would amount to an oppression of the minority, especially by an alteration of the articles.[6]

The view held in the U.S.A. is similar.[7] Certain European legislations provide that shareholders who have a personal

[1] R.G.Z. 132, 33.
[2] Greenwell *v.* Porter (1902), 1 Ch. 530; Puddephatt *v.* Leith (1919), 1 Ch. 200.
[3] North-West Transportation Company *v.* Beatty (1887), L.R. 12 App. Cas. 589.
[4] East Pant Du United Lead Mining Company *v.* Merryweather (1864), 2 H. and M. 254.
[5] Cook *v.* Deeks (1916), 1 A.C. 554.
[6] Allen *v.* Gold Reefs (1900), 1 Ch. 656.
[7] Cf. Ballantine 175*a*.

interest in a given question cannot vote on that question at the constituent meeting, though the provision was not expressly extended to subsequent meetings, and in this way the question became a matter of dispute.

The German Commercial Code of 1897 (§ 252) provided that no shareholder may vote on the question of his release from liability as a manager or supervisor, or from any debts and obligations, or on a contract which was to be made with him, or on the question whether an action should be brought against him. The law of 1937 dropped the limitation in respect of contracts between the company and its members (§ 114 (5)).

The Swiss O.R. only debars shareholders who have taken part in the management from voting on questions concerning their release (695).

76. Nominees

For various reasons, mostly as a matter of convenience, shares in Great Britain are fairly often registered in the name of nominees, so that the register of members does not indicate their beneficial ownership.

It is assumed that this device is frequently used in order to deliberately conceal the true ownership. It has been alleged that in this way "foreigners may be able to acquire control of essential British industries without anyone being aware of it", and that even if the question of foreign nationality did not arise, it would be harmful if, for instance, the control of the press were concealed from the general public; that directors, by acting under the cloak of nominees, would find it easier to conceal speculative dealings based on inside information; and lastly that the knowledge of beneficial ownership would in any case be useful to all shareholders who wish to consult their fellow shareholders in regard to the company's affairs.[1]

Public opinion felt so strongly on the possible and actual dangers of nominee holdings that this question was one of the most conspicuous matters put before the Cohen Committee. Evidence showed that these apprehensions were exaggerated. One of the London Clearing Banks stated that of the 72,436 nominee holdings of its nominee companies, 13,317 were bene-

[1] Report of the Cohen Committee, p. 41.

ficially owned by persons residing outside the United Kingdom, and only 437 nominee holdings were such as could involve concealment.[1]

Even if it be admitted that holdings for brokers, jobbers, trust companies and so on could "include concealment from motives to which objection could properly be taken", the material produced did not in our view support the contentions. Nevertheless the Committee recommended the establishment of a register of beneficial ownership, and on the basis of these recommendations a highly complicated procedure was set up in the Bill. This was subsequently dropped in the House of Lords, in favour of a proposal to give the Board of Trade power to investigate ownership should the public interest require it.

By sec. 172 of the Companies Act, 1948 (re-enacting sec. 46 of the Companies Act, 1947), the Board of Trade has the power to order investigation of the membership of a company or its other circumstances for the purpose of determining the true persons who are or have been financially interested in the real or apparent success or failure of the company or are able to control or materially influence its policy.. It is left to the Board of Trade to order the investigation where there appears to it to be good reason to do so.

Not less than two hundred members of a company, regardless of their holdings, and likewise one or more members holding not less than ten per cent. of the shares issued (sec. 164 (1), (2)) may apply to the Board of Trade for an investigation in respect of particular shares or debentures of the company. The Board, however, may refuse the application if satisfied that it is vexatious. The investigation is made by one or more competent inspectors appointed by the Board, but in case of an application by shareholders one inspector is to be appointed.

The Board may define the scope of the investigation, e.g. in respect of the period or the matters to which it should extend, and in particular may limit it to matters connected with particular shares or debentures.

In the case of an investigation on the application of shareholders, none of the matters sought to be included by the applicants shall be excluded except in so far as the Board of Trade find it unreasonable.

Subject to the terms of the appointment the investigation shall

[1] 78, at p. 40.

extend to any circumstances suggesting the existence of an agreement or understanding which, though not legally binding, was or is observed or likely to be observed in practice, if it is relevant to the purposes of the investigation.

The investigations are under the same rules as investigations into the affairs of companies,[1] and the inspectors shall have the power to examine all persons of whom they have reasonable cause to believe that they are or have been financially interested in the real or apparent success or failure of the company or any body corporate whose membership is investigated with that of the company, or able to control or materially influence its policy, including persons who are concerned only on behalf of others. On the other hand the Board of Trade is not bound to furnish the company or the applicants with a complete copy of the inspectors' report, if it is of the opinion that there is good reason not to divulge its contents, and likewise it may withhold at its discretion any part of the report.

The expenses of investigations into the membership are to be met in every case by the Board of Trade (sec. 172 (1)–(6)).

Should the Board find that it is unnecessary to appoint an inspector, its power extends to require any person whom it believes to be or to have been interested in shares or debentures of any company or to act or have acted as a solicitor or agent of any person interested therein to give any information as to the present or past interest in the shares or debentures.

For the purposes of such inquiry not only the owners of the shares and debentures are deemed to be interested, but also persons who have the right to acquire or dispose of the share and debenture, or have any interest therein, or have a vote in respect thereof, or whose consent is necessary for the exercise of any right therein, and even persons who have the right to request those who are actually interested to follow their instructions or are accustomed to exercise their rights in accordance with their instructions.

Failure to give the information as required, or false information given knowingly or recklessly, makes the person concerned liable to imprisonment not exceeding six months or to a fine not exceeding £500 (sec. 173).

Moreover, the Board of Trade may issue an order directing that the shares or debentures shall be subject to certain restrictions, if it appears in connection with an investigation that it is difficult to

[1] See § 89.

find out the relevant facts, and the difficulty is due wholly or mainly to unwillingness to assist the investigation as required by the Act. The restrictions are:

(*a*) That any transfer of the shares or debentures concerned shall be void, and the same shall apply in case of unissued shares or debentures to any issue and any transfer of the right to be issued.

(*b*) No voting rights shall be exercisable in respect of the shares concerned.

(*c*) No further shares shall be issued in right of the shares or in pursuance of any offer made to their holders.

(*d*) No payment shall be made by the company whether in respect of the capital or otherwise except in a liquidation.

The company or any other person aggrieved may apply to the Board for the lifting of the restriction, and both in the case of the issue of a restricting order and of a refusal to lift the restriction any person aggrieved may apply to the Court for an order to terminate the restriction imposed or maintained by the Board. The termination ordered by the Board of Trade or the Court respectively may comprehend all the restrictions or may be limited to allowing transfers and the exercise of voting rights.

The violation of any restrictive order by the exercise of transfers or voting rights, if made in knowledge of the restriction, incurs liability to imprisonment for a term not exceeding six months or to a fine up to £500 or both, and the issue of shares or debentures in contravention of the restriction to a fine up to £500.

In England, however, no prosecution shall be instituted except by or with the consent of the Board of Trade (sec. 174).

The machinery provided by the Act appears to be apt to secure the ascertaining of the true membership of companies. It is doubtful, however, whether it will be frequently put into operation.

77. Records of Meetings

Regular business practice demands that the proceedings of general meetings should be recorded. Many companies did this from the earliest days, and many legislative systems expressly provide for the keeping of such records.

In Great Britain the Act of 1929 (sec. 120 (1)) prescribed that every company shall cause minutes of all proceedings of general meetings to be entered in books kept for the purpose. The minutes are to be signed by the chairman of the meeting or of the following general meeting, and by the person who prepared them, usually the secretary. Any minute entered in the minute book purporting to be signed by the chairman of that or the next succeeding general meeting shall be evidence of the proceedings (subsec. (2)), and until the contrary is proved the meeting shall be deemed to have been duly convened and held, the proceedings to have been duly had, and all appointments shall be deemed to be valid (subsec. (3)). The minutes are therefore *prima facie* evidence which may be rebutted or supplemented.[1]

The minute book is to be kept at the registered office of the company. The members have the right to inspect it without charge at the times fixed by the company in its articles or in general meeting; any restrictions imposed must be reasonable, and at least two business hours must be allowed. Members may demand copies at a charge not exceeding sixpence for every 100 words, to be delivered within seven days. In case of default or delay the Court may enforce these rights, and the company and every officer in default shall be liable to a fine (sec. 121). No right to inspect the minute books is granted to debenture holders or to the general public.

A wider measure of publicity is provided for special and extraordinary resolutions, for unanimous resolutions of all the members relating to matters which otherwise would have had to be dealt with by special or extraordinary resolutions, for any resolutions by a special class of shareholders affecting their rights, whether carried unanimously or by majority vote, and for resolutions to wind up the company voluntarily. These resolutions are to be printed and a copy forwarded within 15 days to the Registrar of Companies and recorded by him. A fine of £2 is imposed for non-compliance (sec. 118).

The Companies Act, 1947, amended the law in two respects. A fine is imposed for failure to make minutes of general meetings (sec. 8); on the other hand private companies exempted from the duty to file balance sheets and profit and loss accounts (see § 93) need not print the resolutions mentioned, but may forward a copy to the Registrar in some other form approved by him

[1] Fireproof Doors Ltd. (1916), 2 Ch. 142.

(sec. 7). These provisions are now re-enacted in secs. 145 and 143 of the Act of 1948.

Some American statutes deal expressly with minutes of general meetings. Thus the law of California prescribes that a book of minutes is to be made and kept at the corporation's principal office or at such place as the board of directors may order. The minutes have to contain the time and place of meeting, whether the meeting is regular or special and if special how authorised, particulars as to notice, the names of those who were present or represented, the amount of their shares, and the proceedings. The book of minutes may be inspected by the members on the same conditions as the books of account (see § 89).

Under French law the only express requirement is that a list is to be made of those who are present or represented, which must contain the amount of the holdings of each member (art. 28). The Order of 31 August 1937 prescribed that this list is to be certified by the chairman, the keeper of the minutes, and usually by two shareholders, and is to be kept at the company's principal office; it is to be open to inspection by anyone on request. Otherwise the practice requires that the minutes shall give the essence of the discussions and resolutions. It is usual to record the minutes in a book, but their validity is not affected by their being made on a separate sheet. The document is *prima facie* evidence which may be rebutted.[1]

Continental legislations are generally satisfied with minutes in writing. German law, however, requires a judicial or notarial document in which every resolution whether carried or defeated, the results of polls and the declarations of the chairman are to be recorded. The list of shareholders present or represented is to be attached, and documentation as to the calling and notice of the meeting is to be either attached to or included in the minutes. It is not necessary to record the debate; declarations of protest, however, are to be included, and also requests of a specific minority in so far as they are admitted, e.g. in respect of an action for damages against the promoters, members of the management and of the board of supervision (§§ 110, 111, law of 1937). Although notarial and judicial documents are conclusive evidence, it is held that the contents of the minutes may be rebutted by extrinsic evidence.[2] The management must

[1] Req. 28 February 1886, D. 88, 1, 427, cf. Pic 1306–10.
[2] Gadow, p. 467.

forward immediately a legalised copy of the minutes to the Court, even if the resolutions carried were not such as to require registration (§ 111 (5)).

It is obvious that publicity in corporate matters is not achieved if the right to inspect the minutes of general meetings is restricted to members (sec. 146 of the Companies Act of 1948), and since we accept the thesis that publicity is one of the main safeguards against abuse, the conclusion that the minutes of every general meeting should be made accessible not only to members, but also to debenture holders, creditors and the general public seems inevitable.

78. Protection of Minorities

Protection of minorities is one of the most controversial questions of company law. At one time it was generally assumed that shareholders are in the position of partners and should therefore enjoy similar protection. But with the growth of corporate enterprise the right of the majority to decide the business policy of the enterprise was increasingly recognised as the over-riding consideration. This tendency was enhanced by the doctrine of the institutional character of corporate enterprise, particularly in Germany. Extreme stress was laid on this tendency by the doctrine of the company or enterprise as such. It appeared in the legislative field when it was made possible for a company, which formerly could not alter its charter or memorandum of association save by a special legislative act or by unanimous consent, to effect major changes by a majority vote, even though such power was not given it by the articles. This new principle was strengthened and extended until even special privileges attached to a given class of shareholdings could be altered by a special majority vote of the shareholders concerned.

Parallel with this, public opinion became more and more unfavourable to shareholders insisting on their rights; as N. D. Lattin succinctly said, "disgruntled shareholders acquired the reputation of being a nuisance, and highway robbers".[1] Shareholders, it was said, are not only excluded from control but are in fact no longer owners of the corporation, and the suggestion was made that "the stockholder of to-day is more in the nature

[1] 45 H.L.R. 237.

of a lender of money to the corporation than a member actively interested in its welfare". If this be so, it may reasonably be said that "if his nature has changed to that of a small banker, then he should have the banker's usual security on his loan and an assurance that he will get a banker's interest, and possibly the investment banker's generous profits".[1]

The main proposition of this book is that the position of a shareholder is still that of a member, and that while the effective pursuit of the company's purposes ought not to be hindered by obnoxious or selfish actions on the part of individual shareholders or minorities, and the making of necessary changes in the corporate structure by real majorities should be possible, yet shareholders are to be effectively protected in their right to participate in profits, and, at the final distribution, in the assets of the company.

With the adoption of the doctrine that a majority may change the company's structure and bring about major changes in the memorandum, charter and articles, even substituting new purposes, the various legislations sought guarantees against the infliction of possible injury on the shareholders. The first step was that more than a simple majority was required. The specific or qualified majority thus adopted was generally three-fourths of the votes; but there are fundamental differences between the various legislations. If what is required is a majority of those voting in general meeting, the demand is not very onerous. The situation is not much improved if the required majority is to be reckoned on the basis of holdings represented at the general meeting, regardless of whether their votes are exercised or not, since it may be that, in view of the well-known apathy of shareholders, only a small fraction of the capital is represented. Moreover under most legislations an unscrupulous board of directors has ways and means of fixing the place and time of general meetings if they so choose, in such a way as to evade the shareholders' notice. Thus where no special quorum for attendance at general meetings called to decide upon major changes is required, the specific majority does not by itself give an effective guarantee against injurious resolutions.

The position is better if the requirement is that a definite quota of the capital should be represented, either by shareholders in person or by proxies, beside the requirement of a specific

[1] Lattin, *loc. cit.*, p. 245.

majority. For example, two-thirds of the capital might be required with a majority of at least three-fourths of those present. To the objection that such a requirement would obstruct schemes urgently necessary for the efficient carrying on of the business, it may be argued that the board of directors generally finds the means to collect enough proxies to ensure the passing of a resolution, unless the scheme be one whose utility cannot be made clear to the shareholders. A further guarantee is to require adequate notice of such meetings and resolutions. This applies first of all to the contents of the notice; it is not enough merely to announce the subject of the proposed change by quoting the relevant section of the articles, as is frequently done; its merits also must be explained.

A further requisite is the prescribing of a sufficient period between the publication of the notice and the general meeting. The Companies Act of 1929 lays down a minimum of 21 days. Even this term, however, seems insufficient if we bear in mind the time that is necessary to become acquainted with the proposed scheme, to discover the reaction of the financial press and to organise the shareholders. The more widely dispersed the ownership of the company's capital, the more time will be necessary to ensure that informed shareholders participate in the general meeting. Four weeks seems the minimum desirable. It is of course essential that the legal requirements as to quorum, majority, contents and term of the notice should be minimal. If the law were to allow the articles to reduce these requirements, all regulation would be futile; directors and company lawyers would endeavour to reduce them to the utmost.

Even if company law met these postulates, the possibility of injury to the minority still remains. Against such injuries two kinds of remedy are conceivable: to give an action to dissenting shareholders, or to call for the co-operation of the public authority. Legislative experiments have been made in both directions.

The Companies Act of 1929 requires the Court's approval for any change in a company's objects or for the reduction of its capital. Even if the required majority is obtained, the change proposed cannot be effected unless the Court has sanctioned it. In exercising its powers the Court does not content itself with a scrutiny of the formalities, but goes to the root of the matter.

We cannot look upon it as an advance that the Companies Act, 1948, abolishes this requirement, and replaces it with a regulation by which only a minority holding at least 15 per cent. of the issued share capital is entitled to apply for the cancellation of the alteration (sec. 5). The holders of debentures secured by a floating charge, if issued or first issued before 1 December 1947, are entitled to the same notice of any special resolution altering the company's objects as the shareholders, and holders of not less than 15 per cent. of such debentures have the same right to object (sec. 5 (2) (*b*) and (5)). If such an application is made, the Court, while confirming the alteration, will have power to impose terms and conditions at its discretion in order to facilitate arrangements for the purchase of the interests of dissenting members. In case of an arrangement or amalgamation, dissident shareholders could be, even under sec. 155 of the Companies Act of 1929, bought out by a majority comprising 90 per cent. of the issued share capital. The new Act entitles the dissident minority to demand the purchase of their shares (sec. 209 (2)).

Lastly, the power to wind up the company for just and equitable cause may give protection in case of oppression, and the amending provisions of the 1948 Act will considerably improve the position. Moreover, although the company's articles may be altered by special resolution, the resolution may be attacked if it would amount to fraud on the minority.[1]

On the other hand, it is held that shareholders cannot sue the directors in their own name and in that of the other shareholders where the company declines to take action.[2]

Under sec. 152 of the 1929 Act (now sec. 205 of the Act of 1948), all agreements to relieve a director of his liability for breach of trust, breach of duty, default or negligence are void, even though such exemption is stipulated in the articles, or in any contract with the company or otherwise. Nevertheless the power of the majority to refrain from action in such a case seems to be absolute, and except in case of fraud the minority is helpless. It is of course open to any shareholder to take action on the basis that the legal requirements for a resolution have not been complied with; but the expediency of the resolution cannot be attacked.

Under the Common Law of the U.S.A. it was held that shareholders may sue in equity and may enjoin a proposed change

[1] Menier *v.* Hooper's Telegraph Company (1874), L.R. 9 Ch. App. 350.

[2] Foss *v.* Harbottle (1843), 2 Ha *re* 461; MacDougall *v.* Gardiner (1875), 1 Ch. D. 13; but Cooke *v.* Deeks (1916), 1 A.C. 554, seems to qualify this rule.

contrary to the charter or otherwise injurious to their rights. Thus it has been held that the Court may interfere if the directors or the majority intend to carry through a sale of all assets, although the corporation is in a position to carry on business successfully. Similarly it has been held that a merger—if its conditions and terms were unsatisfactory—could be enjoined in equity. Under Common Law, i.e. without any statutory basis, some courts gave dissenting shareholders the right to demand the purchase of their shares in such a case. The purchase could be made by the corporation or by the majority shareholders, and the Court could ensure the satisfaction of the claim by enjoining the transaction unless the shares were purchased and the purchase price paid.[1]

Under the influence of these tendencies a number of States have enacted provisions to this effect. It is provided in many States[2] that in case of mergers, or sales of all or a substantial part of the company's assets, dissenting shareholders have a right to request an appraisal of their shares and payment for them in cash, generally within a short time limit. The appraisal is usually to be made by a board of appraisers; in some States the value of the shares is to be determined by the Court. The statutes provide for the basis of the appraisal in various ways; some require compensation at value or at a fair value. Others prescribe the market value, fair or full, and others combine the two by saying that fair value is to be paid, but not less than the market value.

In any case it is a difficult question to ascertain what the real or fair value is. Market values, if the shares are quoted, give some indication, but only if quotations over longer periods are available. Otherwise prices influenced by passing incidents may be used, and thus either the dissenting shareholders or the company would be harmed. In many cases a valuation of the company's assets will be necessary, and for this all questions discussed in connection with balance sheets will arise. In such cases, however, the real question to be solved is what the assets would bring by sale as a going concern under normal conditions. For this, book values cannot be decisive; the absence of generally adopted standards is a factor which would in itself exclude their adoption. This is especially so if the company has on its books a valuation based upon replacement; and the courts are generally

[1] Cf. Ballantine 277-8. [2] Cf. N.D. Lattin, 45 H.L.R. 233-70.

inclined to disregard such a valuation. The earning power of the enterprise is an important factor, and the future prospects, if certain and not mere guesswork, may also be taken into consideration.

Some examples will illustrate the difficulties of appraisal. In Allied Chemical *v.* Steel and Tube Corp. [1] the book value of the assets amounted to $94,767,000. The appraisal of net assets showed $95,737,000; nevertheless the sale price of $73,000,000 was held to be fair in view of the earning power of the plant and the future outlook of the business. In Jackson *v.* Gardiner Investment Co.[2] the market value was $975 per share; the valuation based on the net sales value of the assets was $1174·94, and the replacement value $2721·25. A merger based upon the market value of $975 was held to be fair. In a case of merger the goodwill should also be taken into account, but this is not always done. In Colby *v.* Equitable Trust Co. of New York,[3] goodwill was entirely disregarded and a merger with Mercantile Trust Co. based on book values minus cost of liquidation and on the earning power was approved.

How difficult appraisals may be, and what long drawn out litigation may be necessary, was shown in Jones *v.* Missouri-Edison Electric Co.[4] where 11 years elapsed between the first and the last judgment of the Federal Courts. It is true that in this case not only was the ratio of the values of the two companies merged to be found, but also the increase in values in consequence of the merger, since the Court held that the shareholders of the merged companies were entitled to participate in such increase.

The dissenting shareholders are entitled under the appraisal statutes to demand payment in cash, but it was held in Geddes *v.* Anaconda Copper Mining Co.[5] that shareholders may be required to take stock in case of mergers if the shares have a wide and general market.

In the application of the different appraisal statutes many other questions arise, e.g. whether dissenting shareholders have a right to dividends declared between the passing of the resolution or their declaration of dissent and the final confirmation of the transaction. Further, from what time onwards have they a right

[1] (1923), 14 Del. Ch. 1.
[2] (1914), 217 Fed. 350 C.C.A. 1st.
[3] (1908), 124 App. Div. 262.
[4] (1916), 233 Fed. C.C.A. 8th.
[5] (1921), 254 U.S. 590.

to interest? It is disputed whether the company may retract and cancel the transaction if it is informed of the number of dissenting shareholders and the amount of their holdings, and lastly, what is to be done if the company is not able to pay cash in order to satisfy dissenting shareholders. It is to be expected that all these questions will be settled satisfactorily either in the practice of the Courts or by legislative amendments. The outstanding question is whether the remedy of appraisal is exclusive, or whether the Common Law remedies still exist.

It is obvious that the question of appraisal can arise only if the transaction is valid in itself. It is therefore to be assumed that shareholders still have a right to attack the transaction and to sue in equity for injunction if either the requirements for the validity of the resolution have not been complied with, or there is a case for a suit based on breach of trust against the directors of the corporation. Actually this has been held, if the power of the directors or of the majority is exercised for personal profit, or the minority is excluded from consultations as to the agreement. In Homer *v.* Crown Cork Seal Co.[1] it was held that in the absence of *ultra vires*, illegality or bad faith, the transaction cannot be attacked. The inadequacy of the price, however, was not held to be in itself evidence of fraud, and the error in judgment of directors gives no action.[2]

Where the principle of the parallel existence of both remedies is recognised, a further question arises as to the possibility of exercising them both simultaneously. It is obvious that since the two remedies are based upon different facts, shareholders should have the choice either of attacking the transaction and enjoining it on the basis of illegality or bad faith, or of accepting it and demanding appraisal and payment. Before the passing of the statutes in question the possibility of alternative demands was in some cases recognised; and we may accept the proposal of Prof. Lattin, that appraisal statutes should be drafted in such a manner that shareholders should not be deprived of the possibility of demanding appraisal if they have already brought action for injunction. The necessity of short terms for demands for appraisal may cause some difficulties, but these can and should be met. It seems that on the whole the remedy of appraisal is beneficial, and will be even more so if the doubts and controversies are settled.

[1] (1928), 155 Md. 66. [2] Koehler *v.* St. Mary's Brewing Co. (1910), 228 Pa. 648.

In cases of fraudulent rescission or breach of contract, omission to take action, mismanagement in general, operation and control of the corporation for the benefit of another corporation or individual, an equitable remedy is available. The essential question is always whether the corporation and through it the shareholder or shareholders taking action have been defrauded. In all these cases the minority may sue for injunction, or in a proper case for the rescission and cancellation of the contract. They may sue the officers or the majority for damages caused by their fraudulent action or their omission. They may likewise sue a third party involved. The action of the minority shareholders is in principle on behalf of the corporation, a so-called representative action.[1]

It is therefore necessary that the corporation should have a right of action whether the action is based on law or on equity, but this is not sufficient, as at present minority shareholders are generally not entitled to intervene in suits brought by or against the corporation. It is necessary for the failure to take action or the refusal to defend to be contrary to good faith; otherwise the minority shareholders cannot intervene.[2]

If minority shareholders are entitled to intervene, they may make use of all the defences which the corporation might have set up. Their action or intervention is always based on equity; therefore consent or acquiescence, or participation of the shareholder, deprives him of the action or intervention.[3] This qualification has been extended to *ultra vires* acts, but not to illegal acts. Whether laches is a bar in the case of illegal acts is controversial, and it may be argued that illegality cannot be cured by laches, since express assent is not sufficient to cure illegality.

The defence of the third party is frequently based upon the argument that the shareholder suing on behalf of the corporation has an improper motive for his action. The majority rule seems to be that the motive is immaterial. It has been said that the courts have nothing to do with the motives of plaintiffs, and the reason for their coming to Court is a matter beyond the province of the Court.[4] On the other hand it has been held that when a corporation refuses to sue the directors for secret profits, a shareholder who before he sued had requested the directors to give

[1] Ballantine, 143-157.
[2] Bronson *v.* Lacrosse (1865), 2 Wal. 283; further, Fletcher 5853, n. 9.
[3] Dimpfell *v.* Ohio (1883), 110 U.S. 209; Fletcher 5862, n. 72.
[4] *Re* Cleland (1910), 218 U.S. 120.

him a share in such secret profits cannot subsequently sue after it has been refused him.[1] But it is universally accepted that bad faith as to motive is no defence if the action of the corporation is based on right. A special line of defence is that the share or shares have been bought for the purpose of bringing the suit. The question is controversial; on the other hand it is generally held that a defence based on the fact that the suit was brought in the interest or for the benefit of a rival, or generally of another corporation, would be good. The view of the Courts as to the extent of the plaintiff's holding is divided. The U.S. Supreme Court held that the smallness of the holding is immaterial,[2] but there are decisions to the contrary. To illustrate the position it may be quoted that a minority shareholder holding one per cent. of the total stock was held entitled to sue,[3] and that in the case of a mining corporation two shareholders holding 200 shares out of 1,500,000 were similarly held entitled to an injunction against the transfer of the property of the corporation.[4] On the other hand it was held that the holder of one share out of a total of 156,000 cannot enjoin the election of directors; [5] and similarly that the extreme smallness of the loss sustained may be a reason for dismissing the suit.[6] The Supreme Court upheld the opinion that the smallness of the holding is immaterial.[7] But even courts holding this view regarded the fact that the plaintiff's holding was small and that other shareholders did not join in the suit as a reason for suspicion of his good faith and good judgment, so that in such a case plaintiff has at least to show a very satisfactory reason for relief. Thus it was held that a suit brought by about three per cent. of the shareholders, the holders of 6617 shares out of 270,000, is pertinent in determining their equities.[8]

It is disputed whether a shareholder may sue if the act was committed before he had acquired an interest in the shares. The Equity Rule of the Federal Court 27 provides that the bill of the shareholder must contain the allegation that he, or his predecessor from whom the shares devolved on him by operation

[1] Fullerton *v.* Crawford, 50 Dom. L. Rep. Can. 457.
[2] Zabriskie *v.* Cleveland (1874), 23 How U.S. 381 and Fletcher 5885, n. 95.
[3] Gordon *v.* Brucker, 208 Ill. App. 188.
[4] Forrester *v.* Butte and M. Consol. Copper and Silver Mining Co., 21 Mont. 544, quoted by Fletcher.
[5] Greenough *v.* Alabama G.S.R. Co., 64 Fed. 22.
[6] Albers *v.* Merchants Exchange of St. Louis, 45 Mo. App. 206, quoted by Fletcher 5885, n. 97.
[7] Ashwander *v.* Tennessee Valley Authority (1937), 297 U.S. 288.
[8] Aldrich *v.* Union Bag and Paper Co., 81 N.Y. Eq. 244; Fletcher 5585, n. 98.

of law, was a shareholder at the time of the transaction. This rule is based on Hawes *v.* Oakland,[1] maintained in Dimpfell *v.* Ohio and M.R. Co.[2] and Quincy *v.* Steel,[3] and is followed by the Federal Courts and by a minority of State Courts. Many of the State Courts maintain that the time of acquisition is immaterial; in other words, a purchaser of shares acquires the right to sue on the basis of wrongful acts done previous to his purchase, unless his vendor or an earlier owner of the shares was prevented from taking action by his assent or other similar act calculated to constitute a case of acquiescence, estoppel or laches.[4] It may rightly be presumed that the uncertainty of the law in these and the related questions is an obstacle to the effective protection of minorities.

The rule that a shareholder is not entitled to complain of acts or omissions previous to his purchase is, however, a more effective preventative of blackmail and malicious acquisition of shares with a view to suing the corporation than any other consideration of the interests involved. It is generally held that the statute of limitations does not apply in equity. Nevertheless it would be an awkward consequence of this doctrine if actions on behalf of the corporation were admitted without regard to the time when they are brought. Therefore it would be advisable to recognise the application of the statute of limitations to such actions in principle. This is already done in some cases, at least on the basis of laches.[5] It is obvious that if the suit of the shareholder is brought at a time when the corporation would be debarred from action in consequence of the limitation, the shareholder is equally debarred from action even under the present rule.

The action of the shareholder on behalf of the corporation may be directed to the enjoining or the cancellation of the act in question, and where an injunction or cancellation would have no effect, to obtaining damages for the corporation. The suit is one in equity, even if it is directed to the recovery of damages, and is to be distinguished from the action for damages suffered by plaintiff himself in connection with the wrongful act, and such action cannot be conjoined with an action on behalf of the corporation, although it has been held that before suing on behalf of the corporation plaintiff has to apply to the corporation. It is accepted, however, that such previous demand on the corporation is not

[1] (1882), 104 U.S. 450. [2] (1883), 110 U.S. 209. [3] (1887), 120 U.S. 241.
[4] Fletcher 5980. [5] Fletcher 5875.

necessary if the request would clearly be useless, e.g. if the control of the corporation is obviously hostile.[1] The demand is as a rule to be addressed to the directors; it may be made to the body of the shareholders if the plaintiff has failed with the directors. Whether such a demand on the shareholders is necessary is disputed. Generally, however, the Court has wide discretion to excuse the failure as to the previous demand.[2] The demand is regarded as useless especially by reason of hostile interests or guilty participation on the part of the directors, or the existence of an interested majority.

This derivative suit of the shareholders has been substantially curtailed by the legislations of New York (1944), New Jersey and Pennsylvania, under which a specific minority of five per cent. is entitled to sue. New York and New Jersey extend the right to sue to shareholdings amounting to not less than 50,000 dollars, or alternatively make it depend on security for costs. The remedy may even earlier not have been very effective; this curtailment tends to exclude it altogether.

Many European states accepted the majority rule without qualification, so that even the regulation in respect of alteration of the articles was left to the company. Thus the articles might provide that such major changes could be made by simple majority vote, and no quorum was prescribed by law.

German legislation provided in 1884 that such changes should require a three-fourths majority; but the law did not demand a quorum. It therefore remained possible for a small fraction of the capital to effect such changes, provided only that the qualified majority was secured. The only change made in 1937 was to require that the majority be reckoned on the basis of the capital represented at the general meeting and not merely on the basis of those shares in respect of which the right to vote was exercised. Even with this structure the legal guarantee does not amount to much. On the other hand under German law shareholders owning at least ten per cent. of the capital are entitled: (*a*) to attack the balance sheet and to resist the formation of hidden reserves; (*b*) to request investigation of the company's affairs; (*c*) to bring suits against promoters, incorporators, members of the boards of management and supervision for damage caused to the company.

[1] Stewart *v.* Washington and A.S.S. Co. (1902), 187 U.S. 466; Hawes *v.* Oakland (1882), 104 U.S. 450; Fletcher 5963, n. 4.

[2] Fletcher 5975, n. 22.

As to the rights of individual shareholders, we have seen that certain defects relating to a resolution may make it void. On the other hand shareholders may bring action to void a resolution of the general meeting if this has been carried by violating the law or the articles. It has been held that in such a case the Court has only the power to examine whether the resolution attacked was in fact contrary to law or to the articles; it cannot go into the question whether the resolution was or was not reasonable from the point of view of the company's interest. Furthermore, German law required that actions should be brought within one month after the general meeting. Not only were shareholders who voted for the resolution barred from action, but also those who were present but did not vote against the resolution and did not put their protest on record. Consequently in some cases actions otherwise well founded were dismissed for non-compliance with these requirements.[1]

In course of time German Courts became less and less favourable to such actions. The same prejudice developed against minority shareholders, especially those with small holdings, who attacked resolutions of general meetings, as in the U.S.A. In some cases this might be justified; but led to the result that the right of action given by the legislator in the interest of the general public became less and less effective.

On the other hand it is recognised that if a resolution of the general meeting violates an individual right of shareholders, they have the right to assert their claim regardless of the resolution. We must mention in this connection the provision of the German law excluding the right to a vote in cases of conflicting interest (see § 75). German practice had begun to give an action in cases in which a shareholder used his right to vote in order to promote his own interest to the detriment of that of the company or the shareholders. This is qualified by the doctrine that such interest must be not mere self-interest, but an interest hostile to that of the company (*Gesellschaftsfremd*). There were very few decisions in this direction, and the whole question was somewhat obscure. Nevertheless the German law of 1937 incorporated this rule (§ 197 (2)). No information was available as to its practical application up to 1939, and whether this provision suffices to make good the absence of equitable remedies may be doubted.

We have seen (§ 19) that French law only gradually recognised

[1] Cf. Jadow, pp. 850-58.

the power of the general meeting to alter the articles by majority resolutions, but even at present the protection of minorities is stronger than in Germany. Any alteration of the articles is allowed, except that the nationality of a company is unalterable and the obligations of the shareholders cannot be increased.

There are two requirements for validity: a quorum and a specific majority. For alterations in general, the quorum is two-thirds of the capital. Should this quorum not be present, a new meeting may be convened which may adopt the motion if attended by shareholders representing half the capital. Failing this, there may be a third meeting, at which the quorum is one-third of the capital.

If, however, the proposed alteration relates to the objects or the form of the company, the quorum is three-fourths of the capital, and this applies to the second or any subsequent meeting. The specific majority required is always two-thirds of the shares represented at the meeting. Furthermore, at any meeting convened to resolve on an alteration of the articles every shareholder has the right to attend, and limitations of the voting right provided for in the articles are inoperative, unless they apply equally to every share and every class of shares. Motions for alterations must be available in printed form for inspection at least 15 days previous to the meeting.[1]

The law of 1867 granted to shareholders of *commandites par actions* and of *sociétés anonymes*, representing five per cent. of the issued capital, the right of action against the directors (*Gérants* or Administrators respectively) and the members of the councils of supervision for misfeasance or non-feasance, though at their own expense.[2] The articles in many cases contained restrictive provisions, such as that before bringing action the minority shareholders must inform the company, or even that they must seek authorisation of the shareholders in general meeting. On the other hand it was held that a release from liability is possible by a resolution in general meeting.[3]

The Order of 31 August 1937 declared all these restrictive provisions void, and provided that resolutions of the shareholders in general meeting cannot release the directors and the members of the councils of supervision from their liability. In so far as

[1] Art. 31 of the law of 1867 as amended by the laws of 1 May 1930 and 13 April 1935.

[2] Arts. 17 and 39.

[3] Cf. Pic 1582–5.

the action is based upon a fact revealed in one of the reports submitted to the general meeting, it is to be presented within a year of the meeting. At the same time the term of limitation was reduced to three years, to be reckoned from the perpetration of the fact involving the liability of the directors or supervisors, and only for cases in which a penal delict was committed did it remain ten years.

The regulation of the Swiss law is in some respects similar. Vested interests, or in the words of the law of 1936 "well acquired rights" of the shareholders, cannot be affected by majority resolutions. Such rights are those of membership, the vote, the right to dividends and the liquidation quota, and the right to contest the validity of resolutions in general meeting (646). A majority of two-thirds of the capital is required for resolutions purporting to alter the company's purposes, to relax the requirements fixed in the articles for resolutions in general meetings, or to issue shares with plural votes. Resolutions restricting transfer of shares become binding upon registered shareholders who did not vote for the resolution only after six months following their publication in the *Gazette* (648). On the other hand this specific majority is not required for the extension of the company's objects to similar ones within its purposes, for their restriction, for mergers, for the extension of the time limit provided in the articles, for an earlier dissolution, for an alteration of the company's name or the transfer of its seat (domicile). In these cases there is a quorum of two-thirds of the capital, which is reduced to one-third for a second meeting which may be held only eight days after the first. The articles, however, may provide otherwise, both in respect of the quorum and the date of the second meeting (649). Any shareholder may sue the members of the management or of the supervision (*Kontrollstelle*) for damages caused by misfeasance or negligence, and if the injury is done to the company, for payment thereto (754). In other words, any shareholder has a representative action. This action is not affected by a resolution in general meeting releasing defendant from his liability, provided the writ of action is presented to the Court within six months after the resolution. No shareholder has such action if he voted for the resolution or acquired his shares with notice thereof.

The time limitation is five years from the date on which plaintiff obtains knowledge of the facts, or of the responsibility of defendant, and ten years without such knowledge (757, 760).

79. Directors and their Powers

(a) General

The persons through whom a corporation may perform its acts are generally called directors. Every company has one or more directors, usually in addition to other officers.

In Great Britain under the Act of 1929 every company, except private companies, must have at least two directors (sec. 139). Almost every company has at least one other officer, the secretary; even private companies usually appoint a secretary, who may himself be one of the directors or even the sole director. The secretary always plays an important part in the management: he is usually the company's chief officer after the director or directors, and he is responsible for the notices and minutes of meetings, the register of members, the transfer books and for correspondence with members.

The Companies Act, 1947, provided that every company shall have a director and a secretary, and that a sole director shall not be secretary also. This applies to private companies also (sec. 26). The position under the Act of 1948 is that every public company registered after 1 November 1929 has to have at least two directors, whereas public companies registered earlier, and private companies, shall have one director (sec. 176), and every company whether public or private must have a secretary, and a sole director shall not be secretary also (sec. 177–8).

The articles may in certain cases give other titles to persons who act on the company's behalf, and sec. 455 (1) provides that any person occupying the position of a director shall be so regarded, by whatever name he is called.

Many companies have more than two directors, in which case one or two of them act as managers and are responsible for the permanent carrying on of the company's business. These are usually known as managing directors, but there is no legal rule as to the nature and extent of their duties. The appointment of managing directors is in the power of the directors as a whole; they may also elect a chairman, and may delegate any of their powers to committees consisting of one or several directors.

Directors make their decisions, at least in major matters, by meeting together as a board. Under sec. 120 (1) of the 1929 Act, now re-enacted in sec. 175 (1) of the Act of 1948, minutes must be kept of all meetings of directors and managers, and the 1947

Act made the company and every officer in default in this respect liable to a fine (sec. 8 (now sec. 145 (4) of the Act of 1948)). If a chairman is elected, he frequently not only presides at meetings but also takes some part in the management. Any company may, and most in fact do, employ other persons whose duties, authority and remuneration may be fixed by the directors.

It is for the articles to define the directors' powers; in the absence of provisions to the contrary they may exercise all the powers of the company which are not reserved to the general meeting, and it is usual for the articles to give them such power (clause 80, Table A). The company in general meeting may regulate and restrict their powers. In many cases their borrowing powers are limited in proportion to the capital.

The position in the U.S.A. is similar. There, however, it is usual to make a distinction between directors who act as permanent managers and those who only take part in decisions on policy and in general direction. The managing director is usually called president, his deputies in the executive vice-presidents. Many companies have a chairman who presides at meetings of the board of directors, with a president and several vice-presidents as executives. The powers of these executives as to contracts and otherwise are discussed at length in the text-books and in judicial decisions.

Some statutes require that a company must have a president and a treasurer or secretary. The directors may appoint a general manager, who may or may not be a director; his powers are limited to making contracts and to other acts incidental to the ordinary business of the corporation. They may be extended or restricted by the terms of his appointment.[1]

Despite differences in detail, the English and American systems have one thing in common: there is one body to represent and act for the company, and to appoint executive officers, namely, the managers. They may appoint officers from among themselves or from outside the board, but they may not transfer or delegate their power.

Under the French system the management was entrusted to one or more directors, called *administrateurs*, or *gérants* in the case of *commandites par actions*, who formed the council of directors (*conseil d'administration*). It was usual to appoint a manager who was not a member of the council, and further to delegate a

[1] Cf. Ballantine 42–8.

director to exercise continuous supervision over current business, an *administrateur délégué*. This example was followed in many other countries.

German legislation, however, made a break in 1870 by establishing the board of management (*Vorstand*) and the council of supervision (*Aufsichtsrat*), the former to act for the company and to represent it as against third parties and public authorities, the latter to supervise the management. The original idea was that the board of supervision should have supremacy over business policy, the board of management running the business and acting as its executive organ. In practice the trend was the reverse, as we saw in § 15.

The present position is briefly as follows. The company must have at least one manager, or a board of management consisting of several members, as the articles may provide (§ 72, law of 1937). In that event the board of supervision must appoint a president. The members of the management are appointed by the board of supervision, which is appointed by the general meeting. This board must have at least three members, but the articles may provide for more. The law of 1937 restricted the membership according to the amount of share capital; companies with a capital up to 3,000,000 marks may have a board of supervision of seven members, those with up to 20,000,000 one of twelve, with over 20,000,000 twenty members.

The board of management has to carry on the business of the company on its own responsibility in such manner as the interests of the enterprise and its employees and the common good of the people and the Reich may require (§ 70 (1)). This power may not be limited or restricted as against third parties, any restrictions in the articles being merely instructions with internal effect only (§ 74), and the shareholders in general meeting may pass resolutions in respect of the management only if the management so requests (§ 103).

The board of supervision must choose a chairman and at least one deputy chairman; the board deliberates at meetings, but committees may be appointed to prepare for the meetings and supervise the execution of the resolutions. The board must supervise the management and may at any time require information therefrom concerning the affairs of the company and its subsidiaries. Their special duty is to examine the books of account and records, and to check the company's cash, securities and stock-in-trade. They may not be entrusted with any managerial duties, but it may be provided that certain classes of contracts cannot be made without their consent. The board of supervision is empowered to call a general meeting whenever the interests of the company require it (§§ 92–5). The only cases in which the board of supervision acts for the company are in making contracts between the managers and the company, and in lawsuits against managers, provided that the initiation of such proceedings has been resolved upon in general meeting or is necessary to avert the liability of any of its own members (sec. 97).

The Vichy legislation adopted in substance provisions similar to the German legislation (see § 24).

Under the Swiss O.R. the affairs of the company are managed by the administration (*Verwaltung*). One administrator is enough; if there are several, they form the board of administration (*Verwaltungsrat*). The board has to carry on the business of the company, to act for it, and to represent it as against third parties. As a rule all its members are equal.

If the articles so provide, the management as a whole or as to certain departments may be entrusted to one or several members of the board, or to managers (*Direktoren*) who are not members of the board, but at least one member of the board must take part in the management. The appointment is to be made by the members in general meeting, or by the board, if so provided by the articles.

(B) APPOINTMENT AND TERM OF OFFICE

In Great Britain the original directors may be, and usually are, named in the articles, which may provide that the names of the first directors shall be determined in writing by a majority of the subscribers (Table A, clause 75). If the articles exclude clause 75 and the subscribers have not appointed directors, two or more members holding one-tenth of the shares may convene a meeting for this purpose (sec. 134 (*b*)). The appointment may be for any term, and in the case of private companies is sometimes for life. Usually, however, especially in the case of public companies, the appointment is for terms of or under five years and it is provided that all the directors shall retire at the first general meeting (clause 87, Table A). Thereafter the power to appoint directors belongs to the general meeting.

It was formerly usual for the appointment of all the directors to be elected to be made by a single resolution, but sec. 28 of the 1947 Act, incorporated in sec. 183 of the Act of 1948, provides that except in the case of private companies the appointment of directors is to be voted on individually, unless it is otherwise agreed unanimously at the meeting, and a resolution in contravention shall be void even though the contravention was not objected to at the time.

On the other hand in accordance with the earlier law it is provided (sec. 180) that the validity of the acts of a director or manager cannot be contested, notwithstanding any defect that may be discovered in his appointment or qualification.

It is permitted, however, for the articles to give an outsider power to appoint one or more directors; this occurs particularly in favour of vendors. Such a provision is to be complied with and may be enforced, but the company may object on reasonable personal grounds.[1] The articles generally provide that the board shall have power to appoint additional directors, who shall retire at the next annual general meeting (Table A, clause 95). They are also usually empowered to fill casual vacancies, in which case the appointment is for the remainder of the term of office of the director who is being replaced (clause 95). It is usual to provide for a rotation in office, and clause 89 of Table A provides that one-third of the directors shall retire yearly. In this way the normal term of office is fixed at three years, but the company, by ordinary resolution, may determine the rotation (clause 94).

Formerly the articles sometimes provided that directors might assign their office, and some agreements also contained such stipulations. Sec. 204 provides that such assignment is ineffective unless approved by a special resolution.

In America the power to appoint directors is vested in the general meeting; their term of office is left to the articles; but certain statutes prescribe annual election, others a maximum term of office, usually with rotation.

Some of the Continental laws allow the first directors to be appointed by the founders, usually for a limited period, generally of three years; otherwise their appointment is vested in the general meeting.

[1] British Murac Rubber Syndicate *v.* The Alperton Rubber Co. (1915), 2 Ch. 186.

As we have seen, however, in Germany the members of the board of management are appointed by the board of supervision, whereas the board of supervision is to be appointed by the general meeting. The articles may, however, provide that some part, but not more than one-third of the whole, may be appointed by certain shareholders, or a certain group, provided they hold nominative shares transferable only with the assent of the company (§ 88). The term of office of the managers is limited to five years (§ 75); the members of the first board of supervision hold office for the first financial year, but subsequently they may be appointed for four financial years (§ 87). In the absence of an appointment, one may in cases of emergency be made by the court, and is valid until a new one is made by the board of supervision or the general meeting respectively (§§ 76, 89).

Under Swiss law the first directors may be appointed for no more than three years; subsequent appointments may be for not more than six years (706).

(c) QUALIFICATION

Companies in Great Britain may appoint any persons as directors, whatever their nationality or residence. Companies or other corporate bodies may also be directors (sec. 201 (1)).

Most U.S.A. laws provide that at least one of the directors must be a citizen and resident of the State concerned.

Swiss law provides that the sole director of a company, and if there are more, the majority of the directors, must be of Swiss nationality and domicile. For holding companies, if their main purpose is investment outside of Switzerland, the government may grant exemption. Violation may give cause for judicial dissolution (711).

The question whether directors must be qualified by shareholdings is in Great Britain left to the articles. Clause 77 of Table A leaves the matter to the company in general meeting; the articles may either require a specific holding or dispense with one altogether. Actually, most articles provide for a qualification by shareholding, but the amount required is usually small, often not exceeding £100 nominal.

Failure to comply with the qualification is governed by sec. 182 to the effect that a director not already qualified must obtain his qualification within two months or such shorter time as the articles may fix, his office being vacated if he fails to comply. He may not be reappointed until he obtains the qualification. Holdings of bearer warrants are not to be regarded as shareholdings.

In the U.S.A. some statutes provide that directors need not be shareholders, unless required by the articles or by-laws.[1]

Other States, e.g. New York, prescribe that directors must be shareholders, unless provided otherwise in the certificate of incorporation or by-law.[2] In New Jersey a director must be a *bona fide* stockholder of the corporation or of another corporation holding at least 25 per cent. of the stock, but the amount of a director's shareholding is to be determined by the certificate of incorporation or the by-laws.[3]

Swiss law provides that directors must be shareholders, though the extent of their holding is not prescribed.

(D) RE-ELECTION

Retiring directors may generally be re-elected. Clause 76 of Table A provides that a retiring director is eligible for re-election, and clause 92 provides that a director retiring in the course of rotation, if he offers himself for re-election, shall be deemed to be re-elected unless the resolution for his re-election was lost or it was expressly resolved at the meeting not to fill the vacated office. According to clause 93, no other person than a director or retiring director shall be eligible for election as a director unless he was either recommended by the directors or named in a written notice of a shareholder entitled to attend and to vote at the meeting, deposited at the registered office of the company not less than three and not more than 20 days before the meeting.

(E) PUBLICITY

The requirements as to publicity have been discussed in § 40, and we have only to summarise here the position in Great Britain in the light of the reforms introduced by the Act of 1947.

Under the 1929 Act every company had to keep at its registered office a register of the directors and managers, containing their present and any former Christian name and surname, their nationality, and if this has been changed, their nationality

[1] California Civ. Code, § 305, as amended by Law 1933, c. 533, sec. 13.
[2] Stock Corporation Law, § 55. [3] R.S. 14, 7–2.

of origin, their occupation, if any, and if a director or manager has no occupation but holds any other directorships, the particulars of at least one of these directorships. In respect of corporate directors or managers, the register had to contain the corporate name and the registered or principal office of the company or corporate body holding such office (sec. 144 (1)). Similarly every company registered after 23 November 1916, and every company licensed under the Moneylenders Act, 1927, whenever registered, was bound to state on all its catalogues, circulars, showcards and stationery, in respect of any corporate director its corporate name, in respect of an individual his present and former Christian names or the initials thereof and his present and former surname, his nationality, if not British, and the nationality of origin if changed, the Board of Trade being empowered to grant exceptions (sec. 145 (1)).

By sec. 27 of the 1947 Act the register of directors is to include particulars of the secretary or secretaries, but not particulars of such managers as are not at the same time directors of the company. In future particulars of all other directorships are to be entered in the register with the exception of directorships in wholly owned subsidiaries of the company, or its parent company owning all its shares, or wholly owned subsidiaries of that company. In the case of companies to which the age limit applies (see (*g*) below), the register is to include the date of birth of every director. Former Christian names and surnames are not to be included in the register if the change occurred before the person concerned attained the age of 18, or the former name has been changed or disused for a period not less than 20 years. This provision applies equally to all directors, whereas under the Act of 1929 a former name could be omitted only by natural-born British subjects, and only where the change was made or the former name disused before the person concerned attained the age of 18 (sec. 145 (*e*)). The nationality of origin need no longer be included in the register or stated in the catalogues, etc.

(F) DISQUALIFICATION

Under British law the question of disqualification was until the Act of 1947 left to the articles. Clause 72 of Table A provided that the office of director shall be vacated if the director—

(*a*) ceases to be a director by virtue of sec. 141 of the Act; or (*b*) without the consent of the company in general meeting holds any other office of profit under the company, except that of managing director or manager; or

(*c*) becomes bankrupt; or

(*d*) becomes prohibited from being a director by reason of any order made under secs. 217 or 275 of the Act, which will be discussed presently; or

(*e*) is found lunatic or becomes of unsound mind; or

(*f*) resigns his office by notice in writing to the company; or

(*g*) is directly or indirectly interested in any contract with the company or participates in the profits of any contract with the company. Provided, however, that a director shall not vacate his office by reason of his being a member of any corporation which has entered into contracts with or done any work for the company if he shall have declared the nature of his interest in the manner required by sec. 149 of the Act, but such director shall not vote in respect of any such contract or work or any matter arising thereout, and if he does so vote his vote shall not be counted. An undischarged bankrupt, however, could not act as a director without the leave of the Court (sec. 172).

The Companies Act, 1947, amended secs. 217 and 275 of the Act of 1929, and sec. 188 of the Companies Act of 1948, re-enacting sec. 33 of that Act, provides that where a person has been convicted in connection with the promotion, formation or management of a company, or where in the course of the winding-up of a company it appears that a person has been guilty of any offence of fraudulent trading, whether convicted or not, or has been otherwise guilty of any fraud or any breach of trust in relation to the company, the Court may make an order that he shall not be a director or take any part or be concerned directly or indirectly in the management of a company without the Court's leave. Such order may be made for a period specified therein not exceeding five years. There is an appeal against such order in the same way as against a conviction; contravention involves liability on conviction on indictment to imprisonment for a term not exceeding two years, or on summary conviction to imprisonment not exceeding six months, or to a fine up to £500, or both.

(G) AGE LIMIT

Many complaints have been voiced against the holding of directorships by aged persons. The Cohen Committee agreed that there were undoubtedly cases in which it would be beneficial to enforce the retirement of men who do not themselves realise that the time for retirement has come, and with whom their colleagues would feel it difficult to raise the question (131, p. 80).

The Companies Act, 1947, on this recommendation, imposed for public companies an age limit of 70 years, so that no person over that age shall be capable of being appointed, and every director on attaining that age must retire at the next annual general meeting. If an existing company's articles provide some other age limit, its provisions remain unaffected both in respect of future appointments and of vacation of office. Furthermore, when an appointment has been made or approved by ordinary resolution and the age of the appointee was disclosed to the meeting, the appointment will be valid, nor has the director to retire. Every director or prospective director must disclose his age when he has attained the age limit of 70 years or the age as defined in the articles, being otherwise liable to a fine not exceeding £5 for every day of violation. There are detailed regulations for the application of these provisions to appointments existing at the time the Act comes into force.

Companies first registered after 1 January 1947 may provide otherwise in their articles, and companies registered before that date may alter their articles in respect of the age limit and provide for a higher age (secs. 30, 31 (secs. 185 and 186 of the Act of 1948)).

The importance of the whole question seems to be exaggerated. There are methods of overcoming the operation of the provision through disclosure of age, and we do not think that such disclosure or non-disclosure makes any difference in respect of the decision in general meeting. Those who propose the appointment and whose vote is decisive know not only the age but also the other qualifications of the candidate fairly well, even without disclosure. On its merits an age limit would be justified in respect of managing directors. For directors who only take part in deciding business policy age plays a subordinate role; experience and sound judgment are much more important, and these often increase with age. Actually many companies make use of the facilities provided by the Act and thus the age limit finds in many cases no application. On the other hand it is to be regretted that neither the qualification of directors by a minimum holding nor the question of interlocking directorates was considered by the Committee, and that on neither of these matters were any steps taken.

80. Removal of Directors

Directors, with their almost unlimited authority, are in a position to bind the company by their contracts *intra vires*. They can therefore benefit it if they exercise their authority skilfully and conscientiously, and injure it if they act with negligence or in bad faith. If the only remedy for this is an action for damages, it may happen that such action is brought only after the mischief has been done and damages are no longer recoverable. It is therefore important for the company to have power to revoke the appointment of directors if the shareholders fear that they may in future injure the company by their acts or omissions. For corporations in general it has been said that the power of removal is incidental to a corporation and "is a power essential to the good order and management of the company without which it is not to be seen how the business of a corporation could be satisfactorily carried on".[1] Halsbury [2] formulates the rule as one "which is generally to be applied to corporations and without a limitation or qualification of the power to remove". But it is to be noted that in the case quoted, which was one of a municipal corporation, the rule was stated in the form that the power of removal exists only for reasonable cause.

In the case of companies this power was until 1947 even more limited. The power to remove a director was held to exist only if the articles contain a clause giving such power to the shareholders in general meeting.[3] It is otherwise with companies governed by the Companies Clauses Act, where the provision to remove is warranted by sec. 91. The articles actually contain such authorisation in most cases, and clause 80 of Table A provided that the company may by extraordinary resolution remove any director before the expiration of his term of office. Most companies

[1] Booth *v.* Arnold (1895), 1 Q.B. 571.

[2] *Laws of England*, Vol. 8, sec. 61, p. 38.

[3] Imperial Hydropathic Hotel Co. *v.* Hampson (1882), 23 Ch. D. 1; Browne *v.* La Trinidad (1887), 37 Ch. D. 1.

either adopted this provision expressly or by the general clause to the effect that the provisions of Table A will be regarded as operating.

In the case of most companies, therefore, a resolution of removal would be carried by a vote of three-fourths of those present at an extraordinary general meeting. But there are some companies, older ones especially, whose articles provide that a director may be removed only for reasonable cause; in such a case removal without reasonable cause is not admitted. But it is held that it is for the shareholders in general meeting to decide what is a reasonable cause, and the Court will not as a rule interfere with their decision.[1] In the case last quoted in the note, it was held that the Court will interfere if a case can be made out for an unfair or arbitrary exercise of the power, and that in the absence of evidence to the contrary the Court will assume that directors acted reasonably and *bona fide*. It seems therefore that as to the operativeness of the resolution the qualification contained in the articles does not amount to a virtual limitation of the power to remove.

If the articles contain no clause as to the removal of directors, the shareholders in general meeting cannot remove by resolution. It is held, however, that the shareholders may alter the articles to this effect by a special resolution, and insert a removal clause which will confer such power for the future.

If the company has power to remove, and this power is validly exercised, a director removed without reasonable cause may claim damages for loss of office, but the resolution as to removal will stand.

In the U.S.A. it is held that the power of a corporation to remove a director is inherent at common law where the director is elected with no definite term of office.[2] If, however, the term of office is determined, i.e. the director has been elected for a definite time, his removal without reasonable cause is not admissible.[3] But if a director has been removed without reasonable cause, his office is nevertheless terminated, though he may claim damages for the remaining term of his office. The dispute is more or less pointless, because most articles and by-laws and

[1] Inderwick *v.* Snell (1850), 2 Mac. and Gor. 216; Osgood *v.* Nelson (1872), L.R. 5 H.L. 636; Gresham Life Assurance Society *in re* Penney (1872), L.R. 8 Ch. App. 446.

[2] Fletcher 351–3.

[3] Fletcher 352; Ballantine 185.

many statutes prescribe that directors shall be appointed for a definite time, and thus the case of an election for an indefinite term will rarely arise.

A reasonable or just cause for removal will be either malfeasance, i.e. wilful breach of trust, or non-feasance, i.e. gross neglect. It is significant that temporary absence is not as a rule held to be a ground for removal.[1]

Under the statutes it is generally left to the articles to provide for the removal of directors, and this power is generally vested in the general meeting by special resolution, i.e. one with notice and a specific majority; some statutes provide otherwise, and it is held that the power may be delegated to the board.

The Court as a rule has no jurisdiction to remove directors. Some statutes give such power, but only in case of an action by the Attorney General. In New York, e.g. it is held that this power may be given by the charter (articles) to other authorities or persons.[2] The Attorney General will as a rule not bring action without a relation (complaint) unless the State is directly interested or a public wrong or violation of a fundamental principle of public policy is committed. Where the statute empowers the Court to remove the director on the action of the shareholders, it is as a rule reluctant to give judgment for removal.[3]

If a director has been removed, he may apply to the Court only on the ground that power to remove was lacking, or that he had no opportunity to be previously heard, or that faith and fairness were absent in the proceedings; otherwise the Court will not interfere with the removal.

The removal terminates the office, and therefore the authority of the director. It has been held [4] that if the removal was without justification in law or in fact and only to secure control, it will be void.[5] But this opinion is contrary to the general rule applying to all officers of a corporation, that a removal—even without justification—in any case terminates the office and will give action only for damages, if any.

On the European Continent the French law of 1867 provided (art. 22) that directors (*administrateurs*) are revocable. This provision has been construed as one of public policy, so that the articles cannot deny or qualify the revocability of directors.[6]

[1] Fletcher 356. [2] People *v.* Powell, 201 N.Y. 194. [3] Fletcher 359.
[4] *In re* Korff, 198 N.Y. App. Div. 553. [5] Fletcher 362.
[6] Cour de Cassation Civ. c. 30, April 1878, D.P. 78, 1, 314, and Requ. 20, Dec. 1910, D.P. 1912, 1, 441.

Furthermore the removal may be resolved upon in general meeting even without previous notice at its convocation.[1] This view is followed by nearly all Continental legislations. On this view the following principles may be stated:

(1) The election of a director gives him the power to act as such as long as he is not removed.

(2) The fact that a director is elected for a definite term of office, say three years or more, does not affect the power of the general meeting to revoke the election.

(3) No specific or reasonable cause is needed to make the revocation valid.

(4) The articles cannot qualify or limit the power to remove; they cannot provide that the removal should be valid only where there was reasonable cause for removal.

(5) The removal terminates the director's office and his authority to act for the company. He may claim damages.

In this respect, however, there is no unanimity, and it is sometimes held that he may claim damages only if he had a contract of employment with the company, i.e. if he was an executive director with a salary, and that he cannot claim compensation if he was entitled only to director's fees (*tantièmes*). Some authorities, however, hold that a director removed without reasonable cause is entitled to director's fees for the term for which he was elected even in the absence of a contract of employment and a salary. The German law of 1937 also broke in this respect with the trend of Continental law. According to § 75 (3) the removal of a manager (director) may be made by the board of supervisors, whereas before this law it was left to the articles to provide by whom the removal was to be made, and they could also provide that the general meeting should be competent for the removal. Furthermore removal is now admitted only for substantial cause, such as especially gross negligence or incapacity for the regular management of affairs. The right of the general meeting to remove a director has thus been eliminated. If the shareholders are not satisfied with the management of the directors, they are not even in a position to instruct the board to remove them. Their only power is to remove the board and to elect another which is willing to comply with their wish.

[1] Civ. r. 5, July 1893, D.P. 91, 1, 41, and 15, July 1895, D.P. 96, 1, 31. Cf. Pic 1117-21.

Such a resolution, however, requires a majority of at least three-fourths of the votes (§ 87 (2)). This qualification may be increased but not reduced. Thus the removal of directors in Germany under Nazi law became practically impossible. This was in accordance with the leader principle, but essentially contrary to the spirit of Company Law.

Even in the absence of such abnormalities of legislation the removal of a director is a very difficult business. Even if the right to remove is absolute, as it was under French law and most European legislations, there must be some definite reason to induce shareholders to organise themselves and to be present at the general meeting so that such a resolution may be carried. Directors are always in a position to obtain a substantial number of proxies and to use them to defeat the motion. It is therefore exceptional to obtain the removal of a director who is prepared to oppose the motion and fights for his position. The case of Standard Oil of Indiana, where John D. Rockefeller, Jr., succeeded in removing James Stewart from the directorate, is, as already mentioned, quoted as a very exceptional one, although the participation of Stewart in the oil scandal gave ample justification for his removal, and it is said that without the exceptional means at Rockefeller's disposal the removal could not have been achieved.

If the management of a business corporation requires that the directors should have wide and unrestricted discretionary powers, it is a matter of necessity that there should be a power to remove them without any limitation as to reasonable grounds. The position of director is, and must remain, a highly confidential one; loss of confidence therefore must be sufficient ground for removal.

Quite different is the question of compensation. A director who has been removed without reasonable cause should not lose his claim to salary or director's fees for his term of office, be he a director with a contract of employment, a managing director or simply a director without such contract.

The Companies Act, 1947 (sec. 29), provided that a company may remove a director before the expiration of his term of office by ordinary resolution, i.e. by simple majority vote, notwithstanding any provision in the articles or any agreement between the director and the company. Therefore the power to remove will be inherent and may be exercised by simple majority. This is not to apply in the case of a private company in respect of directors who on 18 July 1945 held office for life.

The notice of motion to remove a director is to be given to the company at least 21 days before the meeting, and the company is to send a copy thereof to the director concerned and to notify the members either by advertisement or in any other way allowed by the articles not less than 14 days before the meeting. If this has been duly done, it is immaterial that the notice of motion was given later than 21 days before the meeting.

The company in general meeting may without notice appoint another person to the vacant place, and if the vacancy is not filled at the meeting it may be filled as a casual vacancy and the appointment will be for the remainder of the term of office of the removed director. The removal does not in itself deprive the removed director of any compensation or damages due to him in respect of the termination of his appointment as director or any appointment terminating with that as director (sec. 184 of the Act of 1948).

81. Duties and Responsibilities of Directors

The crucial point in company management has always been that of the duties and liabilities of the directors. The various legislations grant wide powers to directors by their statutes, and these may be extended by the articles. These extensions are most far-reaching under the laws of the U.S.A., where the powers of the board of directors are generally much wider than under English or any European legislation. They cover not only the management of the company's business, but extend without exception to the declaring of dividends and the final arrangement of the balance sheet and the profit and loss account. Beside these customary powers and competences, corporation practice has evolved methods of extending them, by the articles as originally drawn up or subsequently altered, to other important matters, such as the issue of authorised stock with the power to lay down the conditions and especially the consideration for the issue, the granting of preferential rights and the alteration of those laid down in the articles, the sale of the business as a whole, i.e. of all the assets of the company, the making of long-term contracts and leases and lastly the sale of the assets against stock. It is obvious that in view of the wide extent of these powers the question of responsibility for their exercise, and of liability for defects therein, is even more important in the United States than in countries which do not recognise such delegation of powers. But even without such abnormal extensions the power of the management is paramount.

We have seen that it is characteristic of Continental legislations that, although the power of the general meeting was declared to be supreme, and—at least until the German law of 1937—the board of management had to comply with instructions given by the general meeting, the validity of contracts made by the management could not be contested by the company, however injurious and damaging they might be. The courts recognised exceptions in case of collusion, i.e. fraud, provided the other party took an active part therein. But this exception could not in most cases be of much avail, and mere knowledge—actual or constructive—was held not to be sufficient for such defence. Therefore even where a contract was made in contravention of a resolution in general meeting, it was binding on the company, the only recourse being an action against the managers guilty of such contravention; a poor remedy in view of the amounts involved in serious cases of breach of trust.

The other factor to be considered is that normally managements are in a position to obtain either powers for executing specific contracts or ratification of their acts from the general meeting, and it is exceptional for their acts to be disapproved by a majority. It is not surprising therefore that the question of the measure of diligence, the spirit in which these powers should be exercised, and the consequences of breach of trust are a matter of much controversy.

In Anglo-American law this question is generally discussed under the heading of trusteeship. By some it is asserted, and by others denied, that directors are trustees.

Obviously they are not trustees in the technical sense, since trusteeship cannot exist without legal ownership, and this is vested not in the directors, but in the corporation. Decisions, especially earlier ones, that directors are trustees, were wrong if this was meant in the strict technical sense, but correct if the term was used in the sense of a fiduciary relation, for the powers conferred on directors by their election are granted in the expectation that they will be exercised in the interest of the company and not that of the directors themselves, or of any outsider.

A further question is, for whom are the directors trustees? That they are trustees for the company as a legal entity is correct, but may be regarded as a truism. Our difficulties begin when we examine the details of the question closely.

One thing is undoubtedly clear: the consideration of their personal interests by the managers is contrary to their fiduciary relationship. Nevertheless even in this regard the rights of the company and the corresponding duties and liabilities of the directors are not always recognised. We shall deal with this point in connection with the remuneration of directors, with the question of loans granted to them by the company, and their dealings in the company's shares and other securities. In each of these cases neither practice nor law gives full protection to companies, though on principle there is no doubt that directors are not given and may not use their powers in order to fill their own pockets. The real question of principle begins when the interest of the company is contrasted with that of the shareholder. One approach is that the directors are in a fiduciary relationship only with the company; another, that they are fiduciaries of the shareholders also, and that in case of a conflict of interests that of the shareholders must prevail. The sharpest formulation of this line of thought is that directors are fiduciaries solely of and for the shareholders. The adherents of the doctrine that directors are fiduciaries of the corporation itself sometimes broaden this view to mean that directors must look not only to the interests of shareholders but also to those of the employees and workers of the corporation, as well as to those of consumers, and generally of all third persons who come into relation with the company, and finally to those of the community, as set forth in the German law of 1937.

In the American literature this question has been thoroughly discussed by A. A. Berle, Jr., and M. E. Dodd.[1] Prof. Berle's arguments were subsequently incorporated in the well-known book by Berle and Means: *The Modern Corporation and Private Property*. Berle asserts that all powers granted either to directors or to groups of shareholders are connected with responsibility. However absolute the powers granted by the articles, they are at all times exercisable only for the proportionate benefit of all the shareholders, and consequently such powers are subject to equitable limitation if and when they have been exercised to the

[1] Harvard Law Review, vols. 44 and 45.

detriment of their interests. In Berle's view the same equitable limitation applies also to powers granted by statute, and consequently every exercise of power is subject to a double test: (*a*) whether the technical rules as to the extent of exercise of the power have been complied with; (*b*) whether the exercise of power is or is not equitable according to rules somewhat analogous to those governing the exercise of the power of a trustee. We are not here concerned with the powers granted to groups of shareholders, or more exactly the majority; this question is discussed elsewhere (§ 78), and we must confine our present discussion to the exercise of powers by directors. Berle asserts that his rule applies to every corporate power, but he restricts the evidence to five apparently absolute corporate powers: (1) to issue stock; (2) to declare or withhold dividends; (3) to acquire stock in other corporations; (4) the reserved power to amend the charter (articles); (5) to transfer the corporate enterprise to another corporation. He asserts that the American Courts have already applied the equitable rule in each and all of these instances. We have not to examine this question in detail, since all five powers are discussed under the respective headings. We may, however, state in brief that the attitude of American Courts is not quite consistent, and the equitable limitation of powers was recognised only with certain important qualifications. On the other hand it seems that Professor Dodd is right in his remark that all the limitations applied in the practice of the American Courts may be interpreted on the basis of contract. The position with regard to a legislative policy test, i.e. whether the rule should be accepted for the future and incorporated as such in the statutes, or accepted by the Courts, is quite different. In this regard the thesis is to be fully supported. It is just and equitable that in cases where boards of directors are empowered to issue additional shares at their discretion, such issues should be made in such a manner as to protect the rateable interest of existing and prospective shareholders. This means that additional shares should not be issued for a consideration disproportionate to their value and to the interest which will be acquired by their purchase. This rule should apply also to treasury stock. The question of rateable interest is crucial where shares are issued for property or services. In such a case the discretion of the directors is practically unlimited, and we think that no such issue should be made without an appraisal by independent experts.

As to shares issued for cash, the interests of existing shareholders could be to some extent protected by recognising their pre-emptive rights; Berle, however, is not in favour of the rigid enforcement of this right. From a historical point of view he asserts that in Gray *v.* Portland Bank,[1] the early decision which was the basis of the doctrine of pre-emptive rights, the Court did not intend to accept the rule as a rigid one, applicable to every case, but only as an equitable rule under which the issue is to be disallowed if and when the equitable interest of the existing shareholders is violated. He finds a statement of this rule in Luther *v.* Luther Co.,[2] in which case the Court considered the unissued stock merely as property over which the powers of the directors are the same as over any other asset of the company, namely, to sell to whom and at such prices as to them shall seem best for the corporation and all its stockholders in the honest exercise of the discretion vested in them. It follows from this rule that shares cannot be issued at a nominal price or at a price which is not in accordance with the existing equities of shareholders.

Berle, however, is of the opinion that the exercise of the power should be allowed even in disregard of technical rules if there is some interest which would justify such procedure. Consequently he thinks that additional shares may be issued in disregard of pre-emptive rights, and even for a consideration which is not in accordance with existing equities, if there is some advantage for the company in allotting the shares to the purchaser in question. In this regard he quotes with approval decisions in which the issue of shares with the exclusion of pre-emptive rights and at prices less than would accord with values has been allowed.

The shareholders usually consider the question of responsibility in management in general meeting. Under the European legislations this is a special subject for the agenda, and a resolution concerning it must be carried at the annual general meeting. The resolution may be that the directors, or where there are such, the boards and councils of supervision, are released in respect of the past financial year, or that release is refused, or lastly that the decision is suspended pending further investigation. The release is held to extend to any matter which was known at the time the resolution was carried, and Courts have held, especially in Germany, that by it the question of liability is settled for good

[1] (1807), 3 Mass. 364. [2] (1903), 118 Wis. 112, 124.

and the company is deemed to have renounced any claim in respect of liability which it might have had.[1] Moreover the persons concerned have an action to request release.[2]

There has been much dispute over what omissions or breaches of trust were known or had to be known to shareholders who voted in favour of the release. The law of 1937 provided that release can be given only in connection with the consideration of the accounts and reports (§ 104), and therefore a release given in respect of one or more single acts of management will be inoperative [3]; it may or may not be valid as a renunciation. Moreover, the law provides (§ 84) that any renunciation in respect of claims against members of the two boards is inoperative if carried during a five years period after such claim arose, whether known or unknown.

Owing to the importance of resolutions relating to releases certain European legislations provide that no shareholder may vote on the question of his own release. The leader in this respect was the German law,[4] maintained by the law of 1937 (§ 114 (5)). The same provision is made in the Swiss O.R. (697).

It is of course generally recognised that directors are liable for wilful acts injuring the company, or in English terminology for breach of trust, i.e. misapplication of the company's funds, and for misfeasance, i.e. other breaches of their duties.

The liability for negligence is much more complicated. In Great Britain the measure of diligence required from directors was frequently discussed, the question being obscured by the fact that the articles of many companies contained provisions exempting directors from liability, except in cases of dishonesty or wilful neglect or default, which stipulation was held to be valid.[5]

In Turquand *v.* Marshall,[6] where the main charge against the directors was that they made a loan to one of their co-directors, L. C. Hatherley said that the directors' "trust to an undue extent was not a matter with which they could be fixed, unless there was something more alleged, as—for instance—that it was done fraudulently and improperly and not merely by a default of judgment". In the same case James, L.J., said that "directors

[1] R.G.Z. 106, 258, 115, 246.
[2] R.G.Z. 89, 396.
[3] Gadow, p. 435.
[4] Commercial Code of 1897, § 252.
[5] Cf. *re* Brazilian Rubber Plantations and Estates (1911), 1 Ch. 425; *re* City Equitable Fire Insurance Co. Ltd. (1930), 2 Ch. 293.
[6] (1869), L.R. 4 Ch. App. 376.

are not to be made liable on those strict rules which have been applied to trustees", and Brett, L.J., said that a director must be "guilty of such negligence as would make him liable in an action. Mere imprudence is not such negligence. Want of judgment is not".

Lindley, M.R., said in Lagunas Nitrate Co. *v.* Lagunas Syndicate,[1] that if directors act within their powers and "if they act with such care as is reasonably to be expected from them having regard to their knowledge and experience", they are not liable. Further, he said in this case and also in National Bank of Wales,[2] that the directors' negligence "must be not the omission to take all possible care, it must be much more blamable than that, it must be in a business sense culpable or gross negligence".

The diligence of men with an ordinary degree of prudence, acting on their own behalf, was adopted as the measure of diligence required from directors in Merchants' Fire Office *v.* Armstrong.[3] In Brazilian Rubber Plantations and Estates Ltd.,[4] Neville, J., held that the reasonable care required from directors is to be measured by the care which an ordinary man might be expected to take in the circumstances, on his own behalf.

Homer, J., rightly stated *in re* City Equitable Fire Insurance Co.,[5] that the authorities do not give any very clear answer to the question what particular degree of skill and diligence is required from directors, and he stresses the rule that "a director need not exhibit in the performance of his duties a greater degree of skill than may be reasonably expected from a person of his knowledge and experience".

Continuous attention to the company's affairs is not required from directors. A director is "not bound to attend every meeting of directors, and it is not part of the duty of a director to take part in every transaction which is considered at a board meeting".[6] Absence from meetings was repeatedly excused and not held to be ground for liability.[7]

Jessel, M.R., said *in re* Forest of Dean Co.,[8]: "Probably an ordinary director, who only attends meetings occasionally, cannot be expected to devote as much time and attention to the

[1] (1899), 2 Ch. 392. [2] (1899), 2 Ch. 629. [3] (1901), W.N. 163.
[4] (1911), 1 Ch. 425. [5] (1930), 2 Ch. 293. [6] Perry's case (1876), W.N. 170.
[7] *Re* Denham and Co. (1883), 25 Ch.D. 752, Marquess of Bute's case (1892), 2 Ch. 100; *re* City Equitable Fire Insurance Co. Ltd. (1930), 2 Ch. 293
[8] (1878) 10 Ch. D. 450.

business of the company as the sole managing partner of an ordinary partnership", and Stirling, J., stated *in re* Denham and Co., *supra*, that "neglect or omission to attend meetings is not the same thing as neglect of a duty which ought to be performed at those meetings".

Romer, J., in the City Equitable Fire Insurance Co. case,[1] summarised the state of law as follows: "A director is not bound to give continuous attention to the affairs of his company. His duties are of an intermittent nature, to be performed at periodical board meetings and at meetings of committees of the board upon which he happens to be placed. He is not however bound to attend all such meetings, though he ought to attend whenever in the circumstances he is reasonably able to do so." Consequently, absentee directors were relieved in many cases.

Moreover, it is held that in order to ascertain the duties of a director "it is necessary to consider not only the nature of the company's business, but also the manner in which the work of the company is in fact distributed between the directors and the other officers of the company, provided always that this distribution is a reasonable one in the circumstances and is not inconsistent with any express provision of the articles of association".[2]

Consequently there is a tendency to exonerate a director who relied on information given to him by the chairman, by co-directors or officials. In the case of Dovey and Cory,[3] a director was exonerated from liability in respect of a fraudulent balance sheet and improper loans, on the ground that he could rely on the information given to him by the chairman and the managing director. Lord Davey said that the director "was bound to give his attention to and exercise his judgment as a man of business on the matters which were brought before the board at the meetings which he attended", and that "he was entitled to rely upon the judgment, information and advice of the chairman and general manager, as to whose integrity, skill and competence he had no reason for suspicion". In the same case Halsbury, L.C., was of the opinion that there is no duty of detecting frauds; "if there is such duty it must render anything like an intelligent devolution of labour impossible". It cannot be expected of a

[1] (1930), 2 Ch. 293.
[2] *Per* Romer, J., *in re* City Equitable Fire Insurance Co. Ltd. (1930), 2 Ch. 293.
[3] (1901), A.C. 477.

director "that he should be watching either the inferior officers of the bank or verifying the calculations of the auditor himself. The business of life could not go on if people could not trust those who are put in a position of trust for the express purpose of attending to the details of management".

In an earlier case,[1] a director was held liable for negligence in respect of a cheque signed by him on behalf of the company, because he failed to make inquiries, trusting his co-directors. It was said that he acted in his own right, but—as Romer, J., said [2]—"in respect of all duties, that having regard to the exigencies of business and the articles of association may properly be left to some other official, a director is, in absence of grounds for suspicion, justified in trusting that official to perform such duties honestly".

The onus of proving negligence is on plaintiff,[3] and as Lord Davey said,[4] "it must be proved that the director did not give his attention and did not exercise his judgment on the matters brought before the board".

As already mentioned, the widespread use of exemption clauses in the articles gave protection in many cases against liability for negligence, and this position led in 1928 to a legislative reform. By sec. 152 of the Companies Act, 1929, any provision of the articles, or any contract made which exempts any director, manager, officer or auditor of the company from any liability imposed by any rule of law in respect of negligence, default, breach of duty, or breach of trust of which he may be guilty in relation with the company has been declared to be void. The same applies to any provision or stipulation indemnifying any such person against such liability.

On the other hand, under sec. 372 of the Act of 1929, the Court has power to relieve any director, manager, officer or auditor of a company from his liability in respect of negligence, default, breach of duty or breach of trust, wholly or partly, on such terms as it may think fit. Such relief may be granted if it appears to the Court that the person concerned, though he is or may be liable, acted honestly or reasonably, and that having regard to all the circumstances of the case, including those connected with his appointment, he ought fairly to be excused.

[1] Joint Stock Discount Co. *v.* Brown (1869), L.R., 8 Eq. 381.
[2] *Re* City Equitable Fire Insurance Co. Ltd. (1930), 2 Ch. 293.
[3] *Re* Liverpool Household Stores (1890), 59 L.J. Ch. 616.
[4] *Re* Dovey *v.* Cory (1901), A.C. 477.

Such relief may be granted either in the course of the proceedings for enforcing liability, or on the petition of a person who has reason to apprehend that a claim to enforce liability will or might be made against him.

The Companies Act of 1947 introduced no new regulation of directors' liability for management, though its reforms include the strengthening of the liability for mis-statements in prospectuses and for defective accounts, and secs. 152 and 372 are re-enacted in secs. 205 and 448 of the Act of 1948.

In the U.S.A.[1] there is much dispute about the standard of care and diligence. In many cases directors have been held liable only for gross negligence; in other cases the Courts held that the standard required is the care and diligence which an ordinary prudent man would exercise in the management of his own affairs.[2] The Pennsylvania Business Corporation Act, 1933, provides [3] that directors must use "that diligence, care and skill which ordinary prudent men would exercise under similar circumstances in their personal affairs". Certain Courts, however, held the true standard to be the degree of diligence which an ordinary prudent director could reasonably be expected to exercise under similar circumstances.[4]

A similar objective rule is contained in the law of Michigan: "The directors and each of them have to give the attention and diligence, care and skill, that prudent men use in like or similar circumstances." [5] This rule is approved in the literature.[6] On the other hand, it is stressed that the decision whether directors have complied with their duties or are guilty of negligence, depends rather more on the actual circumstances of the case than on a general formula as to the care required. In this respect it is obvious that in recent years the courts have taken a less lenient view than in earlier times.[7]

It is noteworthy that directors of banks and financial corporations are sometimes held under duty to apply a higher degree of care and diligence than directors of other business corporations, and that in some cases the position of the chairman and executive directors was held to involve more extensive duties, particularly in respect of supervision. It was stressed in this respect that

[1] Cf. Ballantine 62–5; Dodd and Baker, pp. 472—503.
[2] E.g. Hun *v.* Cary (1880), 82 N.J. 65.
[3] § 408.
[4] Ballantine 63, at n. 11.
[5] § 47.
[6] Fletcher 1070; Ballantine, p. 158.
[7] Cf. Briggs *v.* Spaulding (1890), 141 U.S. 132; and the cases quoted by Dodd and Baker, pp. 483–4.

directors "were not bound by virtue of the office gratuitously assumed by them to call in the passbooks and to compare them with the ledger" and they "hardly could have seen" that their failure to look at the ledger opened the way to a fraud "committed by the cashier".[1]

Failure to attend meetings was generally regarded as ground for liability, and residence in another State as not justifying absence.[2]

The model for State Business Corporation Acts, drafted by the Corporation Law Committee of the American Bar Association (1946) does not attempt to define the standard of care required from directors, leaving the question to be governed by common law. It suggests, however, that a director shall not be liable, if he relied and acted in good faith upon the balance sheet or profit and loss account presented by the president or officer of the corporation having charge of the books of account or certified by an independent or certified public accountant to reflect fairly the financial condition of the corporation.[3]

French law contains no special regulations as to the liability of directors for negligence, and the question is governed by the rules on agency of the Civil Code. According to art. 1992, the agent is liable, beside fraud, for all negligence, though a less strict view is to be taken in respect of unpaid agents.

Since in France directors (*administrateurs*) generally receive compensation in form of fees or a percentage of profits (*tantièmes*) they are liable for all and not only for gross negligence, measured by the standard of care of a *bonus pater familias*. The Courts, however, take a rather lenient view,[4] and tend to exonerate directors in cases of slight negligence. If, however, the directors delegate their powers to a general manager or *administrateur delégué*, they are responsible for his acts or omissions, unless they apply reasonable care in respect of the supervision of his activities.[5]

The German Code of Commerce of 1897 (§ 241) requires from a member of the board of management the care of "a careful man of business" and the same standard is prescribed (§ 249) for the members of the board of supervision. The law of 1937 (§ 84) defines the care required as that of "a careful and conscientious manager of a business" and expressly imposes the duty

[1] *Per* Holmes, J., in Bates *v.* Dresser (1920), 251 U.S. 524.

[2] Bowerman *v.* Hamner (1929), 250 U.S. 504.

[3] § 42.

[4] Cf. Pic 1197–1200.

[5] Cf. Pic 1201.

of secrecy in respect of confidential statements. According to an express provision, the onus of evidence is imposed on the managers; the company has only to prove that damage was caused. The sued manager has to prove that he applied the required diligence. The same was held under the Commercial Code.[1] The company is not entitled to sue for damages if the act or omission is warranted by a lawful resolution in general meeting, whereas the consent of the board of supervision is no excuse.

The liability as against creditors is—apart from certain wrongful acts such as unlawful repayment of capital or unlawful payment of dividends—restricted to cases of gross negligence. Moreover creditors have an action only if they are unable to get satisfaction from the company, but the existence of a resolution in general meeting is no defence against their claims. The same measure of diligence is prescribed for the members of the board of supervision (§ 99). Already under the earlier law it was held that the articles cannot grant exemptions or provide for a lower standard of care.[2] The cases in which violation of the law involves liability are summarised in § 84 (3) of the law of 1937.

Satisfactory as these provisions may seem, their effect is largely nullified by the difficulty of enforcing liability against an unwilling majority. Thus the problem of protecting the company and its members against mismanagement is not in any way solved.

82. Restrictions on Directors

To ensure that directors shall devote their activities to the company's interests, various restrictions have been thought desirable, and some of these have by certain legislations been actually imposed.

Whether a director may or may not engage in business in general, particularly in the company's own line of business, usually depends upon the contract. From the standpoint of Anglo-American law this is a natural consequence of the structure of the board, on which directors who act for the company only in their quality as members of the board, and directors who are at the same time salaried executives, have seats on the same footing.

[1] Staub-Pinner, p. 355.
[2] R.G.Z. 46, 61; Staub-Pinner II, p. 354; Gadow, p. 319.

In the case of executives, contracts usually provide that managers, i.e. directors who are at the same time managing directors, technical managers, experts, and so on, must devote their whole time and activity to the company's interests, and not engage in other business or take part in partnerships. In the absence of such a contract express or implied there is no such restriction. This may operate to the detriment of the company, and the question arises whether such restrictions may be held to be implied in view of the fiduciary character of their position. This consequence has in some cases been drawn in the U.S.A., and we may note some decisions by which such a duty was held to exist. The old English case of Keech *v.* Sandford [1] may be quoted as the basis of this doctrine. In Young *v.* Columbia Oil Co. of West Virginia,[2] action was brought against directors who entered parcels of land adjoining the company's property for the production of natural gas, and after having struck gas, sold the output to the company at the regular prices. The Court held that the directors could not retain the profits, and that the shareholders who had no knowledge of the transaction and had not approved it were entitled to recover a proportionate part of the profits, even though the company itself could not have acquired the property in question, since under the law of the State it had no right to occupy more than 20 acres for each discovery. The company was therefore not a loser; moreover the shareholders in general meeting had ratified the transaction. This seems to go too far. On the other hand the rule that directors may not retain profits from transactions which the company itself might have undertaken is fully justified.

Even if this rule is fully recognised there will be ways in which directors may profit by virtue of their position in cases where neither the company nor its shareholders have suffered losses. Stanton *v.* Schenck [3] was a case in which directors acted as middlemen for the sale of a block of the company's shares owned by a shareholder and were able to earn a large commission. In consequence of the transaction the control of the company was transferred to a new group. Minority shareholders sued for the recovery of the commission earned by the directors in a representative suit for the company. The action was dismissed because the transaction itself, i.e. the transfer of the control, did

[1] (1726), Sel. Cas. Ch. 61.
[2] (1931), 110 W. Va. 364.
[3] (1931), 140 Misc. 621, N.Y.

not harm the company; on the other hand the company was not in a position to make the profit, since there were no treasury shares and a new issue was not practicable. It was further stressed that the director did not act *qua* director but only in his personal capacity. While the first two reasons may be appreciated the last is very dangerous; it will always be difficult to decide whether in a given case a director has acted *qua* director or in his personal capacity, quite apart from the consideration that if the transaction is one which the company is in a position to undertake, the director has certainly no right to act otherwise than on its behalf.

The dangers connected with such reasoning are obvious in cases where a conflict of interest is likely to arise. Kline *v.* Thompson,[1] was a case in which the president of a company employed the plaintiff in its service and at the same time sold him part of his own stock. After having been dismissed by the company the plaintiff sued for damages, and it was held that he could not recover from the company.

If it is assumed, as is often done, that directors are in a similar position to trustees, their duties are yet definitely less extensive than those of a trustee. A trustee may make no profit out of his trust. This rule was precisely stated in Magruder *v.* Drury and Maddox [2]: "the rule springs from his duty to protect the interests of his estate and not to permit his personal interest to conflict in anywise with his duty in that respect. The intention is to provide against any possible selfish interest exercising an influence which can interfere with the faithful discharge of the duty which he is owing in a fiduciary capacity". "It therefore prohibits a party from purchasing on his own account that which his duty of trust requires him to sell on account of another, and from purchasing on account of another that which he sells on his own account. In effect he is not allowed to unite the two opposite characters of buyer and seller, because his interests when he is the seller or buyer on his own account are directly conflicting with those of the person on whose account he buys or sells."[3] "It makes no difference that the estate was no loser by the transaction or that the commission was no more than the services were reasonably worth. It is the relation of the trustee to the estate which prevents his dealing in such way as to make a profit for himself."

[1] (1931), 206 Wis. 464. [2] (1914), 235 U.S. 106, 119–20.
[3] Michmond *v.* Giro (1846), 4 How. 503, at 555.

We shall see that in the case of contracts with a company there are opinions to the effect that the same rule applies, whereas a widespread opinion holds that in so far as the contract is fairly reasonable for the company it cannot be attacked.[1]

Of the European legislations, Germany adopted for the management (*Vorstand*) the system of a positive measure of restriction. This was provided by the Code of 1861 and maintained by the Code of 1897 (§ 236) and subsequently by § 79 of the Companies law of 1937. Under this law the members of the board of management may not engage in trade (this of course includes industry and banking); further, they may not enter a partnership whatever its object. They are likewise prohibited from undertaking transactions on their own account or for third parties in the line of business in which the company is engaged. All this, however, may be permitted by the board of supervision, in which case the manager is free to act on the basis of such permission. Under this restriction managers are prohibited from the regular carrying on of business ; they are not, however, prohibited from undertaking an occasional transaction, unless it be in the same line of business as the company's.

A special question arises as to the purchase and sale of securities. The report of the Reichstag Commission on the Commercial Code of 1897 asserts (979) that speculative transactions in securities are prohibited if the company is itself engaged in business of this kind, and therefore a bank manager, i.e. a member of the board of management of a banking company, is not entitled to make speculative sales or purchases of securities. It is of course very difficult, if not impossible, to decide what makes a purchase or sale a speculative transaction. Quite apart from this, during all the years since the report was published not a single case has been reported in which action was taken before German Courts against a manager on this ground, although it is common knowledge that many German managers were regularly engaged in speculative transactions in securities both of their own and of other companies.

The consequences of transgression are clearly defined : the company is entitled to claim damages or to request that the transaction in question should be dealt with as if it had been made on the company's behalf. It may therefore demand the surrender of the profits. The action, however, must be brought

[1] Cf. Ballantine 66-72*a*. Dodd and Baker pp. 498-531. Berle and Means pp. 220-232.

within three months of the day on which the members of the boards of management and supervision learnt of the transaction. After five years the action is extinct by limitation, regardless of whether and when the transaction came to light.

There is no restriction with regard to the board of supervision. Its members may engage in business, may compete with the company, and transact business whether regular or occasional of the kind carried on by the company. No wonder therefore that the positions of managers and of members of boards of supervision were so coveted in Germany and all countries with similar company laws. Moreover the laws of Austria, Hungary and Switzerland did not contain the restrictive provision of the German law, since they did not separate the board of management from the board of supervision. In these countries directors *qua* directors were under no restriction, and only in so far as they were salaried executives did they come under contractual or in some cases legal restrictions.

A special question arises as to transactions by directors in securities of their own company. Such transactions are frequently on the border-line. Directors as a rule have intimate knowledge of the state of affairs of their business, its results and prospects and its future outlook, whether favourable or not. In the light of this knowledge they may purchase shares when the outlook seems favourable, and sell if events not yet known to the public are likely to bring about a fall in price. Changes in the general trend of prices may upset such calculations, but nevertheless it will generally be profitable to act on inside information. Such abuses were widespread, especially in times of violent repercussions on the security market, in times both of boom and of slump. The possibility of purchases on low margins and of bear operations, i.e. the sale of shares not yet owned by the seller, makes effective influencing of the market possible. This was extensively carried on during the railway period ; the operations of railway kings and "robber barons" form a memorable chapter in the history of American corporations. Such notorious personalities as Jay Gould had an accomplished technique and at that period the activities of directors were aimed rather at the promotion of their own speculations than the administration of the companies they dominated. In those days the executives played a very subordinate and impoverished role in the life of their companies; the field was dominated by the directors, who regarded speculation as their real and main occupation. In consequence of these activities the general public and the management of the companies in question suffered equally. Similar manipulations occurred elsewhere, though not on the same large scale. It is often asserted that with the great concentration of economic power following on the amalgamation of railway systems and in industry on trustification this stage has definitely passed away. Investigation subsequent to the collapse of 1929, however, showed that this was not so everywhere, and large-scale operations of directors were discovered.

As to possible remedies, the position is as follows. In English law there are none; a company has no right to sue a director and recover from him profits earned by speculative transactions in the company's securities, nor have the shareholders any action.

Under European laws the question was never specifically focussed on transactions in securities of the company itself. As to the general rule, as already mentioned, there is the opinion expressed by the German Reichstag Committee according to which bank managers are not entitled to speculate in securities whether those of their own or of other companies. Actually this principle was never enforced: no actions or judgments against members of banks or boards of management are recorded, and the alleged rule was not meant to apply to managers of industrial and trading companies, or to members of the boards of supervision.

The initiative was taken by the American Courts and subsequently by the New Deal legislation. The practice of American Courts shows the beginning of a movement in favour of the recognition of an overriding principle: that of the fiduciary position of directors in regard not only to the company but also to the shareholders. Whereas in earlier times it had been held that directors are entitled to deal with shareholders at arm's length and have no special duties in transactions whose object is a block of securities of their own company, it is now held by many courts that they are under obligation to reveal their personal knowledge if that is relevant to the transaction. Furthermore there have been cases in which directors who sold their own holdings at enhanced prices, while inducing shareholders to accept lower ones, were obliged to let them participate in the difference. But these are only beginnings, and moreover this rule is not yet generally accepted. A positive step, however, has been taken by the New Deal legislation. Directors and officers of corporations whose securities are listed by one of the National Stock Exchanges, and those of public utility holding companies and investment trusts even if their securities are not so listed, have to report their holdings in shares of their own companies and any change therein. The companies are entitled to recover any profit earned by transactions in such securities, provided that the purchase and sale thereof is effected within six months.

It is an advantage that holdings by directors and officers in the securities of their own companies are made known both to the company and through it to the shareholders and also to the public through the office of the Securities and Exchange Commission (S.E.C.). The recognition of the principle that directors and officers have no right to retain profits resulting from speculative transactions in the securities of their own companies is a definite advance. It is also an advantage that the Acts give a simple and clear definition of speculative transactions, though it may be that the rule can easily be circumvented by postponing the sale to a date beyond the six months' period.

The Cohen Committee recognised the importance of this problem in Great Britain, and concluded that the law should be altered so as to discourage improper transactions based on inside information. It was felt, however, that the best safeguard is disclosure and that a high standard of conduct could be maintained by ensuring disclosure in full measure.[1] The Companies Act, 1948 (sec. 195), re-enacting sec. 37 of the Act of 1947, provides for this by enacting that every company shall keep a register showing as respects each director the number, description and amount of any shares in or debentures of the company or any other body corporate, being the company's subsidiary, or a subsidiary of the company's holding company, which are held by or in trust for him or of which he has any right to become the holder (whether on payment or not). Where any shares or debentures fall to be or cease to be recorded in the said register in relation to any director by reason of a transaction entered into by him after the coming into force of this section and while he is a director, the register shall also show the date of the agreement, the price or other consideration for the transaction. This register is to be kept at the company's registered office and to be open to inspection by any member or debenture holder of the company

[1] Rep. 86–7, pp. 45–6.

during business hours, subject to such reasonable restrictions as the company may by its articles or in general meeting impose, so that not less than two hours in each day be allowed for inspection, but only during the period of 14 working days immediately preceding the company's annual general meeting and three working days after its conclusion. Further, it shall be open to the inspection of any person acting on behalf of the Board of Trade at any time, and the Board may at any time require a copy of the said register, or any part thereof. It shall also be produced at the commencement of the annual general meeting and remain open and accessible during the meeting to any person attending. In case of refusal the Court may compel an immediate inspection of the register, and there are fines for default and refusal.

While it may be assumed that abuses in respect of transactions in companies' securities in Great Britain were exceptional and not serious, we think that the example of the U.S.A. should have been followed. The statement of the Committee that the American practice requiring the disclosure of directors' transactions "does not appear to have had unfortunate results" is true also in respect of the recovery of profits resulting from speculative transactions of this kind.

The Act of 1929 provided that the accounts shall show the particulars of any loan made to directors during the respective period by the company or by any other person under the guarantee or the security provided by the company, including the amounts repaid, and further the amount of any loan outstanding at the end of the financial year whenever made. This applies to loans given to officers of the company with the exception of loans not exceeding £2000, if the directors certify that the loan was made in accordance with the practice adopted or to be adopted by the company in respect of loans to its employees.

The duty as to disclosure does not apply if the ordinary business of the company includes the lending of money and the loan was made in the ordinary course of the company's business (sec. 128). There is no prohibition in respect of such loans.

The Companies Act, 1947, however, extended the prohibition to loans to directors of the company or of its holding company, and against giving a guarantee or security for loans made by other persons. Loans by companies whose ordinary business includes the lending of money or giving guarantees are excepted. Loans to directors may, however, be made with the approval of the general meeting, where the director concerned requires the loan to meet expenditure incurred or impending with a view to enable him properly to perform his duties as a director or officer and the purposes of the expenditure are disclosed to the members before approval is given. This prohibition does not apply to exempt private companies (sec. 37).

The provisions of sec. 128 of the Act of 1929 as to disclosure of loans made to directors were accordingly amended, and the duty to show the particulars of loans, etc., is extended to such as were made during the financial year to any person before he was appointed as director or officer (sec. 39; now secs. 197 and 198 of the Act of 1948).

Whether it would not have been more adequate to prohibit loans to directors and officers generally future experience will show.

The law of Great Britain neither prohibits the making of contracts between directors and companies, nor debars the director with whom such a contract is to be made from voting on this matter at the meeting; his only duty is to disclose his interest at the meeting of the board of directors (sec. 149).

In spite of complaints on this question, which by the way induced the London Stock Exchange Committee to withhold permission to deal unless the articles contain a prohibition against the voting of interested directors except on a limited class of contracts, the Committee did not recommend a general prohibition (95, p. 50), and the Companies Act, 1947, refrained from introducing one. The only amendment to sec. 149 of the Act of 1929 was that if a director is interested in a specific firm so that he may be regarded as interested in any contract made with that firm and he in a general notice discloses this interest, such notice shall have no effect unless it is given at a meeting of the directors, or he takes reasonable steps to secure that the notice be brought up and read at the next meeting of the directors (sec. 41 (5), now subsec. (3) para. 2 of sec. 199).

Special rules apply to compromises with creditors and members, but with these we are not here concerned.

83. Directors' Remuneration

The question of the remuneration of the persons who manage the affairs or direct the policy of a corporation is necessarily a very delicate one.[1] Legislation and public opinion alike require

[1] See: George T. Washington, H.L.R. 54, pp. 733-771.

that those who perform these functions should exert themselves in the corporation's interest and abstain from seeking their personal advantage and profit; they should be liable for both damaging acts and omissions, for both malfeasance and non-feasance. In view of these obligations and liabilities it is but just and equitable that they should receive adequate compensation. We exclude here all those who are merely employees of a corporation but not its officers or, in German terminology, "organs".

In Great Britain it is usual to compensate all directors, whether executives or not, for their activities. They receive fees, with the difference that those who also perform managerial functions, as general managers, managing directors, chief engineers and the like, are compensated for their special work by separate salaries and other emoluments. It is not unusual to give special compensation to chairmen.

The British practice as to the compensation of managing directors or executives is very elastic. Sometimes managing directors beside their fees as members of the board of directors receive compensation under various headings, such as a fixed salary and a percentage of the profits, and in exceptional cases a percentage of the turnover, remuneration for expenses connected with their office and so on. It is also not unusual to conclude contracts of employment for several years.

In the U.S.A. the practice is for executives not to have contracts for long terms. Their compensation consists mainly in a salary fixed by the board, and a bonus fixed likewise by the board either in advance or at the end of each year. These bonuses were originally intended to be proportionate to the results. Members of the board of directors who do not exercise managerial functions do not usually receive fees, except nominal fees for attendance at board meetings.

On the Continent the system of compensation is similar to the British. Where besides directorates there are separate boards or councils of supervision the fees of their members are as a rule on a much lower scale, and consist mostly in a compound sum. The German Aufsichtsrat is an exception in this respect; its remuneration may and usually does include fees in the form of a percentage on the profits.

On the actual fees paid there is little information. Relatively much attention has been given to this subject in the U.S.A., and although exact official statistics are not available, there are several valuable studies for different periods. F. W. Taussig and W. S. Barker[1] investigated the question in the light of information collected for the years 1904–13 and 1905–14 respectively from 400 manufacturing companies chosen with the special aim of excluding those which enjoyed a monopoly. Of these 400 companies, one hundred had a capital of $250,000 or less, the second hundred a capital between $250,000 and $750,000, the third from $750,000 to $1,500,000 and the last hundred over $1,500,000. As a rule executives received no compensation other than salaries; the average salary in the respective groups amounted to $3885, $5195, $6897 and $9958 per person. The smallest individual salary was $1200, the largest $100,000. The number of executives varied from one to 15. In the group with the smallest capital many companies had only one executive, who in many cases had other duties to perform apart from management. In a few exceptional cases larger companies made regular conditional payments to managers; about five per cent. of all the companies concerned had a regular system of such extra payments; four per cent. made payments with no regular system, and one per cent. paid occasional lump sums. The investigation did not bring out the total amount paid in salaries in relation to the profits earned, but only to the capital invested. This ratio of course increases inversely to the capital. In the largest companies with an average invested capital of $9,000,000 the ratio was 0·42 per cent.; in the lowest group it was a little over six per cent.

The investigations of the U.S.A. Senate known as the Pecora hearings revealed that during the inter-war period many executives were able to obtain not only vast salaries but also ample bonuses which constituted the major part of their remuneration. Some of these cases have a more than temporary interest.

The American Tobacco Company in 1912 adopted in its by-laws a scheme under which the president was entitled to a bonus of 2·5 per cent. on profits and the five vice-presidents to 1·5 per cent. each, so that 10 per cent. of the profits were payable, an amount exceeding the whole profits of the year 1910. This plan was retained without alteration after the capital of the company had been doubled and profits increased to 500 per cent. Thus in 1930 the president beside a fixed salary of $168,000 received a cash bonus of $842,507·72 and special credits amounting to $273,470·76. The five vice-presidents received pro-

[1] 40 Q. J. Econ., pp. 1-51.

portionate amounts. Besides these emoluments the executives benefited immensely by share subscriptions. Although the by-laws were of course known the precise amounts were never disclosed.

Similar data came to light in the case of the National City Bank of New York, where the procedure was if possible even more irregular. Here the board in 1921 adopted a plan by which the executives "responsible for the management" were to receive 20 per cent. of any profits in excess of eight per cent. of the invested and employed capital. The plan was never submitted to the shareholders; it was stated generally that there was a management fund, but no details were given. A characteristic offshoot of this affair was that the same agreement applied to the National City Company of New York, which was at that time affiliated to the Bank, its shares being held in trust by the Bank for the shareholders. The shareholders, however, were never informed of the agreement. The bonuses of the president amounted in 1927 to $1,156,230, in 1928 to $1,417,150 and in 1929 to $1,345,335. It is significant that although 20 per cent. was surely high enough, and yielded the executives quite extraordinary incomes, they resorted to manipulated accounting so as to exclude losses and thereby increase their bonuses artificially. Thus, though the Bank suffered considerable losses in Cuban sugar investments, these losses were not taken into account on the pretext that the executives were not responsible for the deal and could not have saved the Bank from loss.

The third remarkable case was that of Bethlehem Steel. This company had a bonus plan from the beginning, by which the executives were to receive bonuses on a progressive scale according to the amount of profits, rising from 3·34 to 8 per cent. Dividends on the preferred stock were to be considered, but depreciation and obsolescence were not to be deducted. The distribution of the bonus among the executives was left to the chairman. Significantly shareholders received less and less information when the profits increased during the First World War and the boom of the twenties. The chairman reserved a modest portion for himself; the president, however, in 1929 received $637,754. Apart from this bonus substantial salaries were paid.

Little information is available about other companies for this period. From information relating to subsequent years it appears that on the whole salaries and bonuses were highest in the case of companies controlled by the management, i.e. where there were no controlling majority groups.

Beside salaries and bonuses, compensation used to consist in valuable rights to subscribe for or purchase shares in the company. Several companies extended such facilities to all their employees, manual and clerical workers alike. Such plans have been belauded as a new kind of social reform, likely to secure fuller harmony in industrial production.

The U.S. Steel Corporation proudly showed cases of such purchases by which some of their employees were able to secure property for themselves for their old age. On the whole, however, such schemes of employee shareholdership were not successful. Employees were generally rather distrustful of the proposals of their corporation, however well meant these might be. Moreover the inequality of contractual relations in such schemes is even more accentuated than in respect of bonuses. Employees are seldom in a position to pay cash for their shares; long-term instalments are necessary. It is usually provided that if an employee leaves the corporation, he loses his right to claim the stock, and has to be content with the repayment of the instalments already paid, at most with interest. Some contracts provided that the company might decline to surrender the shares on payment of the remainder, even if the termination of the service contract was due to notice given by the company. There may or may not be a proviso that in case of unmotivated dismissal the corporation is not entitled to call for surrender. In practice, however, employee shareholders could very seldom obtain their shares after leaving the company's employment. There is only one recorded case in which an employee—in that case a sales manager—succeeded.[1] On the other hand it is reported that an employee of Standard Oil of Indiana lost his case, though he was dismissed only three months before the expiration of the instalment terms under which he had paid instalments over a period of many years.

The position of executives in this respect also is quite different. They are in a position to secure for themselves shares from treasury stock at favourable prices and conditions. In some cases shareholders were never informed of such placements.

A conspicuous example of such practices was shown in the

[1] Day Elders Motor Corp. *v.* Nexter (1920), 92 N.J. Equ. 258.

Tobacco case. The executives of the American Tobacco Company obtained a substantial allotment of shares without the knowledge or approval of the general meeting. In 1930 a plan was submitted to the general meeting under which the board was empowered to distribute 56,712 shares among the employees, not excluding directors actively engaged in the business. The fixing of the price was left to the directors, the only limitation being that the shares were not to be issued below par. Under this ruling the directors allotted to the executives 37,730 shares out of 56,712 at the issue price of $25, the market price being at that time $112.

Under English law the directors have no claim to remuneration unless it is provided for in the articles.[1] In practice, however, all articles do so. Clause 76 provides that the remuneration shall from time to time be determined by the company in general meeting. In such a case a director has no power to vote on director's fees either for himself or for any other director.[2]

The amount of the fees is in no way limited, and under the Act of 1929 it could be provided in the articles that they be paid free of income tax, though without such provision the directors may not pay the income tax out of the company's funds.[3]

All that the 1929 Act required was disclosure in the profit and loss account of the sums paid to directors as remuneration, whether such sums were paid as fees, percentages or other emoluments, including those paid by a subsidiary (sec. 128 (1) (*c*)). The amount of remuneration was to be shown as an aggregate without disclosure of its distribution. This provision, however, did not apply to salaries of managing directors or of any other director who holds any salaried employment or office (sec. 128 (3)).

Under the Common Law of the U.S.A. it was held that directors have no right to demand compensation for services. This rule was extended by some Courts even to executives, i.e. such members of the boards as were at the same time active in various capacities, such as presidents, vice-presidents, managers, treasurers, secretaries and so on. The majority rule, however, was that such persons are entitled to compensation for special

[1] Dunston *v.* Imperial Gas, etc., Co. (1832), 3 B. and Ad. 125; Hutton *v.* West Cork Rly. Co. (1883), 23 Ch. D. 654; Stroud *v.* Royal Aquarium Society (1903), 89 L.T. 243.

[2] Kerr *v.* Marine Products Ltd. (1928), 44 T.L.R. 292.

[3] Boschoek Proprietary Company *v.* Fuke (1906), 1 Ch. 148.

services, i.e. such as are not incidental to their office.[1] The practical effect of these and similar disputes matters little, since the statutes and by-laws generally give the right to remuneration. It was held that it is for the general meeting to decide the amount of compensation, unless this power was delegated to the board. This in fact was frequently done, the board thus fixing the salaries and other compensations of executives and other officers of the company. Further it was held that a director is not entitled to vote salary or other compensation to himself, and there must be a quorum of uninterested directors in order to obtain a valid resolution. In practice the procedure was that where the number of uninterested directors was not sufficient, the vote on salaries was split, and directors who were to receive salaries voted salaries for others and *vice versa*. In a case where four out of six directors were executives, whereas the quorum required under the by-laws was three, a director C who was to receive a salary would vote with the uninterested directors and A B on D's salary, while D would vote with A and B on the question of C's salary. Some Courts held that resolutions by interested directors were void, others that they were merely voidable, and some even restricted voidability to cases in which the compensations voted were unfair or unreasonable.

In regard to salaries voted by general meetings the general rule according to which self-interest does not exclude the right to vote and does not make the resolution either void or voidable was accepted without qualification. On the other hand the Courts hold that neither directors nor stockholders may abuse their powers, and therefore resolutions granting disproportionate compensations which amount to waste of the company's assets or simply to gifts may be attacked in equity. Up to 1930 the cases in which Courts decided in suits on the remunerations of directors related rather to small or medium-sized companies, and to those in which all or most of the directors were executives. Furthermore the compensations involved were relatively small, most of them not exceeding $5000; nor was it difficult to decide what the services of the executive in question were worth. The view taken by the Courts was on the whole sound. Thus in Nichols *v.* Olympia Veneer Co,[2] where the directors were all executives and voted themselves, after one of them died, wages of $8 per working day instead of $4 which they had formerly

[1] Ballantine 73. [2] 139 Wash. 305.

received; the widow of a former director was awarded a dividend of $2 per working day. In contrast with these simple cases the Courts engaged in the suits against the giant corporations mentioned had to decide disputes of a very complicated character. How should the Court fix the salary of an executive, especially if the compensation could not be attacked on the basis of interestedness or for some other technical reason!

In the case of the American Tobacco Company suit against the stock subscription plan, the suit was dismissed below, and the Supreme Court did not go into the matter for formal reasons.[1] As to the cash bonus the Supreme Court in another case reversed the decisions below and ordered proceedings to inquire into the question of fairness.[2] Subsequent to the decisions of the Supreme Court the share subscription plan was renounced. In the case of cash bonuses [3] the suit was not proceeded with in consequence of a compromise with the plaintiff. For 1931 and 1932 somewhat smaller but still substantial bonuses were paid; from 1934 onwards they were on a more moderate scale, and thus it cannot be said that the attack was not successful. In subsequent proceedings it became known that plaintiff had received a substantial amount by way of settlement out of Court and most of the amount was paid out of the funds of the corporation. The factual power of the executives was significantly shown in 1940, when a motion to fix the maximum compensation was defeated by the overwhelming majority of nearly 97 per cent. The president did not attend the general meeting although he influenced it by the threat to resign.

In the case of the Bethlehem Steel Corporation the board—to counter the proceedings—collected proxies for the general meeting to which the question of ratification was submitted, and succeeded in procuring 72 per cent. of the votes. The Court, however, granted an injunction, and the general meeting could not resolve upon the matter. In Berendt *v.* Bethlehem Steel Corporation,[4] the Court had not to decide on the merits, because a new plan was accepted under which salaries were to be fixed by directors who did not participate in compensation, and depreciation including obsolescence and depletion were to be deducted. From that time on complete disclosure was made,

[1] Rogers *v.* Guaranty Trust Co. (1933), 288 U.S. 123.
[2] Rogers *v.* Hill (1933), 289 U.S. 582.
[3] Rogers *v.* Hill, *supra.* [4] (1930), 108 N.J. Equ. 148.

and in 1936 a second plan was adopted under which five per cent. of the net profits were to be placed in a special compensation fund to encourage efficiency.

In the case of the National City Bank of New York [1] the Court adopted the view that the directors have the power to fix compensation of executives, and their decision is final, except in case of oppression, bad faith or other breach of trust. In the course of an inquiry ordered on the basis of the opinion of a referee it was found that the officers concerned had received the substantial amount of $1,703,703·23 to which they were not entitled under a correct construction of the plan and which they had to repay. The Court was influenced by the fact that a considerable number of disinterested directors voted for the plan, and also that prominent members of the board, such as the former president of the company, Stillman, found the bonuses reasonable. The evidence of expert witnesses was contradictory. This case also raised an awkward point: although the suit was successful, the corporation had to pay the fees of plaintiff's counsel, amounting to $480,000, and $20,000 to the referee. Nevertheless the litigation had some permanent consequences for the company; compensation became based on fixed salaries, which were moderate in comparison with the exorbitant bonuses paid during the boom period. In spite of public opinion it was not only in the National City Bank case that the Courts were favourable to the claims of directors. An interesting instance was that of the National Cash Register Company. This company reinstated its former general manager in order to solve its difficulties. The said manager secured for himself a fixed salary of $100,000 and an option to take at his choice at any time within five years up to 50,000 shares of the corporation at the price of $9·80. The shares rose to $38 and at the time of the litigation had a market value of $13·25. The suit of a shareholder attacking the option was dismissed by the 4th C.C.A.[2]

Under the legislations of Continental Europe the determination of remuneration is generally left to the articles. Some of them, however, attempted a more stringent regulation. Under German law the salaries and other emoluments of the members of the board of management are to be fixed by the board of supervision, whereas those of the latter board are to be fixed in the articles or by the company in general meeting. An alteration

[1] Gallin *v.* National City Bank of N. Y. (1934), 152 Misc. 679.
[2] McQuillen *v.* National Cash Register Co. (1940), 112 F. 2nd, 877.

of the articles to reduce the remuneration may be carried by a simple majority. But there is a compulsory rule in respect of remunerations fixed as a percentage of the profits which applies equally to members of both boards. Such remuneration, the so-called *tantième*, is payable only from that part of the profits which remains after the amounts for writing off, putting to reserve and paying a four per cent. dividend are deducted. The board of supervision may, however, grant *tantièmes* on the part of the profits which is applied to strengthen free reserves. The other rule is that *tantièmes* should be in proper relation to the amounts allotted for the staff and welfare purposes. It is the duty of the board of supervision to exercise control in so far as the managers are concerned. On the other hand the Public Prosecutor is empowered to bring a civil action (§§ 77, 78 and 98 of the law of 1937). Little is known of the practical effect of this regulation. The analysis of certain company accounts shows that salaries and fees still absorbed about 10–12 per cent. of the profits.

German legislation had a strong influence on the regulations of the Vichy régime, which are still in force.

The Swiss law lays down the same rule as the German for the amount of *tantièmes* (677). It further provides that if the company should become bankrupt, the directors must repay the amounts received as *tantièmes* during the three years previous to the declaration of bankruptcy, and also any other remuneration in so far as it exceeds the proper value of their services, and with a cautious drawing up of the balance sheet should not have been paid. The judge has free discretion in the consideration of all circumstances (679).

The New Deal legislation in U.S.A. provided that all amounts paid as salaries of directors and officers in excess of $25,000 yearly are to be reported to the S.E.C. The consequence of default may be that the securities of the defaulting corporation are removed from the lists of the National Exchanges, a consequence which may injure innocent stockholders. On the other hand publicity as secured by these provisions is not sufficient, since the reports submitted to the S.E.C. are not published; copies of the documents may be obtained, though at considerable expense. There is no provision for communicating to shareholders details as to salaries and compensation.

In the absence of compulsory disclosure the position of the

shareholder will remain difficult. If there is no "self-dealing" (vote by interested directors), shareholders who sue have to prove that the salaries paid to executives are so excessive as to amount to waste. Such evidence will be available only in quite exceptional cases.

Much stress has been laid upon the power of the revenue authorities to disallow salaries and compensation as expenditure in computing the profits of corporations. This, however, would penalise the corporation and not the directors concerned.

Nevertheless the consequences of popular agitation and of the legislation were not negligible, as appears from the investigation of R. Gordon. His examination covered 149 large non-financial corporations, whose ownership had been investigated earlier by Berle and Means and by Gordon himself. The omission of 51 corporations was due in 45 cases to various reasons and in six to the fact that they refused to consent to the publication of the particulars of compensations. This investigation took into account [1] particulars of compensations paid to 264 chief executives. This term was taken to include in every case the president or chairman and any person or persons holding approximately similar positions as to salary and other compensations. Of the corporations in question 80 were industrial, 35 railroads and 34 public utilities; no banks, unfortunately, were included. We learn that in 1935 the median income of 161 executives of 80 industrial companies was $79,200. Only 17 industrial executives received less than $37,500; 30 industrial executives had more than $112,500, and two of these received salaries between $362,500 and $387,500. The results obtained by Gordon are corroborated by the income tax data for 1938. In that year there were altogether 650 corporate employees whose salaries exceeded $75,000, but 125 of these were not executives. The peak salary was $688,368. It is further recorded that General Motors paid in 1934 to their highest-paid executive $459,041, and Bethlehem Steel in 1944 $221,648. High as these salaries are, they are moderate in comparison with those paid in 1929–30.

The possibility of a revival of former abuses in the future cannot be excluded. In this regard we have to bear in mind that the grossest abuses came to light only in consequence of the hearings before the U.S.A. Senate.

[1] Q.J. Econ. 54, 3 May 1940, pp. 455-73.

In may be that in some cases the struggle for power within the board will lead to revelations, as was the case with the Texas Corporation, where the board split into two factions which fought each other violently; as a consequence a committee of investigation was elected. Its work revealed that the board, the majority of which consisted of executives, adopted two profit-sharing plans under which large amounts were distributed in excess of the salaries. Shareholders were not informed at all at first, and subsequently only to an inadequate extent. After the collapse of the stock market the excutive committee of the board gave authority to certain members to grant loans from the funds of the company to executive directors and employees in order to relieve them from loans which they had made with banks against collateral. This resolution was not communicated to the board, and the secretary was directed not to report. Among the loans granted under this resolution was one made to the chairman of the executive committee without security, of about $2½ millions.

The minutes of evidence of the Cohen Committee record strong remonstrances against the present state of affairs, as well as misgivings in respect of the drawbacks of compulsory disclosure. The possible dangers from competitors if the full amount of remunerations were to be disclosed were greatly stressed. The Committee, however, recommended both disclosure and the prohibition of tax-free salaries.

The Companies Act, 1947, provides that it shall not be lawful to pay a director any remuneration free of income tax or surtax or to make his remuneration vary with the amount or rate of his tax liability. This applies to any remuneration, whether as a director or otherwise, e.g. as manager or for other services. This rule does not apply to contracts already in force on 18 July 1945 if there is express provision in the contract not by reference to the articles to this effect (sec. 34; now sec. 189 of the Act of 1948).

In any accounts laid before the general meeting the following amounts are to be shown: the aggregate amount of the directors' emoluments, salaries whether fees, percentage expense allowances chargeable to U.K. income tax, contributions to pension schemes and the estimated money value of any other benefits not in cash. The same applies to pensions of directors and past directors, unless they are paid under a pension scheme maintained by contributions; likewise to the aggregate amount of any compensation paid to directors or past directors for loss of office. All this applies also in respect of subsidiaries (sec. 38; now sec. 196 of the Act of 1948). Furthermore, it shall not be lawful to pay any director any compensation for loss of office or in connection with his retirement from office without disclosing the particulars to the members and without their approval in general meeting (sec. 6; now sec. 196 of the Act of 1948).

There can be no doubt whatever that these amendments will prove highly beneficial.

84. Accounts

No business can be carried on without the keeping of proper books of account, and the safe keeping of the correspondence and other documents. It is also essential to draw up from time to time statements showing the financial position of the business.

It was a matter of course that companies as the most highly evolved form of enterprise should develop the principles of commercial book-keeping to the highest degree. Accounting and book-keeping are nowadays an agglomerate of very intricate systematic rules; and this applies not only to the keeping of day-to-day accounts, but even more to the preparation of periodical financial statements, the balance sheets and profit and loss accounts.

Accounting in general and company accounting in particular has given birth to a considerable literature. Here we are concerned only with its legal aspects.

It is obviously for the the law to define the duty of directors to keep proper accounts; the various legislations, however, have not devoted much care in the past to this matter, and such provisions as they have made are far from satisfactory.

Until the Companies Act of 1929 codified it, the law in Great Britain did not contain any express provisions as to accounting; but even before this it was held that the directors as agents of the company were under duty to keep accounts of their receipts and payments, dealings and transactions on the company's behalf. L. C. Eldon stated [1] that it is one of the first duties of an agent to keep a clear account and to communicate its contents to his principal.

When by the Act of 1900 the auditing of accounts became

[1] White *v.* Lincoln (1803), 8 Ves. 363.

compulsory it was implied that proper books and accounts must be kept.

Under the Companies Act of 1929 (sec. 122), every company must cause proper books of account to be kept with respect to all sums of money received and expended by it, the matters in respect of which the receipt and expenditure takes place, all sales and purchases of goods and all assets and liabilities. This section is supplemented by sec. 274, which deals with the liability of directors and officers for any default in keeping proper books and accounts. It is provided (subsec. (2)) that proper books of account shall be deemed not to have been kept if they are not such as to exhibit and explain the transactions and financial side of the trade or business, including books containing entries from day to day in sufficient detail of all cash received and paid out, and where the business of the company involves dealings in goods, statements of annual stocktakings and of all goods sold and purchased, showing the goods, the buyers and sellers thereof in sufficient detail to enable the persons concerned to be identified. Although these provisions are aimed only at the event of winding-up, they obviously operate to compel the directors and managers to observe these rules carefully, since the possibility of a liquidation can never be excluded. Clause 97 of Table A simply repeats the provisions of sec. 122 (1).

This enumeration of books is clearly not exhaustive, and the position would be very awkward if it were assumed that the directors have complied with the law by merely keeping a record of all sums of money received and expended and of all sales and purchases of goods. It has been rightly observed that on this assumption the directors would have done their duty if they kept such books but did not prepare and keep records, e.g., with regard to cost accounting, whereas a modern business of any size must provide for exact cost accounting and keep all the records necessary for that purpose. Again, the provisions of the Act are too narrow in mentioning only books, since in 1929 mechanical systems of account and book-keeping were already widely used; they have since become even more popular and are nowadays indispensable. In business circles these mechanised accounts are regarded as equivalent to books, although the question has so far not been decided by the Courts.

A closely connected question is whether a right exists to inspect the books and accounts, and if so, who may exercise it.

By the Act of 1929 that right is granted to the directors. Under sec. 122 (2) the books of account shall be kept at the registered office of the company or at such other place as the directors think fit and shall be open to inspection by the directors at any time. Under this section each director is entitled to inspect the books at any time. Under Table A (secs. 97–98) the provisions of sec. 122 of the Act are simply reproduced, so that most companies have in their articles rules identical with the provisions of the Act.

It has been held that if the articles provide that the books wherein the company's proceedings are recorded may be inspected, this does not cover the minute book of directors' meetings.[1] The right of inspection, if given, includes the right to make extracts.[2]

If under the articles a shareholder has a right to inspect the books, it is absolute, and the company is not entitled to refuse his request on the ground that he did not give reasons, or that the cause stated was not reasonable.

May the directors refuse inspection if they are able to show that the shareholder has motives adverse to the interests of the company, or that he is merely a nominee, e.g. of a rival company? This question has been discussed in connection with the register of members which the shareholder has a right to inspect by law (sec. 98 (1)). The decision was in the negative.[3] It may be doubted whether the same would be held to apply to the inspection of books of account, but the question is in any case not practical, for in most companies the individual shareholder has no such right of inspection.

As long as the company is solvent the duty to keep proper accounts is not subject to the control of the Court. But if the company is wound up and it appears that proper accounts have not been kept for the preceding two years, every director, manager or officer who was knowingly a party to or connived at the default is liable to imprisonment on conviction on indictment for a term not exceeding one year and on summary conviction for a term not exceeding six months, unless he shows that he has acted honestly or that in the circumstances under which the business of the company was carried on his default was excusable (sec. 274).

[1] Regina *v.* Mariquita etc. Co. (1858), 1 E. and E. 289.

[2] Mutter *v.* Eastern etc. Co. (1888), 38 Ch. D. 92; Nelson *v.* Anglo-American Land etc. Agency (1897), 1 Ch. 130.

[3] Holland *v.* Dickson (1888), 37 Ch. Div. 669.

American Common Law [1] has no definite rules as to accounts. Many statutes make provision in this respect; thus California [2] prescribes that every corporation shall keep and maintain adequate and correct accounts of its properties and business transactions including its assets, liabilities, receipts, disbursements, gains, losses, capital, surplus and shares. Any surplus, including earned surplus, paid-in surplus and surplus arising from a reduction of stated capital, shall be classified according to source and shown in a separate account. The books of account shall at all reasonable times be open to inspection by any director.

In certain States this question is dealt with in general terms. Thus, New York [3] only says that every stock corporation shall keep at its office correct books of account. Lastly, some statutes omit to define what books and accounts shall be kept. For public utilities Congress has enacted special and very elaborate provisions.

On inspection American law takes a view fundamentally differing from English and indeed from all other legislations. It is generally held that the right to inspect the books and records of the corporation is an inherent right of the shareholder incidental to his ownership of the shares. The corporation must permit inspection, and the Courts will assist the shareholder if the corporation does not comply with his request. The corporation may, however, show that the shareholder is moved by improper motives, e.g. by malice, or is seeking information in the interest of a rival, etc. The corporation has to show good cause for this contention, otherwise the Court will allow inspection.

The statutes as a rule recognise the right of inspection; but in some States it is limited, e.g. to matters in which the shareholder is individually interested, or the right is even reserved to a specific shareholding so that the individual right of inspection is excluded. Thus, e.g. in California,[4] it is provided that the books of account shall be open to inspection by every shareholder or holder of a voting trust certificate at any reasonable time and for a purpose reasonably related to his interests as a shareholder or holder of such certificate. Holders of ten per cent. of the shares represented at any meeting may request that the books be exhibited at any time, even outside the meeting, by written

[1] Cf. Ballantine 223, 159–166.
[2] C.C. § 353.
[3] S.C.L. § 10, as amended by L. 1933.
[4] C.C. § 355, as amended by L. 1933, c. 533, § 54.

demand addressed to the president, secretary, assistant secretary or general manager.

In Continental Europe the duty to keep proper books of account is either expressly enacted or follows from the rule that a corporation is deemed to be a merchant even if the subject of its enterprise is not within the sphere of commerce in the legal sense. Thus the German Companies law of 1937 provides (§ 82) that the management must cause the necessary books to be kept. The Commercial Code of 1897 provides that a merchant is under duty to keep books and to record therein his contracts and his financial position according to the principles of regular book-keeping (§ 38).

At the commencement of business a detailed inventory of all the assets and liabilities and a balance sheet are to be prepared. Copies of business letters sent and received are to be kept for ten years. It is provided (§ 43) that the books are to be kept in a living language and in the letters of such language. Thus the keeping of books, e.g. in Latin, or the use of ciphers, is not admitted. The books should be bound and the pages numbered. The use of mechanical records was formerly illegal; nowadays the question is disputed. In practice most of the larger companies make use of mechanical book-keeping methods.

Under Continental laws the right of inspection is generally withheld from individual shareholders.

From the legislative point of view it is necessary and sufficient to declare by law that the directors are under duty to keep proper books of account. But it is neither necessary nor advisable to go into detail, and to determine what is to be understood under that name. In view of the constant changes in and evolution of book-keeping and accounting methods it is better to leave it to the accountancy profession to decide what systems and methods of accounting are at any time sufficient. The requirements will change with practical experience. Any system or method may be used which can ensure that all the company's transactions and its financial position are apparent at any time from the books and records.

It is advisable to provide that the directors may be compelled by the Court to comply with this duty, and that in the case of an application on the part of a shareholder or other interested person the Court should have power to compel the directors to comply under pain of fine. The granting of the right of inspection to the individual shareholder is not be to recommended. If the Courts are reluctant to compel the company to comply with the request for inspection it is on the whole not operative. On the other hand it might be harmful for the company to be compelled to grant the right of inspection to shareholders without a substantial interest in the company.

The Companies Act, 1947 (sec. 12 (1)), provides that proper books of account shall not be deemed to have been kept with respect to the matters specified in sec. 112 (1) of the 1929 Act if they do not give a true and fair view of the company's affairs and do not explain its transactions. The Act in this respect followed the recommendations of the Cohen Committee,[1] and the Act of 1948, whilst re-enacting in sec. 177 (1) the provisions of the Act of 1929, incorporates in subsec. (2) the same requirement. It was thought impracticable to set out a comprehensive list of the matters in respect of which books of account should be kept and which would fit the circumstances of every company.

The use of mechanical book-keeping is now legalised; any register, index, minute book or book of account may be kept either by making entries in bound books or by recording the matters in question in any other way. In the latter case adequate precautions shall be taken for guarding against falsification and to facilitate its discovery (sec. 119; now sec. 436 of the Act of 1948).

Companies which keep their books of account outside the country must provide for the forwarding to a place in Great Britain of such accounts as will disclose with reasonable accuracy the financial position of the business at intervals not exceeding three months and will enable a balance sheet and a profit and loss account to be prepared in accordance with the law (sec. 12 (2), (sec. 147 (3) of the Act of 1948)).

85. The Balance Sheet

The practice of drawing up from time to time a statement showing the financial results and position of a commercial enterprise over the period concerned—usually a year—arose naturally and not under legal compulsion. From early days this statement became known as a balance sheet. The last item of the statement would show the excess or deficit as compared with the

[1] 109, p. 64.

previous financial statement—that is, the profit or loss. The profit or loss so shown is merely the closing item of the revenue account, traditionally called the profit and loss account. Although companies availed themselves of this method of accounting without legal compulsion, the law gradually came to concern itself therewith.

The balance sheet and profit and loss account are interdependent. No balance sheet is complete without a statement of profit or loss as the case may be; the profit and loss account in turn is influenced by the valuation of the assets and liabilities given in the balance sheet. There have been frequent disputes over which of these two statements of account takes precedence. Much could be said for the proposition that the supremacy belongs to the profit and loss account; especially under those legislations which do not require the drawing up of a balance sheet at the commencement of business. Nevertheless it seems convenient to deal first with the balance sheet.

Under the Companies Act of 1929 the first balance sheet is to be prepared not later than 18 months after the incorporation of the company, and subsequent balance sheets at least once yearly, i.e. the company is free to draw up balance sheets for a shorter period, say half-yearly or quarterly, but may not extend the period for over 12 months. In practice it is unusual for companies to prepare balance sheets more often than once a year, since this involves a considerable amount of work; it is usual, however, to draw up provisional statements for shorter periods.

The date to which the balance sheet is made up should not be earlier than nine months previous to the general meeting; in the case of companies carrying on business or having interests abroad this is extended to 12 months, and the Board of Trade may extend these periods in special cases if it thinks fit. It thus appears the Board of Trade has no power to dispense with the requirement of a yearly balance sheet, though it may extend the time limit for the first balance sheet to 18 months (sec. 128 (2)).

The balance sheet is to contain a summary of the authorised and of the issued share capital of the company. The share capital is to be included among the liabilities, though from the legal point of view it is not a liability of the company. On the other hand the company must always show any excess of net assets over liabilities, or if there is a deficit, the excess of liabilities over assets. The statement must also show whether the share capital is intact or not. For the same reason the reserves must also be shown among the liabilities, regardless of whether they can be freely disposed of by the company or are not distributable. In the words of the Act (sec. 124 (1)) the balance sheet is to contain a summary of the company's assets with such particulars as are necessary to disclose their general nature.

The Act requires a distinction to be made between the amounts of fixed and of floating, or as they are nowadays generally called, current, assets.

It is of course of great importance to make a fair and correct valuation of the assets; this is left to the discretion of the directors, who are free to value them as they will provided they can satisfy the auditors that the valuation is in accordance with sound commercial principles. All that the directors have to state is how the values of the fixed assets have been arrived at.

It has been observed that this state of the law is not quite satisfactory. To state the principles of the valuation of fixed assets is not sufficient; the floating assets, i.e. the circulating capital, are also important, and both shareholders and creditors have a right to know something about the basis on which these are valued, especially the stock-in-trade and the debts. Under the Act of 1929, however, valuation was left to the discretion of the directors subject to the approval of the general meeting.[1]

The question how far directors have to go in giving particulars of the valuation of fixed assets was discussed in Galloway *v.* Schill, Seebohm & Co. Ltd.[2] In this case the balance sheet contained the following items: Goodwill, trade marks, machinery, furniture and fixtures, £100,007 16*s.* 5*d.*, with the following clause: goodwill and trade marks at the sum at which they were taken over by the company; buildings, machinery and fixtures at cost less depreciation. The Registrar objected to the balance sheet on the ground that it did not comply with the law as then existing. The stipendiary magistrate who heard the case in the first instance found that the objection could not be upheld. On appeal the Court took the view that the balance sheet was contrary to law; Lord Alverstone thought that different assets had been valued in different ways, and it was not disclosed to what extent those different ways (cost less depreciation and price of acquisition by the company respectively) had been applied,

[1] Young *v.* Brownlee (1911), S.C. 677. [2] (1912), 2 K.B. 354.

whereas Pickford, J., held that the values of the tangible and intangible assets should have been stated separately.

Under the Act of 1929, with its somewhat different wording, the question has not been decided. The trend in practice, mainly under the influence of the accountancy profession, is towards giving further details.

It is provided (sec. 124 (2)) that: (*a*) the preliminary expenses of the company, (*b*) any expenses incurred in connection with any issues of share capital or debentures, (*c*) the amount of the goodwill and of any trade marks and patents paid for by the company in connection with the acquisition, and any property are to be shown separately, i.e. under separate headings, provided they have not been written off. It is to be remarked in this connection that the Act gives companies a free hand in deciding to write off all these expenses and all the amounts paid for goodwill, patents and trade marks. The only requirement is that the respective amounts be shown in the balance sheet.

Special provisions apply to amounts invested in subsidiary companies and to the holdings of holding companies. It is more convenient to discuss these in connection with holding companies in § 92. Further, in respect of amounts loaned to directors or officers of the company special provisions apply. These provisions, and the disclosure of the amounts paid to directors, have already been discussed.

The balance sheet is to be signed on behalf of the board by two of the directors, or by the sole director if there is only one. For banking companies registered after 15 August 1879 the balance sheet must be signed by the secretary or manager, if any, and by all the directors; or, if their number exceed three, by at least three directors.

Although the balance sheet should as a rule be considered by the board, whoever may have prepared it, the directors were in some cases not held liable for it if they did not take an active part in its preparation. This is far from satisfactory, since it is the duty of all directors to take an active interest in the preparation of the balance sheet, and if they fail to do so they should be liable in the same way as those members of the board who took an active part in the preparation of a balance sheet which is deceptive either by falsity or by lack of due disclosure.

United States Common Law makes no provision regarding the form and contents of the balance sheet, and such statutory provisions as deal with this question do not go beyond those of the British Companies Act. On the other hand, the practical trend in America is very exacting both as to the details and information to be given in the balance sheet and as to the principles of valuation. The measures taken by the Acts passed under the New Deal have been discussed in § 22.

The legislations of Continental Europe have long contained detailed provisions with regard to balance sheets; the most elaborate are to be found in the German Companies law of 1937. This provides that with regard to assets it should be stated under separate headings whether any contributions by shareholders are unpaid; if so, they are to be shown as an asset of the company. Fixed assets are to be stated under separate headings for landed property built up as business or residential premises, or factory (plant) buildings, other buildings, undeveloped land, machinery and fixtures, tools and other factory or business equipment, licenses, patents, patent licenses, trade marks or similar rights, securities. These last, whatever their character, are to be included in the category of fixed assets if it is intended to hold them permanently; not a very distinctive basis of classification.

Current assets are to be detailed under 16 separate headings. Under liabilities the capital of the company is to be stated, and if there are several categories of shares, every class separately; if some of the shares entitle to a multiple vote, their votes and also the votes of all other shares are to be stated. Reserves are to be a further item, legal and free reserves being stated separately. Corrections in the values of assets may be stated as a separate item among liabilities. It is, of course, allowable to make necessary corrections by writing off part of the amount of the relevant asset.

The law distinguishes between reserves, corrections of valuation, and provision for uncertain liabilities, and prescribes that such provisions are to be stated separately.

The law requires the division of the liabilities proper into ten separate headings. Of these, loans, mortgages, advances, i.e. payments made by purchasers in advance, amounts due to banks and those arising from endorsements of bills of exchange or from issue of promissory notes are to be stated separately. Liabilities arising from guarantees and suretyships are to be stated at their full amounts, whether they are secured or not (§ 131).

The law likewise contains detailed provisions as to valuation. Although the assets cannot as a rule be valued higher than their cost or purchase price or their value at the end of the financial year, whichever is less, it is permitted to evaluate fixed assets regardless of their value at the cost or purchase price, provided an adequate amount is written off for depreciation. Preliminary expenses and expenses connected with the issue of shares and bonds cannot be reckoned as assets; they are to be written off immediately. The expenses of equipment may be valued as assets, but under a separate heading, and are to be written off in yearly instalments.

Goodwill may be treated as an asset only if and in so far as something has been paid for it, or the amount of the assets acquired is less than the consideration paid for them. In such a case the difference may be accounted for as an asset, but it is to be written off by yearly instalments.

If bonds have been issued at a discount, the difference between the par value or the amount of redemption and the issue price may be accounted as an asset, subject to writing off by instalments over the period of their circulation.

These provisions have perhaps the disadvantage of too minute detail, and beside these elaborate regulations the government was empowered to issue special instructions for companies or special categories of them. But in practice the provisions were not always fully observed, and there were many published balance sheets whose details were not informative, at least not to the degree necessary to enable the shareholders and the general public to form a definite and clear view of the company's position.

Other Continental laws, while providing for detailed balance sheets and giving rules as to evaluation, do not go into so much detail, and some of them, especially that of Switzerland, had actually a fair measure of success in securing information on the accounts for the public.

By Continental law it is the duty of the board of directors, or in Germany of the board of management, to prepare the balance sheet, which as a rule must be signed by all the members of the board. Consequently all the directors, or in Germany all the managers, are responsible for it.

A member of the board of directors (managers) who wishes to free himself of responsibility must express his disagreement with the balance sheet and communicate his protest to the board of supervisors or to some other authority designated by the law in question, e.g. the general meeting or the Court.

Until 1937 it was generally held on the Continent that the balance sheet, as drawn up by the board, is merely a draft, and that the general meeting may resolve either to accept it in the form and with the contents submitted, or to make alterations, or even to instruct the board to prepare a new one. In 1937, however, the German Companies law made a fundamental alteration in the law, providing that balance sheets are final if the board of management and the board of supervision are in accord. The general meeting therefore became powerless and disenfranchised, with power to resolve on the balance sheet only if the board of supervision did not accept it as drafted by the management.

The resolution on the balance sheet is of course one of the most important events in the life of a company; it is decisive in respect of dividends and the formation and strengthening of reserves, material factors of financial policy. In this regard the general meetings of German companies have lost all their power, since it could not be expected that the board of supervision will be inclined to disagree with the board of management, save in isolated cases. Consequently shareholders could obtain an alteration of the course adopted by the managers only by dismissing the board of supervision. How seldom this could be done we have already seen.

The question of future regulation was extensively discussed before the Cohen Committee both in memoranda submitted and by witnesses. Business circles and also to some extent the professional organisations of accountants were of opinion that "businesses are so varied in their nature that there must be flexibility in the manner of presenting accounts, and a standard form to suit every commercial and industrial undertaking is neither practicable nor desirable".[1] Nevertheless the representative bodies of the accountancy profession agreed that the position of auditors would be strengthened if legislation were to prescribe "a minimum of information to be disclosed in all balance sheets and profit and loss accounts". The Committee made certain recommendations, but refrained from suggesting standard forms of accounts.

Beside its recommendations the Institute of Chartered

[1] 65, recom. of the Institute of Chartered Accountants.

Accountants published in 1944 and 1945 detailed recommendations on accounting for its members, which it is worth while to consider.

Three rules were recommended: (*a*) the various items should be grouped under appropriate headings in order to facilitate a more ready appreciation of the financial position; (*b*) the principles of accounting should be consistently applied; (*c*) in order to facilitate the appreciation of the trend the comparative figures of the previous period should also be given. The Institute means that the use of general headings of assets and liabilities is inappropriate and unnecessary.

The use of these two general headings accepted by the practice of several centuries is, however, extremely simple, and serves the needs of swift appreciation. It is true that the capital of the company and its reserves are not liabilities in the strict sense of the word; nevertheless the two items show the amounts which are to be taken into account before the net profit of the financial period can be ascertained. On the other hand, though the company does not owe the amount of the capital and of the reserves to the shareholders, or for that matter to anybody else, it has to preserve them intact in the interest both of shareholders and creditors.

There are certain items regularly shown as assets which are not such in the proper sense of the word, but here too the grouping is very illustrative and should be preserved. If there were no other reason for retaining the customary headings, their constant use would amply justify it.

As to share capital the Institute recommends that beside stating the amount of shares authorised and issued, the shares should be grouped according to separate classes, if such exist, and the redemption date of the redeemable preference capital, if any, stated. In view of the importance of the widest possible publicity, this recommendation is surely to be approved, as is the recommendation that if there is any option on unissued capital, it should be mentioned in an appropriate clause.

If the company's preferred shares are cumulative, its status and the prospect of dividend on ordinary shares cannot be clearly seen without reference to arrears in the dividends of cumulative shares. Therefore we are in agreement with the recommendation (68), that in such a case the gross amount of dividends in arrear for the date up to which such dividends have been paid should be stated.

Recommendation 69 stresses firstly that amounts which are designed to meet some liability, contingency, commitment or diminution in the value of assets should not be stated as reserves. This is undoubtedly sound, as is the recommendation that reserves not available for distribution as dividends should be shown separately from reserves or surplus which are designed to be distributed or are available for distribution at the discretion of the general meeting or the directors, or whatever agency has authority for such decision.

In this direction we cannot approve the deduction of any adverse balance or profit and loss accounts from undistributed profits; this practice leads to the concealment of the actual results of the financial year in question, and should be barred.

Lastly there is a recommendation (70) that the sum total of the share capital and reserves be shown, to indicate the members' interest in the company. There is no objection to this; it is merely an addition of the two items.

It is recommended (71) that debentures, mortgages and other long-term loans and liabilities should be separately shown. Long-term liabilities in the Institute's view are such as are due for payment only after one year from the date of the balance sheet. It is further recommended that the dates and terms of redemption should be stated wherever practicable.

With the question of accounting of subsidiary undertakings, corporate or non-corporate, we shall deal in § 92; here we state only that it is recommended that amounts going to subsidiary undertakings should be shown either under separate headings as long-term or current liabilities, as the case may be, or as a separate group, but in any case segregated from other liabilities. Under current liabilities are understood amounts due within one year from the date of the balance sheet. It is recommended (74) that items belonging to this group should be classified with disclosure of the nature of the liabilities and the amounts included. The Institute recommends the following classification:

(*a*) trade liabilities, bills payable and accrued charges;
(*b*) bank loans and overdrafts;
(*c*) other short-term loans;
(*d*) interest accrued on debentures and other long-term liabilities;
(*e*) provision for current taxation;

(*f*) provision for specific commitments or contingencies where the amounts involved cannot be determined with substantial accuracy;

(*g*) provision for proposed dividends.

It is to be remarked, however, that the proposed dividend, so long as the proposal is not accepted by the general meeting, is not a liability of the company. It is certainly of interest to show its amount, but it is more adequate to show the net profit, and as to the proposed appropriation to attach a separate note, as is usual and as was recommended in certain memoranda and by some expert witnesses.

Recommendation 75 deals with commitments for capital expenditure and advises the indication in a suitable note of commitments of material amounts existing at the date of the balance sheet. It may be doubted whether indication in a note would be sufficient. Such commitments may constitute real liabilities, and if so they should be shown as separate items among liabilities. On the other hand the accruing capital assets should be shown among the fixed assets.

The same applies to contingencies on guarantees, bills under discount, partly paid shares and similar items. In the Institute's view, dealing with them in a note is satisfactory. Since these items constitute real and true liabilities they should be shown as such. The claim of the company for reimbursement may be shown among the assets as a separate item. This mode of accounting is not only more practical but is even necessary in all cases where it is not certain whether the company will be reimbursed by the debtor or whether the security given is adequate.

Both fixed and current assets are defined. Current assets are those held by the company for realisation in the ordinary course of business (81). All other assets are fixed assets, i.e. are held with the object of earning revenue and not for the purpose of sale in the ordinary course of business. It is recommended (77) that (*a*) goodwill, patents and trade marks, (*b*) freehold land and buildings, (*c*) leaseholds, (*d*) plant, machinery and equipment, (*e*) investments acquired and intended to be retained for trade purposes, should be shown separately, each group under separate headings. It would be advisable to show separately both as to freeholds and leaseholds the amounts charged for the land and for buildings. The same is proposed with regard to shares and other interests in subsidiary undertakings.

In respect of current assets it is recommended that there be stated separately: (*a*) stock-in-trade and work in progress; (*b*) trade and other debtors, prepayments and bills receivable; (*c*) investments held as part of the liquid resources of the company; (*d*) tax reserve certificates; (*e*) bank balances and cash. These recommendations are in accordance with the usual practice of those companies which do not avail themselves of the possibility afforded by the present law of showing a so-called omnibus item in their balance sheet. It is further recommended that debts of material amounts not due within one year from the date of the balance sheet should be separately grouped and suitably described (82).

The Institute recommends (83) the inclusion of particulars and amounts of expenditure such as preliminary expenses, issue expenses and discount on capital issues not written off. The question how these expenses should be written off is left open. As we said above, it would be advisable to prescribe a time limit within which such expenses should be met from current earnings and accordingly written off. For preliminary expenses some legislations provide a five-year term for extinction by writing off in equal instalments.

Where issues of shares below par are admitted at all, the discount should be extinguished in the year of the issue, otherwise the balance sheet would give a wrong view of the financial position of the company. The extinction or writing off may be done either from the current earnings of that year or from a reserve (surplus). In case of a discount on a bond issue the writing off might be effected over the whole term of the issue, i.e. the time within which the bonds are to be redeemed in equal yearly instalments.

The question of valuation for both assets and liabilities is a most difficult and important one. If the assets are valued at a higher level than the circumstances warrant, the balance sheet would give a false picture and would show the financial position in too favourable a light. This would encourage the payment of larger dividends than are advisable, and might eventually lead to insolvency. On the other hand should the valuation be at a lower level than the actual value, we might arrive at an undervaluation, a kind of secret, hidden reserve, which in our view is also dangerous, not for the creditors but for the actual and prospective shareholders.

In respect of fixed assets it is not usual to account at the end of the financial year their actual sale value; neither an increase nor a decrease in their value is normally taken into account. To increase the valuation because the land values have risen or the building and equipment would yield a higher price owing to an increase of replacement costs would be equal to an accounting of unrealised profits; dividends would be paid without real profits, and in case of a relapse of values the financial position of the company would be undermined.

It would surely be sound to reduce the valuation if the value of fixed assets has undergone a reduction, at least in cases in which such reduction seems to be more than a transitory fluctuation. But in the case of such fluctuations generally and even in cases of definite decrease or slumps many companies refrain from a correction in order not to strain the current profits, from which such corrections have necessarily to be met. In any case companies have to and do in fact meet depreciation.

The Institute defines depreciation as representing "that part of the costs of a fixed asset to its owner, which is not recoverable when the asset is finally put out of use by him". The depreciation is partly a consequence of use; every building, machine or tool has a certain life during which it is capable of use. Adequate conservation and constant repair may prolong this life, and negligence may shorten it; but in any case it is restricted. In economic matters a further point has to be taken into account: the use must be sufficient to serve for economical production. We have to consider therefore the useful life of fixed assets and not their absolute life, which latter may only be of importance for an owner who is not in economic competition. A factory building may still be habitable after it has become useless as a factory in view of disproportionate maintenance and repair costs, or can no longer serve the methods of production adopted by competitors. The same applies to machinery, equipment and all other classes of fixed assets.

There is yet another possibility: methods of production may have changed, owing, perhaps, to new inventions, to such a degree that the equipment, though in good condition, has become obsolete and cannot compete successfully with other equipments constructed with a view to the new inventions.

Depreciation from constant use may be estimated within more or less wide limits; obsolescence cannot be estimated, because it cannot be foreseen. Production as a whole is in constant progress, but this progress is not evenly distributed over its different branches, nor is it constant in time. It may happen that one branch of industry is stable in its methods and machinery for some years or even decades; in other branches innovations may occur more frequently, and in consequence of some new invention revolutionary changes may at any time take place which make the old method of production and the machinery in use uncompetitive. The right way to meet these changes is to provide regularly for depreciation and to create reserves against obsolescence.

As to the former, practical experience has shown within what time limits the various kinds of fixed assets lose their practical usefulness with the result that their commercial life comes to an end. Technical experts can discover whether a factory building can be used for its purpose for say, 50 years, a machine for ten, and a tool for five. It is therefore possible to fix with some certainty the amount needed to meet depreciation. Against obsolescence no such calculation is possible.

For the apportionment of depreciation several methods have been employed. The first of these is the so-called straight-line method. By this the amount of depreciation is spread over the expected useful life of the asset and in each financial period an equal amount for depreciation is provided from current earnings. Taking the above-mentioned example: 2 per cent. of the original cost of buildings, 10 per cent. of the cost of machinery and 20 per cent. of the cost of tools would be written off. Another method is that of the reducing balance: the percentage of the reduction or correction in values is applied on the basis of the value as stated at the beginning of each financial period, e.g. it is agreed that for buildings 3 per cent. is to be written off yearly, not from the original cost, but from the amount at which the building is valued at the end of the preceding, or the beginning of the current, financial period. It is obvious that if the depreciation is to be met within the same time limit as under the straight-line method, higher percentages must be applied. Taking the example of machines which lose their utility after ten years, the result under the reducing balance method, if the percentage were not altered, would be that at the end of ten years the machine assumed to be worthless would still figure at about 34·3 per cent. of its cost value. The Institute (94) says that this fact is not generally realised, and rates of depreciation fixed on this basis may tend to be inadequate.

In the U.S.A. and Canada the first method is in almost universal use. In Great Britain it is widespread, but some enterprises still make use of the second method.

A third method endeavours to set aside funds for depreciation, and these funds are accumulated with compound interest to meet the cost of the assets in question at the end of their useful life.

In some cases these amounts are invested outside the business, e.g. in government securities; in others, and indeed in the majority, inside the business as working capital. This method has the disadvantage that the rate of interest may not be maintainable during the whole period, and therefore depreciation may not be fully met by the amounts set aside with their accrued interest. This method is hardly used in industrial and commercial concerns, but is sometimes followed in public utility undertakings in Great Britain.

There is also the renewals reserve method. This means that round sums, not necessarily computed according to the useful life of the assets, are set aside as a general provision for the cost of future renewals. These amounts are sometimes fixed according to trading results, in good years larger, in bad years smaller amounts being set aside for renewals. If the amounts set aside do not reach the sum required for depreciation, the financial position of the company is artificially improved; if on the other hand they exceed the amount called for by the actual depreciation, a secret reserve may be formed, which is equally undesirable from the point of a correct and true balance. There is no objection to the formation and strengthening of a reserve for renewals; but it should be made quite apart from depreciation, and openly, with the knowledge of the shareholders and with their consent by way of a resolution in general meeting.

Although the Institute regards the straight-line method as the most adequate, it refrains from suggesting that it should be made compulsory (101). Accordingly, companies should be free to use one or the other method at their discretion; their only duty would be to make it clear which method has been used, and of course no change should be made from one year to another (cf. 104 and 99).

No recommendation is made for any limit on the valuation of goodwill. The only remark is that its depreciation does not arise from its use in business, and that amounts set aside to provide for diminution in value do not constitute a normal charge against revenue and should be shown separately in the profit and loss account. This point of view cannot be accepted. Goodwill should not be allowed to be included in the balance sheet as an asset, unless the company has paid for it or has had expenses in connection with the acquisition of the business. An arbitrary valuation of the goodwill in the balance sheet as an asset, and similarly any valuation exceeding the amount actually paid or the expenses actually incurred, should on principle be prohibited. Furthermore, it will always be a point of sound financial policy to write off the goodwill item as soon as possible. A definite rule cannot be suggested because, as the Institute rightly states, depreciation of the goodwill item does not arise through use corresponding to the lapse of time from the creation and commencement of business or its acquisition.

Freehold land does not depreciate through use, but it may do so in consequence of a general slump in land values or a decrease in value of adjoining or neighbouring land. Since the company does not intend to sell the land, it is not necessary to provide for a compulsory correction of the value from year to year. It would, however, be sound policy to take into account such decreases in land values in order to avoid losses when the freehold in question is to be sold, e.g. in the course of winding-up or when the company acquires new land for its industrial or trading purposes and the old land becomes redundant. It is recommended that amounts set aside for the reduction of freehold land values should be shown separately in the profit and loss account.

There is nothing special as to provisions for depreciation of freehold buildings, plant and machinery, tools and equipment, ships, transport vehicles and similar assets (101), but additional provisions may become necessary, and companies should from time to time examine the question whether the rate of depreciation applied is satisfactory. We may agree with the recommendations that any additional provision should be stated separately in the profit and loss account, and that fixed assets in existence at the date of the balance sheet should normally be shown at cost and the aggregate of the provisions for depreciation, amortisation and depletion should appear as a deduction therefrom (99).

Assets of very short effective life, such as loose tools, jigs and patterns, may be dealt with by other methods, especially by revaluation. The Institute does not suggest that in consequence of revaluation such items may be valued in excess of their cost; nevertheless it would be unsound to disregard the principle of systematic writing off within their normal commercial life, and this speaks against the method of revaluation. Consequently, if the company writes off in excess of the rate of depreciation provided, this should be shown in the profit and loss account. If on the other hand any asset of this group has been sold within the period in question, the loss suffered (of course so far as it exceeds the amount covered by depreciation provisions) should be shown separately in the profit and loss account as an actual loss.

For leaseholds, patents and other assets, which become exhausted by lapse of time, a provision for amortisation is recommended, adequate to the legal or useful life of the asset. Similarly, allowance should be made for the estimated cost of dilapidation at the end of a lease. This latter item may be covered by a leasehold redemption insurance policy. In such a case the annual premiums are to be included in the profit and loss account as a current expense, and this may provide a satisfactory method of amortisation.

It should be provided that patents cannot be assessed in the balance sheet at more than the price paid for them or the expenses incurred on experimental and other similar work connected with the development. This amount should be subject to systematic writing off in equal instalments over the term of the patent right. Current expenses for the maintenance of the patent should be accounted for under current expenses and any increase in valuation should be prohibited.

Trade marks as a rule are not restricted in their validity or are at least renewable as a matter of right. Consequently a systematic writing off within a definite period is not necessary, although it is a matter of sound policy to write off their purchase price and the expenses incurred in respect of their acquisition within a short time.

With regard to mines, oil-wells, quarries and similar assets it is in many countries a general rule that provision for depreciation and dilapidation should be made according to the estimated exhaustion of the asset. This is widely accepted in Great Britain; nevertheless some companies make no such provision. The

Institute does not recommend the prohibition of this, and requires only that the practice should be made clear in the accounts in order that the shareholders may know that dividends in part represent a return of capital. It is, however, not only the shareholder but also the creditor who is interested in this question. If there is no provision for depreciation and depletion it may happen, if the mine is exhausted sooner than was expected, that the rights of creditors may be impaired. Furthermore, if accounts are to be made informative to the general public, the balance sheet should always take the rate of depreciation and depletion into consideration.

Where a different method is adopted for the future it will frequently not be practicable or desirable to make a change in the case of assets already in the company's ownership at the beginning of the financial period, and the Institute therefore suggests that the new method should be followed only for assets subsequently acquired. This suggestion cannot be recommended, since it would then be many years before such balance sheets became really informative.

With regard to current assets the problem is even more difficult. These include stock-in-trade, work in progress, and also liquid assets temporarily invested, e.g. in government or other securities. The leading principle is that the valuation should not include any elements of profit not yet realised, and on the other hand due consideration must be given to any element of risk which by circumspect observation may be foreseen. It is therefore a requirement of prudent management that the valuation should not exceed either the cost or the market value prevailing at the date of the balance sheet.

This leading principle is a very simple one; its application, however, is difficult, since both cost and market value are frequently hard to ascertain. The elements making up the cost are, first the purchase price of the goods, stores, and in the case of processed stock materials used in manufacture; second, the direct expenditure incurred in bringing stock-in-trade to its existing condition and location. Besides these there are indirect expenses, that part of overheads or general expenses which is incidental to the stock-in-trade in question.

To include in the calculation of the cost price the proportionate fraction of the overhead expenses is a widespread practice; but this tends to increase the value of the stock existing at the date of the balance sheet, and cannot be recommended. Another point stressed by the Institute is that overhead expenses cannot be ascertained with substantial accuracy, and are always a matter of calculation. Furthermore they will fluctuate from one period to another with the volume of goods produced. Consequently their inclusion may lead to a distortion of the results. In some cases fixed annual charges are excluded from the calculation, in others only that amount is included which is based on the normal production of the unit concerned.

The Institute further gives a summary of the various methods used in accounting the cost price. These are: (1) Unit cost method: each article, batch or parcel is valued at its individual cost. In the case of bulk stock this method is not always applicable, and the recording of the expenses may be complicated. In the Institute's view this method may not be practicable in respect of partly processed stock or in the case of finished products where the individual units lose their identity.

(2) First in, first out; it is assumed that those goods have been sold or consumed which have been longest on hand; in other words, the quantity remaining in stock represents the latest purchases. This method dispenses with the necessity for identifying the different units of stock, and has the effect of keeping the valuation of unsold stock in the closest possible relation with the replacement price. The Institute considers, however, that in certain manufacturing or producing businesses it would be difficult to apply this method accurately through the various stages of manufacture or production.

(3) Average cost method: the book value of stock at the commencement of the financial period is increased by the addition of the cost of goods acquired or produced during this period and reduced by the deduction of consumption or sales at the average price realised. This simplifies accounting, and is said to have the further effect of smoothing out distortion of results arising from excessive and frequently quite accidental fluctuations in purchase prices and production costs. It is held to be particularly suitable for manufacturing businesses with several processes.

(4) Standard cost: the stock is valued at a predetermined cost per unit fixed on the basis of a careful budgeting. With the evolution of cost accounting methods this valuation has recently come into commoner use, especially in the case of industries with several manufacturing or processing operations. The applica-

tion of this method leads to a substantial simplification in the case of mass-production lines.

(5) Adjusted selling price: the stock is estimated by its pricing at current selling prices with deduction of the normal profit margin and the estimated cost of disposal. This method is very simple; but there is a danger that possibilities not yet realised may operate to decrease the values.

(6) Base stock method: certain basic stock is permanently retained at its original cost, i.e. a fixed price not exceeding the original cost, provided it does not exceed the market price.

(7) Last in, first out method: the remaining stock is valued at the latest purchase prices, and the profit or loss is calculated on the basis of the difference between the sale price and the actual replacement cost.

The Institute rightly does not recommend any rule as to the use of one method or the other. In our own view the cost price is to be controlled by the market value of the stock held. The market value can easily be ascertained in the case of quoted prices. It is more difficult if the goods are not dealt in in open market; in such cases it is mainly a matter of estimation. The price is to be found at which the stock can be realised in its existing condition or incorporated in a product which may be normally sold. In the latter case the expenditure necessary for the incorporation and in both cases the expenses of disposal are to be deducted. Another method, also very usual, is the ascertainment of the replacement price of the goods concerned. It is generally held that the lower price calculated on the basis of the market value or the cost is to be taken as the basis of the valuation.

There is dispute, however, whether this should be made a compulsory requirement or be left to the discretion of the directors and auditors. According to the general attitude taken in this work towards the requirements of the balance sheet and the profit and loss account it does not seem advisable to omit the legislative enunciation of this rule. The suggestion that certain businesses, such as steel and rubber producing, and mining companies, which usually value their stocks of products at the price subsequently realised after deducting the selling costs, should be free to retain this practice, cannot be accepted.

A special case is that of work in progress on the basis of a long-term contract. It is usual in many cases to disperse the profit of such work proportionately over the whole period of production. It is asserted that in this way the extraordinary concentration of profit in the last year of production is avoided, and that in principle it is more just and suitable to account the profit in that year in which any part of the work was finished. This view is attractive, especially if a company has only one contract for work in execution, e.g. one bridge or one factory to construct or one building to erect. But if a company has two or more contracts for work in execution at the same time, as is the normal case, the argument loses much ground. It is to be presumed that in the constant flow of work and contracts the company will constantly be finishing one or several of them in consecutive years, and therefore there will be no year without a final accounting of one or more contracts. With a normally operating company the hypothesis that the company will show profits only in certain years because in others no work will have reached its conclusion will hardly arise; but in any case the accounting of profits on the basis of estimation would mean that unrealised profits would be shown and distributed, for whether a work is executed at a profit or at a loss cannot be determined before its conclusion. Experience shows that in many cases the final accounts show a result widely differing from that expected. Therefore we cannot accept the suggestion that it should be left to the directors whether they will account for a part of the profits proportionate to the amount of work done during the financial period.

Losses foreseen at the date of the balance sheet should always be accounted for in the valuation of work in progress; their disregard cannot be advocated. The same applies to contracts of sale or purchase at a fixed price if the current market value of the goods in question at the date of the balance sheet shows the probability of a loss.

In this connection we have to deal with the valuation of securities held as investment for liquid assets. This should not exceed the purchase price or the market value at the date of the balance sheet, whichever is lower. In case of securities quoted on the Stock Exchange it is very easy to find the market value; in the case of unquoted securities it can be found by other means, e.g. by ascertainment of actual sales. It is of course true that even the current quotation at the Stock Exchange or market value, however carefully ascertained, is not absolute evidence of the possibility of a sale at that price. It may be that, e.g. in the case of a large amount, the quoted price could not be obtained for a forced sale. Nevertheless the quoted price and market value is the nearest approach to the real value, and a higher valuation should not be allowed. Any prudent management will of course consider the difficulties of a possible sale.

No special recommendations were made in respect of debts due to or from the company. There are, however, certain observations to be made on this question. As a rule debts due to the company are to be accounted at their nominal value. The interest accrued during the financial year is treated as revenue even if it is not paid. This is not objectionable except where the debt has become a bad one. Bad debts are to be written off as current losses. If a debt has become dubious, either a suitable part is written off or provision is made for such contingency. Both methods are equally acceptable. The possibility of creating hidden reserves easily arises in respect of such assets, and can hardly be avoided, since the matter is necessarily in the discretion of the management.

If a debt written off is subsequently paid, this is a profit of the company, and the same is true where a dubious debt partly written off is paid in larger part than was valued. Such items were frequently accounted for by being set off against writings off which became necessary during the financial year. This is not to be recommended, since it is apt to obscure the real position.

Debts due by the company are always to be accounted at their full nominal amount. If the company contests the claim in whole or in part, it is more advisable to account the amount claimed among liabilities and put up a reserve item, or to show the debt at the estimated amount and create a provisions item for contingency among the liabilities. Sometimes companies deal with debts by setting off the compound amount of debts due to and from the company, and showing only the balance among the liabilities or assets, as the case may be. Such a practice is objectionable.

The Cohen Committee adopted many of the recommendations of the accountancy profession, and most of them were embodied in the Companies Act, 1947. Its provisions were intended to supplement the provisions of the existing Act, and it was stated (sec. 13 (3)) that the contents of the new Act shall be without prejudice to the requirements of the Act of 1929 unless expressly provided. The provisions of secs. 12 and 13 of the Act of 1947 are now contained in sec. 149 of the 1948 Act.

The technique adopted is that only some leading principles are embodied in the text of the Act, whereas all the details are put into a Schedule, the Eighth Schedule to the Act, which deals with the balance sheet in Part I.

The aim of the balance sheet is (sec. 149 (1)) to give a true and fair view of the state of affairs as at the end of the company's financial year.

The term "floating" assets is replaced by the term "current" assets (clause 4 (1) of the Eighth Schedule, Part I).

A distinction is to be made between provisions and reserves. Provision shall mean any amount written off or retained for depreciation, renewals or diminution of value of assets or for any known liability whose amount cannot be determined with substantial accuracy. The expression liability shall include all liabilities in respect of expenditure contracted for and also disputed or contingent liabilities. In so far as provisions are in excess of what in the opinion of the directors is reasonably necessary for that purpose, the excess shall be treated as reserve. This, however, shall not apply to amounts written off before the coming into force of the new provisions. Lastly, capital reserves shall be distinguished from revenue reserves, and the former shall not include any amount regarded as free for distribution through the profit and loss account (Eighth Schedule, Part IV).

As to the contents and arrangement of the balance sheet it is provided that reserves, provisions and liabilities shall be classified under headings appropriate to the company's business; the same applies to the assets, with the proviso that fixed shall be distinguished from current assets. If, however, the amount of any class is not material it may be included under the same heading as some other class, and where assets are not separable from assets of another class, they may be included under the same heading.

In respect of fixed assets the method or methods used to arrive at their amount shall be stated under each heading. Generally their amount shall be the difference between the cost, or where they stand in the books at a valuation, the valuation and the amount provided or written off since the acquisition or valuation for depreciation or diminution in value. For assets acquired before the coming into force of the Schedule for which these figures cannot be obtained without unreasonable expense or delay the amount may be based on the net amount at which they stand at that date in the books of the company. Furthermore the above-mentioned rule shall not apply to assets for which the figures relating to the period beginning with the coming into force of the Schedule cannot be obtained without unreasonable expense or delay, or to assets whose replacement is provided for wholly or partly by making provisions for renewals and charging the cost of replacements against the provision or to revenue.

It is not necessary to show the cost price and the amount deducted for depreciation or diminution of value of investments where their market value, or if there is no market value, their value as estimated by the directors, is shown either as the amount or by way of note.

The particulars of the method or methods are to be shown in detail for each heading; thus in the case of provisions for replacement the means by which the replacement is provided for and the aggregate amount of the provisions made but not used are to be stated.

The requirement as to the statement of capital reserves, revenue reserves and any provisions other than those for depreciation, renewals or diminution of value is qualified by two exceptions. In so far as the amounts are not material no separate heading is required. Furthermore the Board of Trade may give dispensation where it is satisfied that the separate statement is not required in the public interest and would prejudice the company, but any heading stating an amount arrived at after taking into account a provision other than as aforesaid shall be so framed or marked as to indicate that fact.

Where the amount of reserves—capital or revenue—or that of provisions other than those for depreciation, etc., shows a material increase at the end of the financial year, the source from which the increase was derived is to be shown. In the case of a decrease of the reserve, and similarly where the amount of provisions other than those for depreciation, etc., exceeded at the end of the financial year the aggregate amount of the sums applied during the financial year and the amounts still retained, the application of the amounts derived from the difference is to be shown. But this is not necessary if the particulars in question are shown in the profit and loss account or in a statement or report annexed thereto.

Trade investments shall be shown under a separate heading,

and other investments shall be divided into quoted and unquoted investments.

Goodwill, patents and trade marks may be shown as a single item. If only a part of the amount of goodwill, patents and trade marks is shown or is ascertainable from the books, contracts and documents relating to the stamp duty payable for such contracts, that part which is so shown or ascertainable must be stated.

Likewise under a separate heading are to be shown the aggregate amount of bank loans and overdrafts and the aggregate of dividends recommended after deduction of income tax.

If any of the company's debentures are held by a nominee or trustee for the company, their nominal amounts and the amount at which they are stated in the books of the company are to be shown.

If there are options for the subscription of any shares of the company, the number, description and amount of the shares, the period during which such option is exercisable, and the price to be paid for them are to be shown in a note or statement, or in a report annexed or otherwise.

If any fixed cumulative dividends of the company's preference shares are in arrear, the amount of the arrears is to be stated before deduction of income tax, and in the case of tax-free dividends the amount shall be shown free of tax, and the fact that it is so shown is to be stated.

The following new requirements as to liabilities are introduced. Statements are to be given in respect of—

(*a*) Particulars of any charge on the assets of the company to secure the liabilities of any other person, including, where practicable, the amount secured.

(*b*) The general nature of any other contingent liabilities not provided for and their aggregate amount or estimated amount if material.

(*c*) The aggregate or estimated amount of contracts for capital expenditure in so far as they are material and not covered by provisions.

Where any of the current assets in the opinion of the directors have not a value on realisation in the ordinary course of business at least equal to the amount at which they figure in the balance sheet, this opinion is to be stated.

The market value of the company's quoted investments other than trade investments is likewise to be given where it differs from the amount of those investments as stated.

If any foreign currencies have been converted into sterling, where the amount of assets and liabilities affected is material, the basis on which the conversion was made is to be given.

If any amount was set aside for United Kingdom income tax the basis on which it was computed is to be shown.

The corresponding amounts for the immediately preceding financial year are to be shown for all items of the balance sheet except in the case of the first balance sheet after the coming into force of the Schedule. In practice, however, many companies gave the corresponding figures of the last financial year, and few availed themselves of the exception.

There are exceptions, especially for banking, discount and insurance companies, which will be considered in the appendix to the following section.

All the amendments introduced may be regarded as beneficial. Whether they are sufficiently far-reaching future experience will show.

86. The Profit and Loss Account

Corporation accounts have also the purpose of ascertaining the results of the management for the period fixed by the articles. Under the Companies Act of 1929 this period must not exceed 12 months. It provides (sec. 123 (1)) that the directors shall at least once in every calendar year lay before the company in general meeting a profit and loss account; the articles may provide for a shorter but not for a longer period. For the first profit and loss account the maximum period is 18 months from incorporation; the Board of Trade may extend these periods for some special reason. These provisions fix the so-called financial year of the company, which may or may not be identical with the calendar year.

It is important that the accounts should be presented to the shareholders in general meeting as soon as possible after the end of the financial year. The Act is fairly liberal, providing that the profit and loss account is to be made up to a date not earlier than nine months—or in the case of a company carrying on business or having interests abroad, 12 months—preceding the general meeting. In either case the Board of Trade may grant extension at its discretion.

Although the profit and loss account is of great importance, and it has been usual since the last years of the 17th century to prepare such accounts and to lay them before the general meeting, it was only by the Companies Consolidation Act of 1928 and subsequently by the Companies Act of 1929 that the drawing up of a profit and loss account was made a legal duty of the directors. Even then the law provided no fixed rules for the form and contents of the account. Indeed, apart from some special matters the only mandatory rule of the Act was that the profit and loss account must be made up to the same date as the balance sheet. The directors therefore had an even greater discretion in the drawing up of the profit and loss account than in the case of the balance sheet, for which, as we have seen, at least certain leading principles were laid down. The only limitation is the duty of the directors to procure an audit of the profit and loss account. It depends mainly therefore on the views of the accountancy profession whether the auditor of the balance sheet and the profit and loss account accepts them or not, or whether he requires some alterations.

In the United States, apart from the New Deal legislation, the legal requirements are even slighter. By common law the whole question of accounts, the profit and loss account included, is left to the discretion of the company, i.e. of the directors. Some rules are laid down by statute, but even these do not go further than the English Companies Act of 1929.

In both countries there are certain classes of companies, particularly railway and public service (public utility) companies, which are subject to special rules.

In Europe profit and loss accounts are generally not regulated to the same extent as balance sheets. The German Companies law of 1937 is an exception and contains (§ 132) very detailed provisions. Losses are to be set out under nine headings. These are: (1) wages and salaries; (2) social welfare contributions; (3) writings off and corrections of value in respect of fixed assets; (4) interest and similar expenses—it is, however, allowable to state only the difference between interest paid and received; (5) income tax, taxes on gross receipts and capital levies, with the exception of income tax paid by deduction at source; (6) contributions to trade associations in so far as membership is legally compulsory; (7) amounts of (*a*) depreciation, (*b*) other losses for which the legal reserve has been used; (8) extraordinary expenditure not included under other items; (9) all other expenditure.

With regard to profits, separate headings are prescribed for: (1) the compound gross profit; all expenditure not detailed under the aforementioned headings may, however, be deducted beforehand; (2) profits from participations; (3) interest and similar items of income, provided they exceed the interest and similar items paid by the company; (4) extraordinary profits, including any resulting from the dissolution of reserves; (5) amounts taken from legal reserve in so far as that may legally be done; (6) extraordinary payments received.

The net profit or loss, as the case may be, is to be stated under a separate heading as the last item of the profit and loss account. The law also requires a separate statement of the carry-over of profit or loss from the preceding fiscal year (§ 132).

All these rules are in accord with the general principles accepted by accountants in Germany and, for that matter, in every other country. But the law, in contradiction to the leading principles declared by the Government when introducing it, did very little to secure full information about the results from the management. Especially noteworthy is it that with regard to profits it suffices merely to state the balance of profits over expenses, apart from the aforementioned classes which are to be stated separately. German industrial or trading companies still retained freedom under the law to deduct all expenses, especially those for raw materials, goods, transport, manufacturing costs, etc., beforehand, and it is only wages, salaries and taxes which have to be stated separately. Furthermore the law allows them to state merely the balance of interest and similar items, whereas to secure full knowledge of the financial status a separate statement of interest paid and received would be necessary. Under these circumstances it is not surprising that the balance sheets of German companies, so far as they were available from the Press, gave even after 1937 very scanty information about the real results of management.

From a legislative standpoint the question of profit and loss accounts requires special consideration. Much material exists, mainly in the literature of accountancy and the transactions and discussions of the professional associations. The practice of companies of giving superficial information as to their profits and losses was strongly criticised, especially the widespread use of the so-called omnibus clause, "profit after deduction of costs of production, overhead expenses, taxation, other expenses and provisions for contingencies". Such a clause does not give any information; even the general trend of business cannot be ascertained. By the use of hidden reserves the profits realised in one year may be increased or reduced by taking from or appropriating to reserve.

Under the influence of public opinion, and especially as a result of the insistence of the accountancy profession, a more truthful method of accounting and of constructing the profit and loss account gradually came into use. Nevertheless even those companies which give more information generally refrain from showing the trading results, i.e. gross trading revenue and expenses. The main argument against giving an exact picture of the business is that rivals may get information therefrom, and thus the more information is given in the published accounts the more harm may be done to the company.

This argument is not well founded. In most cases rivals can secure all the information they need from other sources than the profit and loss account submitted in general meeting, published in the Press and preserved in the files of the Registry. It is only the small shareholders, actual or prospective, who are denied information regarding the true trend of profits.

The Institute of Chartered Accountants recommended the following separate headings: (*a*) trading results; (*b*) gross income from other investments; (*c*) depreciation and amortisation of fixed assets; (*d*) interest charges on debentures and long-term liabilities; (*e*) credits on charges in respect of provisions for contingencies whose amounts cannot be closely estimated; (*f*) national defence contribution and excess profits tax; (*g*) credits or charges which are abnormal in nature or relate to previous periods; (*h*) income tax and the basis thereof; (*i*) amounts set aside for redemption of share or loan capital; (*j*) reserves made or withdrawn; (*k*) dividends paid or proposed, showing separately those dividends which are subject to confirmation by the shareholders; (*l*) balances brought and carried forward.

The Institute did not suggest that the giving of supplemental details of trading results should be prescribed, but that the separate statement of the items mentioned should be the minimum (18). Generally the profit and loss account should be presented in such a form as to give a clear disclosure of the results of the period and the amount available for appropriation (16).

"This implies substantial uniformity in the accounting principles applied as between successive periods." If such changes were made and their effect were to alter the results in consequence of their material nature such as a variation of stock valuation or in the method of providing for depreciation or taxation, the change should be disclosed (17).

The recommendations of the Cohen Committee (Report, pp. 61–2) were largely based on the proposals of the accountancy profession and were embodied in the First Schedule, Part I, B, of the Act of 1947 (now clauses 12–14 of the Eighth Schedule, Part I, of the Act of 1948). There shall be shown: (*a*) the amount charged to revenue by way of provision for depreciation, renewals or diminution in value of fixed assets; (*b*) the amount of the interest on the company's debentures and other fixed loans; (*c*) the amount of the charge for United Kingdom income tax and other United Kingdom taxation on profits, including, where practicable, as United Kingdom tax any taxation imposed elsewhere to the extent of the relief, if any, from United Kingdom income tax and distinguishing where practicable between income tax and other taxation; (*d*) the amounts respectively provided for redemption of share capital and for redemption of loans; (*e*) the amount, if material, set aside or proposed to be set aside to, or withdrawn from, reserves; (*f*) the amount, if material, set aside to provisions other than provisions for diminution in value of assets or, as the case may be, the amount, if material, withdrawn from such provisions and not applied for the purposes thereof; (*g*) the amount of income from investments, distinguishing between trade and other investments; (*h*) the aggregate amount of the dividends paid and proposed.

The following matters shall be stated by way of note if not otherwise shown:

(1) If depreciation or replacement of fixed assets is provided for by some method other than a depreciation charge or provision for renewals, or is not provided for, the method by which it is provided for or the fact that it is not provided for.

(2) The basis on which the charge for United Kingdom income tax is computed.

(3) Whether or not the amount stated for dividends paid and proposed is for dividends subject to deduction of income tax.

The corresponding amounts for the immediately preceding financial year are to be shown for all items, except in the first profit and loss account after the coming into force of the Schedule.

If any item is affected by a transaction not usually undertaken by the company or by circumstances of an exceptional or non-recurrent nature, this is to be stated separately. Lastly, any change in the basis of accounting should be stated.

Many companies began to apply the rules recommended by the Committee following the publication of the report even before the introduction of the Bill, and in this way the recommendations had a beneficial effect even before the change in legislation was effected. Whether the reluctance to require details in respect of trading results will be justified is in our view doubtful. The stressing of possible dangers was obviously of great influence.

These arguments were fully appreciated and in our view even overrated by the committee, and led to the following exceptions:

By sec. 13 (4) of the Act of 1947, re-enacted by sec. 149 (3) and (4) of the Act of 1948, the Board of Trade will have power on the application and with the consent of a company's directors to modify the requirements laid down in the Schedule for the balance sheet and the profit and loss account for the purpose of adapting them to the circumstances of the company, but such modifications must not affect the requirement of giving a true and fair view of the state of affairs of the company at the end of its financial year in the balance sheet and of the profit or loss for the financial year.

Furthermore the Board of Trade may direct that a company shall not be obliged to show the amounts set aside for depreciations and the other purposes aforementioned if it is satisfied that "it is not required in the public interest and would prejudice the company, but in such case any heading stating an amount arrived at after taking into account the amount set aside is to be so framed or marked as to indicate that fact" (Eighth Schedule, Part I, clauses 6 (*b*) and 12 (2).

Special exemptions are granted to banking and discount companies. Whether a company is to be treated as a banking or discount company as regards the application of the Eighth Schedule shall be decided by the Board of Trade. In respect of the balance sheet such companies are not under duty to disclose a number of particulars which are required from other companies. In particular they do not have to state the method of arriving at the amount of fixed assets, the aggregate amounts of capital reserves, revenue, reserves and provisions respectively, the aggregate amount of bank loans and overdrafts, or the aggregate market value of the company's quoted investments other than trade investments where they differ from the amount of those investments as stated. In their profit and loss accounts such companies have to state separately only the aggregate amount of dividends paid and proposed, and by way of note if not otherwise shown, whether this amount is for dividends subject to deduction of income tax, or for tax-free dividends. But where the company, availing itself of the exemption, does not state separately its capital reserves, revenue reserves or provisions, the heading shall be so framed or marked as to indicate that the respective amount was arrived at after taking into account such reserve or provision.

Similarly the profit and loss account shall indicate by appropriate words the manner in which the amount stated for the company's profit or loss has been arrived at (Eighth Schedule, Part III, clause 23).

If there is, generally speaking, something to be said for a relaxation of the duty to disclose hidden reserves and provisions in the case of banking companies, the exemption envisaged by the Act goes in our view too far.

Assurance companies, in so far as their annual accounts comply with the requirements of the Assurance Companies Act of 1909, have been able to deliver to the Registrar of Companies the accounts deposited with the Board of Trade instead of accounts drawn up in accordance with the Companies Act (sec. 110 of the Act of 1929). This position was maintained by the 1947 Act, and it is now provided in clauses 24 and 25 of the Eighth Schedule, Part III, that assurance companies within the meaning of the Assurance Companies Acts, 1909–46, shall enjoy the same exemptions as banking or discount companies. Furthermore they shall not be bound to show separately their trade and other investments quoted and unquoted, charges to secure liabilities of other persons, the general nature and amount of their other contingent liabilities, the aggregate amount of contracts or capital expenditure so far as not provided for, and the directors' opinion on the realisation value of the current assets. If the business of an assurance company includes some other business to a substantial extent, it depends upon the discretion of the Board of Trade whether and how far these exemptions shall apply.

By sec. 454 (1) of the Act of 1948 the Board of Trade shall have power to alter or add to the provisions of the Eighth Schedule, and such alterations are to be made by statutory instrument. If, however, an alteration would render the requirements of the Eighth Schedule more onerous, the regulation shall not be made unless a draft thereof has been laid before Parliament and approved by both Houses, whereas other regulations made in respect of the requirements of the accounts are subject to annulment in pursuance of a resolution of either House of Parliament.

87. Directors' Report, Signature of the Accounts

It follows from their confidential relationship to their companies that directors ought to report regularly to the shareholders on the state of the company and on all important events which have occurred during the period to which the accounts refer. This is the usual practice, and it existed even before it was imposed by legislation.

In many countries the report is made in writing on behalf of the board and signed by its members; it is sent out to the shareholders before the general meeting. The communications made in the report are not then supplemented by speeches made on behalf of the board at the meeting unless dissatisfied or inquisitive shareholders demand further explanations.

In Great Britain, however, it has from early times been usual for the chairman, before embarking on the agenda of the meeting, to make a speech.

The Act of 1929 (sec. 123 (2)) required only that the directors' report should explain the state of the company's affairs, the amount of dividend proposed and the amount—if any—which the directors propose to put into reserve. This provision is re-enacted in sec. 157 of the Act of 1948. These requirements are very modest, and a report restricted to them could hardly be called informative. Although many companies try to give informative reports, others are quite uninformative and, in the words of the Committee, "merely summarise the profit and loss account, giving the specific information mentioned and the names of the directors and auditors who retire and will be proposed for re-election". This is not satisfactory, and things are not much improved by the fact that the chairmen's speeches in most cases give more information, since a large majority of shareholders do not attend the general meetings and even those who do are not in a position to form a judgment on what is discussed. Proceedings of general meetings were in many cases not printed and sent to shareholders; this was especially so in times of paper shortage. Therefore the chairman's speech cannot be regarded as a satisfactory supplement to the report. Nevertheless the Committee did not recommend any extension of the directors' report. The provision of sec. 19 of the 1947 Act, now contained in sec. 157 (2) of the 1948 Act, according to which the report shall deal with the changes occurring during the financial year of the company in so far as it is material for the appreciation of the company's affairs by its members and will not in the directors' opinion be harmful to the business of the company or any of its subsidiaries, encourages reticence rather than disclosure. We cannot agree with this attitude, since there is a strong inclination on the part of directors to restrict publicity as far as possible, and public opinion alone, without legal remedies, cannot assert itself against this tendency. Even in Great Britain, where business standards are generally so high, reports and chairmen's speeches are often reticent.

The Act of 1929 (sec. 129 (1)) provides that the balance sheet shall be signed on behalf of the board by two directors, or if there is only one, by that director, and this is maintained in sec. 155 (1) of the Act of 1948. In the case of banking companies registered after 15 August 1879 the balance sheet is to be signed by the secretary or manager and by at least three directors or where there are not more than three by all the directors (sec. 155 (2)).

In the U.S.A. the statutes generally do not regulate this question. The State of California, however, which is also an exception in providing that the balance sheet and the profit and loss account are to be a part of the annual report, prescribes moreover that both statements shall be certified by the president, secretary or treasurer or a public accountant.[1]

European laws generally provide either expressly or by implication that the balance sheet and the profit and loss account shall be signed by all members of the board, and, where there is a board of supervision, by the members of both boards.

[1] C.C. 358, as amended by L. 1933, c. 533, § 357.

The matter of signature, however, is a formality: the main question is whether and how far the directors are responsible for the accounts by virtue of their office. According to the view already submitted the board should be made responsible for both balance sheet and profit and loss account. It should be the duty of the directors to do everything which is reasonable under the circumstances to ascertain the correctness of the accounts and to see that legal requirements as to accounts are complied with. In accordance with this duty directors should be liable for the accounts, whether they have examined them or not; and the defence that a director has not examined the accounts should not be admitted.

This proposal is aimed at ensuring the correctness of the accounts and also at increasing the possibility of recovering damages when shareholders or third parties are injured by their incorrectness. Should a director not approve the balance sheet, he would refuse his signature, and the account submitted to the general meeting should contain a note explaining the fact and the reason for the absence of such signature.

Following the recommendations of the Committee (101, p. 63), sec. 21 of the Companies Act, 1947, now sec. 156 (1) of the Act of 1948, provides that the profit and loss account shall be annexed to the balance sheet and approved by the board of directors before the balance sheet is signed on their behalf. Compliance is secured by a fine not exceeding £50.

The penal clause of sec. 123 (3) was somewhat amplified by sec. 13 (6) of the Act of 1947, re-enacted in sec. 157 (3), which provides that it is an offence if a director fails to take all reasonable steps to secure compliance with any of the requirements of the report and its presentation. The penalty will be, on summary conviction, imprisonment not exceeding six months if in the opinion of the Court the offence was committed wilfully, or a fine not exceeding £200; if not wilful, the fine alone.

The accounts are to be circularised, i.e. communicated to the shareholders. This requirement applies on principle to both the balance sheet and the profit and loss account. But since the importance of the latter has only been recognised relatively recently, some legislations do not extend to it the provisions for the circulation of accounts. This was the case in Great Britain under the 1929 Act, which provided (sec. 130) only that a copy of every balance sheet should be sent to all persons entitled to receive notice of the general meetings of the company not less than seven days before the date of the meeting. It was further provided that any shareholder, whether entitled to be invited to the general meeting or not, and any debenture holder of the company, may demand a copy of the balance sheet without charge.

It is not reasonable to make a distinction between shareholders as to whether they are entitled to notice of the general meeting or not. On the recommendation of the Committee (107, p. 63) the law was amended to the effect that a copy of every balance sheet and every document to be attached thereto shall be sent to every member and every debenture holder of the company whether he be entitled to receive notice of the meeting or not, and that not less than 21 days before the meeting, with the proviso that a copy need not be sent to any person of whose address the company is not aware or to more than one of the joint holders of shares or debentures (sec. 21·(3) of the Act of 1947; sec. 158 of the Act of 1948). Moreover, every member and every debenture holder may request a copy of the last balance sheet and of every document to be attached thereto without charge (sec. 158 (3)).

88. Supervision of the Accounts: the Audit

It is obvious that company accounts cannot be properly checked and supervised by the general meeting in view of the difficulties and the time needed for so doing. It is therefore necessary to institute some organisation and procedure in order to reassure the shareholders that the accounts as presented by the directors are truthful and reliable. The various legislations have sought to attain this result in different ways.

The first was the French method, which consisted in legal provisions for the election of a board of supervision from among the ranks of the shareholders. Under this system the general meeting has to elect a certain number of members of the board of supervision for a certain period. Their number is at least three, their term of office short, they must themselves be shareholders. This system has been adopted by a number of Continental legislations, especially the Italian, Belgian, Austrian and Hungarian.

The laws in question aimed at securing the independence

of the supervisors usually by providing that they may not be given other functions than that of supervision. The supervisors were to check the books and records of the company, and especially the accounts, i.e. the balance sheet and the profit and loss account. It was usual to provide that they should sign the accounts and make a report of the result of their examination to the general meeting, which without such report might not approve the accounts and resolve upon the distribution of dividends. Most of these laws made it a duty of the supervisors to oversee the management constantly and to convene a general meeting and report to it if and when they found any irregularity. In case of failure to fulfil these duties, liability for damages and more or less severe penalties were imposed.

In spite of this careful regulation the board of supervision did not prove an efficient body. The main defect observed was that nowhere was it truly independent; the supervisors were usually elected on the recommendation of the directors. They were as a rule retired employees of the company, retired civil servants, or simply people whom the directors for one reason or another wished to attach to the company, though they were not important enough to be elected to the board of directors. They were usually paid a fixed fee, voted by the general meeting or laid down in the articles, and normally fairly moderate. As a rule they had no knowledge or experience of book-keeping and accounting; those who were experts were mostly dependent on the directors, and nearly all of them were keen to retain their position for the sake of the fee attached to it. It is therefore not surprising that supervisors in great majority were seldom anxious to examine the books and records even in so far as they were capable of doing so. The checking of the balance sheet and the profit and loss account was at best superficial, and in many cases purely formal. At most company insolvencies it appeared that the defects of the management, the concealment of losses and grave irregularities might have been discovered by careful examination, and the losses inflicted upon shareholders and creditors thus averted.

In Germany a very curious situation arose. The Commercial Code of 1861 did not provide for a board of supervision, but nevertheless many companies had supervisors beside the board of directors. Their authority and duties were defined by the articles of the companies and not by law. The law of 1870 provided for the separation of the board of management (*Vorstand*) from the council or board of supervision (*Aufsichtsrat*). The latter's function, however, was actually not the checking and examination of the accounts and the management as a whole sequence of the business activities, but the fixing of the business policy and the giving of assent to extraordinary acts of the board of management (see § 15). Therefore the board of supervision under German law had in practice very little to do with supervision, such as, i.e. the auditing of accounts, but the original functions of the board of directors had been split into two parts: one part, executive action, strictly speaking, was left to the board of management; the other, the settlement of general business policy, was the task of the board of supervision. As in this way the board of supervision had no special duties as to the examination of the accounts, the general meeting could not rely on the *Aufsichtsrat* any more than on the *Vorstand* for the correctness of the accounts.

A quite different method was followed by Anglo-American legislation. The board of directors has always within its competence not only executive acts but also the business policy. Long before legislation took up the matter it was usual to entrust the supervision and auditing of the accounts to independent experts with skill and experience in book-keeping and accounting. Accounting became a recognised profession, and professional bodies of accountants were established. In England and Wales there are the Institute of Chartered Accountants, the Society of Incorporated Accountants and Auditors, and the Association of Certified and Corporate Accountants, while in Scotland there are Councils of Chartered Accountants which form a Joint Committee. All these bodies admit members after training and examination. They all exercise professional discipline over their members, and an accountant guilty of professional misconduct would be expelled from the body of which he is a member.

Until 1879 only companies governed by the Companies Consolidation Act were obliged to audit their accounts. In that year compulsory auditing was introduced in respect of banking companies, and it was extended to all other companies in 1900. The inclusion in the annual return of a statement in the form of a balance sheet became obligatory only in 1908.

By the 1929 Act every company was bound to appoint at each annual general meeting an auditor or auditors to hold office until the next general meeting (sec. 132 (1)). The first auditors may be appointed by the directors at any time before the first general meeting to hold office until that meeting, but they may then be removed by the general meeting and others appointed in their place (subsec. (7)). Directors may fill any casual vacancy in the office of auditor, but the surviving or continuing auditor may act (subsec. (5)).

No director or officer of the company or (except for private companies) partner or employee of an officer of the company may be appointed as auditor. Furthermore a body corporate is disqualified, but this disqualification does not extend to firms, though in Scotland firms may be regarded as corporate bodies (sec. 133). Otherwise no qualification is prescribed for auditors. It is therefore within the discretion of the general meeting to appoint whom they wish, whether he is a member of any of the professional bodies of accountants or not.

For Societies registered under the Industrial Assurance Act, and similarly for Collecting Societies subject to the Industrial Assurance Act, there is a list of public auditors appointed by the Treasury, and these societies cannot appoint any auditor who is not on this list.

In practice the vast majority of companies appoint only auditors who are members of one of the professional associations, and we may assume that this question would long have been settled by legislation had there been unanimity between the members of the accountancy profession as to the necessary qualifications.

Should a company fail to appoint auditors at any of its general meetings the Board of Trade may on the application of any member of the company appoint an auditor for the current financial year (sec. 132 (2)).

The remuneration of auditors is to be fixed by the general meeting, except for the fees of the first auditors and those appointed to fill casual vacancies; these may be fixed by the directors. The fees of those appointed by the Board of Trade may be fixed by that department. The intention of the Act was to make the auditors as independent of the directors as possible. In view of the concentration of power in the board this is itself a hard task, and in respect especially of the auditor's fees the intention of the legislature is largely vitiated by the practice of general meetings empowering directors to fix the remuneration of auditors at their discretion. In the opinion of the Committee (113, p. 66), the legality of this practice is doubtful; in our view it is contrary to law to delegate this power to the directors. Nevertheless the only recommendation made is that, if the remuneration is fixed by the directors, this should be specially stated.

The Companies Act, 1947 (sec. 24 (8); re-enacted in sec. 159 (7) (*b*) of 1948), clarified the position by providing that the remuneration of auditors appointed in general meeting shall be fixed in general meeting or in such manner as the general meeting may determine.

In order to ensure stability in auditing and at the same time to strengthen the independence of auditors, it is provided that no person other than the retiring auditor may be appointed unless a member has given notice of his intention to nominate another person for the office at least 14 days before the meeting, and the company has sent a notice to the retiring auditor, and communicated the notice to the members by advertisement or in any other manner allowed under the articles not less than seven days before the meeting or, if an annual general meeting is called, 14 days or less after the notice has been received, at the same time as the notice of that annual general meeting (sec. 132 (3)). A gap in the Act is that the retiring auditor has not the right to put his views before the meeting.

The auditors shall make a report to the meeting on the accounts examined by them and on every balance sheet laid before the company during their term of office. In order to be able to make the report every auditor shall have access at any time to the books, accounts and vouchers of the company, and shall be entitled to call for the necessary informations and explanations from its directors and officers. He should state in his report whether he has or has not obtained all the information and explanations demanded.

The main part of the report is on the balance sheet; the auditors have to state whether in their opinion it is properly drawn up so as to exhibit a true and correct view of the state of the company's affairs to the best of their information and the explanations given them and as shown by the books of the company (sec. 124 (1), (2)). It is to be noted that the Act mentions only the balance sheet as the subject of the auditors' examination and report. This is not surprising, since the profit and loss account, as we have seen, was altogether neglected by the Act of 1929. But it is obvious that the examination of the balance sheet is necessarily incomplete without that of the profit and loss account, and no auditor can report on the balance sheet unless he has enquired into the correctness of the profit and loss account. This is rightly criticised in the Report (114, p. 66). On the other hand the expression used in sec. 134 (1) (*b*) "as shown by the books of the company" tends to induce auditors to restrict their activities to a comparison of the accounts with the books and possibly to certify the balance sheet, though the books give only incomplete information.

The auditors shall be entitled (sec. 134 (3)) to attend any general meeting of the company at which any accounts of the company examined and reported upon by them are to be laid before the company. At such meetings they have the right to make any statement or give any explanation they desire with respect to the accounts. But they are not entitled to attend any other meeting of the company.

In performing their duties auditors must apply reasonable care and skill. They must make themselves acquainted with their duties under the Companies Acts,[1] and see "what exceptional duties are cast upon them by the articles". "Ignorance of the articles and of exceptional duties imposed by them would not afford any legal justification for not observing them."[2] On the other hand they are "not bound to exercise more than reasonable care and skill even in case of suspicion" and "may rely on the opinion of an expert where special knowledge is required", and in the view of Lopes, L.J.,[3] "auditors must not be made liable for not tracking out ingenious and carefully laid schemes of fraud where there is nothing to arouse their suspicion". In one case,[4] it was held that although the auditors failed in their duty they were protected by the articles.

The duty of an auditor is to the company, and in case of breach he may be sued by the company.[5]

Auditors may be made liable for misfeasance and compelled by the Court to make amends under sec. 276 of the Act, but only if they are officers of the company.[6] An auditor who is merely

[1] Republic of Bolivia Exploration Syndicate (1914), 1 Ch. 139.
[2] *Per* Lindley, L.J., in Kingston Cotton Mills Co. (No. 2) (1896), 2 Ch. 279 at 284 C.A.
[3] In the same case, at 290.
[4] *In re* City Equitable Fire Insurance Co. (1925), Ch. 407.
[5] Leeds Estate Buildings and Investment Society *v.* Shepherd (1887), 36 Ch. D. 787.
[6] *In re* London and General Bank (No. 2) (1895), 2 Ch. 673 C.A.; Kingston Cotton Mills Co., *supra.*

to audit the accounts is not an officer.[1] The provision of sec. 152, however, by which directors, managers and other officers may not be exempted from any legal liability for negligence, default, breach of duty or breach of trust, or indemnified against such liability, any contrary provisions of the articles or of a contract or agreement being void, applies to persons employed as auditors, whether they be officers of the company or not.

The Companies Act, 1947, introduced a number of amendments mainly based on the recommendations of the Committee, which are now embodied in the Act of 1948. It is expressly provided that the auditors must report on every profit and loss account laid before the general meeting beside the balance sheets and accounts examined by them.

Auditors shall expressly state in their reports:

(1) whether they have obtained all the information and explanations which to the best of their knowledge and belief were necessary for the purposes of their audit;

(2) whether in their opinion proper books of account have been kept by the company so far as appears from their examination of those books and that from branches not visited by them proper returns adequate for the purposes of their audit have been received;

(3) whether the company's balance sheet and profit and loss account dealt with by the report are in agreement with the books of account and returns;

(4) whether in their opinion and to the best of their information and according to the explanations given by them the said accounts give the information required by the Act in the manner as required and give as required a true and fair view in the case of the balance sheet of the company's affairs as at the end of its financial year and in the case of the profit and loss account of the profit or loss account of its financial year or give a true and fair view subject to the non-disclosure of any matter the non-disclosure of which is justified (Ninth Schedule of the Act of 1948).

The provisions of sec. 362 of the Act of 1929 penalising false statements apply also to the auditors' report (sec. 22 (1) of 1947 Act; sec. 438 and Fifteenth Schedule of the Act of 1948).

[1] Western Counties Steam Bakeries and Co. (1897), 1 Ch. 617 C.A.

The rights of the auditors are considerably extended: (*a*) it shall be for them to judge what is necessary as regards information or explanations; (*b*) they shall be entitled to attend any general meeting, to receive all notices and other communications which any member is entitled to receive, and to be heard at any general meeting on any part of the agenda which concerns them as auditors; sec. 162 (3) and (4) of the Act of 1948).

It is provided that a person shall not be qualified for appointment as auditor of a company unless either—

(*a*) he is a member of a body of accountants established in Great Britain and for the time being recognised for the purposes of this provision by the Board of Trade; or

(*b*) he is for the time being authorised by the Board of Trade to be so appointed either as having similar qualifications obtained outside Great Britain or as having obtained adequate knowledge and experience in the course of his employment by a member of one of the recognised bodies of accountants, or as having before 6 August 1947 practised in Great Britain as accountant; but this does not apply to an exempt private company (sec. 23 (1) of the Act of 1947; sec. 161 (1) of the Act of 1948).

The disqualification (sec. 135 of 1929 Act) is extended to servants of the company and to partners and employees of directors (sec. 23 (2) of the Act of 1947; sec. 161 (2) of the Act of 1948).

The disqualification of corporate bodies (sec. 133 (1) (*c*) of the Act of 1929) remains, but in Scotland a Scottish firm of accountants is qualified for appointment as auditor of the company if all its partners are qualified for such appointment (sec. 23 (4) of the Act of 1947; sec. 161 (2) (*c*) and (4) of the Act of 1948).

It is provided that any appointment of an auditor shall be valid until the conclusion of the next annual general meeting (sec. 24 (1) of the Act of 1947; sec. 159 (1) of the Act of 1948); thus certain doubts and disputes are settled.

In order to ensure stability, the new Act provides that at any annual general meeting the retiring auditor shall be reappointed without any resolution being passed, unless—

(*a*) he is not qualified for reappointment;

(*b*) a resolution has been passed at that meeting that he shall not be reappointed, whether or not the resolution appoints some other person in his place; or

(*c*) he has given the company notice in writing of his unwillingness to be reappointed;

and where at an annual general meeting no auditors are appointed or reappointed, the Board of Trade shall appoint a person to fill the vacancy. The company shall, within one week of the Board's power becoming exercisable, give them notice of that fact, and if the company fails to give such notice, the company and officer of the company who is in default shall be liable to a fine.

A resolution that a retiring auditor shall not be reappointed without the appointment of another person in his place, shall require the same notice to the company as would have been required had the resolution extended to the appointment of another person instead of him; and where notice of the intention to move such resolution is given to the company the company shall give notice thereof to the auditor and the members of the company as if it had extended to the appointment of another person.

The notice to be given to a retiring auditor of an intended resolution that he shall not be reappointed or that some other person shall be appointed instead of him, shall be given forthwith after receipt by the company of notice of the resolution.

Where notice is given of such intended resolution and the auditor makes with respect thereto representations in writing to the company (not exceeding a reasonable length) and requests their notification to members of the company, the company shall, unless the representations are received by it too late for it to do so:

(*a*) in any notice of the resolution given to members of the company state the fact of representations having been made; and

(*b*) send a copy of the representations to every member of the company to whom notice of the meeting is sent, whether before or after receipt of the representations by the company;

and if a copy of the representations is not sent because it has been received too late or because of the company's default, the auditor may (without prejudice to his right to be heard orally) require that the representations shall be read out at the meeting (sec. 24 of the Act of 1947; sec. 160 of the Act of 1948).

These provisions are undoubtedly substantial improvements and are calculated to strengthen the independence of auditors. We think, however, that a much simpler solution would be to provide for a three-year term of office with the proviso that the auditors may be removed by a resolution in general meeting.

Influenced by the results of the audit as it worked in Great Britain under the Companies Acts and in the U.S.A., certain Continental legislations have introduced compulsory auditing. The first was Germany, by the Emergency Order of 19 September 1931. This was repeatedly amended, and its provisions were embodied in the law of 1937. The company in general meeting must appoint one or more auditors; only qualified accountants, authorised by the government, may be appointed (*offentlich bestellte Wirtschaftsprüfer*). Members of the two boards, employees of the company and those of a member-company of the same group are disqualified. But companies formed for the purpose of auditing and supervising (*Wirtschaftsprüfungsgesellschaft*) are allowed, provided that at least one of their managers is a qualified accountant. The board of management, the board of supervision or the holders of at least ten per cent. of the shares may object to the appointment. In such event the Court has to decide. If the company fails to appoint an auditor during the financial year, the management is bound to apply to the Court for the appointment. The appointment may be revoked by the general meeting; auditors appointed by the Court may be removed on application by an Order of the Court.

The auditor or auditors must examine the balance sheet and the profit and loss account, and the report prepared by the management, before they are submitted to the board of supervision. Failure so to examine involves the nullity of the balance sheet and profit and loss account. The examination is to extend to the question whether all legal requirements relating to the accounts and the report have been complied with, and shall not be restricted to a comparison with the books and the inventory. In case of disputes between the auditors and the management a special tribunal is to decide.

The managers must give all information and explanations necessary for a careful performance of the auditors' duties. They have to give them access to the books and records of the company;

they may also check the company's cash and stock. They are to prepare a report for the boards of management and supervision which is subsequently to be put before the general meeting. If they are satisfied that the accounts are in compliance with legal requirements, they are to certify them with an adequate clause. In the event of objection they are to refuse or restrict certification. They are entitled to do this although the balance sheet and profit and loss account have been found correct, if the report is likely to give a false picture of the course of business and the state of affairs of the company.

Strong provisions are enacted to ensure professional secrecy on the part of the auditor. In the case of a corporate body acting in the capacity of auditor this extends to the board of supervision of that company; its chairman and his deputy may inspect the reports, but are also bound to observe secrecy. In case of violation the auditors are liable for damages, which are limited in case of negligence to 100,000 marks.

Under the Swiss O.R. every company has to appoint in general meeting one or more persons as supervising board (*Kontrollstelle*). They may or may not be shareholders; corporate bodies may also be appointed. The term of office for the first board is one financial year; subsequently the appointment is limited to three years.

In examining the balance sheet and the profit and loss account the supervising board are to ascertain whether the company has kept adequate books of account, and whether the report of the directors on the results of the business and the state of affairs of the company is in compliance with legal requirements. They must prepare a report and lay it before the general meeting; without such report no resolution with regard to the balance sheet may be carried. They are to attend the annual general meeting.

Should the supervising board observe any irregularities in the course of their examination, they are to inform the superior officer of the respective department of the company and the chairman of the board. In no case, however, are they entitled to give information to individual shareholders or third parties.

These are minimum requirements; the articles may provide for further examinations, especially for interim audits. The members of the *Kontrollstelle* must not be entrusted with any managerial duties (727–31).

The liability of auditors is governed by the provisions relating to the liability of directors. Companies with a share capital of 5,000,000 Swiss francs or more, and such as have debentures outstanding or offer to the public to accept money on deposit have a further duty in respect of auditing. Under § 723 of the law, such companies must present their balance sheets to independent accountants for examination. This may be done by trust companies or corporate bodies formed for the purpose of auditing. The report of these auditors is to be sent both to the directors and the supervisors (*Kontrollstelle*) of the company.

PUBLICITY OF THE ACCOUNTS

We have here to remember that under most legislations the yearly accounts, i.e. the balance sheet, profit and loss account, reports of directors and minutes of general meetings are to be filed with the Registrar or the public body administering the register of companies. These are open for inspection either by the general public or, under certain legislations, by members and debenture holders of the companies, or by persons otherwise interested. Moreover, some legislations prescribe the publication of the approved balance sheet and profit and loss account in the official *Gazette* and sometimes also in a newspaper circulating at or near the place of the registered office of the company.

89. Investigation and Inspection

As shown earlier (§ 84), the old common law right of the shareholders to inspect the corporation's books and records and to investigate its affairs is practically extinct. Most legislations expressly provide that the individual shareholder has no such right, and even where it is still recognised in principle it is ineffective in practice. The demand for the right of inspection is resisted on the ground of the suspicion of malicious intent. If the onus of proving absence of such intent is imposed on the shareholder, it may be very difficult for him to show that he is actuated by honest and rightful motives. If it is on the company, there is the danger of protracted and expensive proceedings, which to many of the shareholders will not be acceptable. Again, few shareholders have either the knowledge or the experience necessary to carry the inspection to a successful result, whereas the employment of an accountant, if allowed at all, is usually impossible in view of its expense.

Where inspection is denied to the individual shareholder, it is usually granted to a specific minority, say to one or several shareholders who own a definite part of the share capital.

The right to request inspection of the affairs of companies was granted in Great Britain by the Act of 1908 to holders of one-tenth of the share capital, but with the proviso that the expenses are to be paid by the applicants, unless the Board of Trade otherwise direct. This factor acted as a deterrent. The Act of 1929 amended the law in several directions. Holders of not less than one-tenth of the shares issued may apply to the Board of Trade to appoint one or more competent inspectors to investigate the affairs of a company and to report thereon. In the case of a banking company this right may be exercised only by holders of not less than one-third of the shares issued. The application must be supported by evidence showing that the applicants have good reason for their request and are not actuated by malicious intent. It is within the discretion of the Board to order or refuse inspection. Before appointing inspectors the Board may also require security for the costs of the inquiry not exceeding £100.

If inspectors are appointed it is the duty of all officers and agents of the company to produce for their use all books and documents in their custody or power, and the inspectors may examine on oath the officers and agents of the company in relation to its business. It has been decided that an officer of the company is bound to answer the questions put to him by the inspector.[1] Refusal to produce the books and documents or to answer the questions of the inspector is to be treated as contempt of Court.

After the conclusion of the inspection a report is to be made to the Board of Trade, which shall be written or printed as the Board may direct. A copy of the report shall be forwarded to the company and a further copy, at their request, to the applicants.

Should the Board of Trade find that any officer of the company has been guilty of a criminal offence, they shall refer the matter to the Director of Public Prosecutions, or in Scotland to the Lord Advocate.

The Director of Public Prosecutions, however, will prosecute

[1] *Re* Gaumont British Picture Corporation (1940), Ch. 506.

only where he considers it in the public interest that the proceedings should be conducted by him. If he institutes a prosecution all present and past officers and agents of the company, including bankers, solicitors and auditors employed by the company even if they are not officers, are bound to give all reasonable assistance. The expenses are to be defrayed by the Board of Trade if a prosecution is instituted. In any other case the Board has power to decide whether the expenses are to be paid by the company or by the applicants, or partly by each of them (sec. 135 (6)).

In the United States many statutes give holders of 10 per cent. of the shares a right to inspect the books of account, but in some States a smaller percentage suffices, e.g. in Michigan, where the holding of two per cent., or of two per cent. of any class if more than one class of shares is issued, is sufficient. Generally, just cause has to be shown.

Under Continental laws the usual requirement is a ten per cent. holding. The appointment of inspectors is in the competence of the Court. The exercise of the right to request investigation and inspection, however, is strongly curtailed.

Under the German Law of 1937 the holders of ten per cent. of the shares may apply to the Court only if a motion for investigation has been rejected by the general meeting. They must give *prima facie* evidence by a declaration before the Court or a notary public under oath that they have held their shares for at least three months. Moreover the shares are to be deposited with the Court pending its decision. Inspection will not be ordered unless it is shown by the applicants that there is reason to suspect breach of trust or gross violation of the law or the articles on the part of the management. The Court may require security for damages if it is shown that the company may suffer by the wilfulness or gross negligence of the applicants. The investigation, if ordered, is restricted to the previous two years. The inspectors are not entitled to include in their report details which the managers have communicated to them under seal of secrecy justified by the interest of the company or common weal of the people or the realm. The inspectors are entitled to refuse the inclusion of details for similar reasons.

The report is to be forwarded both to the managers and to the Court. It is to be put on the agenda of the next general meeting, which is to decide whether the expenses shall be met by the company or the applicants. Since the whole machinery is set in motion only where a majority has previously defeated the motion for investigation, it is hardly to be expected that they will take over the expenses at the company's charge (§§ 118–121).

The Swiss O.R. grants every shareholder the right to call the attention of the *Kontrollstelle* to ambiguous items in the balance sheet and to ask for explanations. Although the members are denied inspection of books and correspondence without the express authorisation of the general meeting or of the management, the Court has power to make an order on application for giving information as to relevant facts, by furnishing authentic copies or extracts from the books of account or the correspondence. Such information should not impair the interests of the company. This right to supervision cannot be denied or restricted by provisions in the articles or resolutions in general meeting (697).

Owing to the aforementioned limitations and particularly to the burden of expense the right to investigation and inspection was hardly, if ever, effective. Even in Great Britain, where the law is more liberal than in any other country in Europe, the regulations are so framed as to restrict the use of the machinery to a large extent.

It is extremely difficult to assemble a ten per cent. holding, especially in the case of large companies, whereas the requirement of one-third of the capital, as provided for banking companies, is simply prohibitive. To produce evidence of good reasons for the inspection and to prove the absence of malicious motives is not easy, and the danger that the expense of the investigation may be subsequently imposed upon the applicants is also a deterrent. There are minor defects in the regulations, especially with regard to subsidiaries: the inspectors appointed by the Board of Trade have no right under the Act to investigate the affairs of a subsidiary of the company whose affairs are under investigation.

According to the Cohen Report, in the 15 years from 1930 to 1944 there were altogether 70 applications for investigation; of these eight were for the investigation of a single group of companies, and if these eight applications are regarded as one, the total number of applications was 63. Of these 63 applications 34 were refused, 19 were withdrawn or not proceeded with, one is still under negotiation, and only nine resulted in the appointment of inspectors.

Convinced as we are of the high standard of British companies, a procedure by which on the average hardly more than one investigation is ordered in every two years cannot be regarded as satisfactory. Many complaints were voiced before the Committee, and its recommendations in several directions were extensive (pp. 154–60; 98–100). They were incorporated in the Companies Act, 1947, and re-enacted in the Act of 1948. The amendments are as follows. Inspectors may be appointed not only on the application of holders of at least one-tenth of the issued shares, but also if 200 members apply for it regardless of the amount of their holdings, and both conditions are to apply equally to banking companies. On the other hand it is not necessary to show that the applicants are not actuated by malicious motives in requesting the investigation. The other requirement of sec. 135 (2) of the Act of 1929, evidence that the applicants have good reason to make the application, is still maintained, though if there are certain reasons the Board of Trade may act on its own initiative and may appoint inspectors if it appears that there are circumstances suggesting that a company's business is conducted with intent to defraud its creditors or the creditors of any other person or otherwise for a fraudulent or unlawful purpose or in a manner oppressive of any part of its members or that it was formed for any fraudulent or unlawful purpose; or that persons concerned with its formation or the management of its affairs have in connection therewith been guilty of fraud, misfeasance or other misconduct towards it or towards members; or that its members have not been given all the information with respect to its affairs which they might reasonably expect (secs. 42 and 43 of the Act of 1947; secs. 164 and 165 of the Act of 1948).

In future past officers and agents are in all cases of investigation to be under the same duty as those who at the time of the investigation are in office or employment, and the expression "agents" includes bankers, solicitors and auditors (sec. 42 (3) of the Act of 1947; sec. 166 (5) of the Act of 1948). Solicitors, however, have not to disclose any privileged communication, except the address of their clients and any person for whom the client acts or has acted, and bankers have not to give any information of the affairs of other customers. The duties of the persons concerned are defined more precisely: besides producing the books and documents of, or relating to, the company which are in their custody or power, they have also to give to the inspectors in other respects all assistance in connection with the investigation which they are reasonably able to give.

Furthermore, if an inspector appointed under sec. 164 or 165 thinks it necessary for the purpose of his investigation that a person whom he has no power to examine on oath should be so examined, he may apply to the Court, which if it sees fit may order that person to attend and be examined on oath before it on any matter relevant to the investigation; and on any such examination: (*a*) the inspector may take part therein either personally or by solicitor or counsel; (*b*) the Court may put such questions to the person examined as it thinks fit; (*c*) the person examined shall answer all such questions as the Court may put or allow to be put to him, but may at his own cost employ a solicitor with or without counsel, who shall be at liberty to put such questions as the Court may deem just for the purpose of enabling him to explain or qualify any answers given by him. Notes of the examination shall be taken down in writing, and shall be read to or by, and signed by, the person examined, and may thereafter be used in evidence against him.

The inspector may, and if so directed by the Board must, make interim reports in addition to the final report, and the Board may, if it thinks fit, on request and on payment of the prescribed fee, furnish a copy of the report to any member of the company, and to any creditor whose interests are affected.

Lastly the Board may cause any report to be published, whereas under the principal Act it had only power to cause it to be printed.

The Board of Trade shall be empowered to present a petition for the winding-up of a company if as a result of the investigation it comes to the conclusion that it would be just and equitable that it should be wound up. In future the Director of Public Prosecutions shall commence proceedings in any case in which he finds that a prosecution ought to be instituted, and shall not make his action dependent upon the consideration that it is of public interest. In this way the existing difference between England and Wales on the one hand and Scotland on the other will be eliminated. The Board of Trade shall also have the right of action or other proceedings on behalf of the company and in its name if it appears from the investigations that the company suffered damage in consequence of fraud, misfeasance or other misconduct in connection with its formation or the management of its affairs, or any of its property has been misapplied or wrongfully retained, provided the proceedings for the recovery of damages or of the property are in the public interest. In such a case the Board of Trade shall indemnify the company against any costs or expenses incurred by or in connection with such proceedings (sec. 42 of 1947 Act; sec. 169 of 1948 Act).

The Board of Trade shall appoint inspectors if the Court declares by order that the affairs of the company shall be investigated by an inspector appointed by the Board (sec. 44 (1) (*a*); sec. 165 (*a*) of the Act of 1948), in which case a copy of the report is to be forwarded to the Court. The burden of expenses is to some extent eased, since those of the inspection shall be defrayed in the first instance by the Board of Trade. Nevertheless the company will be liable for the expenses if the inspector was appointed otherwise than by the Board of Trade unless the Board otherwise directs. On the other hand the applicants may also in future be made liable for the expenses to such extent as the Board may direct, and they have at the request of the Board of Trade to give security for the costs up to £100 (sec. 45 of the Act of 1947; sec. 164 (2) of the Act of 1948). The risk in respect of the expenses, though mitigated, still falls on the applicants.

If a person is convicted and ordered to pay damages or to restore any property to the company, he may be ordered to pay the expenses of the investigation wholly or in part, and a company in whose name such proceedings were instituted will be liable for the amount recovered (sec. 45 (1); sec. 170 (1) of the Act of 1948).

These reforms will certainly contribute to make investigations both more frequent and more effective. But it may be questioned whether a reduction of the quota of shareholding to, say, five per cent. would not have been better. The requirement of 200 members, on the other hand, may in the case of smaller companies be excessive, while in that of large units it does not involve an interest of any importance. Whether the extension of the powers of the Board of Trade will be able to supplement the still greatly fettered initiative of the minority seems doubtful.

So far we have only considered investigations in the absence of or against the will of the majority. That the majority is always in a position to insist on an investigation seems obvious. In some legislations it is so. There are Company laws under which this is held in the absence of express provision;

other laws declare that the shareholders in general meeting may carry a resolution for investigation. Thus the German law of 1937 provides that shareholders in general meeting may carry such a resolution by a simple majority (§ 118). This provision is in accordance with § 266 of the Commercial Code of 1897; whereas, however, the Commercial Code allows of resolutions as to investigation both in respect of occurrences in the management of the company's affairs and the balance sheet as a whole as well, § 118 of the law of 1937 limits the investigation to definite events, especially those connected with the procuring of capital and reduction of the share capital. On the other hand investigations may be instituted in respect of the formation of the company.

The Companies Act of 1929 required a special resolution, the carrying of which is much more difficult. If such resolution is carried and one or more inspectors are appointed, they have the same rights and duties as inspectors appointed by the Board of Trade. The company in general meeting has power to choose the inspectors and is not bound by any provision as to qualification. The inspectors have to report to such persons and in such manner as the company in general meeting may direct (sec. 137). A copy of the report of any inspector authenticated by the seal of the company is evidence of the opinion of the inspectors in any legal proceeding in all matters contained in the report (sec. 138).

It seems that sec. 137 was practically inoperative. In our view this was due to the requirement of a special resolution. The Committee did not think so, but felt that inspectors appointed by the general meeting should not have the wider powers which were envisaged for the future (160, p. 106). The new Act following this recommendation provides (sec. 43 (1) (*a*); sec. 165 (*a*) of the Act of 1948) that if the company in general meeting resolves by special resolution on investigation, it is reserved for the Board of Trade to appoint the inspector or inspectors and to direct the manner in which the report is to be made. In such a case the same rules apply as to other cases of inspection, and in this way the resolution is rightly termed a declaration that the company's affairs ought to be investigated.

Investigation into the membership of companies is considered in § 76, and the matter of groups of companies in § 92.

90. Increase of Capital

(a) issue of additional shares

The capital requirements of corporations cannot be fixed in advance. Even if the purpose of the enterprise is strictly defined, the expenses of organisation may be wrongly estimated. Thus in the time of the canal companies and in the early railway age additional amounts were often needed for constructional purposes. Even in the case of corporations not in need of large capital assets, additional current means are often required.

So long as the principle of limited liability was not generally recognised additional capital was mainly obtained by calls; members of companies were called upon to pay amounts proportionate to their shareholdings and thus to provide for the corporate needs. As we have seen earlier, even in the case of a company for which limited liability was an incident of its creation by charter it was held possible for the company itself to make calls and to compel its shareholders to make the payment required, on pain of forfeiture of their shares.

With the acceptance of the principle of limited liability not only as against creditors but also as between the company and the shareholder it came to be otherwise. Companies could no longer make calls if and when the par value of the shares subscribed had been fully paid up.

In order to make possible the satisfaction of urgent needs for additional capital, companies had two alternatives: they might either at the formation fix the capital at an amount far in excess of their actual requirements, thereby creating authorised but unissued capital, or they could insert a clause in the charter, deed of settlement, or articles, giving power to increase the capital. In course of time, however, this procedure was found inconvenient.

Where the principle of a rigidly fixed capital was followed, no means of increasing it were available. Consequently in time all legislations allowed the capital of companies to be enlarged by a subsequent issue of additional shares, even though the original Act of incorporation did not foresee or provide for this. But there were variations as to the method to be adopted, and differing requirements as to the issue of additional shares.

The British Act of 1929 provided that a company limited by shares, or one limited by guarantee but with a share capital, may increase its capital by issuing new shares, provided it is authorised by its articles to do so (sec. 50 (1) (*a*)). This had already been enacted by the Companies Act of 1862 (sec. 12). For power to increase the capital an authorisation by the articles is required, but in the absence of such special authorisation the company may amend its articles so as to insert the necessary clause. If authority to increase the capital is contained in the articles (sec. 50 (2)), a simple resolution in general meeting suffices, unless the articles provide otherwise, whereas for an amendment of the articles to insert the authorisation, a special resolution is required.

It was held in Campbell's case [1] that if a company has passed a special resolution authorising the creation and issue of additional shares, such resolution will provide the necessary authority, i.e. will operate as an amendment of the memorandum and articles, and further will give the directors power to exercise that authority.

Otherwise the Act of 1929 contains few provisions for and consequently few limitations on the increase of capital. It requires only that if a company has increased its share capital, it shall, 15 days after the passing of the authorising resolution, give notice thereof to the registrar (sec. 51 (1)). The notice shall include particulars as to the classes of shares affected and the conditions of issue of the new shares. Together with this notice a printed copy of the resolution is to be forwarded. The requirements therefore are: (*a*) a resolution of the general meeting; (*b*) the notice to the registrar accompanied by a copy of the resolution. Otherwise the company has a free hand. The regulation under the Act of 1948 (secs. 61 and 63) is identical.

The capital may be increased even though the original authorised capital is not fully paid up. The company may offer new shares to the existing shareholders or may exclude pre-emptive rights; it may fix the issue price and other conditions and terms at its discretion. The par value of the new shares need not be the same as that of the existing shares; it may be either greater or less. The company in general meeting may also empower the directors to fix the time and terms of the issue subsequently at their discretion.

Finally, the device of authorised capital may also be made use of to increase capital. The company has power to resolve in general meeting on an increase of capital, i.e. the creation of

[1] (1873), 9 Ch. App. 1, at 21.

additional shares, and at the same time to provide that for the time being only a certain part of them should be issued. In this way, although the original authorised capital may be exhausted, the creation of additional authorised capital is still possible.

If the issue is made for cash the same rules as to payment of commissions and brokerage apply as at the formation of the company. The issue of additional shares at a discount is admitted under the Act of 1929 (sec. 47, now sec. 57 of the Act of 1948), subject to the sanction of the Court. But for companies to resort to this expedient is exceptional.

An issue may be made for property, in which case it is governed by the rules already discussed in connection with the formation of companies.

The new shares may be ordinary shares ranking *pari passu* with the shares already existing; but it is possible to issue preference shares, and if a company already has preference shares, to give to the new shares preferential rights as against not only the ordinary, but also the preference shares already issued, as was shown in § 61.

In America [1] the general rule at Common Law was that a corporation has no inherent or implied power to increase its capital, unless such power has been expressly conferred on it by statute, or expressly reserved by the charter or by special act of the legislature.[2] In the absence of such authorisation no increase could be made even with the consent of all the shareholders, and any unauthorised increase was void. In practice, however, this rule is considerably modified, since in most cases the corporation is authorised to make an increase by its valid charter. If the authorisation is restricted to a certain amount, the increase will be valid within the limits prescribed; any further increase would be null.

In the case of National banks the capital may be increased with the approval of the Comptroller of the Currency by a vote of shareholders owning two-thirds of the capital.[3]

Many State legislations require as a prerequisite for any increase of capital that the existing capital should be fully paid up; where such a rule is adopted, the increase is void until the existing capital is paid up in full.

[1] Cf. Ballantine, 1st ed., 133, 134.

[2] See Chicago City R. Co. *v.* Allerton (1873), 18 Wall. 233; Scovill *v.* Thayer (1881), 105 U.S. 143; State decisions, Fletcher 5129, n. 93.

[3] See Act of 25 February 1927, c. 191, sec. 5.

The increase of capital is generally made by an issue of new shares against cash. In such cases it is mostly provided that the additional shares are to be taken in full and that until the payment is completed no share certificates may be issued, nor are the subscribers or purchasers of the new shares entitled to exercise any rights belonging to shareholders, especially the right of voting.

In some cases the increase is effected by paying stock dividends,[1] i.e. besides or instead of a dividend paid in cash the shareholders receive a dividend in the form of a distribution of new shares. A simple case would be as follows: the corporation increases its capital by ten per cent., and to this end issues new shares numbering ten per cent. of those already existing. The shares so issued are distributed among the shareholders so that each shareholder receives one new share for every ten he already holds. In such cases special provisions have to be made for holdings of less than ten shares, which question has been considered separately. The rule that every increase of capital without payment must be covered by surplus (free reserve) of course extends also to this method of increasing capital.

The rule that the new shares must be covered either by payment or by existing surplus (free reserve) does not exclude an increase for property or services; and this is generally allowed. The dangers of and objections to this method of increase are the same as we have already seen in connection with the creation of corporations.

In some cases the increase of capital is made dependent upon the assent of some public authority. This is the case with railways, electricity, gas or waterworks corporations.

If the increase of capital is authorised by statute, it is generally in the power of the general meeting. Many laws require the assent of a substantial quorum, e.g. two-thirds, or a specific majority, e.g. three-fourths, of those who vote at the meeting. In the latter case, i.e. where the quorum is governed by the number of shares represented at the meeting, specific regulations are often provided for the convocation, the time and the notice of such meetings. Some legislations allow of power to increase the capital being delegated to the board. In the author's view such delegation is not desirable and should be barred.

French law was originally governed by the principle that an

[1] Cf. Ballantine 208.

increase of capital is a fundamental alteration of the company's structure and therefore, unless allowed by the original articles, requires the unanimous assent of all shareholders. On the other hand it was held that the articles may provide for a subsequent increase in the sense that the shareholders shall be bound later to contribute further amounts to the company. This could be done by an authorisation to increase the par value of the shares, with the consequence that the shareholders must effect the payment of the increase according to the resolution of the general meeting or—if the necessary power has been given—to the board of directors following their decision. Another possible way was to divide partly paid up shares into two or more shares of the same par value. It was thus possible to compel shareholders to make additional payments. But it is to be remembered that unless such power were reserved in the original articles no such alteration could be carried out save by unanimous consent of the shareholders.

Gradually, however, the way was paved by several amendments for the possibility of amending the original articles by majority resolution, and this was made available *inter alia* for effecting an increase of capital. A short summary of the evolution was given in the sketch of the history of French Company law. Here it is sufficient to state that by the law of 1 May 1930, amending art. 31 of the law of 1867, a general meeting has power to amend and modify the original articles in any respect, except as to the nationality of the company or an increase of the obligations of shareholders. The fundamental principle that shareholders cannot be compelled to make larger contributions than provided by the original articles has been maintained.

Apart from this the capital may be increased even though the original articles have excluded it. The only requirements for the validity of such resolutions are: (1) that the printed text of the resolution proposed should be placed at the disposal of the shareholders at latest 15 days previous to the general meeting (law of 30 April 1935); (2) a special quorum and regulation of voting powers; it has been provided that in general meetings carrying resolutions of this kind every shareholder has the right to vote, even if under the articles his share or shares would not entitle him to do so. Furthermore at least two-thirds of the capital is to be represented, and the resolution is valid only if the majority includes at least two-thirds of the holdings represented. Even if the general meeting does not resolve upon an alteration of the articles which could affect the purpose or form of the company, at least two-thirds of the share capital is to be represented, and in the absence of this quorum a second general meeting may be held. For this second general meeting a quorum of 50 per cent. is sufficient, and should the second meeting be abortive, yet a third meeting with a quorum of one-third is possible.

It was held under French law that the principle of equality among shareholders cannot be affected by a resolution for the increase of capital. Originally the issue of preference shares, if not provided for in the original articles, was held to violate this principle. Since 1903, however, this is no longer the case.

As to the formalities of such issues, the new shares are to be subscribed and the subscription must cover the whole of the new issue; failure in this respect makes the subscription void. It is held, moreover, that fictitious subscriptions involve the nullity of the whole issue. On the other hand it is held that a company may reserve the right to limit the issue to any amount covered by subscriptions, provided that the minimum amount is fixed in the resolution. The alteration of the articles and the report of the completed issue are to be drawn up in notarial form and filed with the Court. As under the British Companies Act of 1929 and under American law, issues of additional shares may be made for property.

German Company law since 1884 has provided an elaborate machinery for increase of capital. The law of 1937 adopted the existing law with many details settled by decisions of the Reichsgericht; it has also supplemented German law with two devices, authorised capital (*genehmigtes Kapital*) and conditional increase of capital.

As we have already seen, German law operated from the beginning with the system of a rigidly fixed capital. Under this system the whole capital of the company is to be fixed at its formation; for the company to be incorporated the whole capital must be subscribed; each and every share must be covered by subscription and a payment of at least 25 per cent. of its par value. The company may increase this capital by a resolution in general meeting. At any moment, however, the capital is a fixed amount and before the law of 1937 the company could not have authorised but unissued capital, and it was even held that a provision of the articles to this effect and the shareholders' assent to a subsequent increase was void. The reform introduced in 1937 makes it possible for the company to provide by its original articles that it may issue additional shares, and such an issue may be made by the board of management. The additional shares cannot exceed 50 per cent. of the original capital, and the authorisation is valid for five years. A similar authorisation may be resolved upon by a subsequent general meeting. The issue should be made with the assent of the board of supervision; but the validity of the new shares is not affected by the absence of such assent.

A fundamental prerequisite of any increase of capital is that the par value of every share already issued be fully paid up; but insurance companies may provide otherwise, and relatively insignificant amounts may be neglected and do not prevent a new issue. Any resolution to increase the capital requires a majority of three-fourths of the capital represented at the general meeting; the articles may provide for a larger or smaller majority. In the case of a resolution relating to the creation of additional authorised capital a higher but not a lower majority may be required. The new shares are to be subscribed; the requirements of the subscription are fixed by the law (§ 152). The main requirements are: the issue price of the new shares, instalments, if any, and any additional obligations, and the time at which the subscription becomes invalid if the completion of the increase is not entered in the register.

The new shares may also be issued against contributions in property; in such cases the law requires that the consideration in property, the person of the transferor and the par value of the shares to be given for such property are to be included in the resolution as to the increase of capital. There is no requirement as to the valuation of the property, as there is for similar issues at the creation of the company.

Those requirements are to be applied to all issues of additional shares made within the first two years after registration.

It is hard to understand why the legislature thought fit to dispense with the guarantees against overvaluations and watering of stock after the two first years of the company's existence have elapsed. It is true that the Court, under § 151 (3), may refuse to register the increase if it is obvious that the value of the property does not reach the par value of the shares to be given for it. This sounds like a guarantee; but the promoters will be sure to take care that the discrepancy between the value of the shares and that of the property shall not be obvious.

After the resolution as to the increase of the capital has been carried, it is to be reported to the Court for registration. Subsequently, after the complete placing of the new issue, a new report is to be made to the Court, the documents showing the subscription are to be presented, and the expenses of the issue reported. After due examination the increase is to be registered. The Court may refuse registration if the legal requirements have not been complied with and, as already mentioned, when the additional shares are issued fully or partly for property, if the value of the property is obviously less than the par value of the shares issued in consideration. With the registration of the increase the procedure comes to an end, and accidental defects do not affect the validity of the shares, provided the shareholder in question has exercised his rights or performed his obligations based on the subscription. Any share issued before the fact of the increase is entered in the register is void (§§ 149–58).

The third type of increase of capital introduced by the law of 1937 is conditional increase. This is destined to cover cases where convertible bonds have been issued, and may also be used for the preparation of mergers; it gives power to issue shares up to the amount of demands based upon claims for conversion or in pursuance of mergers. The general meeting may give the power to issue shares to the maximum amount of 50 per cent. of the capital already existing at the time the resolution is carried. Such a resolution requires the consent of at least three-fourths of the capital represented in general meeting. The articles may require a higher majority and impose other conditions. Together with the resolution the purpose of the issue, the particulars as to claims on such shares, and the issue price are to be fixed. The issue of shares for property is also possible in such cases; the requirements are the same. The persons who receive the new shares must complete a declaration as to the exercise of their claims based on the ownership of convertible bonds, or shares in companies to be amalgamated. The procedure, i.e. reporting of the resolution authorising the conditional issue, and report on the exercise of the power, is on the whole identical with that for a normal capital increase. The report on the actual issue is to be presented at latest once yearly within one month after the end of the financial year, but there is no time limit for the exercise of the power. This is, of course, to be understood in cases where the shares are issued for convertible bonds; as to amalgamations, it gives the management unlimited power (§§ 159–68).

Both the device of conditional capital increase and that of authorised capital increase were meant to give German companies the opportunity to attract additional capital without delay, if and when market conditions should allow. The introduction of these devices was urged especially before the crash of 1929 by bankers, baffled by the progress of the capital markets in the U.S.A. In 1937 these reforms, quite apart from their merits, had no longer any meaning at all for German companies. Attraction of capital from abroad was made impossible by currency restrictions, and the inland market was discouraged by the constant neglect of shareholders' interests and the violation of their rights. In any case the law only came into force on the eve of the German aggression leading to the new world conflagration.

The Swiss law (650–653) contains provisions which are both simpler and give more guarantees than the German. The leading rule is that a company may increase its capital only in accordance with the rules provided for the formation of companies. Consequently, if additional shares are to be issued for property, the company has to draw up the same report as is required when shares are issued at the time of incorporation.

Any increase of capital is to be resolved upon in general meeting; if the shares are offered to the public, a prospectus containing all particulars is to be issued. Although only the last balance sheet and profit and loss account are to be included, the dividends paid during the five years last preceding the issue are to be disclosed. Instead of a separate prospectus, the particulars required may be inserted in the subscription lists to be signed by the subscribers.

Swiss law requires two general meetings in connection with an increase of capital. The first is to carry the resolution authorising the new issue, the second to record its completion, i.e. the placing of the shares for cash or property. There is no objection to the holding of both meetings on the same day, provided the additional shares are immediately subscribed and paid in. The concentration of both steps within the competence of the general meeting undoubtedly helps the security of capital readjustments.

(B) PRE-EMPTIVE RIGHTS OF SHAREHOLDERS

If a company increases its capital by the issue of additional shares, it is to be assumed that the new shares should be offered to the members; in other words the right of the existing members to take up any new shares in proportion to their holdings, the pre-emptive right as it is called, should be recognised. This follows from the general nature of membership; moreover any issue of additional shares to outsiders affects the interests of the members in the financial future of the company and their proportionate participation in control.

In earlier times this was held to be the general rule; gradually, however, legislation began to discard it, and to leave it to the companies to grant the right of pre-emption in their articles or not as they thought fit.

In Great Britain the Act of 1929 (sec. 50 (1) (*a*)) does not mention the right of pre-emption at all; it merely provides that a company may "increase its share capital by new shares of such amount as it thinks expedient". Under this provision the terms of the issue may be fixed by the company, and if the articles do not otherwise provide, the new shares may be placed with whomsoever the company may choose. Clause 27 of Table A (1862) provided that the new shares should be offered to the members; clause 35 of Table A (1929), however, prescribes this only "subject to any direction to the contrary that may be given by the company in general meeting". The position under the Act of 1948 is unchanged; moreover Table A contains no provision similar to clause 35. It is exceptional for articles of companies to exclude or limit this freedom of choice. This does not mean that shareholders in British companies are actually deprived of their pre-emptive rights; as a rule new shares are offered to the shareholders by companies of standing; nevertheless in most cases this is not compulsory, and business practice may change.

In America[1] the Common Law rule is that stockholders are entitled to subscribe for new shares issued in connection with an increase of capital in proportion to their respective holdings in the stock.[2] Whether non-participating preferred shares confer

[1] Cf. Ballantine 109; Dodd and Baker, pp. 1257–86; V. Moravetz, H.L.R. 42, pp. 186–97; H. S. Drinker, Jr., *ibid.* 43, pp. 586–616.

[2] Gray *v.* Portland (1807), 3 Mass. 364; Gibbons *v.* Mahon (1891), 136 U.S. 549; Miles *v.* Safe Deposit and Trust Co. of. Baltimore (1922), 259 U.S. 247; see also the State cases quoted by Fletcher 5135, n. 85.

such a right is disputed. Further, it is disputed whether the right of pre-emption operates in respect of treasury stock and of stock authorised but unissued.[1]

If the new shares are issued for property, the pre-emptive right is usually held to be excluded, though the authority of Meredith *v.* New Jersey Zinc and Iron Co.[2] was denied in Wall *v.* Utah Copper Co.[3] by the same judge. It was generally held that the charter may provide otherwise, and only a minority of the Courts have held that the pre-emptive right is inherent. The tendency of statute law is towards curtailing the right of pre-emption. Thus the law of California [4] provides that the board of directors may issue shares or securities having conversion or option rights without first offering the same to shareholders of any class or classes. In many States the right of pre-emption may be denied or limited by the charter.

In practice, it seems that this possibility was frequently used to the detriment of the existing shareholders or a part of them. Prof. A. A. Berle, Jr., has asserted [5] the doctrine that any increase of capital excluding pre-emptive rights should be made with full regard to the rateable equity of existing shareholders. With this doctrine as basis he asserts that a shareholder wronged by violation of his rateable interest has an equitable action. Such action should lie not only against directors who make an inequitable use of their power to issue and to place shares, but also against the majority which has carried resolutions to this effect.

It is to be admitted that in certain cases of obviously gross abuse some Courts have sustained actions for damages against directors and even against majority shareholders on this ground. But such cases are exceptional, and the Courts were only too inclined to accept explanations, as e.g. that the company had a substantial justification for placing the shares in the hands of new owners from whom it might expect valuable gains in the form of possible financial assistance or other advantages. If we further take into consideration the difficulties and expenses of such proceedings, we must admit that this remedy will be of no avail save in exceptional cases (see § 78).

Under German law, as already seen, pre-emptive rights are

[1] Cf. Ballantine 209, n. 96.
[2] (1897), 55 N.J. Eq. 211.
[3] (1905), 70 N.J. Eq. 17.
[4] Civ. Code, § 297, as amended in 1931.
[5] In his essays reproduced subsequently in *The Modern Corporation and Private Property* by Berle and Means.

recognised in principle, but may be excluded by the resolution as to the increase of capital. It is true that the exclusion requires a three-fourths majority vote of the capital represented at the meeting, but no quorum is fixed, and experience has shown that it is always possible to secure the necessary votes. In this way many instances of injurious increases of capital occurred under § 282 of the German Commercial Code of 1897. Especially during the inflationary period following the First World War it was only in a few exceptional cases of gross abuse that the Courts gave relief.

If a company excludes the right of pre-emption and thereby deprives the existing shareholders of their chance to invest their money favourably, especially if the issue is below the market value of the shares, the exclusion of pre-emptive rights may affect the position of the existing shareholders by altering their proportionate share in control. If they have to abide by an offer of the additional shares to third parties, it is inevitable that their control should be weakened. It is true that so long as the shares are in the market they may purchase them on the Stock Exchange or through brokers in sufficient quantity to preserve their proportionate interest; but it is not a matter of indifference to them that they have to make exertions for the acquisition, since the market price may be artificially increased by their urgent demand. The equitable remedy as given by some Courts in the U.S.A. is operative only in exceptional cases, and even then is very difficult to obtain. These difficulties and especially the relatively exorbitant expenses involved make this remedy in practice illusory. We have further to take into account that all legislations admit the possibility of issuing additional shares for property, and that it is generally held that pre-emptive rights do not apply in such cases. The same is true with regard to mergers.

From the point of view of expediency the power of general meetings to refuse pre-emptive rights is strongly defended. It is said that the management is thus enabled to bring necessary increases of capital to a swift conclusion, and the company will benefit by the sale of the whole issue to a powerful group both by securing higher issue prices and a placement of additional shares, which will be less dependent upon the daily variations of the market. According to the adherents of this point of view the financial advantage would be sufficient to justify the disregard of pre-emptive rights, quite apart from the possibility already mentioned of obtaining valuable commercial or industrial connections through new shareholders. On the other hand it is undoubtedly true that shares of corporations which respect pre-emptive rights and offer their new issues regularly to their shareholders are more popular, and their popularity results both in a higher price in proportion to their dividends and also in the fact that their holders generally adhere faithfully to their holdings, which therefore remain to a higher degree in permanent hands.

From the standpoint of legislative policy it seems preferable to reserve pre-emptive rights for the original shareholders. If a company is able to attract new groups, this can be done by inducing the prospective members to purchase shares on the market. Furthermore there are always shareholders who are willing to sell their rights for cash, i.e. to refrain from taking up the new shares and to assign their exercise of pre-emptive rights to others. This procedure may be cumbersome for the prospective new group, but it is not to be assumed that it will prevent the transaction. On the whole and in the long run the interests of the company will be better guaranteed by giving shareholders an absolutely fair deal in respect of new issues.

(c) INCREASE OF CAPITAL BY ADDITIONAL PAYMENTS

Modern corporation law is based upon the principle that shareholders cannot be compelled to make additional payments. Some legislations apply this principle with absolute rigidity to the effect that even the articles cannot impose such an obligation; others allow it and regard provisions in the original articles imposing such liability as enforceable.

It is to be remembered that under legislations which allow of corporations with unlimited liability or with liability limited by guarantee, e.g. to some multiple of the par value, this principle applies only to corporations with limited liability. The correct formulation of the rule is, therefore, that shareholders cannot be compelled to contribute to the company any amount exceeding the limit of their liability. Consequently additional payments will seldom in practice be found. But shareholders may be willing to make additional payments in order to further the success of the enterprise. Such additional payments may be so made that the new amounts will increase the par value of the shares. In some cases such payments have not affected the par value of shares and consequently the nominal capital, but have been applied to strengthen reserves, in the same way as if the shares had been issued originally with a premium. In such a case there is technically, of course, no increase of capital.

During the financial crisis of the first decade of this century a particular procedure was used by certain German companies: companies in financial distress placed before their shareholders schemes under which any who were willing to make additional payments could convert their shares into cumulative and participating preference shares. This was mainly done in connection with a reduction of capital. The capital of the company concerned was to be reduced and at the same time increased by the additional payments. Shareholders who were willing to make the payment required would on surrender of their shares receive preferred shares as described. German Courts, and especially the Reichsgericht, declared this procedure legal where those shareholders who were unwilling to pay the amounts in question would not be penalised in respect of the reduction of capital. Those schemes, however, which attempted to induce shareholders to pay by a more favourable accounting in respect of the reduced and increased capital were annulled. Thus, if it were proposed to reduce the capital in view of losses and depreciation by 50 per cent., and at the same time to invite shareholders to make additional payments to the same amount, such reorganisation was held to be valid if shareholders willing to make the payment received an increase of the par value of their shares equal to the payment, with or without preferential rights. If, however, under the scheme they would receive more in par value, or shareholders unwilling to make the payment would have to suffer a larger reduction in par value, the resolution was held to be void (see § 61).

(D) INCREASE OF CAPITAL BY READJUSTMENT

A company which has reserves may apply them to increase its capital. This can be done by increasing the par value of the shares, or by the creation of new shares to be distributed among the existing shareholders in proportion to their holdings. Such transactions are possible only when there is a real reserve, i.e. where the value of the net assets exceeds the capital, and when the reserve in question is not earmarked for some special purpose. The rights of creditors are not affected by such a transaction;

from the shareholders' standpoint it is generally regarded as advantageous.

The requirements under most legislations as to formalities are the same as in the case of an increase of capital by the issue of additional shares. It is immaterial whether the reserve in question originates from share premiums or from earned profits. In neither case is any interest of creditors involved, since there is no direct or indirect repayment of capital. It is rather favourable to creditors, since if reserves are used to increase the capital their use for any other purpose is prevented.

91. Reduction of Capital

The reduction of a corporation's capital may involve any of four quite different transactions: (1) a rectification of the capital item in the balance sheet; (2) the liberation of the shareholders from a part of their obligation and liability; (3) the redemption of shares; (4) the distribution of part of the assets among the shareholders.

(1) The corporation may have lost a part of its capital, and the net value of the assets no longer cover the par value of the shares. In such a case the corporation may hope to recover the loss in the course of its business, and as a rule, though not under all legislations, it cannot pay dividends until the loss is made good. If the shareholders are not willing to wait, they will insist on a rectification of the balance sheet by reducing the capital sufficiently to wipe out the loss. If in a given case a company with a capital of £100,000 suffers a loss amounting to £38,000, a reduction of 40 per cent. might be proposed; after the reduction the corporation will have a capital of £60,000 and a surplus or reserve of £2,000. Therefore it will be in a position to pay dividends if a profit is earned in the current financial year. The sound practice will be not to use the surplus for the payment of dividends, and under certain legislations there is a legal prohibition against doing so.

A reduction of this kind will obviously be sought in cases where there is no hope of a speedy recovery from the losses, and correction of the balance sheet is desirable for the sake of accuracy. Such a reduction of capital will of course affect the par value of the shares. If, in the case mentioned, the capital of £100,000 consists of 100,000 shares of £1 each, a reduction by 40 per cent., i.e. to £60,000, will reduce the par value of each share from £1 to 12*s*. Where a minimum par value is established by law, difficulties arise if the capital is reduced to such an extent that the par value would fall below that minimum. In such a case some legislations provide that in order to preserve the legal minimum the shares shall be put together. If the legislation requires a minimum of, say, 15 units of its currency and the shares after the reduction would be nominally worth 12, five of the old shares would be put together and converted into four shares of 15 units each. This is quite simple if a shareholder holds five shares or any multiple of five; but if he holds only four shares or less, he is not in a position to receive the equivalent in new shares and there will be a fraction which cannot be converted. In order to satisfy the legal requirement the shareholder would be compelled to buy additional shares to such an extent as was necessary for the supplementation or to sell some or all of his own. The legislations concerned provide that sufficient time shall be allowed for the conversion, and they empower the corporation after the lapse of the time limit to sell the fraction not converted on the Stock Exchange, or if the shares are not quoted, by public auction. Such transactions inevitably cause some impairment of shareholders' rights.

The question of such reductions does not occur in cases where the shares have no par value; this is one of the arguments put forward in favour of no par value shares.

(2) If a corporation's shares are not fully paid up the corporation might find that it will not need the unpaid part of its capital. It would then be pointless to have shares with the latent obligation and liability of future calls. The capital will therefore be reduced by that amount which is not paid up, and the nominal value of the shares will be reduced accordingly to the amount paid in. Thus, if a corporation has a capital of £100,000 divided into 20,000 shares of £5 each, with 40 per cent., i.e. £2 per share, paid up, the corporation reduces its capital to £40,000 and the par value of each share to £2, freeing the shareholders from liability to further payment of £3 per share; the corporation will then have 20,000 shares of £2 each, fully paid up. Such a transaction of course materially affects the position of the existing creditors, since the liability for the unpaid part of the capital will cease.

The only advantage to the shareholders is that they now have shares not subject to any further calls. In the case of well-managed corporations the possibility of calls may be more or less theoretical; a number of big banks and insurance companies in Great Britain, for example, have had for decades shares not fully paid up, in respect of which no calls have been made during all the time. The risk, however, is latent, and the consequences of economic upheavals cannot be foreseen.

(3) The reduction of capital may be made by redemption of shares, and in some cases a successive redemption is provided for by the original articles. Such is the case if the corporation has a franchise limited in time with an obligation to hand over the object of the enterprise eventually to the State or some other public body without compensation. On the European Continent railways, tramways and public utilities generally had franchises valid for a fixed number of years, e.g. 90 or 50; the franchise carried with it the obligation to keep the object in good repair and to turn it over to the State (town, etc.) without compensation at the end of the said period. Such corporations must take the steps necessary to redeem the shares during the validity of their franchise and to repay their par value to the shareholders. This is usually done by providing for drawings under a scheme of redemption. The amount needed for the redemption is set aside from current profits; the repayment generally takes precedence of dividends. If profits do not allow of redemption, it must be postponed until the next or a later year.

In such cases it was often provided that a share so drawn and redeemed was to be converted into a profit share (*action de jouissance, Genuszschein*) giving the former shareholder a participation in the dividends over a certain amount, say four or five per cent. Such profit shares or profit certificates may or may not give their holders a vote. In these companies redemption is an inherent part of the capital structure, and consequently the shareholders have a right to the drawings, while on the other hand they are under duty to surrender the shares according to the scheme of redemption. The creditors of such a company are under constructive notice of the redemption and cannot object to it.

Apart from such cases as these the management of a corporation frequently assumes that it will not need the whole of its liquid assets for business, and finds it in the interest both of the corporation and of the shareholders to use a part of them for the reduction of capital. This may be done by purchasing certain shares.

Apart from cases of redemption there is of course no obligation whatever for a shareholder to sell his shares or any of them to the corporation unless he chooses. In some cases such sale may be advantageous to the shareholder; purchase by the corporation will then be somewhat of a privilege, and some shareholders may object to the board's power to decide whose shares they will acquire. It has been suggested that in such case the corporation should ask for tenders and accept the most advantageous offers, i.e. those offered at the lowest price. This procedure is in some cases followed and under some legislations is even compulsory.

(4) From the standpoint of equality among the shareholders the fourth alternative, namely, the repayment of a certain amount on each share and the reduction of the par value, is to be preferred.

From the creditors' standpoint repurchase of shares, or payment on each share, are of equal moment. The fund from which they could recover debts due to them is reduced in either case. In view of the importance of the capital structure of the corporation and of any change in it, it is generally required that a reduction of the capital should be possible only by resolution of the shareholders, except of course when the repayment, in accordance with a redemption scheme, is provided for by the charter or articles of the corporation.

Some American States permit the delegation to the board of the power to resolve upon a reduction of the capital. Most legislations, however, do not allow this, and require furthermore special formalities in convoking the meeting and a specified majority for a valid resolution. In the interest of creditors reductions of capital are generally made to depend upon either the assent of creditors, or a decree of the Court or some public authority competent to deal with the question of corporations.

The position in Great Britain under the Companies Act of 1862 was that companies could not reduce their capital as fixed by the memorandum of association. Sec. 12 of the Act provided for an increase of capital if authorised by the articles, but not for a reduction. A company might lose its capital through adverse circumstances, but it was prevented from reducing it, as it was thought that the capital, which in view of the limited liability was the only fund for creditors, could not be reduced voluntarily by the company itself. It soon proved, however, that cases may occur in which circumstances call for a reduction, and that this may be effected without impairing creditors' rights.

The Act 30 & 31 Vic., c. 131, sec. 9 (1867) gave power to reduce the capital by special resolution in general meeting; but laid down no special method of reduction. Jessel, M.R., however, held [1] that the power to reduce the capital does not extend to cases where the capital has diminished through loss or depreciation. The doubt was promptly solved by legislation, and 40 & 41 Vic., c. 26, sec. 3, enacted that the word "capital" includes paid-up capital and any lost capital. It was therefore maintained that companies may reduce their paid-up capital with or without reducing liability. Subsequently Lord Macnaghten stated [2] that Lord Jessel's view was not correct under the Act of 1867.

After 1877 the regulation remained on the whole unaltered, apart from amendments in detail. Under sec. 55 (1) of the Companies Act, 1929, a company limited by shares, or one limited by guarantee but having a share capital, may reduce its capital by special resolution in any way, provided it is so authorised by its articles. An authorisation contained in the memorandum is not sufficient; there must be power in the articles.[3] If there is no such clause in the articles, they may be altered by special resolution, so that in such a case two special resolutions are required; one to alter the articles, the other to reduce the capital.[4] The resolution must comply with the requirements of the Act relating to such resolutions, of which the most important is for a majority of three-fourths of those present and entitled to vote. Although a reduction of capital is necessarily an alteration of the memorandum, the resolution need not be declared expressly to be such.[5] It is, however, necessary to show exactly what is proposed to be done. In general the most usual ways of reduction are mentioned, but the provisions relating to these ways are without prejudice to the generality of the power. Under the Act a company may reduce its capital,

[1] *In re* Ebbw Vale Steel, Iron and Coal Company (1877), 4 Ch. D. 827.

[2] British and American Trustee and Finance Corporation *v.* Couper (1894), A.C. 399.

[3] See *re* Dexine Patent Packing and Rubber Co. (1903), 88 L.T. 791.

[4] See Patent Invert Sugar Co. (1885), 31 Ch. D. 166; Oregon Mortgage Co. Ltd. (1910), S.C. 964.

[5] Campbell's case (1873), 9 Ch. App. 1.

inter alia, by extinguishing or reducing the liability of the shareholders in respect of the share capital not yet paid up. In other words the capital may be reduced by reducing the par value up to the amount of the part not yet paid and extinguishing or reducing proportionately the shareholders' liability and obligation to contribute. In connection with this power, sec. 49 of the Act gives authority to companies to determine that any portion of the share capital not yet called up shall not be capable of being called up in future, except in the event of liquidation and for the purpose of winding-up. In such a case the shareholders remain liable and are obliged to contribute the portion concerned, but so long as the company carries on it has no power to demand the payment of the remainder.

Both this and any other method of reduction involving repayments to shareholders of some part of the paid-up capital should be used only in respect of such part of the capital as is in excess of the debts of the company.

The cancellation of a part of the share capital which has been lost or is not represented by available assets is really not a reduction but a correction of the capital, and the interests of creditors are, or may be, affected thereby only in so far as the company, which would be obliged to refrain from declaring dividends so long as the loss is not made good, may be enabled to pay dividends immediately after the reduction, provided it is earning current profits.

In all these cases the Act requires confirmation of the resolution by the Court. The company under sec. 56 has to apply to the Court. Where the proposed reduction involves a diminution of liability in respect of unpaid capital or a repayment to shareholders, the Court will hear the company's creditors, but it may dispense with such hearing with regard to all or any classes of creditors at its discretion. The Court, as a rule, will require the assent of the creditors, or the giving of satisfaction or security for the debts due to them. But it may dispense even with this requirement. On the other hand it may if it thinks fit require such assent or settlement even in cases where the liability is not affected, nor any repayment proposed. Apart from hearing the creditors, the Court may require that the company should publish the reason for the reduction and such other information as it may think expedient for the proper information of the public.

The Court has full discretion to give or to refuse its confirmation.

If reduction is proposed because part of the capital is lost or the assets of the company have depreciated, the Court will require some *prima facie* evidence of the loss or depreciation.[1]

Although a company has full power and authority to propose the adjustment of its capital, the Court is empowered to refuse confirmation if it is not satisfied that the proposed correction is proper.

After the reduction has been confirmed by the Court it will be registered, and a notice of the registration is to be published in such manner as the Court may direct. Furthermore the company may be placed under obligation to add after its name the words "and reduced" for such period as the Court may direct; but the Court may refrain from imposing this obligation.

In all these cases the reduction affects the position and interests of all shareholders equally. Generally reductions of capital should be all-round ones. But there are cases in which reduction is possible, although not all the shareholders are equally affected by it.

If a company makes shares forfeit for non-payment of instalments or calls pursuant to the articles, this amounts to a reduction of capital, provided the shares are cancelled and not reissued (see clauses 23–9 of Table A; clauses 33–9 of Table A of the 1948 Act). For such a proceeding confirmation by the Court is not required. The same is true if a company cancels shares which have not been taken up or agreed to be taken up. This is a reduction of authorised capital, but technically not a reduction of capital proper, and the Act requires only a simple resolution in general meeting. Notice of the cancellation, however, is to be sent to the registrar (sec. 50 (1) and (3); further sec. 51).

A border-line case is the surrender of shares. This may be accepted by the company as a short cut to forfeiture; but in so far as liability is extinguished by the acceptance of the surrender, its validity without the confirmation of the Court is doubtful. Where shares are taken back on the ground of misrepresentation, it is held that in the absence of confirmation by the Court the case is to be judged on its merits.

Where a company reduces its capital by purchasing a certain number of its own shares, whether fully or partly paid up, the Court's confirmation is undoubtedly required, and a surrender

[1] *Re* Barrow Haematite Steel Co. (1901), 2 Ch. 746; Caldwell *v.* Caldwell and Co. (1916), W.N. 70.

of shares in return for money paid by the company is invalid without the sanction of the Court.[1]

It is of course possible to accept the surrender of fully paid up shares if no payment on the company's part is involved. This may also be done if such shares are surrendered in exchange for other shares.[2] If the surrendered shares were only partly paid up, a surrender involves the reduction of the fund securing the creditors, in view of the cancellation of the liability for the remainder. Consequently the acceptance of such surrender amounts to a reduction of capital, for which the confirmation of the Court is necessary. This question, however, is somewhat disputed. In Teasdale's case[3] it was held that confirmation is not necessary. The contrary was held in a dictum in Trevor *v.* Whitworth[4] and in Bellerby *v.* Rowland and Marwoods, etc., Co.[5]

It is to be noted that any other reduction similarly needs confirmation by the Court. In such cases the same procedure is to be followed as in the three cases mentioned expressly in sec. 55.[6] In the last-mentioned case the company had partly paid shares which were subdivided into shares partly paid and not paid at all. The unpaid shares created by resolution were surrendered to the company for reissue.

If a company has two classes of shares, i.e. preference and ordinary, any loss suffered by it is to fall first upon the ordinary shares, if the purpose of the reduction is to wipe out the loss. But if a company has a more complicated capital structure, and in any case in which the reduction is to affect the shareholders in a way differing from their rights as provided in the articles, each and every class of shareholders has to carry the special resolution by a separate vote. To summarise the position under the Companies Act of 1929, the guarantee provided by the Act is twofold: the requirement of a special resolution with notice to shareholders and with the specific majority prescribed; the necessity of judicial confirmation intended to secure the rights of both creditor and shareholder.

[1] See Trevor *v.* Whitworth (1887), L.R. 12 App. Cas. 409, *per* Lord Macnaghten at p. 438; British and American Trustee and Finance Corporation *v.* Couper (1894), A.C. 399; Bellerby *v.* Rowlands and Marwoods, etc., Co. (1902), 2 Ch. 14.

[2] Cf. Eichbaum *v.* City of Chicago Grain Elevators (1891), 3 Ch. 459; Rowell *v.* John Rowell and Sons Ltd. (1912), 2 Ch. 609.

[3] (1873), 9 Ch. App. 54.

[4] Trevor *v.* Whitworth, *supra.*

[5] Bellerby *v.* Rowlands and Marwoods, etc., Co., *supra.*

[6] See British and American Trustee and Finance Corporation *v.* Couper, *supra*; Poole *v.* National Bank of China (1907), A.C. 229; Louisiana, etc., Co. (1909), 2 Ch. 552, and Doloswella Rubber and Tea Estates Ltd. (1917), 1 Ch. 213.

Under the Common Law of the U.S.A. a corporation has no power to reduce its capital without statutory authority, or powers granted under the charter or articles. This rule is nowadays rather theoretical, since most statutes contain a provision granting such authority, and the charters or articles almost without exception confer the power to reduce.[1]

As already stated in connection with the power of corporations to acquire their own shares, it has frequently been discussed in the decisions of Federal and State Courts what effect is to be attributed to such purchases. The majority rule is that a purchase or other acquisition of its own shares by a corporation is not in itself a reduction of capital. It depends upon the circumstances and the intent with which the shares have been acquired. It is therefore held that without expressed or implied intent as to reduction the corporation may reissue and resell the shares at any time.[2]

American statutes are less exacting in this matter than either British or European law. We may quote as an example the provisions of the Stock Corporation Law of New York: "A stock corporation may reduce its share capital by a resolution approving the reduction by a majority vote of all outstanding voting shares. To the certificate of reduction an affidavit of the corporate officers is to be attached, stating either that no distribution of assets to the stockholders will be made in connection with the reduction or that the actual value of the corporation is not less than the total amount of its debts plus the proposed amount of its capital." The rule as to distributions is that no corporation, except as otherwise provided by law, shall make any distribution of its assets in connection with the reduction of its capital, if its effect will be to reduce the actual value of its assets to an amount less than the total amount of its debts and liabilities plus the amount of its capital as reduced.[3]

The redemption of shares is restricted under the statutes to preferred stock, and the right to redeem preferred shares must be included in the certificate (articles) of incorporation. The redemption is as a rule at the option of the corporation; it may be made by using surplus, or if from capital, only if the effect of the redemption will not be to reduce the value of the assets below the amount defined.[4] Other statutes, such as those of California,

[1] Fletcher 5147.

[2] Fletcher 5148, n. 49.

[3] N.Y. Stock Corp. Law, §§ 37, 38.

[4] Cf. N.Y. Stock Corp. Law, § 28.

Delaware and Illinois, contain similar provisions. Even if the redemption be compulsory, it is disallowed where it would impair the position of the creditors.[1]

Under French law it was held originally that a reduction is possible only by unanimous consent of all the shareholders. Later, however, it was recognised that the reduction is a special kind of alteration of the articles. Consequently, for any reduction the formalities required for an alteration of the articles are necessary. As to the form and methods of reduction there is nothing to be added to the analysis contained above as to British company law. As to procedure and the effect of reductions there are two important differences. Firstly, the Courts have no power to confirm special resolutions of companies for the reduction of capital. They therefore cannot confirm such a resolution by a decree or order, nor have they power to refuse it: the resolution is valid or invalid on its own merits. In case of an attack by shareholders or creditors the Court will declare it valid or void, as the case may be, but always by judgment. The second important difference is that a reduction of capital shall in no case affect the position of creditors whose debts already exist at the time when the resolution was carried. It is only debts originating from a time subsequent to the reduction which are affected by the resolution.[2]

Under German law the possibility of reducing the capital was already admitted by the Code of 1861. At that time, however, the assent of the government was necessary; this state of the law was preserved in Austria up to the *Anschluss*. The law of 1870 dispensed with this requirement; instead thereof a special resolution and registration by the Court was required. As a further guarantee the law provided that where the payment to shareholders was connected with the reduction, no such payment should be effected within one year from the resolution in general meeting.

The Code of 1897 followed the same line in building up the regulation for the reduction of capital. For such a resolution a majority of at least three-fourths of the capital represented at the general meeting is necessary: the articles may impose further requirements. The three-fourths majority may not be reduced. When there are several classes of shares with differing rights, a special resolution of each class is necessary besides that carried by the common vote of all classes. The resolution must state

[1] Cf. Ballantine 266–72.

[2] Cf. Pic 1428–40.

the purpose of the reduction, and particularly whether it is made for repayment of capital to the shareholders, and also its manner (§ 288). Immediately after the general meeting the board of management must report the resolution for entry in the register. Before registering it, the Court has power to investigate whether the resolution is valid, i.e. in compliance with legal requirements, but otherwise it has no power to exercise any control, especially in respect of the creditors and shareholders. The management must insert a notice in the *Gazette* requesting the creditors of the company to report their claims; this is to be published three times. Creditors known to the company are to be informed individually. All creditors whose claims are already existent at the first publication of the notice are to be paid or secured, provided they report their claims to the company. Payment to shareholders is not to be made within a year from the first publication of the notice, and then only if all the creditors who have reported are either paid or secured. The cancellation of liability as to unpaid parts of shares is not effective before the lapse of one year, as mentioned (§ 289). After the reduction of capital has been effected, the management must report it to the Court for entry in the register. Although the supervision by the Court is purely formal, this is done twice: first after the general meeting has carried the resolution, secondly after the reduction is in fact completed.

After the inflation it was provided that a company's capital cannot be reduced below the modest minimum of M5000. Earlier there was no such minimum, but there was a minimum for the par value of the shares. Consequently there was always difficulty when the capital was to be reduced to such an extent that the minimum par value of the shares could not be maintained. In such cases the code gave power to resolve on the conversion of two or more shares into one, complying with the legal minimum for the par value. Thus, if a company had losses necessitating a capital reduction of 50 per cent., it could be resolved that two shares were to be surrendered to the company for one new share. The proportion might of course be a different one. If, e.g., a company made a reduction of 20 per cent., shareholders could be required to surrender five old shares for four new ones. In all these cases the company was empowered to request the surrender within a certain time to be communicated to the shareholders, with the proviso that all shares not presented within the fixed term should be invalid, and the company would be empowered to sell the corresponding new shares on the Stock Exchange for the account and at the risk of the shareholder who should fail to present his shares for conversion. This right was carried to the extent that the company was empowered to use the same machinery if in consequence of the reduction the new reduced par value was to be marked on the share certificate without the creation of fractional shares (§ 290). The German Companies law of 1937 reduced the guarantee for creditors, while at the same time the procedure was on the whole maintained. Instead of one year, as required by the Code, only six months are in future necessary. Since this law prescribes the high minimum of M500,000 for share capital, it was enacted that the capital may be reduced below this minimum, provided it is at the same time increased by the issue of additional shares to at least M500,000. Such an issue, however, cannot be made otherwise than for cash, and the resolution as to reduction and reincrease is void if the whole transaction is not completed within six months (§§ 175–81).

The law also contains provisions in respect of a simplified reduction of capital for cases in which the purpose of the reduction is readjustment for depreciations or losses, or increases of the legal reserve. This form of capital reduction had already been introduced by the emergency legislation by decree in 1930 (see § 24). Such a reduction cannot be made until the legal reserve in excess of ten per cent. of the capital and all the free reserves and funds for depreciation are exhausted. The Ministers of Justice and Economy have power to grant exceptions. In the case of such reductions, amounts originating from reserves and the reduction cannot be applied for payments to shareholders to convert partly paid into fully paid shares, and in this way to wipe out shareholders' liabilities. Furthermore, in cases in which it appears subsequently within two years that losses and depreciation in fact arose only to a lesser extent than was supposed, the difference is to be put into legal reserve. No dividends may be paid until the legal reserve reaches ten per cent. of the capital, and for the first five years no more than four per cent. There are provisions giving additional guarantees to creditors in cases of such simplified capital adjustments in form of reduction. On the whole, however, it is an attenuation of legal requirements and is not without its dangers (§§ 182–91).

Swiss law, in all cases where the capital of a company is reduced without a simultaneous reincrease up to the original amount, requires a report from a corporate body of auditors or a trust company approved by the government showing that the company will be able fully to satisfy all creditors, despite the reduction. Without such report the resolution cannot be carried, and the auditors are to be present at the general meeting. The resolution is to refer to the report and is to state the method of reduction. The minimum of capital is to be maintained, and therefore if the original capital is reduced below the legal minimum of 50,000 Swiss francs it is to be reincreased at the same time, otherwise the reduction is invalid.

The amount of book profit originating from the reduction of capital is to be applied exclusively to the writing off of assets (732). The three notices to creditors give a period of two months for reporting for creditors. The term of two months seems too short, especially in the case of companies whose business relations are more than local. Moreover, the notice to creditors and their payment or securing in case of their reporting may be dispensed with, if the purpose of the reduction is only readjustment. Consequently it is provided that this exemption can apply only if the reduction does not exceed the loss or depreciation suffered (733-735).

In Great Britain the powers given to the Court in relation to sanctioning reductions of capital seem to have worked satisfactorily. At the hearings of the Cohen Committee no complaints were voiced in respect of the working of the regulation of the Act of 1929 in this respect and thus the law remained unchanged (secs. 66–70 of the Act of 1948). Only in respect of redeemed preference shares were amendments recommended, and recommendations pursuant to them included in the Companies Act, 1947. Most of these are of a technical nature. It is to be noted that where the redemption is at a premium, the premium is in all cases to be paid out of profits, and not only where the shares are redeemed out of the proceeds of a fresh issue (sec. 71; re-enacted in sec. 58 of the Act of 1948).

92. Holding Companies

The view of early corporation law was, that one corporation cannot be the member of another, and consequently a company cannot hold shares in another company. L. C. Cairns said: [1] "It is at first sight beyond the province of one trading corporation to become a shareholder and apply its funds for that purpose." This doctrine, however, was abandoned in Great Britain, and Lord Cairns stated in the case mentioned that "there is no reason at common law" as far as he knew "why one corporate body should not become a member of another corporate body", and it was and is still held that a company—if authorised by its memorandum—may acquire and hold shares in other companies. In practice, most—if not all—companies insert in their memorandum a clause to this effect. Furthermore this power may be implied. Thus in one case it was held [2] that the clause of the memorandum giving power to amalgamate covers the case in which the consideration for the assets consists in shares in another company.

In the U.S.A.[3] the Common Law doctrine is that a company has no power to become a member of another company, certain early statutes going so far as to prohibit expressly the holding of shares in other corporations. Corporations may, however, be authorised by charter to acquire and hold shares in other corporations. Thus the Baltimore and Ohio Railroad Corporation was authorised as early as 1833 to acquire stock of another railroad.

The first American statute to depart from the common law doctrine was that of New Jersey (1880). Subsequently the majority of the statutes of the various States declared that one corporation may purchase and hold stock of other corporations. The only difference is that in some jurisdictions it is held that the power to purchase and hold stock is inherent, and exists unless prohibited by the charter (articles), whereas others hold that the charter must authorise the holding of corporate stock, and that without such authorisation the purchase is *ultra vires*. Even in the latter case several important exceptions are recognised. Thus it is held that although a corporation is not authorised to purchase and to hold corporate stock, it may accept such stock as collateral and may acquire the collateral if the debt is not paid; furthermore the corporation may acquire corporate stock as payment by way of a compromise. It is generally provided

[1] Barned's Banking Co. (1867), L.R. 3 Ch. App. 105.
[2] *Re* Thomas (William) and Co. Ltd. (1915), 1 Ch. 325.
[3] Cf. Bohnbright, J. C., and Means, G. C., *The Holding Company* (New York and London, 1932); Ballantine 88; Dodd and Baker, p. 393, 403, n. 3.

that corporate stock so acquired is to be resold within a fixed, usually a short, period.

Under the Continental legal systems the power to acquire and hold such stock has always been considered as inherent in a corporation. Not only banks, but also industrial and commercial corporations exercised this power; its exclusion by the insertion of a clause in the articles, though possible, was seldom if ever provided for.

The holding of shares in another company does not of itself make the former a holding company; we can speak of a holding company only if the holding is substantial. A company may be a pure holding company if it has no other purpose than to acquire and hold stock and debentures of one or more other companies. Beside having such holdings the company may carry on business on its own, and operate one or more plants. Such companies are sometimes called mixed holding companies.

Both the mixed and pure holding companies have one thing in common: their holdings amount to a substantial part, sometimes even the whole, of the other company's capital. It is usual to call these latter subsidiaries and the holding company the parent company, even when the subsidiary was not formed by the holding company but became connected with it later by an increase of capital or by purchase in the open market.

As shown in § 26, holding companies are nowadays widespread. The reasons for this are manifold. Frequently it was desired to form a group in order to have easier access to the security market. If several industrial assets are small and of merely local character, they cannot expect to attract the attention of the investor, except in a small circle. But if a large company holds the capital of a number of such smaller units, the appeal to the investing public is much easier. Thus at the beginning of the electric age plants for producing electric current for light and industrial power and for trams needed substantial capital. The power station of a great metropolis could be financed by the issue of shares and debentures, but not one of modest size and in a remote place. A company holding and managing a number of small and medium-sized enterprises was on the other hand able to place its own shares on advantageous conditions. Such holding companies were frequently formed by industrial firms, which built and equipped power stations and had a great interest in spreading the use of electricity. Nearly every leading firm had its own holding companies for such purposes. Some of these holding concerns extended their operations into many countries: Sofina (Brussels), (the Chade) controlling mainly South American enterprises, the Gesfürel (Berlin), and several Canadian and Swiss companies.

In industry there were other important reasons for the rise of holding companies. If an industrial concern starts a new line of production, e.g. to exploit an invention, it is in many cases convenient to separate the new enterprise from their plant, to provide it with its own accounting and also to limit the risk incurred. In the case of a new invention the inventor will be paid, at least in part, by participation in the share capital, and this can only be done by an independent unit with exclusive interest in the invention. Thus usually a company will be formed, devoted entirely to the development of the invention. In Great Britain this was done by creating a private company; in Germany it was mostly a G.m.b.H. Usually this arrangement will be maintained after the experimental stage has come to an end and the company starts production. In course of time the parent company may find it convenient to convert the subsidiary into a public company, and to increase its capital by placing shares partly with selected friends or among the general public.

The holding company method is also used where a company buys out rivals or acquires substantial blocks of shares in their companies, in this way forming a so-called horizontal combine.

The most convenient way for a company to extend its activities into other fields is either to form a new company, or to purchase shares in existing companies. In this way so-called vertical combines are built up. An iron and steel concern may control through stock ownership iron ore and coal mines, to secure the necessary raw materials; shipping companies for the shipping of raw material and finished products from the plant, and so on. We need mention only the United States Steel Corporation. Many coal-mining companies control brick and cement works, glass factories, electric power plants and even chemical factories which use the by-products of the cokeries for the fabrication of various chemical products. The most amazing instances of such concerns are to be found in the chemical industry. Thus Imperial Chemical Industries, Ltd., the leading British chemical firm, according to the evidence before the Cohen Committee at the end of 1943, had 80 subsidiaries. Even more striking was the case of the leading German chemical concern, I. G. Farben: this at the end of 1939 had not only various chemical plants in its ownership and owned a 100 per cent. participation in other chemical corporations, but also owned stock in factories for explosives, rayon and coal mines; it owned majorities in other coal-mining corporations, various selling agencies, and even a bank. That all these and similar large industrial concerns have widespread interests in foreign countries, controlled and owned through stock ownership, is common knowledge.

There might have been deeper economic reasons for the rise of those big combines, but incidentally from the time at which it became possible for a company to acquire shares in other companies many factors combined to make the use of this device popular with managements.

It was not necessary to provide all the capital needed for the enterprise; debentures could be issued and to a considerable part placed in the market. Moreover it was not necessary to hold the entire share capital; control of the voting power was sufficient. Since the law in many countries did not object to the exclusion of preference shares from voting, and even the issue of non-voting ordinary shares was valid, relatively small financial interest could be combined with control over large groups. Incidentally, in the U.S.A. the absence of Federal legislation was a factor of some importance in promoting the evolution of holding companies and control through stock ownership. Since each State had and has power to legislate concerning corporations, it was convenient to incorporate factories erected or acquired in other States as independent units. Moreover, complete mergers of companies incorporated in different States were difficult in view of differences of legislation. The limits on the objects of corporations as defined in their charters may also have played a part in making control through shareholdings attractive. The result was that holding companies in the U.S.A. attained a very high degree of development.

The use of holding companies, however, is not without dangers, and may make the structure of a concern very intricate. The parent company may take an interest in other companies through one of its subsidiaries; in this way several chains may be formed, with subsidiaries and sub-subsidiaries in the second or an even more remote degree. These subsidiaries in their turn may have an interest in other subsidiaries, and so on.

Even more dangerous is it if subsidiaries acquire shares in the parent company, and financial transactions take place between members of a group. The whole structure may become so involved and complex that no shareholder, if not on intimate terms with the directors, will be able to form a clear view of the position. It was said in certain cases that eventually even the directors were unable to cope with the complexities.

Furthermore, an easy method of dishonest manipulation is to drain the more prosperous members of the group to the detriment of the minority and even to show non-existent profits and pay dividends out of capital in order to influence the market. As long as new shares can be placed and appearances kept up all is well; but if this comes to an end collapse is inevitable. The dangers of such pyramiding became only too obvious in the U.S.A. after the crash of 1929. Many holding companies became insolvent and had to be reorganised with enormous loss to the shareholders. The best-known cases were those of the Insull concern, a public utility holding company in which a vast number of electricity generating and distributing companies were controlled by a minimum of effective investment, and the Van Sweringen concern, a railway holding system of similar structure. In both cases dishonest intentions were absent. Insull was eventually acquitted; in the other case there was no trace of blame, and the two Van Sweringens enjoyed in fact the confidence and favour of J. P. Morgan and Co. The method used proved, however, to be fundamentally unsound, and these events led to special legislation in the matter of public utility holding companies.

The building up of combines through holding companies may be contrary to anti-trust legislation. This, however, is not a question of corporation law or policy.

From our point of view two main questions arise, namely, the prevention of evasion of the prohibition of financial assistance for the acquisition of the parent company's own shares, and that of the accounts.

Every legislation must at first define its object and state what is to be understood by the expression, "holding company". Two legislations attempt such a definition. The German law of 1937 is based upon the doctrine evolved in literature [1] and in the practice of the Finance Court. If two or more formally

[1] Cf. Haussman Z.H.R. 97, 1–40 (1932).

independent enterprises are under a united management, they are members of a concern, whether one of them holds any shares in the others or not. On the other hand if one company on the ground of shareholding exercises a dominating influence direct or indirect over the other, the two companies, the dominating and the dominated, are similarly a concern (§ 15).

The British Companies Act of 1929 (sec. 127) provides that a company is deemed for the purposes of the Act to be a subsidiary company if another company holds more than 50 per cent. of its share capital, or has a holding which gives more than 50 per cent. of voting power, or has power to appoint the majority of the directors. Holding through a nominee is equivalent to direct holding. On the other hand, if the ordinary business of the parent company includes the lending of money, shares held as security shall not be counted in the 50 per cent., and if the power to appoint directors is vested in the parent company only by virtue of a debenture trust or shares issued under a trust deed in pursuance of its provisions, this is not deemed to make the company a subsidiary (sec. 127).

The Cohen Committee held that this definition is too wide, since it includes the holding of preference shares, though they give no votes, and too narrow in respect of the control of the directorate (115 and 118, pp. 69–70).

The Act of 1947 accepted both recommendations. According to sec. 18 (now sec. 154 of the Companies Act, 1948) only the holding of equity share capital is relevant, so that shares which carry no right to participate in distributions (dividends and capital) beyond a specified amount, shall be excluded, i.e. only ordinary and participating preference shares shall be taken into account. As to the control of the composition of the board of directors, the alterations are: (1) the parent (holding) company must be a member of the subsidiary; (2) the control must be such as can be exercised without the consent or concurrence of any other person, so that the power applies both to appointment and removal, and that either a person cannot be appointed without the exercise of the holding company's power, or that appointment to more than half of the directorships follows necessarily from appointment as director of the holding company, or lastly, where a directorship is held by the holding company or by one of its subsidiaries.

The new Act clarifies the position of the so-called sub-

subsidiaries by providing that a company is the subsidiary of another company if the first mentioned is a subsidiary of any company which is a subsidiary of that other company. For the purposes of the Act a company is deemed to be another's holding company only when that other company is its subsidiary under the provisions of the Act. There are some minor technical amendments with which we are not concerned. It seems doubtful whether the exclusion of holdings of non-participating preference shares is justified, since after all such holdings may influence the whole business policy of the company.

Sec. 45 of the 1929 Act, which prohibits any financial assistance in respect of or in connection with a purchase of shares in the company, did not mention the shares of a holding company. Its application to cases in which such shares are or will be purchased was a matter of doubt. Now sec. 73 of the Act of 1947 (sec. 54 of the Act of 1948) expressly provides that the prohibition extends to shares in a company's holding company, just as it applies to the shares of the company itself. At the same time it is made clear that it applies equally to a subscription of shares. Similarly sec. 35 (sec. 190 (1) of the Act of 1948) prohibits loans to directors of the holding company in the same way as to the directors of the company itself. The danger of interlocking holdings was met by sec. 80 of the Act of 1947, re-enacted in sec. 27 of the Act of 1948, which forbids the acquisition of any shares in a holding company by its subsidiary and declares any allotments and transfers in violation of this rule to be void. This rule, however, is not retroactive, so that any subsidiary having acquired shares in its holding company before 1 July 1948 may keep these shares though it will have no right to vote (subsec. (3)). The subsidiary may act as personal representative or as trustee provided neither the holding company nor the subsidiary has any beneficial interest in the shares concerned. This exemption may be appreciated, but not the further exemption of subsec. (2), according to which the subsidiary is not deemed to be interested if the shares of the holding company are held as security for the purpose of a transaction entered into by the subsidiary in the ordinary course of business including the lending of money.

The most important problem in respect of holding and subsidiary companies is that of disclosure. When holding companies and concerns began it was usual for the corporate stocks held by the parent company to appear in the balance sheet under the heading of investments, or in other cases as securities; and the advances made to such companies among the debts due to the parent company. The average shareholder generally had no idea that a more or less substantial part of the investments consisted not of investments of the general type, but of holdings in other corporations. Nor was the profit and loss account more informative; it very often contained only the well-known omnibus clause (see § 86).

The dangers of such a practice are obvious. There might be cases in which one or several of the subsidiaries operated with active profits, others with losses. The parent company had the formal right to account the dividends in its profit and loss account and to make use of them in fixing its own dividend, whereas it was under no obligation to disclose the losses suffered by other subsidiaries. If those losses were substantial and continuous, so that they could not be made good in subsequent years, the parent company's own position would necessarily be weakened. The distribution of dividends in such a case, regardless of the losses suffered by other subsidiaries, might lead even to disaster. All this was possible without disclosing the true position to the shareholder.

It is obvious that this is inconsistent with the idea of conscientious stewardship imposed upon directors. Under the principle of negligence such manipulations should be and presumably are impeachable by the shareholders. On the other hand it is a fact that owing to the honesty of many boards, and to the professional endeavours of accountancy, it gradually became usual to give information to shareholders about the true position of the whole group.

This can be done in different ways. One way, which is sometimes used, would be for the parent company to give a separate disclosure of its interests in subsidiaries in its own balance sheet and accounts. By this method the items relating to the corporate stocks of subsidiaries held by the parent company are stated separately in the balance sheet; similarly the advances made to subsidiaries or debts due to them are separated from those of other creditors and debtors. In the profit and loss account the dividends received from subsidiaries are separated from other dividends. This does not cover the case where subsidiaries are operating at a loss. Such losses are often mentioned in the directors' reports or—especially in Great Britain—in the chairman's speeches. Another way which has become common in recent years is the use of consolidated accounts. The parent company draws up and communicates to its shareholders a consolidated balance sheet in which all the assets and liabilities of the whole group are disclosed, after elimination of all interlocking debts and liabilities. In such a consolidated balance sheet all plants and other fixed assets appear as one item, as do cash and securities, stock-in-trade, debtors and creditors of the whole group as well. In the same way the consolidated profit and loss account will enumerate all revenue and expenditure of the whole group after elimination of the intra-concern expense and income items.

It is a great advance and a very remarkable fact that such an improved practice could develop without any pressure from legislation. Some indeed think that we should be satisfied with such spontaneous evolution. According to this view the managements of the various concerns and the accountancy profession have gone thus far without legal compulsion; it is therefore to be expected that further progress will be made, and the leaving of freedom to directors would have the advantage of elasticity, while the joint efforts of directors and accountants would develop even more adequate systems of accounting.

Before examining this question the present state of the law is to be considered. The Swedish Companies law already provided in 1910 (§ 58 (*a*)) that a company which holds shares in other companies must state its holdings in its balance sheet and must attach thereto a copy of the balance sheet of the subsidiaries.

In Great Britain the 1929 Companies Act (secs. 125 and 126) provided that where any of the assets of a company consist of shares in, or amounts owing by, a subsidiary company or companies, the aggregate amount of these assets, distinguishing shares and indebtedness, is to be set out in the balance sheet of the first-mentioned company separately from all its other assets, and that where a company is indebted to a subsidiary company or companies, the aggregate amount of the indebtedness shall be set out in the balance sheet of the company separately from its other liabilities. Under section 126, in the case of a holding company, defined as a company which holds shares either directly or through a nominee in a subsidiary company or in two or more subsidiary companies, there shall be annexed to the balance sheet a statement stating how the profits and losses of the subsidiary company or companies have, so far as they concern the holding company, been dealt with in, or for the purposes of, the accounts of the holding company and in particular how, and to what extent, (*a*) provision has been made for the losses of a subsidiary company either in the accounts of the company or of the holding company, or of both; and (*b*) losses of a subsidiary company have been taken into account by the directors of the holding company in arriving at the profits and losses of the holding company as disclosed in its accounts. It is not necessary to specify the actual amount of the profits or losses of any subsidiary company, or the actual amount of any part of any such profits or losses which has been dealt with in any particular manner.

In scrutinising these provisions the Cohen Committee points out that: where the profits or losses or any part of them are taken into account in the profit and loss account of the holding company, a statement to that effect, without necessarily disclosing the amounts, is all that is required. Where they are not so taken into account, it must be stated how they have been dealt with, but a mere statement that they have been carried forward in the accounts of the subsidiaries is sufficient, and this gives no real information as to the results of their operations unless particulars of the profits and losses of the subsidiaries are made available. Further, the limited disclosure called for by sec. 125 as to the amount of the aggregate interests in subsidiary companies affords no real information as to their financial position unless particulars of their liabilities, reserves and assets are published to supplement the accounts of the holding company. The Committee therefore recommended that holding companies should lay before the general meeting, beside their own balance sheet and profit and loss account, consolidated accounts, unless this would be inappropriate (Report 122, p. 72).

The Act of 1947 provided several amendments which were re-enacted by the 1948 Act. Where a company at the end of its financial year has subsidiaries, "group accounts" are to be laid before the company in general meeting, when the holding company has to present its own balance sheet and profit and loss account (sec. 14 (1); sec. 150 (1) of the Act of 1948). These "group accounts" are to give a true and fair view of the state of affairs and profit or loss of the "group", the company and the subsidiaries thereby being dealt with as a whole, as far as they concern the members of the company (sec. 16 (1); sec. 152 (1) of the Act of 1948). The group accounts have to contain a consolidated balance sheet and a consolidated profit and loss account.

If the directors are of the opinion that some other form would be preferable to present the same or equivalent information, and would be appreciated by the members, they are free to act in this direction. They may prepare more than one set of consolidated accounts, dealing with the company and one group of subsidiaries, and with other groups respectively. They may, if they choose, submit separate accounts dealing with each of the subsidiaries, or they may expand the information about subsidiaries in the company's own accounts. Any combination of these methods is permitted, so long as it gives a true and fair view of the state of affairs and the profit or loss of the group. Even a partial or whole incorporation of the group accounts in the company's own balance sheet and profit and loss account is admitted (sec. 18; sec. 151 of the Act of 1948).

If the group accounts are prepared as consolidated accounts, they are to be drawn up as far as possible in compliance with the requirements of the First Schedule (now Eighth Schedule to the Act of 1948). If prepared otherwise, they are to give the same or equivalent information, but on the application of the directors or with their consent the Board of Trade may modify those requirements in respect of the company "for the purpose of adapting them to the circumstances of the company" (sec. 16 (3); sec. 152 (3) of the Act of 1948).

The view given by the group accounts is "true and fair" only if it deals with the state of affairs of the subsidiaries at the same dates, and it is desirable that the financial year of each of the subsidiaries should coincide with the company's own financial year. This should be secured by the directors of the holding company, except where in their opinion there are good reasons against it, as e.g. in the case of foreign subsidiaries. If, however, the financial year of a subsidiary does not coincide with that of the holding company, the group accounts shall deal with that subsidiary's state of affairs and its profit and loss account at the end of its financial year ending last before that of the holding company, but the Board of Trade, on the application or with the consent of the holding company's directors, may direct otherwise (sec. 16; sec. 153 of the Act of 1948).

Group accounts are not required if the holding company

concerned is itself, at the end of its financial year, a wholly owned subsidiary of a body corporate incorporated in Great Britain.

Furthermore, the directors may dispense with group accounts or leave out a subsidiary, if they are of the opinion that it is impracticable or would be of no real value to the shareholders, in view of the insignificant amounts involved, or would cause to the members of the company expense or delay out of proportion to the value.

If the directors are of the opinion that the business of a holding company and that of any of its subsidiaries are so different that they cannot reasonably be treated as a single undertaking, or the result would be misleading or harmful to the business of the company or any of its subsidiaries, and they do not wish to deal with the subsidiaries concerned in group accounts, they have to obtain the approval of the Board of Trade (sec. 14 (2); sec. 150 (2) of the Act of 1948); but in such a case a minimum of information is still required, which will be discussed presently.

According to Part II of the Eighth Schedule there shall be shown by way of note on the balance sheet or in a statement or report annexed thereto, the number, description and amount of the shares in and debentures of the company held by its subsidiaries or their nominees, but excluding any of those shares or debentures in the case of which the subsidiary is concerned as personal representative, or as trustee, and neither the company nor any subsidiary thereof is beneficially interested under the trust.

Where group accounts are not submitted, there shall be annexed to the balance sheet a statement showing:

(*a*) the reasons why subsidiaries are not dealt with in consolidated accounts;

(*b*) the net aggregate amount, so far as it concerns members of the holding company and is not dealt with in the company's accounts, of the subsidiaries' profits after deducting the subsidiaries' losses (or *vice versa*); (i) for the respective financial years of the subsidiaries ending with or during the financial year of the company; and (ii) for the previous financial years since they respectively became the holding company's subsidiary;

(*c*) the net aggregate amount of the subsidiaries' profits after deducting the subsidiaries' losses (or *vice versa*); (i) for the respective financial year of the subsidiaries ending with or during the financial year of the company; and (ii) for their other financial years since they respectively became the holding company's subsidiary; so far as those profits are dealt with, or provision is made for those losses, in the company's accounts;

(*d*) any qualifications contained in the report of the auditors of the subsidiaries on their accounts for their respective financial years ending as aforesaid, and any note or saving contained in those accounts to call attention to a matter which, apart from the note or saving, would properly have been referred to in such a qualification, in so far as the matter which is the subject of the qualification or note is not covered by the company's own accounts and is material from the point of view of its members; or, in so far as the information required is not obtainable, a statement that it is not obtainable:

Provided that, in relation to a subsidiary not dealt with in consolidated accounts by virtue of a direction of the Board of Trade, these provisions shall apply only to such extent (if any) as may be provided by that direction.

The provisions as to profits and losses apply only to profits and losses which may properly be treated in the holding company's account as revenue profits or losses, and the profits and losses attributable to any share in a subsidiary for the time being held by the holding company or any other of its subsidiaries shall not be treated as aforesaid so far as they are profits or losses for the period before the date on or as from which the shares were acquired by the company or any of its subsidiaries; and for the purpose of determining whether any profits or losses are to be treated as profits and losses for the said period the profit or loss for any financial year of the subsidiary may, if it is not practicable to apportion it with reasonable accuracy by reference to the facts, be treated as accruing from day to day during that year and be apportioned accordingly.

The balance sheet of a company which is a subsidiary of another body corporate, whether or not it is itself a holding company, shall show the aggregate amount of its indebtedness to all bodies corporate of which it is a subsidiary or a fellow subsidiary, that is a subsidiary of the same holding company, but neither being the other's subsidiary, and the aggregate amount of the indebtedness of all such bodies corporate to it, distinguishing in each case between indebtedness in respect of debentures and otherwise.

The consolidated balance sheet and profit and loss account shall combine the information contained in the separate balance sheets and profit and loss accounts of the holding company and of the subsidiaries dealt with by the consolidated accounts so as to give a true and fair view of the state of affairs and profit or loss of those companies, but with such adjustments (if any) as the directors of the holding company think necessary for that purpose. The consolidated accounts shall, in giving the said information, comply, so far as practicable, with the requirements as if they were the accounts of an actual company.

In relation to the remuneration of past and present directors and other officers of the holding company the requirements as to disclosure shall apply for the purpose of the consolidated accounts as if they were the accounts of the holding company.

The requirements prescribed in respect of auditing, further investigation and inspection apply to subsidiaries as well.

These amendments undoubtedly go a long way to secure fuller information in respect of the affairs of groups of companies. It may, however, be doubted whether it is adequate to require a 50 per cent. holding of the voting shares. In view of the dispersal of share ownership in larger companies (see § 27) a much lower percentage gives actual control even if not exercised or exercisable in respect of the appointment of the board of directors. We think that a shareholding exceeding 25 per cent. of the voting shares should be considered as establishing the relationship of holding-subsidiary.

We have not discussed the position of those companies which devote themselves to catering for the small investor by using their capital for investments dispersed over a wide field, the investment companies or, as they are sometimes called, investment trusts. Their holdings in one and the same company seldom exceed one or two per cent. of the capital, and they have no intention of controlling the respective companies. They have problems of their own; these, however, are quite different from those of holding companies.

93. The Private Company

As corporate enterprise invaded the field of medium and small businesses, the need for some relaxation of legal requirements in respect of the formation and management of these companies soon came to be felt.

Continental legislations met this need by introducing a special form of corporate structure: that of companies, or rather partnerships, with limited liability, which they sought to distinguish from companies proper mainly by prohibiting the issue of share certificates, providing for a simpler method of management and dispensing with filing and publicity for accounts. The initiative was taken by Germany in 1892, and a number of other countries, including France, followed suit.

The legislation of Great Britain chose in 1907 another approach. The ordinary corporate structure was on the whole maintained for private companies, the only difference being the granting of several exemptions. This example was never followed in the U.S.A., where there is only one form of business corporation, though in recent times it has been stressed that for smaller enterprises special regulations should be adopted.

In this section we propose to deal with the private company under British Company legislation, and the reforms envisaged by the Cohen Committee and adopted in the Companies Act, 1947, and subsequently re-enacted by the Companies Act of 1948.

From 1907 the Companies Acts made a distinction between public and private companies based not on size, but on the number of members and the restriction of share transfers.

A company, to be a private company, must in its articles: (*a*) restrict the right of transfer of its shares; (*b*) limit the number of its members to 50; and (*c*) prohibit any invitation to the public to subscribe for its shares and debentures.[1] These three requirements need some elucidation. The restriction of transfer does not mean its exclusion, but simply that it must be dependent upon the assent of the company. Such restrictions may be made by the articles of public companies also, but in the case of a private company they are obligatory. The questions connected with restrictive clauses have been considered in § 59.

The rule limiting the number of members is qualified to the extent that present and past employees are not to be reckoned,

[1] Companies Act, 1929, sec. 26 (1); sec. 28 (1) of the Act of 1948.

and hence the number of members may considerably exceed 50 without depriving the private company of its status as such. A further provision is that joint holders of shares are to be treated for the purposes of the limit as one member (sec. 28 (2)). The prohibition of invitations to the public does not extend to invitations addressed to a restricted circle of persons.

These requirements must be complied with throughout the existence of the company. This means that if a private company alters its articles in respect of one or more of the three requirements, it ceases to be a private company and loses its privileges as such. Secondly, the requirements must be complied with in fact, and in the event of default the company likewise loses its privileges; but where the failure was accidental or due to inadvertence or other sufficient cause, the Court may grant relief on the application of the company or some other interested person, on such terms and conditions as it finds just and expedient. This may also be done on other sufficient grounds (sec. 27 (3); sec. 29 of the Act of 1948).

In order to prove compliance, the private company must submit with its annual report a certificate signed by its director or secretary, stating that it has not during the past financial year issued any invitation to the public to subscribe for shares or debentures, and where the number of members exceeds 50, that the excess consists of present or former employees of the company. On compliance with these requirements the private company enjoys substantial privileges.

The minimum number of members is two instead of seven.

A private company need not have two directors. The Report of the Cohen Committee goes even so far as to state that "as the law stands at present, it need not have any directors" (49, p. 26). Actually most if not all private companies have at least one director, and with the coming into force of the Companies Act of 1948 even a private company shall have at least one director (sec. 176) and a secretary, and a sole director shall not also be a secretary (sec. 177 (1)).

Under the Act of 1929 a private company is not required to file a list of persons who have consented to become directors, or to deliver to the registrar their declarations of consent (sec. 139–40).

A private company is not bound to hold a statutory meeting, or to forward the statutory report to the members and to the registrar (sec. 113 (10)). It is exempt from the duty of issuing a prospectus or a statement in lieu. It is entitled to commence business after registration without any formalities and to allot shares without requirements as to a minimum subscription.

A private company must lay before its members in general meeting a balance sheet and a profit and loss account; the balance sheet is to be audited and the members are entitled to request a copy thereof and of the auditor's report at a charge of sixpence per 100 words. It is, however, exempt from the duty of forwarding to the members a copy of the balance sheet and of the documents annexed thereto seven days before the meeting free of charge, which is obligatory for public companies (sec. 130 (1)) and persons who are partners or are in the employment of an officer of the company are not disqualified from acting as auditors (sec. 133 (1) (*b*)).

Lastly, a private company is not bound to file its balance sheet and the documents annexed thereto (sec. 110 (3)). This is the most essential of the exemptions and privileges of private companies, and the general public has thus no means of ascertaining their actual financial position and the trend of their business results.

Under the impact of this regulation the number of private companies has immensely increased. Not only have many new companies of this kind been formed, but quite a number of public companies have been converted into private ones, especially in the years following the legalisation of this form of corporate enterprise in Great Britain. Nowadays such a conversion is exceptional, whereas if a private company wishes to make a public issue, or its principal members intend to place their holdings wholly or partly with the public, it is converted into a public company, as has been done in a number of cases, especially in periods of prosperity and particularly in the present post-war readjustment of capital structures.

The Report of the Cohen Committee stated (48, p. 26) that from 1939 to 1944 the number of private companies rose from 146,735 to 169,208, while that of public companies declined from 13,920 to 13,303. In the same period the fully paid up capital of public companies declined from £4,117,000,000 to £4,052,000,000, whereas the capital invested in shares of private companies rose from £1,923,000,000 to £1,935,000,000. Both in numbers and in capital invested the proportion of private companies was on the increase.

Although there are many small private companies, it cannot be said that the share capital of private companies is insignificant; in fact the average is about £11,400, and a few of them are of imposing size, such as the Iraqi Oil Company with a capital of £14,000,000.

The exemption of private companies from the duty of filing their accounts gave rise to complaints which were put vigorously before the Cohen Committee. Particularly was it alleged that by making use of this privilege unscrupulous directors were able to obtain credit for companies without substance, and as a matter of fact the so-called long-firm frauds largely occurred in the case of private companies. Furthermore the representatives of trade unions and other organisations stressed that the secrecy of the accounts puts employees and workers in a difficult position in formulating their demands for just salaries and wages.

On the other hand objections were raised mainly in respect of small companies, such as family businesses, on the ground that publicity for their accounts would give valuable information to their rivals, especially to powerful competitors, who, becoming acquainted with their financial position, could easily drive them out of business, whereas the long-established publicity of the accounts of public companies is of little avail to the little man. Besides, it was argued that publicity of accounts is of little help after all in view of their uninformative character. The Committee, after considering all these conflicting arguments, came to the conclusion that the exemption should be maintained save for those private companies whose share capital is beneficially owned by corporations. This and certain minor amendments were adopted in 1947 and are now embodied in the Act of 1948.

Sec. 129 of the Act of 1948, in connection with the Seventh Schedule, provides that private companies must file their accounts if a body corporate is holder of any shares or debentures, or is beneficially interested in such, or is a director of the company, or any person other than the registered holder has any interest in any of the shares or debentures, and likewise if the number of members or debenture holders exceeds 50. The exemption from this duty also ceases if either the company or any of its directors or debenture holders is a party to an arrangement under which the company's policy is capable of being determined by persons other than directors, members or trustees for debenture holders of the company. This rule is qualified in several directions. It is a matter of course that corporations sole are not treated as corporate bodies for this purpose. This exemption from the duty to file accounts is maintained if any share or debenture or any interest therein is subject to a charge in favour of a banking or finance company for money lent in the ordinary course of its business. Holdings by private companies in other private companies shall not deprive the latter of exemption if they themselves, i.e. the relevant companies, are exempted. Similarly, if one or more banking or finance companies acquires and holds either directly or through nominees shares or debentures in pursuance of the ordinary course of their business and by arrangement with the relevant company or its promoters, such holding shall be disregarded in respect of the exemption, unless the banking or finance company or companies have the right to exercise or control the exercise of one-fifth or more of the voting power at any general meeting of the relevant company. It will be appreciated that holdings of personal representatives of deceased share- or debenture holders are to be disregarded so far as the limit as to numbers is concerned, and the same is provided in respect of family settlements.

The introduction of the duty to file accounts in the aforementioned cases is undoubtedly an advance. In our view, however, the Act does not go far enough. It will still be possible to control a large business by holding the voting power through a private company. There is nothing to prevent arrangements by which the holder of shares giving the majority of the voting power in another company is a private company, which is furnished with the financial means to acquire and to hold those shares by way of loans. In such a case it would be easy to arrange for the private company's shares to be in the legal and beneficial ownership of a restricted number of persons, and the exemption could be maintained.

From a technical point of view the structure of the regulation as provided is highly complicated and capable of giving rise to many doubts and disputes. We think further that the arguments in favour of full publicity on the whole prevail, and that legislation had better abandon the exemption of private companies as a whole. It is to be feared that those private companies in respect of which complaints were voiced will not be at all hampered in their fraudulent activities.[1] On the other hand the new Act

[1] O. Kahn-Friend, Mod. L.R. 7, pp. 54–66.

introduces a number of useful technical amendments. Thus, the members will have the right to receive accounts in the same way as the members of public companies, and the requirements in respect of audits will also be equalised to a certain extent.

Many of the reforms, especially the new regulation as to winding-up for just and equitable cause, will benefit the members of private companies to even a much larger extent than those of large public companies.

94. The One-man Company

The leading purpose of corporate enterprise is to unite the capital resources and economic strength of several individuals. Most legislative systems expressly require that no corporation should be incorporated or registered without having a stated number of members. The acceptance of limited liability, however, proved a strong incentive to the creation of enterprises owned by one individual in corporate form, and similarly to the conversion of already existing enterprises into corporations.

Besides the wish to obtain limited liability and thus to free all the entrepreneur's assets other than the capital invested in the corporation from the risks connected with the enterprise, there may be other substantial reasons for choosing a corporate form for privately owned businesses. Such are, e.g., the wish to make the existence of the enterprise independent of the incident of death, greater ease in management and an easier form of alienation. For a long time the incidence of taxation was also important; nowadays, however, the position as to taxation is in most countries the reverse.

Under some, though not all, legislations plurality of shareholders is required for the creation of a corporation and must be maintained during its lifetime; under others it is required only at the time of incorporation. The legal consequences of the absence of plurality differ.

In Britain the Companies Act of 1948 (sec. 1) requires that in order to form a company seven or more persons shall subscribe the memorandum of association. To form a private company the co-operation of two persons is required, and sec. 2 (4) (*b*) requires that no subscriber may take less than one share. Sec. 31 of the Act requires that this minimum number of members is to be maintained. If at any time the number of members falls below seven or two respectively, and the company carries on business for more than six months while the number is so reduced, the members cognisant of this fact are severally liable for such debts of the company as are contracted during this time.

Under this ruling British companies comply with the requirement as to the number of members to the extent that no application for registration is made without showing the required number, and the required membership is invariably shown in the yearly returns. But there are many cases in which an overwhelming part of the share capital is subscribed by one individual. Furthermore, even the single shares subscribed and alleged to be subsequently held by the other six subscribers may be beneficially owned by a single individual, the other six acting merely as his trustees or nominees.

It is now held that the requirement is complied with if the legal ownership of the remaining six shares or, in the case of a private company, of the other share is vested in the subscribers, and the fact that these shares are held beneficially by one and the same person does not affect the existence of the corporation. In Buckley's words (p. 2), "the one-man company is legal; the six holders of one share each may be trustees for a seventh person who holds all the rest". According to Buckley there is nothing in the Act requiring the subscribers to be independent or unconnected or to have a substantial interest, or to have a mind and will of their own, or that there shall be anything like a balance of power in the constitution of the company. The authority for this rule is the judgment of the House of Lords in the case of Salomon *v.* Salomon and Co. Ltd.[1] In this case Aron Salomon converted his enterprise into a limited company for a consideration of £20,007 divided into £1 shares, of which 20,001 were allotted to him, the remaining six being held by his wife and five children, each holding one share. Vaughan Williams, J., held that the company was a mere alias for Salomon, and that therefore he was liable for its unsecured debts. The Court of Appeal, in affirming the judgment, held that the intention of the Companies Act was that there must be seven *bona fide* subscribers or shareholders in association, and that it was contrary to that intention that a company should consist of one substantial shareholder and six others devoid of any real interest. The judgment was reversed by the House of Lords without dissent. Lord Chancellor Halsbury said (p. 30): "The statute

[1] (1897), A.C. 22.

enacts nothing as to the extent or degree of interest which may be held by each of the seven, or as to the proportion of interest or influence possessed by one or the majority of the shareholders over the others". Lord Herschell stated (pp. 45–6) that: "The statute forbids the entry in the register of any trust, and it certainly contains no enactment that each of the subscribers should be beneficially interested in their shares. . . . Whether they are beneficially owners or bare trustees is a matter in which neither the company nor creditors have anything to do". The dicta of Lord Macnaghten at p. 50 are those quoted by Buckley.

Since then this rule has been consistently followed.[1] In Inland Revenue Commissioners *v.* Sansom,[2] one shareholder held 2499 out of 2500 shares, the remaining share being held originally by a friend and subsequently transferred to his daughter. It was held that this fact did not affect the valid existence of the company. The rule therefore is that, provided the number of shareholders is made up in a formal sense, the validity of the corporation is not affected; all the shares may be held beneficially by the same person. Further, although there is no authority for this, it may be argued that from the point of view of sec. 31 the formal existence of six other shareholders, or in the case of a private company of one other shareholder, would suffice to exclude the joint and several liability of the shareholders for the debts of the company. To this, however, there are qualifications. The first is that the transfer of real property to a company may be attacked in case of fraud on creditors under sec. 172 of the Property Act as it was formerly under 13 Eliz., c. 5. The same rule applies in the case of the vendor's bankruptcy within three months from the sale. Such sale is void as an act of bankruptcy of the vendor, although the sale was not entered into with fraudulent intent.[3]

On the other hand the number of shareholders is important from the point of surtax since the coming into force of the Finance Act of 1922, sec. 21 of which, amended by later Finance Acts, provides that such part of the profits of companies as is withheld from distribution in form of dividends without sufficient reason may be treated as income of the shareholders for the assessment of surtax, provided the company has not more than

[1] See Attorney-General for Canada *v.* Standard Trust Co. (1911), A.C. 498, in which case there were four shareholders.

[2] (1921), 2 K.B. 492.

[3] Cf. *re* Fasey (1923), 2 Ch. 1.

50 shareholders and is controlled by not more than five of them.[1]

From the point of international law, especially with regard to wartime legislation, there are other cases in which corporate entity is disregarded. This aspect of the question, however, is outside the scope of our investigations.

In the U.S.A.[2] one-man companies are widespread. Especially is this so with smaller business units, where corporate form is desired in many cases for the sake of limited liability.

Most States of the U.S.A. require a minimum number of shareholders for the creation of a corporation. Only in Iowa and Michigan is the formation of one-man companies expressly admitted. In the other States the requirement of plurality of membership must be complied with, and only subsequently may it occur that the shares are acquired by the majority holder. But there are not infrequent cases in which the one-man company is intended from the beginning, and in such cases the shareholders are generally trustees or dummies of the sole owner of the capital.

The consequences when all the shares of a corporation become the property of a single shareholder are a matter of dispute. In some cases the Courts have held that corporate existence is suspended until the stock ownership is again dispersed.[3] The majority, however, follows the rule in the Salomon case, and holds that the mere fact of exclusive ownership is a reason neither for dissolution nor for denying limited liability. This rule, however, is affected by several qualifications. Thus, if the sole shareholder manages the corporate business in a way which makes the corporation his *alter ego*, or the corporate entity is instrumentally frequently disregarded, he is held to be personally liable for the debts. Thus in Wittmann *v.* Wittingham [4] the sole shareholder was held personally liable to an employee who was employed in the business from a time previous to the conversion into a corporation. It was found that the sole shareholder conducted the business on unaltered lines, and in such circumstances could not evade his personal liability for the obligations of the corporation to its employee. A similar reason for establishing personal liability was found where the sole shareholder made use of the

[1] Cf. Penang and General Investment Trust Ltd. *v.* Inland Revenue Commissioners (1943), A.C. 486.
[2] Cf. Ballantine 128.
[3] Cf. Ballantine 128, and the cases in note 49.
[4] V. W. Fuller, H.L.R. 57, pp. 1373-1406, 85 Cal. Ap. 140 (1927).

corporate assets for his own purposes or was mixing the accounts. In several cases Courts have established personal liability on the ground that the sole shareholder did not observe the formalities prescribed for corporate management. It has been said [1] that the Court will not scrutinise scrupulously whether the sole shareholder has acted on his own or on the corporation's behalf. In cases in which the sole shareholder was at the same time creditor of the corporation the Courts have in several cases refused to recognise the dual capacity and to enforce the debt in concurrence with other creditors. The reasons given differed widely. Failure to keep proper accounts, and the appropriation of corporate assets, also occur in this relation. In some cases inadequacy of the capital was also held to be a sufficient reason to refuse enforcement. Thus in Albert Richards Co. *v.* the Mayfair [2] the holding amounted only to about $6000, of which one shareholder held $100 whereas for the business an investment of $75,000 was required. It was held that the shareholder who held only $100 stock could not enforce the debt in concurrence with other creditors. On the other hand so long as other persons are not interested as creditors or otherwise adversely affected the American Courts are inclined to overlook formal defects and to regard the acts of sole shareholders as binding on the corporation. Even contracts made by the sole owner of the stock with himself have been regarded as valid. This view has of course been taken only if the corporation was not insolvent and was not made insolvent by the contract in question.

The question whether subsequent creditors have the right to attack transactions fully performed earlier is disputed, whereas the enforcement of unsettled claims arising out of such transactions is mostly refused. Transfers of property, if fraudulent, are of course not valid as against creditors.

Another disputed question is whether payments made by the sole owner of the shares to himself may be invalidated. If such payments are made from surplus it is usually held that they cannot be attacked by creditors; if the payment impairs the capital it is considered voidable. There are cases, however, in which it has been held that, provided the corporation was solvent when the payment was made, creditors have no right to attack it, since the owner could easily reduce the capital by observing the for-

[1] McCormick Seltzer Co. *v.* Grizzley Creek Lumber Co. (1925), 74 Cal. Ap. p. 278.
[2] (1932), 287 Mass. 280.

malities required and the absence of formalities does not justify such burdensome consequences.

In view of these disputes and the obscurity of the legal position voices have been heard in the U.S.A. advocating the regulation of the one-man company, the incorporated individual. Thus Professor Fuller [1] complains that American State legislation treats under one heading three different classes of corporations: the quasi-public corporation with a large number of shareholders, the close corporation with a restricted number of members and generally with restrictions on transfer, and lastly the one-man company. In his view each requires different regulations.

Under French law a distinction is made between the case in which the number of shareholders is reduced below seven and the case of the one-man company proper, in which the ownership of all the shares is vested in a single person. In the former case the Court may declare the dissolution of the company on the action of any party interested if one year has passed since the diminution of membership (law of 1867, art. 38). But it is to be remembered that according to the law of 1893 the action is to be dismissed if the required membership had been restored before the action was presented to the Court. Even before the passing of this law it was disputed whether a transitory reduction of membership—if rectified—would justify the dissolution. On the other hand under the law the Court has power to dissolve the company, but is not bound to do so, and may dismiss the action if it thinks fit.

It seems that the Courts regard the attendance lists of general meetings as conclusive evidence of membership, and therefore an action for dissolution could not be based upon evidence that the holding is merely nominal.

Nothing is said about the liability of shareholders, and it therefore seems that in spite of the reduction of numbers it is the company only which is liable for debts.

For one-man companies there is no express provision. Nevertheless it is held that they are contrary to the very idea of an association, which requires at least two members or partners. This rule has been repeatedly applied by the Supreme Court.[2] Consequently in such a case the holder of the shares is held to be

[1] *H.L.R.* 51, pp. 1373–1406.

[2] Cf. Cour de Cassation, 10 April 1864, D. 67, 1, 397, and 7 February 1881 D. 81, 1, 267.

liable for the debts of the company; on the other hand the sole holder of the shares is not entitled to appropriate the company's assets for himself and to mix them with his own property. It is held that he must declare the fact of the devolution of the ownership of all shares as against the public by making proper application to the Court. According to the general rule this is to be done by declaration before a Notary Public. Consequently, although the existence of the company comes to an end with the fact of the sole ownership, its existence is maintained in the interest of creditors who have an exclusive claim for satisfaction out of the corporate assets.

In Belgium the French rule is followed.

The Italian Commercial Code has no express provisions, and the question is disputed. Some opinions hold that any shareholder or creditor may sue for the dissolution of a company whose shares are held by a single person, whereas others, e.g. Sraffa and Bonfante, hold that corporate status is not affected by the acquisition of the whole share capital by one person. The followers of the opposite view are divided: some believe that the present law recognises the one-man company and they suggest only *de lege ferenda* the adoption of the view that its dissolution may be requested by shareholders and creditors, and that in case of a one-man company the holder of the shares should be under absolute and unlimited liability for all debts and obligations of the company. Again, some authors, and *per accidens* the Supreme Court of Rome, adopted the view that under the existing law the liability of the holder of the shares in a one-man company is established and an action for dissolution is given. This view is based on the consideration that individual merchants or partnerships may not limit their liability; consequently this limitation cannot be effected by the roundabout device of a one-man company. Besides this the holder of the whole share capital can at any time transfer the company's property at his free choice and in this way frustrate the rights of creditors. Lastly, one author based his view on the doctrine of simulated contract: simulation involves the application of the rules governing the real contract. He who acquires the whole share capital in fact establishes a single enterprise and the corporate form is simulated.[1]

In Germany there is no rule against one-man companies, and the reduction of the number of shareholders below five, as

[1] Cf. Wieland Z.H.R. 97, pp. 419–21.

required for companies, is held to be of no importance. As a matter of fact one-man companies were numerous, of course more frequently in the case of G.m.b.H.s. It is held that the reduction of the number even to one does not affect the validity of corporate existence, and the assets of the company remain in the sole ownership of the corporation itself. The owner of the whole capital may be indebted to the company or *vice versa.* In order to transfer corporate property to the sole shareholder, or property of the sole shareholder to the company, the same acts of transfer are required as in other cases, i.e. when the company has a number of shareholders. The reduction of numbers below the requirement for the creation of the company, and even sole ownership, do not involve dissolution, and no action for dissolution may be maintained on this ground.[1] The sole owner may appoint himself manager, i.e. a member of the board of management, and even sole manager where the articles permit the board to consist of one member only. In general meeting the sole shareholder is entitled to exercise the vote on all the shares. This is a peculiar feature in view of the elaborate provisions of German Company law with regard to the restriction of votes in cases of conflict of interest. The commentators are not in agreement about the application of those rules to such cases. Some maintain that they apply, but that in spite of this the resolutions passed become valid if not attacked within the prescribed term. Others think that the rules are suspended so long as the sole ownership prevails, and there is an opinion in the sense that the rules do not apply at all. During the time of the sole ownership the sole owner as shareholder will of course exercise his vote in favour of a discharge to himself as manager or supervisor, and also in order to confirm contracts made with himself on behalf of the company. All these possibilities gave many headaches to German Courts and jurists, and the decisions and views are not quite consistent. Thus it has been held that a power of attorney executed by the sole shareholder on behalf of the company is not binding. Furthermore it is assumed that if and when the shares or some part of them are sold, the rights of the company in respect of the avoidance of contracts made by the sole shareholder with himself, resolutions of discharge, and so on, revive. This result is obviously contrary to the view that the acts concerned became valid after expiration of the term prescribed for

[1] R.G.Z. 68, 172; 92, 84; 98, 289.

action. On the other hand the sale of all shares was held in some cases to amount to the sale of all assets, both as to taxation and as to duties of the vendor under the contract. The sole shareholder, however, is generally not held to be liable for the debts of the company; cases of fraud, fraudulent transfers of property and unlawful payments of capital excepted.[1]

Under Swiss law (625) the Court may dissolve the company if the number of shareholders falls below that required for its formation. The dissolution may be decreed on the action either of a shareholder or of a creditor. It is, however, left to the discretion of the Court, and the Court has to fix an adequate time for the restoration of the required membership; dissolution therefore seems not to be compulsory.

In the course of proceedings the Court may order preliminary steps to be taken for securing the rights of creditors or shareholders. There is no provision for the liability of the sole owner; it seems that in the absence of fraud it is not to be assumed.

The Scandinavian Companies laws provide for the dissolution of a company if the membership sinks below the minimum and this situation lasts for more than six months. The Swedish law of 1944 broke with this view: winding-up is no longer compulsory, but the sole owner is liable if he appropriates the assets, or the company becomes bankrupt or insolvent (§§ 32 (*a*), 100 (*a*), 208, 209).

The minute State of Liechtenstein, a favourite place for the formation of holding companies, also provides facilities for the incorporation of one-man companies.

For legislation to require a minimum membership for the creation of corporations but to dispense with this requirement subsequently is undoubtedly a contradiction. In such a case the legal requirement may be quite easily circumvented through a transfer shortly after incorporation, and such transfer may even be stipulated for before, or simultaneously with, incorporation. Furthermore it seems contradictory to allow the use of the corporate form for enterprises owned by single individuals. But quite apart from theory, purely practical considerations recommend a solution in the negative.

In the case of a corporation owned by a single person it is quite impossible to secure guarantees for a management which would exclude the possibility of transfers detrimental to creditors and

[1] Cf. Wieland 124; Gadow, pp. 44–6.

to the public. The sole owner is at any time in a position to transfer assets of the company to himself or to other units in which he is interested. Thus he may lend the company's liquid assets to himself; he may make contracts quite out of the ordinary course of business as to subject or terms; he may vote disproportionate salaries to himself and his appointees, sell to himself or other units controlled by him under market prices or purchase from himself or one of his other concerns at excessively high prices, and in this way disguise the normal results of the business. The dangers to creditors and the impairment of public interests, such as taxation, wages and otherwise, if all this can be done without incurring personal liability, are obvious. It is said that cases of fraud are always excepted; but proof of fraud is in many cases not easy.

We think therefore that in the case of a one-man company the sole shareholder should be made liable for the debts and obligations of the company by the mere fact of his ownership. To restrict liability to cases in which the shareholder has made the company his instrument, as has been held in the U.S.A., would mean that a remedy is given only if and when injury is already proved. It is obvious that such a remedy will in many cases be too late. Nor is it advisable to restrict personal liability to cases in which sole ownership is openly manifest; actually this will hardly if ever happen, because ownership will be camouflaged in order to evade liability.

Creditors or other interested parties should be allowed to give evidence of the existence of beneficial ownership being vested in one person although legal ownership is vested in several.

Lastly, personal liability should not be restricted to 100 per cent. ownership. A concentration of ownership exceeding 75 per cent. or so gives the majority shareholder a control similar to sole ownership. Practical considerations therefore require the adoption of the same liability in such cases; whether it is for 90 or 85 or any other percentage is a question of secondary importance. The maintenance of provisions which make the dissolution of corporations compulsory or facultative in cases of one-man companies or those whose membership becomes less than is required for formation may be beneficial, but their importance is reduced if personal liability is once adopted.

The liability of holding companies as sole owners of the capital of subsidiaries, i.e. the case of 100 per cent. subsidiaries, is similarly disputed. Many, though opposed to the introduction of the personal liability of sole owners, are in favour of such liability if the holding is vested in a corporation so that a double-decked exclusion of liability is established.

95. Dissolution

Under this head we propose to consider in what cases and for what reasons the legal existence of a corporation may come to an end.

This use of the term "dissolution" is not in accordance with English legal terminology. The Companies Acts use this term in speaking of the order of Court declaring that the corporate existence of a company has come to an end when and because its affairs have been completely wound up (sec. 274 of the Act of 1948).

In America and most countries outside the British Commonwealth a distinction is made between the causes for winding-up proceedings and the winding-up itself; the former are discussed under the heading of dissolution. For convenience we here follow this terminology.

Blackstone, who made no distinction between members' and stock corporations, said (I, 485) that a corporation may be dissolved: (1) by Act of Parliament; (2) by the natural death of all its members; (3) by the surrender of its franchises into the hand of the King, which he calls a kind of suicide; (4) by forfeiture of its charter through negligence or abuse of its franchises. It is obvious that the death of the members has no importance at all in relation to the existence of the company, and the aspects of the other reasons mentioned by Blackstone are also quite different. The right of the sovereign power to dissolve a corporation is the natural consequence of the doctrine that corporate existence is due to the charter granted by the Sovereign.

Although nowadays the creation of a company under general corporation laws is rightly to be regarded as an act of the incorporators, the power of the legislature to dissolve a company cannot be denied. On the other hand it is a principle that the State should not interfere with the life of companies unless on some ground based on public policy.

In the United States, however, since the Dartmouth case, it has been held that unless the power to amend or repeal the charter is reserved, the charter, or in other words the franchise, to exist as a corporation cannot be repealed, because the incorporation creates a contract as between the corporation and the State which cannot be terminated by the one-sided act of one of the parties. In practice nowadays this means little, if anything, since following Story's dictum practically all charters were granted with a clause reserving the power to repeal, and since the adoption of general corporation laws a reservation made in the statutes is equally held to be sufficient.

GROUNDS FOR DISSOLUTION

I. *Expiration of time limit.*—The leading idea at common law seems to have been that a corporation cannot be created for a definite period: it must have perpetual succession. This principle, however, was not always observed, and in some cases charters were granted for limited periods only. Thus, the first charter of the East India Company was for 15 years, and subsequently it was renewed only for definite periods.

It was held that statutory companies might be created for definite or indefinite periods, and this of course applied also to cases where the Crown issued a charter under an Act of Parliament. For chartered companies it was only the Act of 1837, 7 Will. IV and 1 Vic., c. 73, which made it clear that the Crown may grant a charter for a definite term of years. Under this Act a number of companies were created for definite periods. Furthermore, there were cases in which charters granted for definite periods were extended before their expiration or even renewed after it. It was held that the Crown has power to do this, but in order to relieve doubts an Act was passed in 1884 (47 & 48 Vic., c. 56), which declared that a charter limited for any term or number of years, or for any other period whatsoever, may be extended or renewed on the same conditions, i.e. unconditionally or conditionally, and this may be done by charter, warrant, or other writing under the sign-manual of the Sovereign. Consequently there are companies chartered for a longer or shorter term of years; e.g. the British Broadcasting Corporation, whose charter was issued in 1927 for ten years and has since then been renewed.

On the other hand it is not very usual in Britain to create registered companies for limited periods; most of them are created under their articles with an intention of perpetual succession, however short-lived they may be in consequence of their economic fortunes. Consequently the question whether the expiration of the time fixed by the articles is a reason for winding-up proceedings, and whether and how this may be averted, does not frequently arise in Great Britain, and sec. 278 of the Act of 1948 treats the expiration of the time limit as a case of voluntary winding-up.

The situation on the European Continent differs both in fact and in law.

In Germany it was usual to grant charters with definite time limits; thus railway companies without exception received charters for fixed periods, and these provided that after their expiration the track, with all buildings, rolling stock and appurtenances, was to revert to the State. The same practice was observed in the case of other public utilities, such as water, gas and electricity companies. Furthermore, it was usual even in the case of companies not directly affected by public interest, e.g. banks, industrial, mining or trading companies, to provide for a definite term of existence. Thus besides companies created for an indefinite time there were others formed for longer or shorter terms. Of this latter type there were some whose articles provided in advance for the possibility of future extensions. An extension was always to be effected by a resolution in general meeting. As to companies whose articles did not so provide, it was held that a resolution for extension of the term might be passed by the general meeting at any time before, but not after, its expiration.

There was dispute, however, about the requirements for such a resolution. Some authors held that it could be carried only by unanimous consent of the shareholders; others maintained that a majority sufficed. This latter view prevailed before the Courts.

It is remarkable that a view was advocated according to which a simple majority vote would be sufficient for the validity of such a resolution. This view was supported on the ground that the wording of the German Commercial Code made a distinction between extensions of time and alterations of the articles. On this basis it was assumed that the majority required for alterations of the articles, i.e. three-fourths of those voting at the meeting, is not necessary. From the coming into force of the law of 1884 the view became prevalent that for an extension of the fixed time limit the specific majority required for the alteration of the articles is necessary, and the revised Code of 1897 made this quite clear. But the rule that an extension must be resolved upon before the expiration of the term, and that in the absence of such a resolution winding-up of the company is compulsory, was maintained.

In the years following the First World War another view was accepted. At first the Courts recognised the validity of resolutions cancelling an earlier resolution of the general meeting on the liquidation of the company. In other words it became possible to resuscitate a company whose dissolution had been decided upon by an earlier meeting, and the entry of the dissolution in the Trade Register could then be cancelled. It is obvious that under these circumstances the former rule by which an extension of the time limit could be resolved upon only before the expiration of the term could not be maintained. Both the Courts and the literature accepted it as a settled rule that, so long as the assets of the company are not distributed, an extension by resolution in general meeting is possible.[1]

The law of 1937 (§ 203 (1)) maintained that the company is dissolved by the expiration of the time fixed in the articles. § 215, however, provides that an extension can be resolved upon by the general meeting until the distribution of the net assets among the shareholders has begun. At the same time it was made clear that such a resolution requires for its validity a majority of three-fourths of the capital represented at the general meeting. The articles may provide for a larger but not a smaller majority than required by the law.

United States laws show great variety; the statutes of several States even to-day limit the lifetime of corporations to a fixed number of years, and in earlier days such regulation was more frequent. When the corporation has been created under such a statutory rule, the extension of the term is possible only by an Act of the legislature. The shareholders, of course, have to apply for such extension, or at least to accept it, since neither the grant nor the extension of a charter is possible without the assent of the incorporators or, in the case of extension, of the corporation, i.e. the shareholders in general meeting. In States where there is no such statutory rule, a corporation may be created either for a definite or an indefinite term, and if for a definite

[1] Cf. Staub-Pinner, II pp. 783–4.

term, the expiration of this term leads automatically to dissolution. Most of the relevant Statutes, however, contain adequate provisions for an extension by resolution of the general meeting, and the filing of the alteration of the articles with the competent authority.

There is no difference in effect between an extension of the charter by legislative Act, and by steps taken by the shareholders; in both cases the corporation continues to exist, and it cannot be said that there is a new corporation; the old rights and obligations remain unaltered. Furthermore the revival of an already dissolved company is also recognised, except where the State's constitution forbids such a step. If such revival is possible by legislative Act or under a general statute, the revived corporation is not a new one; the same rule applies as with an extension of term. In some jurisdictions it is held that if a corporation carries on business after expiration of its term, it is a *de facto* corporation, and may sue and be sued as such; but this rule is not generally accepted. Whether the same rule should apply when the limit is fixed by statute is disputed.[1]

II. *Voluntary dissolution.*—Most legislations recognise that a company may be dissolved by voluntary resolution. For the validity of such a resolution a specific majority is generally required. Thus the British Companies Act of 1948 provides that a company may be wound up by special resolution either voluntarily (sec. 278) or by the Court if so resolved (sec. 222 (*a*)). The same is the position under the Continental legislations.[2]

The American Common Law rule [3] is that a voluntary dissolution is possible only with the assent of the State or other competent public authority. This doctrine is based on the contractual nature of the charter. But it is recognised that general corporation law may authorise the voluntary dissolution resolved upon by shareholders.[4] Actually most of the statutes contain such an authorisation. Generally the authorisation is absolute: it is left to the free resolution of the shareholders to dissolve the corporation by a vote in general meeting. Some statutes require a specific majority; e.g. the National Bank Act [5] provides for a two-thirds majority of the capital. Certain statutes, in requiring

[1] Cf. Ballantine, 307.
[2] See, e.g. German law of 1937, § 203; Swiss O.R. 736.
[3] Cf. Ballantine, 302–3.
[4] See Mumma *v.* Potomac Company (1834), 8 Pet. U.S. 281.
[5] 12 U.S.C.A. 181.

such a qualified majority, make an exception for the case of insolvency, when they are satisfied with a simple majority.

In so far as the dissolution is authorised by a resolution in general meeting, it is left to the discretion of the majority whether they think fit to dissolve the corporation. It might be injurious to the minority if a prosperous corporation were dissolved and the shareholders thus deprived of the profits and advantages arising from the continuance of the business. Nevertheless, if a resolution to dissolve is carried by the required majority, the minority cannot attack it, unless they prove fraud. Such fraud is deemed to have occurred if in the course of the winding-up the assets of the corporation are acquired by the majority. In fact it would be very dangerous to burden the Court with the task of examining whether the dissolution is necessary, convenient and advantageous for the shareholders or not.

Some American statutes authorise the directors to decide upon the question of dissolution, and in such a case they usually provide for a quorum. All that has been said as to the requirements of a resolution in the general meeting and the possibility of attack on the part of dissenting shareholders applies of course to the resolutions of the board of directors.

In some cases, especially for public service corporations, the assent of some public authority is called for, even where corporations in general have power to resolve upon a voluntary dissolution. In respect of companies of this class a resolution to dissolve the corporation voluntarily, and to surrender its charter and special franchises, may be regarded as contrary to the obligations incurred at its creation. Thus a railway company obliges itself, in connection with the charter granted for its specific line, that it will begin and continue the service either without a time limit or for a specific period; similarly an electricity company is obliged to furnish light and power during the period of its franchise. In such a case it may be asserted that the company has no right to evade this obligation by voluntary dissolution. The correct solution in our opinion seems to be that the resolution to dissolve the corporation would be valid but would not affect the obligation incurred, and consequently the State or some other public body will be entitled to sue for specific performance or for damages, as the case may be. Apart from such cases the corporation is generally under no obligation to continue its corporate existence, in so far of course as voluntary dissolution is admitted at all. It may be remembered that the German economist Rathenau asserted that in so far as a corporation has obligations towards the public and has some position of substance in the economic field, its existence is a matter of public interest, and the shareholders cannot be allowed to decide freely upon the continuance or discontinuance of the corporate existence and business.

III. *Involuntary dissolution; Compulsory winding-up.*—Under the British Act of 1948 (sec. 222) a company may be wound up by the Court in any of the following cases: (*a*) if the company by special resolution resolves that it should be wound up by the Court; (*b*) if default is made in delivering the statutory report to the registrar or in holding the statutory meeting; (*c*) if the company does not commence its business within a year or suspends its business for a whole year; (*d*) if the number of members is reduced below seven, or in the case of a private company below two; (*e*) if the company is unable to pay its debts; (*f*) if the Court is of the opinion that it is just and equitable that the company should be wound up. It is to be noted that when a company cannot continue its business by reason of its liabilities and finds it advisable to wind up, it is open to it to resolve upon a voluntary dissolution under sec. 278 (*c*).

The Court orders the winding-up on petition. Those entitled to make such a petition are: the company itself, though there is not much reason for it to do so, since it can at any time carry a resolution for voluntary winding-up; a shareholder or former shareholder, in so far as he is still liable for contribution; or a creditor, including a contingent or prospective creditor (sec. 224). Lastly, a petition for winding-up may be presented by the Board of Trade if in the course of an inspection grave irregularities appear (sec. 224 (*d*)). The Court decides at its discretion; it may reject the petition or defer its decision. In certain instances this is expressly provided for; thus, if the petition is based on default in delivering the statutory report, the Court may direct that the report shall be delivered, and where the default is in holding the statutory meeting, that the meeting be held (sec. 215 (3)).

The winding-up on petition of creditors is a special institution of English law. It is necessary, since a company under English law cannot be declared bankrupt (Bankruptcy Act, 1914, sec. 126), nor is the Deeds of Arrangement Act, 1914, applicable.[1]

[1] *Re* Rileys Ltd. (1903), 2 Ch. 590.

The circumstances which give rise to the presumption that a company is unable to pay its debts are defined (sec. 223) and it was held: "It is not a discretionary matter with the Court when a debt is established and not satisfied to say whether the company shall be wound up or not";[1] but if a debt is *bona-fide* disputed by the company, the petition will be dismissed.[2] Furthermore, the Court may have regard to the wishes of creditors and contributories, may direct meetings to be held, and in considering the result of the meeting shall have regard to the amount of debts and the number of votes of contributories respectively (sec. 346). The Court may dismiss the petition, though the debt remains unpaid, if it finds this equitable, or may direct the petition to stand over if that is found to give better prospects of payment.[3]

The Court has power to restrain proceedings by creditors after the petition was presented (sec. 226), and if an order for winding-up is made or a provisional liquidator appointed, all proceedings are stayed and cannot be proceeded with unless the Court grants leave (secs. 228 and 231). Even in case of a voluntary liquidation executions and other proceedings can be restrained by the Court on application under sec. 307.

The "just and equitable" clause, as now understood and applied by the Courts, covers a wide field, and is not restricted to cases *ejusdem generis* with the categories mentioned in sec. 168 (1)–(5) of the 1929 Act, now contained in sec. 222 (*a*)–(*e*) of the Act of 1948. Winding-up was ordered where the company was a bubble,[4] where the scheme of the company and its management was fraudulent,[5] where full investigation was necessary[6] and where the substratum was gone.[7] Under this clause companies may also be wound up in case of complete deadlock,[8] for the reason that one of the principal shareholders, having the majority of the voting power, refused to produce accounts or balance sheets, or to pay dividends,[9] and where the petitioner was excluded

[1] *Per* Lord Cranworth in Bowes *v.* Hope, etc., Insurance Co. (1865), 11 H.L. Cases 389.

[2] London and Paris Banking Corporation (1875), L.R. 19 Eq. 444; *In re* A. Co. (1894), 2 Ch. 349.

[3] London and Paris Banking Corporation, *supra.*

[4] London and County Coal Co. (1866), L.R. 3 Eq. 355.

[5] T. E. Brinsmead and Sons (1897), 1 Ch. 45, and on appeal (1897), 1 Ch. 406.

[6] Peruvian Amazon Co. (1913), 29 T.L.R. 384.

[7] *Re* Blériot Aircraft Co. (1916), 32 T.L.R. 253.

[8] Yenidje Tobacco Co. (1916), 2 Ch. 426.

[9] Loch *v.* John Blackwood Ltd. (1924), A.C. 783.

from all participation in the business,[1] but even in such a case the Court has discretion.

In cases of oppression the petition to wind up the company may be a very poor remedy, since it may happen, and in some cases has happened, that the oppressed minority suffers considerable losses in consequence of the liquidation, whereas the oppressing majority comes into a position to acquire the assets of the company, possibly at a low purchase price, and in this way is able to appropriate the business with its future chances on favourable conditions.

On the recommendation of the Cohen Committee the Companies Act, 1947, adopted an amendment by which the Court is empowered, where it finds that a winding-up would unfairly prejudice the minority, including the petitioner, to make, instead of the liquidation, such order as to bring to an end the position complained of. Such order may be made for the regulation of the conduct of affairs in future, or for the purchase of the shares of the petitioner by other members, or for the purchase of his shares by the company and a corresponding reduction of the share capital. The power of the Court, however, is not restricted; an order can be made in any other direction at its discretion. If the order involves an alteration of the memorandum or articles, or an addition thereto, these shall operate with the same effect as if they were duly made by a resolution of the company, and the company may not make any alterations or additions which would be inconsistent with those ordered, without leave of the Court (sec. 9 (1), (2), (3) (now sec. 210 of the Act of 1948)). These powers seem adapted to meet every contingency, and a wise administration will bring full relief to any oppressed minority showing their case.

Under the law of the United States compulsory winding-up [2] is dealt with mainly under the heading of forfeiture of the charter. This is entirely different from the case in which a corporation has not been legally created. If the incorporators have not complied with the legal requirements for creation and the corporation is labouring under a defect, e.g. a condition precedent is absent, the State has power to institute proceedings against the corporation mainly by an action *quo warranto*. Until such step is taken, the corporation, as we have seen, has a *de facto* existence,

[1] Thomson *v.* Drysdale (1925), S.C. 311; *re* Davis and Collett Ltd. (1935), Ch. 693.
[2] Cf. Ballantine, 304–10.

provided an attempt has been made to comply with the requirements, and according to the general view a collateral attack is not admitted. In such proceedings, however, the Court has only to enquire whether the creation is in accordance with the law, and if some substantial defect is found, judgment is to be given to the effect that the corporation has no right to exist as such. For a dissolution there must be a corporation which has been legally created, otherwise there would be no case for dissolution.

A case for forfeiture may arise for non-use or misuse of the charter. Story in Terrett *v.* Taylor [1] said: "A private corporation created by the legislature may lose its franchises by a misuser or a non-user of them." This view is constantly upheld by the Courts.[2]

It is an interesting feature of American decisions that the State may base its action upon the illegality of the purpose of the corporation. The fact that the State has granted a charter does not prevent the State from suing to annul the same if the corporation has been created for an unlawful purpose.[3] It would be more consistent to hold that a creation for an unlawful purpose could be attacked by an action *quo warranto*, whereas a dissolution or forfeiture of the charter would lie if a corporation created for a lawful purpose were subsequently to take up some unlawful purpose.

A further basis for forfeiture proceedings is abuse of its charter by the corporation. This occurs if the corporation engages in some purpose which is either unlawful or, although lawful, is not within its power. Lastly the corporation may be dissolved for non-user. In all these cases it is necessary that a clear case of intentional act or omission should be present, which is in some way injurious to the public. On the whole the Courts are averse to declare forfeitures or destroy corporations without abundant reason.[4] Generally a constant and continuous abuse or absence of use of the charter is required. It has been said that such vitiation of the organic law from which the corporation derives its existence and powers, or such non-user of the franchise, should be present as results in a substantial failure to fulfil the design and purpose of the corporation's organisation.[5] The National Bank Act provides that if the directors knowingly violate, or knowingly

[1] (1815), 9 Cranch U.S. 43.
[2] Fletcher 8034, n. 29.
[3] See New Orleans Debenture Redemption Co. *v.* Louisiana (1900), 180 U.S. 320.
[4] Fletcher 8035, n. 37.
[5] Fletcher 8045.

permit any of the officers or servants of the bank to violate any of the provisions of the Act, it will be ground for forfeiture.[1]

Illegality or fraud in the organisation, purpose or conduct of the corporation is a ground for forfeiture. The same is true for breach of conditions subsequent, prescribed by the general statute or by the charter. Such are failure to subscribe or to pay in the prescribed amount of capital, failure to file reports, to pay the franchise tax, to appoint agents on whom process may be served, to maintain general offices within the State. If a corporation, in consequence of death or removal, has no officers, the corporation will be dissolved only if in spite of notice it fails to elect new ones. The same is held in case of failure to hold meetings.[2]

Acts or omissions which, though contrary to law, do not injure the public interest, are no cause for forfeiture. This is held especially with regard to *ultra vires* acts, if they are not injurious from the standpoint of public interest.[3] It is generally held that deadlock in the conduct of affairs is no ground for dissolution, although there are decisions to the contrary. It would, however, be important to give an action for dissolution in such cases if, e.g. there are two equally strong groups of shareholders who do not agree as to the conduct of affairs and therefore no valid resolutions can be carried. It is conceivable that in such a case public interest may not be involved, but on the whole it is injurious to prolong such deadlocks.

It is generally recognised that if fraud and mismanagement occurs in the course of the business, it gives the State the right to declare the charter forfeit. With regard to the right of shareholders to request dissolution for fraud or mismanagement there is considerable controversy. It is recognised that a corporation, if it has failed in respect of the purposes and objects of its creation, or conditions have arisen which render it impossible for it to continue its business and perform the conditions upon which the charter was granted, may be dissolved.[4] Cessation of business is not a sufficient ground for dissolution, unless it has continued for a considerable time. Statutes of some States provide for a fixed period of one or two years. So in Illinois insurance companies are subject to forfeiture for failure to transact

[1] 12 U.S.C.A. 92; see Selma *v.* Colby (1874), 21 Wal. 609.
[2] Cf. Fletcher 7994, 6, 7.
[3] Fletcher 8056.
[4] See Chicago Life Insurance Company *v.* Needles (1885), 113 U.S. 574.

business for one year.[1] The alienation or lease of all the corporate property, at least where it is made for a long period and renders the corporation unable to carry on its business, may lead to forfeiture.[2]

The State exercises its right of action through the proper representative, usually the Attorney-General.

The right of shareholders to enforce dissolution, as already mentioned, is not generally admitted. There are, however, decisions recognising the right of action at least where the purpose of the corporation is impossible of attainment, or in case of breach of trust. Some statutes give the action to minority shareholders, and such statutes are constitutional. An equitable remedy for shareholders without statutory authorisation is not recognised. Therefore, as a rule, shareholders in the U.S.A. have no action either at law or in equity, unless the statute provides otherwise.

Creditors have no means of securing dissolution or forfeiture.[3] The position of third parties is similar. This is rightly so, since creditors can assert their rights by action on debt, obtain judgment and satisfaction by execution, and ultimately by obtaining a decree of bankruptcy or a creditors' liquidation under legislations which make use of this device instead of bankruptcy proceedings in the case of corporations.

The cause of forfeiture may be waived by the State, especially by subsequent legislative act, but also by implication.[4]

The action is to be instituted against the corporation and not against the shareholders. Shareholders, however, may intervene in an action brought by the State, and similarly the State may intervene in those brought by minority shareholders.

The total loss of the corporate property or its alienation, and finally discontinuance of business for a considerable time, may lead to a state of things in which the corporation is to be held to have been terminated. Generally in such cases it is not to be regarded as having been terminated without opportunity having been given to creditors and shareholders to assert their rights. If, however, a corporation has done no business at all for a considerable time, and no assets and liabilities appear to exist, corporation laws generally provide for a short and simple way of ascertaining the absence of corporate existence and of striking

[1] See Ewen *v.* American Fidelity Corporation (1923), 261 U.S. 322.

[2] Fletcher 8072–3.

[3] Fletcher 8078, n. 91.

[4] See Davis *v.* Gray (1872), 16 Wal. 203; Fletcher 8084–5.

off the corporation from the register or other official record, as provided by the law of the State in which the corporation was created. In such cases the general requirement is to be observed that the striking off may not be effected without due notice to creditors and shareholders.

Under Continental legislations the declaration of bankruptcy involves dissolution.[1] On the other hand, in case of a voluntary winding-up creditors are not prevented from proceeding against the company. They may sue, obtain judgment, and enforce it by execution; they may also present petitions to the Court for a declaration of bankruptcy, regardless of the winding-up proceedings.

In Germany, until the law of 1937, the prevailing opinion was that companies cannot be dissolved for misfeasance, except in Prussia, where the law introducing the Commercial Code of 1861 gave such power to the administration, subject to appeal to the Administrative Tribunal. The law of 1937 (§ 288) provides that the Government may bring an action for dissolution if the company endangers the common weal, particularly by the conduct of its officers grossly violating the law or the principles of responsible management of affairs. The Economic Tribunal of the Reich is the competent authority for the proceedings. This tribunal may decide in what manner the affairs of the company may be wound up, and the provisions of the Companies law apply only in so far as the Tribunal has not provided otherwise (§ 288). There is no compensation for loss of corporate existence (§ 291). The implications of the provisions are obvious; we have, however, no information whether and how they were actually applied.

Under Swiss law companies are to be dissolved if the number of members falls below the legal minimum (625, see § 33), and where the provisions of the O.R. as to the nationality of the directors have been violated (711, 4).

IV. *Effect of dissolution*.—The effect of any of the causes of dissolution, apart from the case of bankruptcy, is the winding-up of the company's affairs; corporate existence comes to an end only when the liquidation is completed, the assets are sold, the debts paid and the residue distributed.

The procedure of winding-up is everywhere regulated by legislation. Great Britain has a highly detailed regulation;

[1] German law of 1937, § 203 (1); Swiss O.R. 736, 3.

155 sections of the Act of 1948 dealt with winding-up proceedings, and besides these there are winding-up rules divided into 230 sections. This is to some extent due to the evolution of different procedures for cases of voluntary winding-up on the one hand, and for winding-up by the Court on the other. Furthermore, it is possible to wind up the affairs of a company under the supervision of the Court. The regulations of other legislations in this matter are less elaborate.

Winding-up is in its details a highly technical matter, best discussed in connection with insolvency and bankruptcy proceedings, which are beyond the scope of this work. The aim of these regulations is to secure the liquidation of the company's assets with the best possible results, the equal treatment of creditors by respecting the existing lawfully acquired priorities, mortgages and charges, and a speedy distribution of the net residue among the members. The numerous complaints, however, show that this aim has so far been attained only to a very limited extent.

96. Government Control [1]

Before general corporation laws were passed, corporations were generally held to be under the control of the government which granted them their charter. This supervision was exercised chiefly in order to ascertain whether the conditions laid down in the charter were complied with.

In England, as we have seen already, the Crown could proceed by the writs of *scire facias* and *quo warranto* through the law officers; the necessary consequence was forfeiture of the charter. Members could file an information, on the basis of which the Attorney-General could proceed. Whether the Crown could sue in equity on an information filed by a member in case of the violation of the members' rights is doubtful.

The same was the position in the U.S.A. In Attorney-General *v.* Utica,[2] Ch. Kent held that there is no equitable remedy to prevent an assurance company from engaging in banking business.

With the introduction of general corporation laws the right of the government to supervise the activity of business corporations was maintained only in so far as the legislation reserved

[1] Cf. Roscoe Pound, H.L.R. 49, pp. 369–95.
[2] (1811), 2 Johns Ch. N.Y. 371.

such powers, and these were restricted mainly to the duties imposed upon companies in respect of publicity, registration of charges, presentation of accounts and holding of meetings.

In certain European countries it was customary to appoint Civil Servants as commissioners for the purpose of supervision, and this procedure was maintained for companies already existing, even after it had been abandoned in respect of newly created companies. Generally, however, companies manage their affairs without governmental interference or supervision, and it was up to the shareholders to exercise their rights within the limits of the law. In America this is forcefully expressed in the doctrine of the contractual nature of the charter, which is protected by the contract clause of the Constitution.[1] It is otherwise in the case of companies which operate services of public interest, such as railways, public utilities and so on. This was never doubted outside the U.S.A., and there it was recognised that incorporation does not preclude the legislature from a proper exercise of its police power.[2]

Corporations affected by public interest are subject to more extensive regulation than others;[3] but even in their case governmental power is limited.[4] Furthermore, legislative enactments are subject to judicial review as to their constitutionality.

There are many decisions of the Supreme Court reviewing the validity of Acts of Congress and State laws from this standpoint, and they are of the highest interest. Unfortunately it is not possible to go into details, and we must restrict ourselves to the statement that the general trend of the judicature is in favour of the extension of the limits of the regulative power.

Until the New Deal legislation the police power was mainly exercised in respect of railroads, public utilities, banks, the business of common carriers, grain elevators and warehouses, corporations engaged in inter-State commerce, and many others. The New Deal legislation considerably extended the sphere of governmental supervision, laying down extensive regulations in respect of securities distributed by inter-State mail and establishing the Securities and Exchange Commission with wide adminis-

[1] But Pound, p.c., maintains that the State has still visitatorial jurisdiction.

[2] Boston Beer Company *v.* Commonwealth of Mass. (1877), 97 U.S. 25; Chicago Life Insurance Company *v.* Needles (1885), 113 U.S. 574.

[3] Wolf *v.* Court of Industrial Relations (1923), 262 U.S. 522.

[4] Louisville and N.R.R. Co. *v.* Kentucky (1896), 161 U.S. 677; Cargill *v.* Minnesota (1900), 180 U.S. 452; Cram *v.* Chicago, etc., R.R. Co. (1913), 228 U.S. 70.

trative powers. Public utility holding and investment companies were subject to special regulations likewise to be administered by the S.E.C. As already stated, the impact of these enactments is more in administration than in the rules laid down in the respective Acts.

The Companies Acts of 1947 and 1948 give extensive new powers, and at the same time transfer certain already existing powers from the Courts to the Board of Trade.

In the course of the hearings of the Cohen Committee two suggestions were put forward by Mr. Hargreaves Parkinson, then Editor of the *Financial News*, both very interesting and ingenious. The first was that the Board of Trade should be allotted one share in every public company, or where several classes of shares are issued, one share of each class, which, as public shares, should give the same rights as any other share in the company or class respectively. A Public Shareholder's office should be created under the Crown for the exercise of the rights derived from the shares vested in the office. The Public Shareholder should institute civil actions whenever it should appear that public interest or the better protection of shareholders required it, for misfeasance, fraud, negligence, etc., against promoters, directors, officers, managers, auditors, etc. The Board of Trade should receive any notices and documents which are to be circularised among the members, and this material would enable the Board to approach the company in a proper case in its capacity of shareholder and to take any necessary steps; all the material should be open to inspection at the registrar's office. Every shareholder should have the right to approach the Public Shareholder to suggest a *prima facie* case for his intervention and to lay before him all relevant documents. Where criminal questions arose, the Public Shareholder should be the normal channel of communication with the Director of Public Prosecutions. Lastly, the costs of all civil actions should be met by the Crown.

The other suggestion was that a statutory body should be created, the Shareholders' Standing Advisory Committee, chosen by the Board of Trade to review continuously all matters relating to limited companies, to review the Companies Act in practice, to give advice to shareholders who ask for it before giving their vote, to give the Committee's views to the Stock Exchange on matters of granting, withholding or maintaining facilities for dealing, and to take action when necessary with the concurrence of the departments concerned.[1] Neither of these suggestions was accepted by the Committee, which doubted the wisdom of delegating the initial responsibility for legislation in major matters. Instead the Committee expressed the opinion that a committee, not being a statutory body, would be useful to advise the Board of Trade in matters arising in the administration of the Companies Act.

While we agree with this view, we think that in the aforementioned suggestion there is a sound observation, that the obtaining of more information on company matters would be of public interest, and that therefore it would be advisable to provide that all communications sent to shareholders should be forwarded to the Board of Trade, where this material should be collected and made the subject of scrutiny and study. Such systematic work, combined with more adequate statistics, would enable the Government to obtain a more intimate knowledge of corporate affairs, and if the results of the scrutiny were published from time to time, they would give public opinion the guidance which at present it undoubtedly lacks.

The Government, following the recommendation of the Committee, set up two advisory committees, one of which is to be devoted to accounting.

[1] Memorandum in Minutes of Evidence, pp. 166–71.

CONCLUSIONS

It is assumed that the contents of this book give ample evidence of the role of business corporations as a powerful instrument of economic progress.

By the formation of business corporations able to collect funds from wide circles of the public for definite purposes and independent of the life and economic fate of their members, it became possible to initiate and carry on enterprises surpassing the resources of even the wealthiest individual. Furthermore the idea of regarding and treating corporations as living entities and the development of adequate methods of accounting ensured efficiency in management and results in production and distribution on a scale previously unimagined.

The evolution of giant corporations has a tremendous impact upon the concentration of economic power and the distribution of income. In some circumstances corporations may even exercise undue influence on the political life of the community.

Wholesale nationalisation would eliminate business corporations and supplant them by administrative agencies or publicly owned corporations. Whether such a change would be for the better or the worse is extremely doubtful, since we cannot be certain how far efficiency could be secured on the one hand, and bureaucracy and political interference avoided on the other. An important factor in this respect is the cost of the nationalised sector. No country is able in the long run to afford the luxury of nationalisation for its own sake without impairing the standard of living of the community, if the running of the nationalised industries involves a higher expenditure than is necessary, or that exceeds the cost under private enterprise. Careful accounting and full publicity as to both costs and business policy are therefore of the highest value and importance.

We assume further that in spite of the huge wave of nationalisation since 1945 a large field will still remain for private and consequently for corporate enterprise. Thus the problem how adequate safeguards can be provided against possible abuses of the corporate device and the dangers connected therewith will still remain to be solved.

It seems to us that attention has been focussed rather on the position of corporations *vis-à-vis* the community than on the relationship of corporations to their members, and that the implications of the latter have sometimes been somewhat neglected. Therefore our suggestións for legislative reforms, made on the basis of an examination of the framework of corporation law, are equally directed towards better protection for the rights of members and minorities.

We do not claim that legislative measures are a panacea for all evils, but we expect much from the combined effect of law and public opinion in the improvement of the management of corporations and the attainment of higher standards. This, however, is mainly dependent upon fuller publicity in corporate affairs, which in its turn requires effective legislation for its enforcement.

MAIN SOURCES OF PART II

COMPARATIVE LAW

Hallstein, Walther: *Die Actienrechte der Gegenwart* (Berlin, 1931).

Kuhn, Arthur A.: *A Comparative Study of the Law of Corporations* (New York, 1914).

Lehmann, Karl: *Das Recht der Aktiengesellschaften*, vol. I (1898); vol. II (1904).

Wieland, Karl: *Die Kapitalgesellschaften, Handelsrecht*, vol. II (München and Leipzig, 1931).

GREAT BRITAIN

Buckley [Lord Wrenbury]: *The Law and Practice under the Companies Acts*, 11th ed., by W. G. Brown, R. J. T. Gibson and D. B. Buckley (London, 1930).

Gore-Brown: *Joint Stock Companies*, 40th ed. (London, 1946).

Palmer: *Company Law*, 17th ed., by A. Topham (London, 1942).

Palmer: *Company Precedents*, 15th ed., by A. E. and A. M. R. Topham (London, 1937–8).

Stiebel, A.: *Company Law*, 3rd ed. (London, 1929).

Law Quarterly Review.

Cambridge Law Review.

Modern Law Review.

ON THE COMPANIES ACT OF 1947

Magnus, S. W., and Esterin: Butterworth's *Annotated Legislation Service* (1947).

Palmer, *Company Law*, 18th ed., 1948.

ON THE COMPANIES ACT OF 1948

Buckley, 12th ed. by Hon. D. B. Buckley, assisted by N. Warren and J. Brian Parker, consulting ed. Cecil W. Turner, 1949.

Palmer, 19th ed. by F. A. Topham, 1949.

U.S.A.

Fletcher: *Cyclopaedia*, 1932 ed. with Appendices.

Ballantine, H. W.: *On Corporations*, revised ed. (Chicago, 1946). (The first ed., 1927, is still to be consulted in some matters.)

Berle, A. A., Jr., and Magill, B.: *Cases and Materials in the Law of Corporation Finance* (St. Paul, Minn., 1942).

Dodd, E. M., Jr., and Baker, R. J.: *Cases in Business Associations*, vol. I (Chicago, 1940).

Richards, H. S.: *Cases on the Law of Private Corporations* (St. Paul, 1940).

Corpus Juris, vol. 14 (New York and London, 1919).

Columbia Law Review.

Harvard Law Review.

Yale Law Journal.

FRANCE

Houpin et Bosvien: *Traité Général, Théorique et Pratique des Sociétés Civiles et Commerciales*, vols. I–III (Paris, 1921); *Annales de Droit Commercial* (1900–38).

Pic, P.: *Des Sociétés Commerciales*, vols. I–III (Paris, 1925), vol. I, 3rd ed. (Paris, 1948).

Rousseau, A.: *Sociétés Commerciales*, vols. I–II, 5th ed. (Paris, 1921).

GERMANY

Lehmann, Karl: *Das Recht der Aktiengesellschaften*, vol. I (1898), vol. II (1904).

Düringer-Hachenburg: *Das Handelsgesetzbuch vom* 10. *Mai* 1897, vol. III, 1 and 3, by Hachenburg and others (Mannheim, 1934–5).

Fischer, R.: *Die Aktiengesellschaft* (Ehrenberg: *Handbuch des Gesammten Handelsrechtes*, vol. III, 1) (Leipzig, 1916).

Staub-Pinner: *Staub's Kommentar zum Handelsgesetzbuch*, 14th ed., vol. II (Berlin and Leipzig, 1933).

Wieland, Karl: *Die Kapitalgesellschaften Handelsrecht*, vol. II (München and Leipzig, 1931).

Gadow, W., and others: *Aktiengesetz Kommentar* (Berlin, 1939).

Zeitschrift für das Gesammte Handelsrecht (Stuttgart, 1858–1939).

Entscheidungen des Reichsgerichtes in Zivilsachen (1880–1939).

APPENDIX

To § 22. Legislation of the U.S.A.

In August 1949 a Bill was introduced in the Senate of the U.S.A. by Senator Frear for the amendment of the Securities Exchange Act of 1934. The Bill envisages the extension of the competence of the Securities and Exchange Commission (S.E.C.) to all business corporations with assets of at least $3,000,000, issuing securities regularly traded in by use of mails or any other means or instrumentality of inter-State commerce, even if the securities are not traded in on any of the National Stock Exchanges. Corporations the securities of which are held by less than 300 members shall be exempted, as well as banks as issuers of securities. Furthermore, S.E.C. shall be empowered to grant exemption particularly to corporations the securities of which are held within a single State. The extension of the competence of S.E.C. means that the corporations to which the extension of powers applies are bound to file with the Commission a registration statement containing all the information prescribed by the Act of 1934, and to furnish subsequently the same information and periodical reports which are required from the corporations subject to the control of S.E.C. Should this Bill be adopted by Congress, a burden will be imposed upon the Commission with which it could hardly cope even with a considerably increased staff.

To § 26. Evolution of Corporate Enterprise in Great Britain since 1939

The publication of the General Annual Reports on Companies by the Board of Trade was resumed in November 1947 by the issue of a report for the seven years 1939–45. Since then the reports for 1946 and 1947 have been published.

The particulars of the new registrations are[1]:

Year	*Total Number of New Registrations*	*Companies without Share Capital*	*Public Companies*		*Private Companies*		*Number of Registrations*	*Capital in £*
			No.	*Capital*	*No.*	*Capital*		
				£		£		
1939	11,091	120	82	11,980,648	10,889	46,772,370	10,971	58,753,018
1940	6,422	92	58	4,283,961	6272	23,427,779	6,330	27,711,740
1941	7,298	82	26	2,067,995	7,190	22,957,434	7,216	25,025,429
1942	6,787	103	27	2,081,600	6,657	23,302,959	6,684	23,384,559
1943	6,940	126	19	183,250	6,795	24,249,853	6,814	24,433,103
1944	7,946	110	27	5,106,666	7,809	30,106,814	7,836	35,213,480
1945	10,948	137	38	27,550,812	10,773	62,683,275	10,811	90,234,087
1946	25,217	200	73	14,706,005	24,944	119,194,326	25,017	133,900,331
1947	21,753	168	72	54,876,000	21,573	169,828,000	215,857	224,704,000

[1] The figures for 1947 include increases made during the year amounting to £29,004,000.

On the other hand the number of companies dissolved or struck off the Register was as follows:

Year	1939	1940	1941	1942	1943	1944	1945	1946	1947
No.	9187	4102	2511	4256	3456	2266	2090	2205	2722

The number of companies on the Register, excluding companies in course of liquidation or removal from the Register, and their paid-up capital (including the amounts paid up otherwise than in cash) was on 31 December in the ten years 1938–47 [1]:

Year	*Number of Companies*	*Paid-up Capital in Million £*	*Public Companies*		*Private Companies*	
			Number	*Capital in Million £*	*Number*	*Capital in Million £*
1938	157,576	5,991	14,355	4,097	143,221	1,894
1939	160,655	6,040	13,920	4,117	146,735	1,923
1940	163,556	6,074	13,742	4,113	149,814	1,961
1941	168,566	6,053	13,571	4,105	154,995	1,948
1942	173,249	6,043	13,433	4,088	159,816	1,955
1943	176,656	6,024	13,395	4,078	163,261	1,946
1944	182,508	5,987	13,303	4,052	169,205	1,935
1945	191,729	5,973	13,171	4,044	178,558	1,929
1946	213,915	6,001	13,172	4,078	200,743	1,923
1947	231,651	6,081	13,168	4,110	218,483	1,971

During the whole of this period there was a constant increase in the number of companies, but from 1941 until the end of 1945 there was a decrease in the paid-up capital, which was made good by a considerable increase in 1946 and 1947, so that on 31 December 1947 the paid-up capital of the active companies in Great Britain amounted to £6,081 million, £7 million more than at the end of 1940.

The increase both in numbers and in paid-up capital occurred in the sector of private companies, their number having been increasing from 143,211 in 1938 and 149,814 in 1940 to 218,483, their paid-up capital from £1894 million in 1938 and £1961 million in 1940 to £1971 million at the end of 1947.

The number of public companies decreased from 14,355 in 1938 to 13,168 on 31 December 1947, their paid-up capital from £4117 million in 1939 to £4110 million in 1947, which was by £13 million more than in 1938, but by £3 million less than in 1939.

Thus the trend in favour of private companies continued in spite of the number of conversions from private to public companies:

[1] See Table IV, Report for 1947, p. 11.

Year	*Conversions from Public to Private Companies*	*Conversions from Private to Public Companies*
1938	92	63
1939	58	44
1940	36	14
1941	32	12
1942	26	13
1943	32	18
1944	27	22
1945	30	34
1946	41	187
1947	47	226

The number of new registrations in 1948 was 16,165, with an aggregate nominal capital of £115,704,000; in the eleven months from 1 January until 30 November of 1949, 13,008 with a nominal capital of £76,989,000, showing a considerable slowing down of new incorporations.[1]

To § 29. Publicly Owned Corporations

(a) the gas act of 1948

Following on the nationalisation of the Electricity industry by the Electricity Act, 1947, the Gas industry, that is, the production and distribution of gas, and of coke and other by-products obtained in the process of manufacturing gas, was nationalised by the Act 11 & 12 Geo. VI, c. 67 (the Gas Act, 1948).

For the acquisition of the existing gas undertakings, their maintenance and for the creation of new plants for the production and supply of gas, twelve Area Boards have been established, all of them being corporate bodies. In order to advise the Minister of Fuel and Power on questions of the Gas industry and further to promote and assist the efficient exercise and performance of the functions of the Area Boards the Act provides for the establishment of a Gas Council. The constitution of the Gas Boards and of the Gas Council is similar to that of the British Electricity Authority and the Area Electricity Boards.

The question of compensation also is settled on similar lines. Where undertakings owned by companies have been nationalised, compensation was made payable to the holders of their share securities. The basis of compensation is the average market price quoted on six fixed days of October 1947 or alternatively the average of the prices quoted on the middle day of the six months from February to July 1945, whichever is the higher.

[1] Board of Trade Journal No. 2764 of 10 December 1949, p. 1148.

The special circumstances of the Gas Industry were taken into consideration, in so far as sec. 26 of the Act provides machinery for the increase of compensation where the total sales of the gas company concerned were substantially lower in 1943, 1944 or 1945 than those in 1938, and this by reason of any war damage or of any transfer of population from any part of the company's area due to circumstances arising out of the war, provided that as a result thereof the quotations of the shares were on the relevant dates lower than they would have been otherwise.

In such cases, on representations made by the stockholders' representative of the company concerned, the Minister shall direct that an agreement be made with the stockholders' representative for a proportionate increase of the stock valuation. Should the Minister refuse to give such direction, or if, although he had in fact given the direction, no agreement could be reached as to the amount of the increase, the stockholders' representative may refer the matter to the Gas Arbitration Tribunal for decision. The constitution of this Tribunal and its procedure are regulated on the same lines as was done in respect of the Electricity Arbitration Tribunal by the Electricity Act, 1947.

No consideration was given to the general deterioration of the earning power of gas companies owing to wartime price restrictions.

The payment of compensation is to be effected in Gas Stock. The compensation of local authorities as owners of gas undertakings is made by the taking over of loans contracted for the purposes of those undertakings in the same way as was done in the case of electricity plants owned by local authorities. Moreover, "for the severance of gas undertakings from the other activities of the local authorities concerned, a sum of two million five hundred thousand pounds shall be paid to and divided among them" (secs. 28 and 29 of the Gas Act).

The holders of gas securities suffered further losses owing to the slump in gilt-edged securities in 1949. Under sec. 25 (1) of the Gas Act they are to receive "British Gas Stock of such amount as in the opinion of the Treasury is at the vesting date equal in value to the said securities held by them, regard being had (in valuating the value of the stock so issued) to the market value of government securities at or about the vesting date". Consequently, where the fixing of the compensation was delayed, the holders of securities received stock the market price of which was at the time of issue lower than its par value. It has been estimated[1] that out of a total of about £185 million the holders of £93 million nominal value received their Gas Stock at times when it had on the average a market

[1] Hansard (House of Commons) of 12 December 1949, pp. 2385–7.

value of about 90 per cent., whereas the compensation for holders of about £15 million gas securities is not yet settled. The motion for remedy was defeated in the House of Commons.

The vesting date for nationalisation was 1 May 1949, and so far no authentic information about its effects is available, apart from the fact that the standardisation of the charges for gas tended rather in the direction of increases.

(B) THE NATIONALISATION OF THE IRON AND STEEL INDUSTRY

Though strongly opposed at their initiation, the four Acts of Nationalisation are now, save in respect of long-distance road haulage, accepted as definitive measures by public opinion and by the Opposition Parties as well. The present task is to ensure their smooth working by objective and constructive criticism and to increase the efficiency of the administration of the four giant national enterprises.

Quite different is the position in the case of the Iron and Steel industry. There are signs justifying the assumption that the decision to nationalise this Industry was not made unanimously by the Government and the leadership of the Labour Party. There were weighty reasons for refraining from further nationalisation and concentrating on the improvement of the four industries already nationalised. Economic circles, on the other hand, saw no reason at all for nationalising an industry which had increased its production considerably, had not only reached but surpassed its target, and had retained and even improved its high standards, while nobody could complain of an oppressive private monopoly. Besides this economic argument the two Opposition Parties stressed that the electorate gave no mandate in 1945 for this important legislative measure.

It may be that these facts and arguments were not quite overlooked by the majority party, and caused some hesitation. On the other hand, it is possible that dogmatic Socialism and the belief that every act of Nationalisation tends to increase the influence and power of the Labour Party played a considerable role. Once the decision was taken, however, everything was done to secure the enactment and coming into force of nationalisation within the lifetime of the existing House of Commons and the majority elected in 1945. In order to ensure this it was proposed that the Bill should come into force on the day of its enactment and that the general date of transfer should be 1 May 1950.

In the meantime the Government introduced a Bill amending the Parliament Act of 1911 so as to secure that the two years' term for the enactment of Bills three times rejected by the House of Lords should be reduced to one year. Although it was denied that this step had anything to do with the Iron and Steel Industry Bill, the debates thereon in both Houses of Parliament were overshadowed by the Parliament Bill, and its careful and detailed examination in the House of Commons was largely prevented by the application of the closure machinery. In the House of Lords the majority adopted the line of not opposing the Iron and Steel Bill, although they held it to be superfluous and even dangerous, and wished to amend it and particularly to postpone its operation to a date after the General Election. Their amendments were rejected, and when the Bill came to the House of Lords for the second time, the Lords insisted merely on the amendments that (*a*) the Bill should come into force on 1 October 1950, (*b*) that the general date of transfer should be 1 July 1951.

At this stage the Government, whilst declining to fix a specific date for the coming into force of the Act, proposed that the members of the Iron and Steel Corporation of Great Britain should not be appointed before 1 October 1950 and that the general date of transfer should be 1 January 1951 or such later date as the Minister of Supply might fix.

Since the Opposition in the House of Commons and the majority of the House of Lords had achieved their main purpose, namely that "the Bill should not come into operation until the electors have had an opportunity of expressing their opinion upon it",[1] the Bill was not opposed further, and it became law on 24 November 1949 as the Iron and Steel Act, 1949 (12 & 13 Geo. VI, c. 72).

Thus the future of the nationalisation of the Iron and Steel Industry depends upon the result of the General Election of 1950: should the Labour Party retain their majority in the House of Commons, nationalisation will be carried through; should they be defeated, the repeal of the Act seems to be inevitable. It is therefore premature to analyse the Act's provisions in detail. Nevertheless, it is of interest to note that although the well-known pattern of the previous Nationalisation Acts is followed in many details, the approach to nationalisation is different.

The Iron and Steel Corporation of Great Britain is to be established for the acquisition and administration of the industrial units which are to be nationalised. It will be a body corporate and a public authority with all the attributes and capacities thereof. It will consist of a chairman and not less than six nor more than ten members. Both the chairman and the members will be appointed by the Minister of Supply, and the Minister may appoint from the members of the Corporation one or more deputy chairmen. The appointments shall be made from amongst persons appearing to the

[1] House of Lords' reason for insisting on their amendments, printed on 30 July 1949.

Minister to have acquired wide experience and shown capacity in the production of iron ore or steel, in industrial, commercial or financial matters, in administration or the organisation of workers (secs. 1 (1) and (2)).

The Lords proposed that at least three members should have experience and capacity in the production of iron and steel, and at least one have wide experience as a consumer of iron and steel for industrial purposes; this amendment was rejected by the Commons.

The nationalisation extends to any company engaged in the working, getting and smelting of iron ore, the production of steel and the shaping of steel by rolling, provided its output reaches or exceeds certain yearly minima set out in the Second Schedule to the Act. These are: in respect of working and getting of iron ore 50,000 tons, the smelting of iron ore in a blast furnace with or without other metalliferous materials 20,000 tons, and similarly 20,000 tons in respect of hot-rolling of steel in a rolling mill for changing its cross-sectional dimensions or cross-sectional shape. If a company is engaged in more than one of these processes, the aggregate of the output shall be the determining factor. Companies with an output under the minimum are free from nationalisation, but a minimum output of 5000 tons in any, or an aggregate output of 5000 tons in several, processes shall require a licence.

The Third Schedule to the Act contains a list of the companies which will be taken over. On the date of transfer, which is either the general date or such later date as is fixed by the Minister on the recommendation of the company concerned, after consultation with the Corporation, all securities of the company will become vested in the Corporation, so that the company retains its corporate existence and becomes a publicly owned company. These publicly owned companies are to remain registered companies under the Companies Act, and the Ninth Schedule to the Act provides for certain modifications in their constitution and proceedings. The dividends of the companies are to accrue to the Corporations.

The compensation of the owners of the securities acquired by the Corporation is to be made in British Iron and Steel Stock, which is to be guaranteed by the Treasury but whose interest is to be paid from the dividends of the publicly owned companies and the direct revenue of the Corporation. The provisions for the determination of the amount of compensation and the satisfaction of the claims are on lines similar to those in the other four Acts, although the relevant dates for the valuation of the quoted securities are, of course, not identical.

The Corporation shall exercise all the rights conferred by the holding of the securities of the publicly owned companies and co-ordinate their activities accordingly. The highest degree of decentralisation is specially stressed.

In relation to the consumers it is provided that it is the duty of the Corporation to promote the efficient and economic supply of iron and steel products at reasonable prices and to secure that no undue preference shall be shown to or undue differentiation be exercised against any consumer or any class of consumers.

In order to keep the Minister informed of matters affecting the interests of the consumers in general and in respect of representations of individual consumers, a body is to be established not later than six months after the general transfer, to be known as the Iron and Steel Consumers' Council. This Council shall consist of an independent chairman and not less than fifteen and not more than thirty members appointed by the Minister, and of two members of the Corporation nominated by the Corporation itself. The appointment of the members shall be made after consultation with such bodies selected by the Minister as he thinks fit to represent the interests of the consumers. Organisations representing workers may be included.

(C) THE WORKING OF THE NATIONALISED INDUSTRIES

Up to the end of 1949 the Reports of the National Coal Board for 1947 and 1948 and the Report of the British Transport Commission for 1948 have become available. The Reports of the National Coal Board are dated 30 June 1948 and 17 June 1949 respectively; the Report of the British Transport Commission is dated 19 August 1949. The interval between the end of the year and the publication of the Reports is fairly large, so that they had more or less lost their actuality when they became public.

From a technical point of view the Reports are of high standard and give a large volume of particulars in an attractive form. They give also a fair picture of the progress of the great industries concerned and of the immense work done by the two administrative bodies. No study of the two industries should neglect to consider these Reports. From the point of view of this book, however, we have to focus our attention on the aspects of organisation.

1. *The Coal Industry*

The first problem of the nationalised Coal Industry was to take over the collieries in such a way that continuity of production and distribution should be secured. For this purpose the National Coal Board was appointed in due time so that it was able to make the necessary preparations,[1] whereas the Divisional Coal Boards were all appointed by the end of 1946.

[1] See First Report of the National Coal Board.

The National Coal Board had beside the chairman eight (now 11) members, all of whom have to devote all their time to their office. Apart from the chairman and one member appointed to act as deputy chairman, all the members have departmental functions and responsibilities besides their activities in the formulation of the Board's policy. Three of the original members left the Board during 1947 and 1948. No change was made in its constitution until 1949.

Though by the end of 1946 all the eight Divisional Boards were established, most of them were unable to organise the Area Managements within their divisions and in most parts of the country the collieries had to carry on as before until the Area Organisation could take charge. In this transitory period the collieries worked as "Coal Board Units", administered by Controllers appointed by the Divisional Board, who were responsible to the Divisional Board or—where possible—to the Area General Manager. Special transitory arrangements were necessary in respect of collieries owned by composite concerns. All these difficulties were overcome, the new organisation was built up and neither production nor distribution was interrupted in these months of transition. Of the eight Divisional Boards seven have altogether 48 areas, but in the South-Eastern Division (East Kent) no separate Area Organisation has been created. Each area has a General Manager and each of the collieries, about 1000, a Manager.

At the date of nationalisation manpower in the coal-mining industry was depleted. By the beginning of 1947 there were 692,000 miners on the books of the collieries. Effective recruitment, enrolling 94,190 men, about 6000 of them Polish workers, resulted in a net increase of 26,165, and it was hoped that the substantial increase in wages and the improvement of working conditions would provide sufficient attraction for new entrants. In 1948, however, the net increase was only 7763, slightly less than the number of the newly recruited foreign workers, and in 1949 there was a considerable drop in numbers: on 26 November 1949 the number of workers was 708,900, a decrease of about 16,000 in comparison with the 726,300 men on the colliery books on 31 December 1948. It has been stated, however, that the decrease in the number of face workers was only about 1000.

On the other hand, much has been done for the technical development of the mines, particularly in respect of coalface machinery and the improvement of underground transport. These factors promoted production and productivity, and the output per manshift, which was 1·03 in 1946, rose to 1·07 in 1947 and to 1·11 in 1948, and the Minister of Fuel and Power is confident that it will reach at least 1·15 tons in 1949 and thus surpass the output of 1938 (1·14).[1]

The introduction of the five-day week considerably shortened the

[1] Hansard (House of Commons) of 10 November 1949.

average working time, although absenteeism, which fell from 15·95 per cent. in 1946 to 12·43 per cent. in 1947 and 11·58 per cent. in 1948, was still considerable. In the first 42 weeks of 1949 it was 12·5 per cent., in comparison with 11·5 per cent. in the corresponding part of 1948. According to the explanation given by the Minister in the House of Commons, voluntary absenteeism, distinguished from involuntary, which was 8·4 per cent., fell to 6·4 per cent. in 1947, and to 6 per cent. in 1948, and for the first 42 weeks in 1949 was reported at 5·5 per cent.[1] The output per man-year in 1948 was 271 tons, whereas it was 290 tons in 1938, and this difference cannot be fully explained by the lengthening of the distance from pithead to coal-face.

There were no official strikes, but in 1947 there were 1635 unofficial ones involving 303,452 miners, and in 1948 1528 affecting 190,915 men. The resulting loss in production in 1947 was 1,652,000 tons, and in 1948 1,062,300 tons, a considerable improvement.

Production in 1947 was hampered to a certain extent by the fuel crisis, but the difficulties were soon overcome and the output of coal in February and March was actually 1,100,000 tons more than in the corresponding months of 1948.

In 1947 the total production amounted to 197,000,000 tons, 187,000,000 from deep-mining and 10,000,000 tons from opencast sites. The total output rose in 1948 to 209,300,000 tons, that of deep-mined coal to 197,600,000 and from opencast sites to 11,700,000 tons. Provisional reports[2] show that in 1949 the total production reached 215,125,100 tons, of which 202,685,400 tons were deep-mined coal and 12,439,700 tons from opencast sites. This is in the neighbourhood of the lowest figures given in the forecasts of the Government's Economic Survey for the year. The rate of improvement in 1947 was roughly 3⅓ per cent., in 1948 5½ per cent., and for 1949 a rate of about 3 per cent. may be assumed.

The export of coal was resumed, and in 1947 coal exports totalled 5,394,699 tons, of which 1,056,033 tons were for foreign-bound bunkers. In 1948 exports amounted to 16,132,800 tons, of which 5,391,000 tons were for foreign-going vessels and trawlers and 1,016,800 tons for oversea bunker depots; the export to foreign countries rose from 4,338,656 tons to 9,725,000 tons. For 1949 an export of about 19,000,000 tons was estimated and 19,327,000 tons actually reached. The progress in exports is undoubtedly remarkable, though their total is still far from the 52,000,000 tons of 1937.

The rise in costs was substantial. In 1947 the yearly average of production costs was 41*s.* 3*d.* per ton, in 1948 45*s.* 7*d.*, and in the last quarter of the same year 45*s.* 11½*d.* The Report for 1948 spoke of a prospective fall for 1949, and the Report for 1949 will show whether

[1] Hansard, p. 1434.

[2] See *The Times*, 5 January 1950.

this forecast was substantiated. The rise in cost was due mainly to the introduction of the five-day week, the increase of wages of the lower-paid workers and other improvements. The Board have done magnificent work in improving living conditions and caring for the safety and health of workers. These improvements have naturally involved an increase of costs. The Report estimates that the improvements required in 1947 an increased expenditure of about £24,000,000 and will amount in a full year to £62,500,000.

These increases had to be met by a general increase in the price of coal, which in its turn was a heavy burden on industry. At present exports are giving a good yield, but it cannot be foreseen for how long, in view of the increase of German and Polish coal production. The importance of preventing further rises and the desirability of lowering the price is stressed by the Board. This, however, cannot be achieved without an increase in productivity and strict measures of economy.

The financial results in 1947 were poor. The losses of collieries amounted to £9,203,905, and after deduction of ancillary profits there remained an operating loss of £6,187,300. The Board had to bear the loss on the imports of German and Polish coal, so that with interest and the interim income due to the companies the total loss amounted to £23,255,587. In 1948 there was a colliery profit of £16,172,694, an improvement of about £25,000,000, whereas the ancillary profits declined to £1,342,262. After meeting the charges for interest and interim income, there was a net surplus of £1,657,965. For 1949 the prognosis is for a profit of about £10,000,000, and the hope was expressed that in 1950 the remainder of the deficit will be wiped out.

There have been complaints of over-centralisation in the administration. An object of criticism was the growth of the National Headquarters, due to the fact that the Board's activities were not sufficiently limited to the direction of policy. Further, it was asserted that the establishment of Divisional Boards between the National Headquarters and the Area Managements is superfluous and causes unnecessary delays. From these considerations it was proposed that the number of Areas should be increased, and that the Area Managements decentralised in this way should be directly responsible to the National Coal Board. The attitude of the Board, however, was negative and was upheld by the Government. Even a public inquiry was declined, and instead the Board appointed a Committee under the chairmanship of one of its members. The main proposals of this Committee on Organisation are included in the Report for 1948.[1] They refrain from fundamental alterations, and it is noteworthy that in spite of urgent requests in the Press and in Parliament the report of the Committee itself was not published.

[1] Pp. 233–6.

During 1949 the Coal Industry was twice the subject of legislative enactments. By the Coal Industry Act, 1949 (12 & 13 Geo. VI, c. 53), the maximum number of members of the National Coal Board was increased to eleven, whereby the appointment of part-time members became possible. Five part-time members were appointed by the Minister, among them a prominent industrialist and a distinguished merchant banker. There cannot be any doubt that the inclusion of part-time members who are active in business will be valuable and will improve the relations of the Board with industry and commerce. The Act provides *inter alia* that the National Coal Board may extend its activities to foreign countries, but they may not carry out any activities outside Great Britain without an Order of the Minister conferring authority for this purpose, and such authority is to be given by statutory instrument which shall be laid subsequently before Parliament. Among the other provisions of the Act it is noteworthy that the restrictions imposed by sec. 23 of the Act of 1946 on the disposal of the Government Stock issued as compensation have been lifted.

The Coal Industry (No. 2) Act (12 & 13 Geo. VI, c. 79) became necessary because the assessment of compensation progressed very slowly, and the Coal Industry Nationalisation Act (sec. 22) provided only for the years 1947 and 1948 for the payment of half of the comparable ascertained revenue as interim income. The new Act now provides that for the year 1949 and any later year until the compensation is paid the companies concerned should receive one-third of their comparable ascertained revenue. The Explanatory Memorandum presented by the Government estimates that the payments under this heading for 1949 will amount to not more than £8,000,000 and will diminish thereafter.

As from 1 January 1950 the number of Divisional Boards has been increased by one, the Durham Division, which will include the five Durham Areas, the Northern Division retaining the Cumberland and Northumberland Areas.

2. *The British Transport Commission*

Every necessary preparation had been made to take over the enterprises to be nationalised on the vesting date, 1 January 1948, and this immense task was achieved smoothly. In respect of hotels, refreshment rooms and dining cars an interim regime was established and the Hotels Executive assumed control only on 1 July 1948. The Road Transport Executive began its work on 15 April 1948. The acquisition of existing concerns by way of voluntary agreements was gradually effected and in 1948 248 predominantly long-distance undertakings, owning 8208 motor vehicles, 1717 trawlers and 1867 horse vehicles came under the control of the Executive. At the end of 1948 notices of compulsory acquisition were served on 113 undertakings, and in autumn 1949 it was estimated that 31,000 vehicles were already under the control of the Executive out of the 40,000 eventually expected.

As to organisation, a wise restraint was shown by deciding from the beginning that the British Transport Commission should be a policy-making and directing body not discharging any executive functions, and that the members of the Commission should not be charged individually with functional responsibilities. The Commission made in due time necessary arrangements for the delegation of powers to the five Executives, in order that they might be able to carry out the ordinary business within their competence. In 1949, as a step to further decentralisation, the Road Passenger Executive was formed. In order to meet the difficulties connected with road haulage, eight divisions were formed by the Executive, each divided into districts—as a rule into four—and each district into groups, from five to twelve. The Group Managers are responsible for the operation of the vehicles in order to give personal service. In the forming of groups the larger undertakings were used as nuclei, e.g. Carter Patersons are for the time being still run separately as a national organisation.

The work done by the Commission and the five executives both in overcoming difficult transitional problems and improving transport facilities deserves high praise. Much has been done to rehabilitate the physical apparatus of the railways both as to tracks and structures and in respect of rolling stock. Many improvements were achieved in respect of traffic development; new works on railways and the London Transport system were promoted within reasonable limits. There were also improvements in emoluments of the staff and their welfare institutions.

All this, however, had to be paid for, and in spite of the increases in charges before nationalisation, receipts were not sufficient to meet expenditure. The year 1948 ended with a deficit of £1,714,616; with the sum of £2,487,741 required for capital redemption and certain smaller items the total deficit amounted to £4,732,824, and no provision could be made for the building up of a general reserve. Since the increases in the rates of pay awarded in 1948 required £8,979,000 for a full year, and other costs continued to rise, a larger deficit for 1949 became inevitable, and it was estimated that this would reach about £20,000,000. To meet this deficit at least partly an increase in freight charges is proposed, an increase of the charges on passenger traffic seeming impossible, since receipts from this are already on the decline.

It is hoped that in the long run the integration of transport services, particularly the increase in charges for road haulage, will bring about a balance between receipts and expenditure. How far such a general increase of charges for road transport is possible seems uncertain. The increase of the rates for freight, affecting mainly heavy traffic such as coal, iron and steel, will undoubtedly raise the general price level. Under these circumstances the reorganisation of services, the application of labour-saving devices and the use of every means to reduce costs are of extreme importance.

3. *The Control of Nationalised Industries*

The accounts both of the National Coal Board and of the British Transport Commission have been audited by independent firms of chartered accountants of the highest professional standing, appointed by the Minister of Fuel and Power and the Minister of Transport respectively. These audits, however, were based largely on internal audits, and in the case of the British Transport Commission, also on the audit-reports of the accountants appointed by the Executives. It is too early to judge whether this system of auditing—satisfactory as it seems to be for the time being—needs further improvements.

The control by Parliament may be regarded in our opinion as unsatisfactory. When questioned about current events and measures, the Ministers frequently declined to go into the matter, referring to the independence of the Central Boards and to the fact that Parliament will have ample opportunity to exercise control after the submission of the respective Reports. Actually, however, the Report of the National Coal Board for 1947 was not debated at all; its Report for 1948 and the Report of the British Transport Commission only towards the end of 1949, at a time when many of the complaints and criticisms were past remedy. Moreover, the time allowed was so short that an intensive and fruitful discussion of the problems of these highly important national enterprises was impossible.

In the author's view new means of control should be devised, preferably by setting up standing committees of the House of Commons for each of the nationalised industries, which would be trusted with the supervision of the respective central boards, be authorised to make inquiries, and be under the duty to report to the House both by way of Annual Reports and also during the financial year if they think fit.

To § 38. Corporate Name

The number of applications to use particular words in a company's title (such as "Royal", "Imperial" or any word suggesting connection with a Government Department) was in the following years:

Year	*Applications Made*	*Consent Given*	*Applications Refused*	*Applications Withdrawn*	*Outstanding at end of year*
1939	52	14	38	—	—
1940	34	8	26	—	—
1941	61	40	21	—	—
1942	186	117	59	10	—
1943	163	124	32	6	—
1944	287	210	75	2	—
1945	379	251	102	24	2
1946	557	353	87	111	—
1947	392	206	113	73	—

In the same years approvals of change of name were:

Year	*Applications Made*	*Applications Approved*	*Applications Refused*	*Applications Dropped*	*Applications Still Under Consideration*
1940*	—	459	—	—	—
1941	—	380	—	—	—
1942	—	401	—	—	—
1943	—	542	—	—	—
1944	—	389	—	—	—
1945	—	573	—	—	—
1946	1932	1620	11	301	—
1947	1786	1425	7	351	3

* For 1939 no details are available owing to loss of records by enemy action; for 1940–45 only the number of approvals is shown.

To § 58. Dividend Policy

VOLUNTARY LIMITATION OF DIVIDENDS

The views aired by Mr. Hugh Dalton, then Chancellor of the Exchequer,[1] retained their favour with the Labour Government. Though refraining for the time being from imposing a limitation on dividends by legislative enactment it was expected that companies would voluntarily exercise such restraint and would not increase their rates of dividends. This suggestion was supported by the various organisations of industry and commerce and found a ready response, as shown by a survey [2] of about 2095 selected companies of all kinds. The net profits of the year ending 30 June 1949 rose from the £203,800,000 of the preceding year to £237,300,000, i.e. by £33,500,000 (about 16·4 per cent.), whereas ordinary dividends increased from £94,400,000 to £96,400,000, i.e. by £2,000,000 (about 2·12 per cent.), whilst the dividends of preference shares show a slightly lower increase

[1] See p. 519. [2] *Economist*, 1 October 1949, p. 733.

from £26,000,000 to £26,500,000. If we take into consideration that a certain proportion of these companies had not yet fully recovered their pre-war prosperity, we may undoubtedly accept the statement of the *Economist*[1] that industry has scrupulously observed the undertaking not to increase its payments of dividends, and the complaints and warnings appear to be quite unjustified. It is to be appreciated that three leading organisations, the Association of British Chambers of Commerce, the Federation of British Industries and the National Union of Manufacturers, in a joint statement issued on 20 December 1949, gave their members the advice to maintain the restraint and not to increase dividends.[2]

In this connection it should be taken into account that the profits tax operates as a brake on any increase of dividends. Profits tax on undistributed profits absorbs 10 per cent. of those profits, whereas profits tax on distributed profits has been increased by the Act 12 & 13 Geo. VI, c. 64, from 1 October 1949 onwards by 50 per cent., i.e. from 20 per cent. to 30 per cent. Even without this increase the burden of taxation on corporate profits was high, as is shown by every profit and loss account. Thus, according to the figures given by the *Economist*, the taxes paid by 2095 companies in 1948–49 absorbed £328,200,000, whereas £122,900,000 was paid as dividends (for preference and ordinary shares) and £114,300,000 was retained in the businesses. Under the new Act the profits and income tax on undistributed profits would take 50·5 per cent. and in case of distribution 61·5 per cent. of the profits. Thus the small shareholder not subject to surtax could receive only 38·5 per cent. of that part of distributed profits which accrues proportionately to him. The position is further aggravated by the fact that the allowances for depreciation are not adequate and provisions for the replacement of stocks cannot be made free of tax. To maintain the sound foundations of corporate enterprise under such circumstances is extremely difficult.

To § 76. Nominees

According to the information given by the Insurance and Companies Department of the Board of Trade up to 1 December 1949 no application was made to the Board of Trade under sec. 172 of the Companies Act, 1948, to investigate the ownership of the shares and debentures of any company, nor did the Board of Trade find that there was good reason to order such investigation as provided by sec. 172 (1) of the Act. In one case, however, the Board of Trade required information as to the present and past interest in certain shares and debentures (sec. 173 of the Act), and since it was obtained there was no necessity to appoint inspectors.

[1] 1, i. [2] *The Times*, 21 and 22 December 1949.

To § 88. Appointment of Auditors by the Board of Trade

The power to appoint an auditor if none were appointed at the annual general meeting of a company was exercised and auditors were so appointed during the respective years as follows:

1939	1940	1941	1942	1943	1944	1945	1946	1947
14	2	4	6	6	3	1	—	3

To § 89. Investigation and Inspection

In the years 1943–47 the number of applications for the appointment of an inspector to investigate the affairs of a company and the result of these applications was:

Years	*Number of Applications*	*Number of Appointments*	*Applications Refused*	*Applications Withdrawn or Not Proceeded With*
1939	13	9	2	—
1940	5	—	3	—
1941	6	—	5	—
1942	2	—	2	—
1943	2	—	2	—
1944	2	—	—	—
1945	—	—	—	—
1946	4	—	1	3
1947	1	—	1	—

The particulars for the years 1948 and 1949 are known from the answer of the Secretary for Overseas Trade, given to the question of Sir Waldron Smithers in the House of Commons on 8 November 1949. According to this answer the Board of Trade, under the Companies Act of 1948, and before the consolidation under the Act of 1947, have appointed inspectors to investigate the affairs of companies having a share capital in the following cases:

(1) on the application of members (sec. 164 (*a*) of the Act), in two cases, in one of which the applicants were required to give security for costs to the amount of £100.

(2) In two cases inspectors were appointed following an order of the court declaring that the affairs of the companies concerned ought to be investigated (sec. 43 (*a*) (ii) of the Act of 1947). It is noteworthy that in one of these cases the Board of Trade applied for the order.

Three of these four cases (1) and (2) arose out of the issue of a prospectus.

(3) In the case of a company limited by guarantee the appointment was made pursuant to the special resolution of the company in general meeting (sec. 165 (*a*) (i) of the Act).

(4) The Board of Trade on their own initiative appointed inspectors in eight cases (sec. 165 (*a*) (i)).

It is known that in one of the cases arising out of the issue of a prospectus proceedings have been instituted against two of the directors.

In another case, that of A. Reyrolle and Co. Ltd., the two reports of the Inspector, the late Sir Douglas Thornbury Garrett, were published in November 1949 by the Board of Trade (sec. 168 of the Act). The investigation in this case was ordered on the application of dissatisfied shareholders of A. Reyrolle and Co. Ltd., who complained that in connection with an increase of the capital of Morphy-Richards Ltd., in which company Reyrolles had a considerable interest, an option for one thousand ordinary shares of that company granted to Reyrolles was in fact exercised in favour of the chairman of both companies, and that in this way A. Reyrolle and Co. Ltd. were deprived of a substantial profit. The most careful investigation showed that A. Reyrolle and Co. Ltd. had never had an option in respect of these shares and that the intention of Morphy-Richards Ltd. was exclusively aimed at the acquisition of the shares by the chairman. On the other hand, the Inspector found that both the application to the Capital Issues Committee and the prospectus issued in connection with the offer for sale of the ordinary stock units into which the ordinary shares of Morphy-Richards Ltd. had been converted were inaccurate and misleading, with intent to camouflage the real transaction in order to secure for the chairman a saving of income tax and surtax on the bonus element contained in the taking of the said one thousand ordinary shares at the agreed price. Whether the investigation will lead to further action by the dissatisfied minority of Reyrolles is not known, and it is possible that the transaction would have been equally approved by all persons concerned in case of full information. It is to be appreciated that the two reports of the Inspector are remarkable both from a technical point and equally for the insistence on truthfulness and on the maintenance of high moral standards in corporate affairs.

To § 90. Increases of Capital

BONUS ISSUES OF ADDITIONAL SHARES

On the part of the present Government there was always a bias against the so-called bonus issues, i.e. issues of additional shares without actual payment by the use of free reserves. The Capital Issues Committee, acting undoubtedly under the instructions of the Treasury, gave their consent only sparingly to such issues. There were complaints that the practice of the Committee was not always consistent and that assent was withheld in certain cases without convincing reasons, whereas in others it was granted, though no essential difference as to the merits of the case could be seen. With the deterioration of the national financial position the opposition to bonus issues became stronger, mainly owing to fears that by issue of bonus shares the voluntary limitation of dividends could be evaded and thus the inflatory pressure increased. On 24 October 1949 the Committee were instructed to suspend all recommendations with regard to such issues. On 13 December, however, the Chancellor of the Exchequer, in a letter to the Chairman of the Committee, lifted this absolute embargo and requested that the Committee should recommend such issues only if they were satisfied that they were necessary for the continuation or expansion of the company's production or for the increase of the volume of its exports. The onus of proving such necessity is regarded to be very much lighter when the company exports a considerable percentage of its production to hard-currency markets, and in such cases the Committee is likely to make a favourable recommendation more easily. On the other hand, the Chancellor asked the Committee not to make recommendations for consent to the issue of preference shares on a bonus basis, save in exceptional cases.[1]

To § 93. The Private Company

The average size of the capital of private companies on the Register decreased during the years 1939–47. On 31 December 1938 it was £13,230, at the end of 1947 about £9,020. This was due to the formation of great numbers of small private companies.

The average nominal capital of the newly registered private companies was as follows:

1939	1940	1941	1942	1943	1944	1945	1946	1947
£4295	£3735	£3193	£3501	£3569	£3855	£3819	£4778	about £7890

[1] See written answer of Sir Stafford Cripps on 15 December 1949 (Hansard, House of Commons, Vol. 407, No. 207, pp. 295–6).

SELECTED BIBLIOGRAPHY

ACRES, W. H.: *The Bank of England from Within* (vols. I and II), London, 1931.

AMERICAN BAR ASSOCIATION: *Model for State Business Corporation Acts*, prepared by the Corporation Law Committee of the Association, Chicago, 1946.

ANDREADES, A.: *History of the Bank of England* (English translation), 2nd ed., London, 1924.

BALLANTINE, H. W.: *On Corporations* (Chicago, 1927), 2nd ed., Chicago, 1946.

BALOGH, T.: *Studies in Financial Organisation*, Cambridge, 1947.

BAYKOW, A. M.: *The Development of the Soviet Economic System*, Cambridge, 1946.

Soviet Foreign Trade, Princeton, 1946.

BERLE, A. A., jr., and MAGILL, R.: *Cases and Materials on Corporation Finance*, St. Paul, Minn., 1942.

BERLE, A. A., jr., and MEANS, G. C.: *The Modern Corporation and Private Property*, New York, 1933.

BESSAU and others: *Das bürgerliche Gesetzbuch*, 8th ed. (Commentary of the Judges of the German Supreme Court), Berlin and Leipzig, 1934.

BLANDI, J. G.: *The Maryland Business Corporation*, Baltimore, 1934.

BOGART, E. L.: *Economic History of the American People*, 2nd ed., New York, 1947.

BOHNBRIGHT, J. C., and MEANS, G. C.: *The Holding Company*, New York and London, 1932.

BOSSELMANN, K.: *Die Entwickelung des Deutschen Aktienwesens im Neunzehnten Jahrhundert*, Berlin, 1939.

BRANDEIS, L. D.: *Other People's Money*, New York, 1914.

The Curse of Bigness, New York (the 1935 ed. has been consulted).

BUCHANAN, N. S.: *The Economics of Corporate Enterprise*, New York, 1939.

BUCKLAND, W. W.: *Textbook of Roman Law*, 2nd ed., Cambridge, 1932.

BUCKLAND, W. W., and McNAIR, A.: *Roman Law and Common Law*, Cambridge, 1936.

BUCKLEY, J. B. (Lord Wrenbury): *The Law and Practice under the Companies Act*, 11th ed., by W. Gordon Brown, R. J. T. Gibson and the Hon. D. B. Buckley, London, 1930.

12th ed., by the Hon. D. B. Buckley, assisted by Nigel Warren and George Brian Parker, Consulting Editor Cecil W. Turner, London, 1949.[1]

[1] Published during the printing of this book and thus could not be consulted.

BURNHAM, J.: *The Managerial Revolution*, Pelican ed., London, 1945.

CARR, C. T.: *Select Charters of Trading Companies*, Selden Society Publications, vol. XXVIII, London, 1913.

CARVER, T. N.: *The Present Economic Revolution in the U.S.A.*, London, 1926.

CAWSTON, G., and KEANE, A. H.: *The Early Chartered Companies 1296–1858*, London and New York, 1896.

CLAPHAM, Sir J.: *An Economic History of Modern Britain*, Cambridge: vol. I, 2nd ed., 1930; vol. II, 1932; vol. III, 1938.

The Bank of England, A History, vols. I and II, Cambridge, 1944.

Economic History of Great Britain from Earliest Times to 1750, Cambridge, 1949.

COCHRAN, T. L., and MILLER, W.: *The Age of Enterprise*, New York, 1942.

COHN, M.: *Römisches Vereinsrecht*, Berlin, 1873.

COLE, C. W.: *Colbert and a Century of French Mercantilism*, New York, 1939.

French Mercantilism (1683–1700), New York, 1943.

COOK, W. W.: *The Corporation Problem*, London and New York, 1891.

CUNNINGHAM, W.: *The Growth of English Industry and Commerce in Modern Times*, 4th ed: vol. II, part I, *The Mercantile System*; vol. II, part II, *Laisser Faire*, London, 1925.

DAVIES, E.: *National Enterprise. The Device of Public Corporations*, London, 1946.

DAVIS, J. S.: *Essays on the Earlier History of American Corporations*, vols. I and II, Cambridge, Mass., 1917.

DERNBURG, H.: *System des Römischen Rechtes*, 8th ed. by P. Sokolowski, Berlin, 1911–12.

DOANE, R. R.: *The Measurement of American Wealth*, New York and London, 1933.

The Anatomy of American Wealth, New York and London, 1940.

DOBB, M.: *Studies on the Development of Capitalism*, London, 1946.

Soviet Economic Development since 1917, London, 1948.

DODD, E. M., jr.: *The First Half Century of Statutory Regulation of Corporations in Massachusetts* (Harvard Legal Essays), Cambridge, Mass., 1934.

"American Business Association Law a Hundred Years Ago and To-day" (in vol. III of *Law, a Century of Progress*), 1936.

DODD, E. M., jr., and BAKER, R. J.: *Cases on Business Associations*, Chicago, 1940.

DRUCKER, P.: *Big Business*, New York, 1944.

Concept of the Corporation, New York, 1946.

DUBOIS, A. B.: *The English Business Company after the Bubble Act, 1720–1800*, New York, 1938.

DÜRINGER-HACHENBURG: *Das Handelsgesetzbuch*, 3rd ed., vol. III, 1, Company Law, by M. Hachenburg, J. Flechtheim, and F. Bing, Mannheim, Berlin, Leipzig, 1934.

EHRENBERG, V., and others: *Handbuch des gesammten Handelsrechts*, vol. I, vol. III, 1, Company Law, by R. Fischer, Leipzig, 1916.

ELIASEVICH, R., and others: *Traité de droit civil et commercial des Soviets*. Vol. I—III Paris, 1930.

ENDEMANN, W., and others: *Handbuch des Deutschen Handels-, See- und Wechselrechts*, vol. I, including Company Law, by Primker, Leipzig, 1881.

ENGLISH, H.: *A Complete View of English Joint Stock Companies Formed during the Years 1824 and 1825*, London, 1827.

EVANS, G. H.: *British Corporation Finance, 1755–1850*, Baltimore, 1936.

FAULKNER, H.: *The Quest for Social Justice*, New York, 1931.
American Economic History, 4th ed., New York, 1938.

FEILER, A., and MARSCHAK, J.: *Management in Russian Industry and Agriculture*, London, 1944.

FLETCHER: *Cyclopaedia of the Law of Private Corporations*, permanent edition, 1932, with Supplements.

FORMOY, R. R.: *The Historical Foundations of Modern Company Law*, London, 1923.

GADOW, W.: *Aktiengesetz, Kommentar*, Berlin, 1939.

GIERKE, O.: *Das Deutsche Genossenschaftsrecht*, vols. I–IV, Berlin, 1868–1913.
Die Genossenschaftstheorie und die Deutsche Rechtsprechung, Berlin, 1887.
Deutsches Privatrecht, vol. I, Berlin, 1895.
Political Theories of the Middle Ages, with Introduction by F. W. Maitland, Cambridge, 1900.

GOLDSCHMIDT, L.: *Universalgeschichte des Handelsrechtes*, Stuttgart, 1891.

GORDON, L.: *Public Corporations in Great Britain*, Oxford, 1937.

GORE-BROWN, F.: *Handbook on the Formation, Management and Winding-up of Joint Stock Companies*, 40th ed., London, 1946.

GUHL, T.: *Das Schweizerische Obligationsrecht*, 3rd ed., Zürich, 1944.

GUNTHER, J.: *Inside U.S.A.* (English ed.), London, 1947.

HACKER, L. M.: *Triumph of American Capitalism*, New York, 1940.

HALLSTEIN, W.: *Die Aktienrechte der Gegenwart*, Berlin, 1931.

HALSBURY: *Laws of England*, 2nd ed., by Lord Hailsham: vol. V, Companies, by Mr. Justice Macnaughten, London, 1932.
New ed. based on Companies Act, 1948, edited by Lord Justice L. L. Cohen, London, 1949. (Published during the printing of this book and has not been consulted.)

HECKSCHER, E.: *Mercantilism* (English ed.), London, 1934.

HOAGLAND, H. E.: *Corporation Finance*, 3rd ed., New York and London, 1947.

HOLDSWORTH, W. S.: *History of English Law*, vol. VIII, 2nd ed., London, 1937.

HOUPIN, Ch., and BOSVIEUX, H.: *Traité général des sociétés civiles commerciales et associations*, 5th ed., Paris, 1925.

HUBBARD, E. L.: *Soviet Money and Finance*, London, 1935.
Soviet Trade and Distribution, London, 1938.
The Economics of Soviet Agriculture, London, 1939.
Soviet Labour and Industry, London, 1942.

HUNT, B. C.: *The Development of the Business Corporation in England, 1800–1867*, Cambridge, Mass., 1936.

JOSEPHSON, M.: *The Robber Barons*, New York, 1938.

KESTER, R. B., and INGHRAM, H. A.: *Corporation Financial Statements*, New York, 1940.

KLEIN, F.: *Die neueren Entwickelungen in Verfassung und Recht der Aktiengesellschaften*, Vienna, 1904.

KNIEP, F.: *Societas Publicanorum*, Jena, 1896.

KUHN, A. A.: *A Comparative Study of the Law of Corporations*, New York, 1914.

LASKI, H. J.: *The American Democracy*, London, 1949.

LAVISSE, E.: *Histoire économique de France*, Paris, 1913.

LEHMANN, K.: *Geschichtliche Entwickelung des Aktienrechts*, Berlin, 1895.
Das Recht der Aktiengesellschaften, vol. I, Berlin, 1898; vol. II, Berlin, 1904.

LEVASSEUR, E.: *Histoire de commerce de la France*, vol. I, Paris, 1911; vol. II, Paris, 1912.

LÉVY-BRUHL, H.: *Histoire juridique des sociétés de commerce en France au XVIIe et XVIIIe siècle*, Paris, 1938.

LIEFMANN, R.: *Beteiligung und Finanzierungsgesellschaften*, 4th ed., Jena, 1923.
Die Unternehmungsformen, 4th ed., Stuttgart, 1928.

LILIENTHAL, D. E.: *TVA—Tennessee Valley Authority, Democracy on the March* (Penguin ed.), London, 1944.

LINDLEY, N. C. (Lord Lindley): *Treatise on the Law of Partnerships, including its Application to Joint Stock Companies*, London, 1860–63.

LIPSON, E.: *The Economic History of England*, vol. I, 10th ed., London, 1945; vols. II and III, 5th ed., London, 1931.
The Growth of English Society, a Short Economic History, London, 1949.

LYNCH, D.: *The Concentration of Economic Power*, New York, 1946.

LYON-CAEN, C., and RENAULT, L.: *Traité de droit commercial*, vol. II, 1, 5th ed., Paris, 1927.

McKay, D.: *The Honourable Company*, London, 1937.

Madariaga, S.: *The Rise of the Spanish-American Empire*, London, 1947.

Mead, E., Jeremiah, B. D., and Warrington, W. E.: *The Business Corporation*, New York and London, 1941.

Mitchell, B.: *Depression Decade (The Economic History of the United States)*, vol. IX, New York, 1947.

Mitteis, L.: *Römisches Privatrecht*, vol. I, Leipzig, 1908.

National Resources Committee: *The Structure of American Economy*, Washington, 1935.

Nevins, A.: *The Emergence of Modern America*, New York, 1927.

O'Brien, T.: *British Experiments in Public Ownership*, Cambridge, Mass., 1937.

O'Leary, P. M.: *Corporate Enterprise in Modern Economic Life*, New York, 1935.

Palmer, F.: *Company Law*, 18th ed. (including Companies Act, 1947, by Judge F. A. Topham), London, 1948.
19th ed., based on 1948 Act, London, 1949.
Company Precedents, vols. I–III, 15th ed., London, 1935.

Pardessus: *Cours de droit commercial*, Paris, 1833.

Parker, J. S.: *The Corporation Manual*, edited by J. B. R. Smith, New York, 1943.

Parkinson, H.: *Scientific Investment*, 4th ed., London, 1946.

Passow, R.: *Die Aktiengesellschaft*, 2nd ed., Jena, 1923.
Der Strukturwandel der Aktiengesellschaft, Jena, 1931.

Pecora, F.: *Wall Street under Oath*, London, 1939.

Petrazízkyc, L. J.: *Aktienwesen und Spekulation*, Berlin, 1900.

Pic, P. (Collection Thaller): *Des sociétés commerciales*, vols. I–III, 2nd ed., Paris, 1925; vol. I, 3rd ed., with J. Kreher, Paris, 1940.

Planitz, H.: *Die Stimmrechtsaktie*, Leipzig, 1922.

Rathenau, W.: *Vom Aktienwesen*, Berlin, 1917.

Regelsberger, F.: *Pandekten*, vol. I, Leipzig, 1893.

Renner, K.: *The Institutions of Private Law and their Social Functions* (English ed., with Introduction and Notes, by O. Kahn-Freund), London, 1949.

Richards, H. S.: *Cases in the Law of Private Corporations*, 3rd ed., by S. Johnson, St. Paul, U.S.A., 1940.

Riesser, J.: *Die Neuerungen im Deutschen Aktienrecht*, Berlin, 1900.
The German Great Banks and their Concentration (Amer. ed.), New York, 1911.

Ripert, G.: *Aspectes juridiques du capitalisme moderne*, Paris, 1946.

Ripley, W. Z.: *Main Street and Wall Street*, Boston, 1927.

ROBSON, W. A., and others: *Public Enterprise*, London, 1937.
ROGERS, T.: *The First Nine Years of the Bank of England*, London, 1887.
ROSTOVTZEFF, M. J.: *Economic History of the Roman Empire*, Oxford, 1926.
ROUSSEAU, A.: *Sociétés commerciales*, 5th ed., Paris, 1921.

SAMUEL, H. B.: *Shareholders' Money*, London, 1933.
SCHLESINGER, A. M., jr.: *The Rise of the City*, New York, 1933.
The Age of Jackson, New York, 1946.
SCHLESINGER, R.: *Soviet Legal Theory*, London, 1945.
SCHMOLLER, G.: *Grundriss der Allgemeinen Volkswirtschaftslehre*, 11th and 12th ed., Leipzig, 1919.
SCHUHMACHER, H.: *Die Entwickelung der inneren Organisation der Aktiengesellschaft im Recht bis zum Handelsgesetzbuch*, Erlangen, 1937.
SCOTT, W. R.: *The Constitution and Finance of English, Scottish and Irish Joint Stock Companies to 1720*, Vols. I–III, Cambridge, 1912.
SIEGWART, A.: "Obligationsrecht", vol. V, 5, of *Commentary to Swiss Private Law*, Zürich, 1945.
SLOSSON, P. W.: *The Great Crusade and After*, New York, 1931.
SOLINSSEN, G.: *Probleme des Aktienrechts*, Berlin, 1928.
SOMBART, W.: *Der moderne Kapitalismus*, vols. I and II, Leipzig, 1928; vol. III, Leipzig, 1927.
SONTAG: *Die Aktiengesellschaft im Kampf zwischen Macht und Recht*, Berlin, 1919.
SOULE, G. H.: *The Prosperity Decade*, London ed., 1947.
SPACKMANN, H.: *Statistical Tables of the United Kingdom and its Dependencies*, London, 1843.
STAUB, H.: *Kommentar zum Handelsgesetzbuch*, 6th and 7th eds., Berlin, 1900.
STAUB-PINNER: *Staub's Commentaries*, ed. by Pinner, 14th ed., Berlin and Leipzig, 1933.
STEINITZER, E.: *Ökonomische Theorie der Aktiengesellschaft*, Leipzig, 1908.
STIEBEL, A.: *Company Law*, 3rd ed., vols. I–II, London, 1929.
STRIEDER, J.: *Zur Genesis des Modernen kapitalismus*, 2nd ed., Munich and Leipzig, 1935.
Studien zur Geschichte kapitalistischer Organisationen, 2nd ed., Munich and Leipzig, 1926.

TARBELL, J. M.: *The Nationalising of Business*, New York, 1936.
TEMPORARY NATIONAL ECONOMIC COMMITTEE: *Investigation of Concentration of Economic Power*—Monographs:
No. 9, Taxation of Corporate Enterprise.
No. 11, Bureaucracy and Trusteeship in Large Corporations.
No. 29, The Distribution of Ownership in the 200 Largest Non-Financial Corporations.

No. 30, Survey of Shareholdings in 1710 Corporations with Securities listed on a National Securities Exchange.

Final Report (Document No. 35), presented 31 March 1941, Washington, United States Printing Office.

THRING (Baron Thring): *The Joint Stock Companies Acts, 1856 and 1857*, London, 1857.

THURSTON, J.: *Government Proprietary Corporations*, Cambridge, Mass., 1937.

WEBB, S. and B.: *Soviet Communism, a New Civilisation*, London, 1935.

WEBER, M.: *Wirtschaft und Gesellschaft*, 2nd ed., Tübingen, 1922.

WIELAND, K.: *Handelsrecht*, vol. I, Munich and Leipzig, 1921; vol. II, Munich and Leipzig, 1931.

WILLISTON, S.: *A History of the Law of Business Corporations* (Select Essays in Anglo-American Legal History), Cambridge, Mass., 1905.

JUDICIAL DECISIONS

ENGLISH: Decisions are quoted from the Law Reports.

U.S.A.: The quotations of the Decisions of the Supreme Court refer to the official edition. The Decisions of the Federal and State Courts could be referred to only sparingly from the Reports, otherwise the *Collection Corpus Juris*, ed. 1919, New York and London, has been used.

FRANCE: Dalloz, *Recuëil Repertoire pratique*, Paris.

GERMANY: *Entscheidungen des Reichsgerichts in Zivilsachen*, official edition (R.G.Z.).

PERIODICALS

ENGLAND:

Cambridge Law Journal, Cambridge.
Law Quarterly, Oxford.
Modern Law Review, London.

U.S.A.:

Columbia Law Review, New York.
Harvard Law Review, Cambridge, Mass.
Yale Law Review, Newhaven.

FRANCE:

Annales de droit commercial (founded by E. Thaller), Paris.

GERMANY:

Zeitschrift für das Gesammte Handelsrecht (founded by L. Goldschmidt), Erlangen.

ACKNOWLEDGMENTS

This book owes its coming into being to the initiative of Karl Mannheim, who gave inspiration to so many, together with his competent advice and generous help. The leading idea was to present the position of the Private Corporation as the powerful instrument of capitalistic enterprise in modern society, its economic background and legal framework, giving thereby material for thought to those engaged in the solution of the problems of post-war reconstruction. The outlines of the work had been fixed in frequent conversations with Prof. Mannheim, but his fatal illness and premature death prevented his approval of the completed text, the responsibility for which rests entirely with the author.

The writing was begun in wartime and finished in 1947. Owing to well-known circumstances the collection of material was difficult, and as far as it was successful it was owing to the assistance from various quarters which the author was so fortunate as to enjoy. It is a pleasant duty to express his gratitude and appreciation to the Insurance and Companies Department of the Board of Trade and the Treasury Department of the Federal Government of the U.S.A. for the communication of particulars not yet published at that time; to the Hon. Joseph O'Mahoney, Senator of the U.S.A., Chairman of the Temporary National Economic Committee, for a number of Monographs of the Committee on the Investigation of Concentration of Economic Power in the U.S.A.; to Prof. E. Merrick Dodd, Jr., of Harvard University for valuable advice on the American literature; to Mr. Hargreave Parkinson, then editor of the *Financial News*, for his permission to reproduce the contents of several studies on the dispersal of share ownership in Great Britain; to the Trustees of the British Museum, the Honourable Society of Lincoln's Inn, the British Library of Political and Economic Science, the American Embassy in London and the University of Cincinnati for the use of their libraries; and to a large number of colleagues and friends for the loan of books otherwise unobtainable.

No-one can be more aware of the deficiencies of this book than its author, who nevertheless hopes that he has succeeded in drawing attention to certain problems of vital interest, and whose wish is that others more competent than he may undertake and accomplish their solution.

London, December 1949.

INDEX

INDEX OF ACTS OF PARLIAMENT

INDEX OF CASES REFERRED TO (BRITISH)

INDEX OF CASES REFERRED TO (AMERICAN)

For Product Safety Concerns and Information please contact our EU representative GPSR@taylorandfrancis.com
Taylor & Francis Verlag GmbH, Kaufingerstraße 24, 80331 München, Germany

www.ingramcontent.com/pod-product-compliance
Lightning Source LLC
LaVergne TN
LVHW011103300926
849160LV00008B/269

* 9 7 8 0 4 1 5 8 6 8 5 0 1 *